INNOCENCE LOST

INNOCENCE LOST

An Examination of Inescapable
Moral Wrongdoing

Christopher W. Gowans

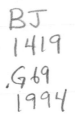

New York   Oxford
OXFORD UNIVERSITY PRESS
1994

Oxford University Press

Oxford   New York   Toronto
Delhi   Bombay   Calcutta   Madras   Karachi
Kuala Lumpur   Singapore   Hong Kong   Tokyo
Nairobi   Dar es Salaam   Cape Town
Melbourne   Auckland   Madrid

and associated companies in
Berlin   Ibadan

Copyright © 1994 by Christopher W. Gowans

Published by Oxford University Press, Inc.,
200 Madison Avenue, New York, New York 10016

Oxford is a registered trademark of Oxford University Press

Library of Congress Cataloging-in-Publication Data
Gowans, Christopher W.
Innocence lost : an examination of inescapable moral wrongdoing /
Christopher W. Gowans
p.   cm.
Includes bibliographical references and index.
ISBN 0-19-508517-5
1. Decision-making (Ethics)   I. Title.   II. Title: Inescapable
moral wrongdoing
BJ1419.G69   1994
170—dc20   93-11593

2 4 6 8 10 9 7 5 3 1
Printed in the United States of America
on acid-free paper

For my parents,
William J. Gowans and June L. Gowans

Preface

Several years ago in a report on public opinion, *The New York Times* observed that "one of every six Americans says simultaneously that abortion is murder and that it is sometimes the best course" (April 26, 1989 p. A1). This might be taken to reveal, what opinion polls sometimes do reveal, that some people have incoherent beliefs. For, if abortion is murder, then it is always wrong; but if it is sometimes "the best course," then on those occasions it would seem to be wrong not to have an abortion. If this were the case, sometimes a woman considering an abortion would act wrongly no matter what she did. Surely, it may be said, this is incoherent. Many philosophers may well have had this reaction upon reading this statement. But it was not my reaction. Without agreeing with the statement, it did not strike me as being an incoherent position. For in my view it is possible for moral wrongdoing to be inescapable.

I came to believe this, or perhaps discovered that I already believed it, a number of years ago while reflecting on Bernard Shaw's *Major Barbara*. In the second act of the play, a Salvation Army shelter devoted to helping the bodies and souls of the poor is faced with the prospect of closing its doors unless it accepts a donation from an unscrupulous arms manufacturer who is willing to sell his product to any country, whether its cause be just or unjust. Major Barbara, thinking perhaps of those unjustly killed by weapons sold to finance the donation, believes it would be wrong to accept it. But her superior, Mrs. Baines, looking at the indigent persons around her, believes it would be wrong not to accept it. Might not they *both* be correct in their respective beliefs? I thought then, and still think, that this might well be the case, that this could be a situation in which moral wrongdoing is inescapable.

Thinking this, I looked to see what moral philosophers had to say on the subject. It turned out that most of them had little to say, except perhaps to note in passing that inescapable wrongdoing was impossible. Yet there were a few who believed it was possible, that in fact it was sometimes actual; and their arguments were starting to attract some critical response. This was the beginning of what has become a rather substantial literature on "moral dilemmas." I have profited a great deal by reflecting on this literature, and in many respects this book is a product of these reflections.

My principal purpose is to defend the thesis that there is a significant sense in which moral wrongdoing is sometimes inescapable. But I also argue that a certain kind of moral conflict is not possible. I have learned that, as a result, I am interpreted by some as supporting those who think there are moral dilemmas, and by others as opposing this view and substituting for it a substantially weaker position. My intention is much closer to the first interpretation. Moral deliberation in a familiar sense aims to decide, from a moral point of view, what to do. The sense in which moral conflict is not possible is roughly this: It cannot be the case that the correct conclusion of moral deliberation is to decide to do one thing and to decide to do another, knowing that one cannot do both. This would mean that the Salvation Army shelter might be correct in deciding to accept the donation and at the same time in deciding to refuse it. As a conclusion of moral deliberation (indeed of *any* deliberation about what to do), this would be incoherent. I doubt that proponents of the idea of moral dilemmas have generally meant to deny this. Insofar as this is true, I do not disagree with them. On the other hand, it does sometimes appear that the moral dilemmas debate concerns the possibility of conflicting conclusions of moral deliberation in this sense. My point in identifying and arguing against these conflicts is to undermine this appearance and shift attention to the real issue.

The real issue concerns the possibility of conflicts in which moral wrongdoing is inescapable. These conflicts do not require that there be conflicting conclusions of moral deliberation. This point has been obscured by the fact that conflicting deliberative conclusions would be sufficient for inescapable wrongdoing in an obvious sense. What needs to be recognized is that they are not necessary for inescapable wrongdoing in a sense which matters greatly to us—namely, that whatever we do we will transgress a genuine moral value. I argue that, though deliberative conclusions may not conflict, there are conflicts in which infringement of a genuine moral value is unavoidable. The shelter may have no choice but to violate its moral responsibility to the indigents of the neighborhood or to violate its moral responsibility to the innocents who stand to be harmed by the unjust use of the weapons of the arms manufacturer. I believe this position is close to what most proponents of the idea of moral dilemmas have had in mind.

Though my primary aim is to argue for this position, my secondary purpose is to direct the discussion of moral dilemmas in certain directions. In this regard, there are several themes of my argument worth emphasizing.

First, it is often supposed that the key issue turns on the possibility and interpretation of moral conflicts in which neither side is morally stronger than the other. In my view, the emphasis on these conflicts is misplaced. What is important is whether or not there are moral conflicts in which wrongdoing is inescapable, even if one moral reason is stronger than the other. The Salvation Army shelter may have a morally better choice. Yet it could still be the case that each choice violates a moral responsibility. Once this is recognized, it becomes apparent that moral dilemmas are potentially a more pervasive phenomenon than is often believed.

Second, it is sometimes thought that the debate about moral dilemmas is primarily a metaethical issue, concerned with questions of consistency and deontic logic. These questions are indeed important. In the final analysis, however, the problem of inescapable moral wrongdoing is as much a normative issue as it is a metaethical one. To a large extent, philosophical opposition to the idea of inescapable wrongdoing is rooted in utilitarian and Kantian perspectives. For this reason, I examine closely the views of Mill and Kant as well as those of their followers, and I develop a substantially different normative outlook to support my position. On my account, we have moral responsibilities to particular persons in virtue of our appreciation of the intrinsic and unique value of each of these persons, and of our connections with them. I argue that when we think of our responsibilities in this way, we have reason to believe that they sometimes conflict and that it is wrong to violate them even when they do conflict. By contrast, in both the utilitarian and Kantian traditions, a conception of morality predominates that at once eliminates genuine moral conflict and tends to displace particular persons as direct objects of moral concern. These traditions succeed in eliminating conflict only at the cost of an inadequate understanding of the way in which particular persons are valuable to us. We cannot resolve the question of inescapable wrongdoing without confronting these fundamental issues in normative ethics.

Third, insofar as it is recognized that normative issues are at stake in the moral dilemmas debate, it is often supposed that what is important is whether or not there is a plurality of kinds of moral values. Proponents and opponents of the idea of moral dilemmas are seen as basing their positions on pluralism and monism respectively. For the most part, my account sidesteps this way of understanding the debate. Though my sympathies are with the pluralists, my argument for inescapable moral wrongdoing does not directly depend on pluralism in this sense. What is required is that we have a plurality of responsibilities to persons; there need not be a plurality of kinds of responsibilities.

Finally, much of the debate about moral dilemmas has involved tacit assumptions about the proper methodology of moral philosophy, with little explicit awareness of the crucial role of these assumptions, much less an attempt at their defense. I devote a chapter to this subject, drawing especially on recent methodological discussions apropos Hare and Rawls, both to show the importance of methodology for the moral dilemmas debate and to develop the methodology that governs my own argument.

In the course of developing these ideas in some preliminary papers and in this book, I have received much helpful advice from many people. For constructive philosophical criticism and suggestions, I would especially like to thank Jonathan Adler, Jeffrey Blustein, Earl Conee, Vincent M. Cooke, S.J., Timothy Gould, Brian Leftow, Terrance McConnell, James McGrath, Mike Morris, Walter Sinnott-Armstrong, Dave Solomon, Michael Stocker, Peter Vallentyne, Margaret Urban Walker, and Michael Zimmerman. I have also benefited a great deal from the thoughtful responses of two anonymous referees for Oxford University Press, members of the audience at various conferences at which these ideas were first presented, and the graduate and undergraduate students in several of my moral philosophy classes in recent years. I would also like to thank Angela Blackburn and Robert Dilworth of Oxford University Press for their assistance in bringing the manuscript to publication, David Kaplan for help in preparation of the bibliography, and Terence Cuneo for aid in proofreading. Portions of the book, mainly in Chapter 4, originally appeared as "Moral Dilemmas and Prescriptivism" in the *American Philosophical Quarterly* (vol. 26, 1989, pp. 187–97). I am grateful for permission to republish. Work on the book was greatly facilitated by two Faculty Fellowships from Fordham University, in the spring semesters of 1988 and 1993.

New York   C.W.G.
April 1993

Contents

INNOCENCE LOST

Close friendships, Gandhi says, are dangerous, because "friends react on one another" and through loyalty to a friend one can be led into wrong-doing. This is unquestionably true. Moreover, if one is to love God, or to love humanity as a whole, one cannot give one's preference to any individual person. This again is true, and it marks the point at which the humanistic and the religious attitude cease to be reconcilable. To an ordinary human being, love means nothing if it does not mean loving some people more than others. . . . The essence of being human is that one does not seek perfection, that one *is* sometimes willing to commit sins for the sake of loyalty, that one does not push asceticism to the point where it makes friendly intercourse impossible, and that one is prepared in the end to be defeated and broken up by life, which is the inevitable price of fastening one's love upon other human individuals.

George Orwell, "Reflections on Gandhi"

Philosophers have insisted, and still insist, that we encounter here the demands of another kind of theory, moral theory, which aims to systematize and simplify our moral opinions. But they rarely even try to answer a real question: what authority is theoretical tidiness or simplicity supposed to have against the force of concerns which one actually finds important? . . . It may be that there are no, or few, purely theoretical pressures to reduce the conflicts in our value-system. Berlin will say that there is a pressure to *not* reducing them, towards remaining conscious of these conflicts and not trying to eliminate them on more than a piecemeal basis: that pressure is the respect for truth. To deny the conflicts, indeed to try to resolve them systematically and once and for all, would be to offend against something absolutely true about values.

Bernard Williams, "Introduction" *Concepts and Categories: Philosophical Essays by Isaiah Berlin*

1

"The Angel Must Hang!": *Inescapable Moral Wrongdoing in Melville's* Billy Budd

Moral conflict is an obvious fact of our experience. Everyone has faced situations in which it appears that some moral reasons support one course of action and other moral reasons support an incompatible course of action. In these situations we sometimes feel that we must choose "the lesser of two evils." Moral conflicts have occasioned a good deal of moral philosophy. Most concerns have been casuistical: They have focused on the questions "What is the correct resolution of these conflicts?" and "How is this resolution to be determined?" My concern is different. I want to consider whether or not there are moral conflicts in which, irrespective of the correct resolution, whatever the agent does he or she will do something that is, in some sense, morally wrong. Many philosophers maintain that in every moral conflict some course of action that is wholly free from wrongdoing is available to the agent (though it may be difficult, and perhaps in some cases virtually impossible, to know what this action is). In my view, these philosophers are mistaken. We may find ourselves in moral conflicts in which, through no fault of our own, we will do something morally wrong no matter what we do. In these situations we may choose the lesser of two evils and hence act for the best. But in acting for the best we still choose an evil, and in this sense we do something wrong. Moral wrongdoing may thus be inescapable. My aim in this book is to defend this position.

This introductory chapter is mainly devoted to an interpretation of Herman Melville's marvelous and disturbing story *Billy Budd*. Through this interpretation I hope to bring to life the philosophical issues that will concern me in the later chapters and to indicate in a preliminary way the nature of my position on these issues. My purpose here is not merely to provide a vivid and colorful introductory example. It is a fundamental part of my argument throughout the book that concrete moral considerations must play a central role in the justification of a position in moral philosophy. The defense of this methodology is the subject of the next chapter. For now I will simply point out that my reading of *Billy*

3

Budd will be representative of an important premise in my argument for inescapable moral wrongdoing.

In the first section I give a brief account of the idea of inescapable moral wrongdoing, and I distinguish it from another idea with which it might be confused. Then, in Section II, I begin my interpretation of *Billy Budd* by reviewing the controversy over its meaning and by proposing, as both the correct reading and an explanation of this controversy, that its central character, Captain Vere, should be understood as being in a situation in which moral wrongdoing is inescapable. This interpretation is then developed through a close analysis of the text in the next three sections. In the final section, I formulate some of the philosophical issues to be discussed in later chapters by reference to my reading of *Billy Budd.*

I. The Idea of Inescapable Moral Wrongdoing

Discussion of the thesis that there are moral conflicts in which wrongdoing is inescapable has not been prominent in the history of Western moral philosophy, but most philosophers in this tradition have assumed that circumstances always make it possible to avoid moral wrongdoing. However, this assumption has not been universally shared by those outside philosophy. Writers of tragedy in particular, from the Greeks to Shakespeare to the present, may be read as exploring the variety of circumstances in which moral wrongdoing is inescapable.[1] Moreover, in recent years several philosophers in the Anglo-American tradition have argued that sometimes wrongdoing cannot be avoided. Their arguments have been received with considerable skepticism by philosophers of otherwise quite diverse moral perspectives, and a debate has ensued about their soundness.[2]

It is important to note at the outset that there has been a persistent equivocation within this debate. Usually it is said that what is at issue is whether or not there are "moral dilemmas," typically defined as situations in which an agent morally ought to (and can) take one course of action and morally ought to (and can) take another course of action, even though the agent cannot take both courses of action. But this definition conceals a significant ambiguity. For the debate about "moral dilemmas" has in fact concerned two distinct issues.

The first has to do with the possibility of irresolvable moral conflicts: Are there circumstances in which there is no moral reason for choosing between two conflicting actions, each of which is supported by some moral ground? I will maintain that the answer to this question is clearly "yes," since conflicting moral reasons are sometimes equal in weight or significance. For example, if a mother can save the life of one, but only one, of her two children, she has a moral reason to save each child, but she may well have no moral reason for saving one child rather than the other. Hence, if a moral dilemma is understood as a conflict between equally strong and hence nonoverridden moral reasons, then it is obvious that there are such dilemmas. Once this is established, a further question arises: Faced with such a conflict, what should a morally conscientious agent, who is trying to decide what to do, conclude about what, in the final analysis, she morally ought to do? I will argue that the answer to this question is, "I morally ought to save one child or the other (so far as deciding what to do is concerned, it does not matter morally which)," thereby leaving the choice as to which child is to be saved to be determined on some nonmoral ground, or else arbitrarily. It would be incoherent to say that the correct decision is to save one child and to save the other, knowing that it is not possible to save both. Hence, if a moral dilemma is understood as a situation in which correct conclusions of moral deliberation conflict, then there are no moral dilemmas.

Much of the debate about "moral dilemmas" has focused on questions pertaining to irresolvable moral conflicts.[3] In my view, no serious philosophical problems are raised by this issue, and apparent controversies about it are likely to be resolved once terminology is clarified. I will be concerned with this issue only insofar as it is necessary to establish the claims of the previous paragraph and to distinguish it from other more important topics.

Intermingled with the discussion of irresolvable moral conflicts, and sometimes confused with it, has been a debate about another issue that poses deep and difficult philosophical problems about the moral life. This issue concerns the truth of the thesis stated earlier: Are there moral conflicts in which an agent will do something morally wrong no matter what he or she does? My position is that there are such conflicts, and my primary aim in this book is to defend this position.

It is important to recognize that these two issues are independent of one another. First, from the fact that conflicting moral reasons are both nonoverridden it does not directly follow that moral wrongdoing cannot be avoided; for it might well be said, and often is, that in such a case the only actual moral obligation is to perform one action or the other, and that so long as this is done there is no wrongdoing whatsoever.[4] Hence, the recognition that there are conflicts between nonoverridden moral reasons requires some further consideration to establish that these are situations of inescapable moral wrongdoing. Second, those who maintain that there are moral conflicts in which wrongdoing is unavoidable have often claimed, correctly in my view, that this may be so even when the moral reason for one action clearly overrides the moral reason for the conflicting action.[5] In these cases, they claim, not only is there moral wrongdoing when acting against the overriding reason, there is also moral wrongdoing in some significant sense when acting in accordance with the overriding reason; so the agent will do something morally wrong no matter what. Hence, even if there were always a resolution of conflicting moral reasons, moral wrongdoing might still be inescapable. In sum, inescapable moral wrongdoing has nothing essentially to do with moral conflicts in which neither reason overrides the other.

I will give a more precise specification of various positions concerning these two issues in Chapters 3 and 5. Because they are often discussed together, however, it will sometimes be convenient to make references without regard for these distinctions. For this purpose, I will occasionally speak of such things as the "moral dilemmas" view, debate, literature, and the like (in each case with quotation marks around 'moral dilemmas') in order to refer to the issue of irresolvable moral conflicts, or the issue of inescapable moral wrongdoing, or both.[6]

The debate about inescapable wrongdoing might seem to be of minor importance, concerned with a few cases on the margin of moral philosophy and having no bearing on more fundamental matters. But once it is recognized that inescapable wrongdoing does not require irresolvable moral conflicts, it becomes clear that it is potentially a more pervasive phenomenon. Moreover, disagreements about the possibility of inescapable wrongdoing often reflect deep differences in the understanding of morality, with respect to both methodological and normative questions.

I will discuss these differences in due course. For now it is important to observe that those who have defended the idea of inescapable moral wrongdoing have commonly emphasized the epistemic value of concrete moral experiences, while those who have opposed this idea have usually relied on more abstract, a priori considerations. In my view, both of these approaches are important, but neither should be given an absolute priority. This is, of course, a controversial methodological stance, and my defense of it must await the next chapter. I mention it here because, in the face of the strong propensity among philosophers in favor of the general and the abstract, I believe proponents of inescapable moral wrongdoing have been correct to emphasize the fundamental importance of our intuitive responses to particular moral conflicts. This is why I think it is appropriate and indeed essential to begin with a detailed consideration of a specific moral conflict.

There are several reasons for focusing on the conflict in *Billy Budd*. Unlike the simple examples ordinarily invoked in philosophy, *Billy Budd* offers us a detailed, intricate, and emotionally engaging narrative that closely approximates the particularity and affectivity of moral conflicts in real life. On the other hand, unlike most examples that might be drawn from someone's actual life, *Billy Budd* is public: It is equally accessible to us all, and it is quite well known. Moreover, though in some respects it approximates actual moral conflicts, as a work of fiction it allows us the luxury of leisurely reflection and critical distance not always available in the circumstances of our everyday lives.[7] Finally, Melville is an author who is especially sensitive to the depth and complexity of the moral life, and the controversy among critics of *Billy Budd* is particularly pertinent to the issue of moral conflicts. None of this is to deny that works of literature have limitations as points of reference in philosophical writing. For example, they typically lack the conceptual clarity required by such writing. Still, keeping in mind that my discussion of *Billy Budd* is only one phase of my overall argument, it is a useful place to begin.

II. The Controversy about *Billy Budd*

Billy Budd was Melville's last work. It was left more or less completed at his death in 1891 but was not published until 1924. What is fascinating about *Billy Budd* is not only the story itself, but the extraordinary diversity of responses it has elicited from its readers. For a preliminary understanding of these responses, it will suffice to state briefly the central events of the story. A young sailor on board a naval ship in time of war is falsely accused of plotting mutiny by an evil officer. In order to test this accusation, the ship's captain compels the sailor to face his accuser and respond. But the innocent sailor is afflicted with a speech impediment, activated in times of stress, and he cannot speak. In frustration, he strikes the accusing officer, who drops dead to the deck. The captain orders an immediate trial of the sailor for this insubordinate act. Before the court the captain grants that the sailor was falsely accused, and he acknowledges that justice and compassion compel leniency. But he argues that the court's higher obligation is to enforce the law, which requires execution, and that no mitigation of this penalty can be allowed in view of the fact that the navy has recently suffered two mutiny attempts. The court reluctantly agrees, and the following morning the sailor is hanged.

Two contrary traditions of interpretation of *Billy Budd* have developed. The dispute between them centers primarily on the moral evaluation of the captain, Edward Fairfax Vere, and his role in the trial and execution of the young sailor, Billy Budd. For some, Vere was a hero who did what was morally, albeit tragically, necessary, while for others he was simply an authoritarian ruler lacking compassion and a sense of justice. For example, for Lewis Mumford, Vere was "a man of superior order,"[8] while for Lawrence Thompson, the captain was "a sinner and a criminal."[9] Over sixty years of interpretation, punctuated by the publication of a definitive text,[10] has done nothing to abate this controversy.[11]

It has been suggested that *Billy Budd* as Melville left it lacks a fully unified vision,[12] and also that its critics simply read their own ideological biases into it.[13] There is some truth in both claims: Melville died before he finished revising the story, and it has been something of a litmus test of its readers' political outlooks. Still, I believe there is a more fundamental explanation of this controversy. We should read Melville as being interested first and foremost in encouraging our reflection on the complex moral nature of Vere's situation, and as being concerned with inviting us to evaluate Vere's response to that situation only in light of this complexity. His situation, I will argue, was morally tragic in this sense: Whatever he did, in the wake of Billy's killing of the officer, he would have committed a serious moral wrong. Because moral wrongdoing was inescapable for Vere, it has been possible for some readers to see his chosen course of action as wrong and for others to see any other course of action as wrong. There is a sense in which both sides are correct. On the other hand, there is also a sense in which they are both mistaken, insofar as they share the assumption that there must have been some course of action open to Vere that was morally unproblematic—wholly and without qualification *the* right thing to do. In this way, the conflicting responses may be explained.

My reading of *Billy Budd* also offers a partial reconciliation of the two critical traditions. The first group of readers were right to stress the tragic dimensions of the story. Raymond Short, for example, accurately saw that "no matter what course of action is taken, not either, but both, good and evil will issue forth."[14] But from the fact that Vere would have done wrong no matter what, it does not follow that any course of action would have been morally as good or as bad as any other. Inescapable moral wrongdoing does not mean the moral reasons supporting each alternative are equally strong. Nor does it follow that what Vere actually did was morally best. Hence, it is compatible with my reading of Vere's situation as tragic to reject the early interpreters' claim that Vere was a moral hero. *Billy Budd* may still be read as a testament of resistance rather than acceptance. In this respect, Karl Zink was right to claim that, though Billy accepted the necessity of his execution, "we are mistaken if we assume that Melville himself accepted it."[15] Though we ought to sympathize with Vere insofar as he was in a tragic situation, we ought also to be critical of how he chose to respond to this situation. Thus, there is merit in some of the reproofs of Vere by readers of the second tradition. Yet I do not see Vere as wholly evil, as some have argued. To be driven to this extreme is to miss what is, in the words of the narrator, "a moral dilemma involving aught of the tragic" (p. 105). It was this dilemma, I maintain, that Melville was chiefly concerned to explore.

III. The Trial of Billy Budd

Essential to any understanding of *Billy Budd* is the fact that it took place against a background of rebellion motivated by a sense of justice against the authority of tradition and law. The scene was the HMS *Bellipotent*, a man-of-war on duty with the Mediterranean fleet of the English navy, during the war with revolutionary France, in the summer of 1797. The previous spring had been the occasion of "The Great Mutiny," an insurrection of English sailors at the Nore, preceded by a smaller revolt at Spithead. "Reasonable discontent growing out of practical grievances in the fleet," the narrator tells us, "had been ignited into irrational combustion as by live cinders blown across the Channel from France in flames" (p. 54). Both outbreaks had been suppressed, but with only partial redress of the wrongs that had inspired them, and "it was not unreasonable to apprehend some return of trouble" (p. 59). Among the crew of the *Bellipotent* were some who had participated in the recent rebellions and some who had been brought into service by impressment—one practice untouched by these rebellions, and untouchable, in that the navy could not be maintained without it. Included in the ranks of the impressed was Billy Budd, taken only recently from a merchant ship, the *Rights-of-Man*, named after Thomas Paine's response to Edmund Burke's indictment of the French Revolution.

By situating the story in this specific political context, Melville clearly intended to raise questions about the basis of political authority as well as the grounds for revolt against it. But he did not mean for his readers to approach the story with unqualified support for either the French or the English. Rather, the setting established a milieu in which the legitimacy of tradition and law, as represented by the English and the English navy, were confronted with the threat of revolt under the banner of human rights, as exemplified by the French and the mutineers. Both sides of this confrontation, I will suggest, merit a mixture of respect and apprehension.

Vere was not confronted with a rebellion from the crew of the *Bellipotent*.

But his need to respond to Billy's deadly but nonmalevolent act brought him face to face with the moral grounds of his own legal authority and compelled him to consider whether he himself might have reasons to rebel against that authority. We are told that Vere was a man of established convictions who felt that these "would abide in him essentially unmodified." They were "as a dike against those invading waters of novel opinion" (p. 62). In particular, Vere opposed the ideas of the French Revolution on the ground that they were "insusceptible of embodiment in lasting institutions, but at war with the peace of the world and the true welfare of mankind" (p. 63). Against these ideas, Vere once declared that for mankind "forms, measured forms, are everything" (p. 128). Still, charged with responsibility for Billy's fate, it might be expected that Vere would have had occasion to modify if not abandon these convictions—or at least consider doing so. For there was another side to Vere: As Billy struggled to make verbal rejoinder to Claggart, the accusing officer, Vere "laying a soothing hand on his shoulder" urged him to take his time in "words so fatherly in tone" (p. 99). It is true that once Billy struck and killed Claggart, "the father in him . . . was replaced by the military disciplinarian" (p. 100). But the repression of Vere's fatherly aspect does not diminish the fact that elements of the larger political conflict were personified in his own character.

For the full disclosure of that character, we need to consider Vere's words and actions before, during, and after Billy's trial.[16] As soon as the surgeon confirmed that Claggart was indeed dead, Vere ordered an immediate "drumhead court." Though the surgeon and other officers thought the case should be referred to the admiral, "in a way dictated by usage" (p. 101), Vere justified his action on the ground that the *Bellipotent* was presently away from the fleet and the claim that "unless quick action was taken on it, the deed . . . would tend to awaken any slumbering embers of the Nore among the crew." This "sense of the urgency of the case," we are told, "overruled in Captain Vere every other consideration," so "he was glad it would not be at variance with usage" to call a drumhead court (p. 104).[17] Vere also decided "in view of all the circumstances" to hold the trial in secret, and for this he was again criticized by some of the officers as well as by the narrator (p. 103).

In this decision to order an immediate and secret trial, there is an early indication of the significance of Vere's passion for order. True, there were two recent mutiny attempts, so it was surely reasonable for Vere to take them into account. But he did not believe Claggart's accusation, and he had no reason to suspect an incipient rebellion aboard the *Bellipotent*. The weight Vere gave to the danger of mutiny thus suggests a man for whom the maintenance of order was an overwhelming concern. The military disciplinarian in him had indeed replaced the father. On the other hand, Billy probably would not have fared any better in either a public trial or a trial before the admiral.

The drumhead court consisted of three officers, selected by Vere, together with Vere himself acting as witness and coadjudicator. From the interrogation of Vere and Billy, the court correctly accepted as truth that Billy bore no malice against Claggart, that Claggart falsely accused Billy of plotting a mutiny, that

Billy struck and killed Claggart, that he would not have struck him if he could have spoken, and that by striking him he did not mean to kill him. It was evident to the court that Billy's character was such that he was incapable of guilty intent either with respect to mutiny or murder. This young sailor, adolescent in appearance, was exceptional for his simplicity and innocence. Of limited intelligence and experience, he was incapable of any form of double-meaning, be it satire or shrewdness. This "child-man" lacked any "intuitive knowledge of the bad" (p. 86). Upon his impressment, he raised no objection, was nearly cheerful about it. Billy was, in fact, "little more than a sort of upright barbarian, much such perhaps as Adam presumably might have been ere the urbane Serpent wriggled himself into his company" (p. 52).

There was perplexity in the court about *why* Claggart had falsely accused Billy. What we know from previous narration, but the court could only suspect, is this: Though outwardly a respectable sort—sober and intelligent, patriotic and deferential to authority, of high social and moral character, without vices— Claggart was in fact "the direct reverse of a saint" (p. 74). He suffered from "a depravity according to nature" (p. 75), an inborn evil mania activated only on occasion by the presence of some particular object of attention. Yet, when possessed by this malevolent obsession, he was capable of executing the most rational of means to achieve its end, and so might appear as one especially subject to reason. The specific object of Claggart's obsession was, of course, Billy. His "significant personal beauty," together with his simplicity and innocence, had inspired in Claggart both envy and antipathy of the deepest and most passionate sort (pp. 77–78). It was this that led him to plot against Billy, the culmination of which was his false accusation of mutiny.

Of these details the court was unaware. But it knew enough to recognize that an officer with evil intentions had falsely accused the innocent Billy of mutiny and that it was on account of this extreme provocation coupled with an inability to speak that Billy struck out, expressing frustration and indignation but no intention to kill. Hence the court knew the essentials of the relevant facts pertaining to Claggart and Billy.[18]

IV. A Tragic Choice

Once the interrogations ended, Vere perceived the three officers of the court to be in a state of "troubled hesitancy," and with this in mind he addressed them as to the proper verdict (pp. 109–13). In this allocution Vere shows intellectual awareness, if not full emotional appreciation, of the fact that the court faces a deep and painful moral conflict. He begins by granting that there are moral grounds for treating Billy with leniency. In support of this conclusion, he refers to "moral scruple," "compassion," "natural justice," "the heart," and "the private conscience." Natural justice in particular compels consideration of more than "the prisoner's overt act" (p. 110). It requires scrutiny of intention and motive, and it is beyond question that Billy "proposed neither mutiny nor homicide" (p.

111). In Vere's mind, there is no doubt that Billy is "innocent before God" (p. 110), that "at the Last Assizes" he shall be acquitted (p. 111).

There is little reason to dispute the moral validity of these considerations. Billy was practically a child, he had been impressed into the navy, he was the object of an evil plot by an officer, he acted under extreme provocation, and he had no intention to kill. Justice and compassion both speak against the penalty of death, even if there are some actions for which death is a just punishment. It does not follow from this that these circumstances favor complete exoneration. After all, Billy did strike and kill a man. The alternative to hanging Billy is thus a set of possibilities ranging from exoneration to some substantial penalty short of death, though I will refer to these with the term 'leniency' as if they were a single alternative. There are then clear and compelling moral reasons for supposing that the officers have a responsibility to Billy to exercise some form of leniency.

On the other hand, Vere continues, according to martial law, if a man "in wartime at sea . . . strikes his superior in grade . . . apart from its effect the blow itself is . . . a capital crime" (p. 111). None of the officers denies that this is the law, and the narrator confirms that Billy's act, "navally regarded, constituted the most heinous of military crimes" (p. 103). So far as martial law is concerned, the only relevant fact of the case is that Billy struck Claggart. Billy's "intent or non-intent is nothing to the purpose." Vere acknowledges that martial law is imperfect in this respect. It "resembles in spirit the thing from which it derives—War." As "war looks but to the frontage, the appearance," so too does martial law (p. 112). Nevertheless, Vere argues, the members of the court, "as the King's officers," have an allegiance to the King and hence an obligation to enforce martial law: "Our vowed responsibility is in this: That however pitilessly that law may operate in any instances, we nevertheless adhere to it and administer it" (pp. 110–11). The narrator again confirms the point: As "a loyal sea commander," Vere "was not authorized to determine the matter" on the basis of "the essential right and wrong involved" (p. 103).

It might be thought that Vere's argument, based on the officers's allegiance to the king, carries no moral weight at all since the regime of the king and its laws are corrupt. There is no question that they are corrupt in some respects; indeed they are portrayed as such (p. 58). In my view, however, we miss the import of the story if we conclude from this that there is no moral conflict. The deeper point to which Melville is calling our attention is that every government is morally imperfect to some extent and that any system of laws will occasionally produce unjust results. Such are the effects of human finitude and fallibility. Yet those charged with administration of the law must be required to enforce it irrespective of whether or not they approve of its results. Without this requirement there would be no government of law at all. And there is a powerful reason to value such a government. In the words given Thomas More in Robert Bolt's *A Man For All Seasons*, "the law is a causeway upon which, so long as he keeps to it, a citizen may walk safely."[19] Since for there to be such a causeway government officials must be required to enforce the law and not their own private conscience, any such official may confront situations in which he or she believes, perhaps rightly, that enforcement, though required, is unjust. Vere and the officers of the court are representative of such a person. The fact that they have a responsibility to the state to enforce the law is thus a genuine moral consideration.

We are thus given reason to think that Vere and the court will commit a serious moral wrong no matter what they do: If they execute the undeserving Billy, they will violate their responsibility to him to exercise leniency, a responsibility rooted in their sense of justice and compassion, but if they show him leniency, they will violate their responsibility to the state to enforce the law. At this point Vere makes a crucial move: He argues that their responsibility to enforce the law preempts all other moral considerations. He says to his officers that "in receiving our commissions we in the most important regards ceased to be natural free agents" (p. 110). Were Billy to be condemned by martial law, "for that law and the rigor of it, we are not responsible" (pp. 110–11). In reference to his earlier observations, Vere says, though "the exceptional in the matter moves the hearts within you . . . let not warm hearts betray heads that should be cool." Finally, he asks rhetorically, leaving no doubt as to the correct response, "tell me whether or not, occupying the position we do, private conscience should not yield to that imperial one formulated in the code under which alone we officially proceed?" (p. 111).

Several issues are raised by these claims. Before discussing them, we need to consider the final step in Vere's argument. One of the officers asks if it would be possible to "convict and yet mitigate the penalty" (p. 112). To this Vere responds, "were that clearly lawful for us under the circumstances, consider the consequences of such clemency." This does not directly acknowledge that clemency would be lawful. Yet if it were not lawful, it would seem that that would be the end of the matter. The fact that Vere goes on to object to clemency on consequentialist grounds suggests that perhaps it would be lawful. In any case, the consequences cited by Vere are these. To the crew, with their "native sense" and inability to "comprehend and discriminate," Billy's deed "will be plain homicide committed in a flagrant act of mutiny" (p. 112). They will wonder why the penalty for that was not imposed, and this will lead them to revert to the recent mutiny attempts. In particular, they will think that we are "afraid of practicing a lawful rigor singularly demanded at this juncture, lest it should provoke new troubles. What shame to us such a conjecture on their part, and how deadly to discipline" (p. 113). In sum, clemency cannot be allowed on the ground that in these exceptional circumstances it would render the command of the ship liable to disobedience if not outright mutiny.

Though such utilitarian reasoning is controversial among philosophers, I believe Melville intended for us to recognize in Vere's argument a valid though problematic moral stance. It was valid insofar as it was legitimate for Vere to consider as morally relevant the consequences of their disposition of Billy's case with regard to the maintenance of order on the ship. This does not mean that the value of these consequences is the only morally relevant factor, nor does it mean that it overrides all other morally relevant factors. But we are surely encouraged to enter into Vere's perspective to the point of seeing that the preservation of order on the ship, and ultimately in the English state, was *a* valid moral consideration for Vere to bring to the court's deliberations.

Vere's argument was morally problematic, however, insofar as it made Billy's execution depend on grounds quite extraneous to the moral quality of his act. That this act did not warrant execution, from the standpoint of justice and compassion, Vere has already acknowledged, and he appears to do so again here when he speaks of "so heavy a compulsion" that is laid upon the court and says, "I feel as you do for this unfortunate boy" (p. 113). The intuitive wrongness of punishing the undeserving because it will have the best overall consequences has, of course, been the bane of utilitarians everywhere. But Melville's point was not simply to weigh in for the deontologist's cause. To the contrary, he meant to force us to confront the fact that evil means may be necessary to achieve good ends, in particular that it may sometimes be necessary to harm the undeserving in order to acquire and maintain political power, even political power committed to serving the public good. Hence, though utilitarian reasoning may be legitimate, when good ends do justify evil means, the means are still evil—something that utilitarians by and large have denied.

At the same time, Melville did not intend to deny that there may be occasions when the evil means are so evil that they must be resisted, even if this means harming the public good. To this extent deontologists are correct; for we are surely meant to at least wonder whether the trial of Billy was such an occasion. Still, refraining from evil means may also be morally problematic, especially for those charged with the responsibility to protect the public good, for refusal to take the necessary means may entail the sacrifice of a great good for others to which one has morally committed oneself. This is itself a form of evil—something which deontologists by and large have denied.

In view of the politically charged readings of this story, it is important to recognize that, though the means-ends issue is a sharp point of contention between utilitarians and deontologists, it is not an issue that per se divides the conservative and revolutionary political ideologies in contention in *Billy Budd.* In addition to Vere's willingness to execute the undeserving Billy in defense of conservative England, and more generally the repressive measures employed by England in establishing and maintaining its colonial empire, we need to consider the role of *la Terreur* in the French Revolution as a means of achieving a society based on *la Déclaration des droits de l'homme et du citoyen* (or, to take a more recent example, Trotsky's claim that "killing old men, old women, and children" is justified when it is the only means of achieving the goal of the socialist revolution).[20] There is, of course, significant disagreement about what ends are politically desirable, and there are those on both the left and the right who maintain that some means are absolutely impermissible in politics. But I take Melville to be making a point that transcends these controversies: that sometimes the good of a political regime, however understood, may be achieved and maintained only by evil means, and that when this occurs, whatever choice is made, whether to use evil means or to sacrifice the general good, there will be moral wrongdoing.[21] In this respect we are encouraged, not to take sides in the dispute between England and France, but to reflect on the moral ambiguities inherent in political rule in a very imperfect world.[22]

V. An Assessment of Vere

I have argued that the situation of Vere and the court regarding Billy Budd was such that they would commit moral wrongdoing no matter what. Either they must execute the undeserving Billy and violate their responsibility to him to show leniency or they must show such leniency and transgress their responsibility to the state to enforce the law as well as to maintain order on the ship. That their situation was a moral tragedy in this sense I take to be the import of Melville's careful articulation of the serious but conflicting moral responsibilities they faced. But this interpretation does not prevent us, or Melville, from being critical of the decision they made. Though moral wrongdoing was inescapable, it is a further question whether their decision to execute Billy was morally the best choice. There are grounds in the text for thinking it was not.

First, we are given reason to question Vere's consequentialist argument. Though Vere thought it was obvious that the crew would be incapable of seeing Billy as anything but a murderer and mutineer, we learn later that it "instinctively felt that Billy was a sort of man as incapable of mutiny as of wilful murder" (p. 131). Moreover, despite the previous mutiny attempts, Vere had no specific reason to think *his* crew was contemplating a mutiny. It may have been more Vere's passion for order than a disinterested estimate of probable consequences that led to his conclusion. His argument is clearly weakened to the extent that he exaggerated the danger of mutiny, and Billy's death was not reasonably required as a means of maintaining order on the ship.

Vere's primary argument, however, is that the members of the court, as the king's officers, have a moral responsibility to enforce martial law, which requires execution, and that this responsibility overrides the moral considerations that compel leniency. This conclusion does not immediately follow from the argument presented earlier that government officials have a moral responsibility to enforce the law irrespective of their personal moral judgments. That argument gives Vere and the court a powerful moral reason to simply apply the law and not consult their own consciences—a reason that ordinarily would override other considerations. But it is compatible with this argument to hold that there are situations in which it is morally best to override the responsibility to enforce the law. These situations would have to be exceptional cases, but this does not mean they are impossible. Even as a people may in certain circumstances be morally compelled to overthrow its government, in violation of the moral responsibility to obey the law, so an administrator of the law may on some occasions be morally required to refuse to enforce the law despite the moral responsibility to do so. In these acts of rebellion and civil disobedience, moral responsibilities to obey or enforce the law need not be rejected as no longer valid. They may be acknowledged and yet violated in the name of a higher moral judgment. So the possibility is open to Vere and the officers to transcend their "station and its duties," and to act, in F. H. Bradley's words, on "claims beyond what the world expects of us, a will for good beyond what we see to be realized anywhere."[23]

Many have argued that this is what Vere ought to have done. Though I will not repeat their arguments here—they depend largely on giving considerable weight to the innocence of Billy's character and the gross injustice of the situation in which he was placed—there is some merit in what they have said.[24] But it is important to emphasize that Melville did not make it obvious that this was the case. For Vere to have followed this course would have been to take an extraordinary and perhaps even heroic step. It would have meant not only acknowledging a fundamental flaw (or at any rate, limitation) in his moral universe, but, more practically, might have resulted in his having to resign his position as well as being regarded as a traitor. For Vere, in whom there is no better example of Bradley's conception of a moral self being defined through fulfillment of its "station and its duties," this would have been a step of monumental proportion. Hence, it is more accurate to say that Vere failed to take a morally courageous action than that he made a straightforward moral error.

In any case, Melville was more concerned with encouraging reflection on the nature of moral tragedy than he was with prompting judgments about what Vere should have done.[25] This suggests that there is a further, and perhaps more important, perspective from which we may evaluate Vere's response to Billy's act. Irrespective of his decision, to what extent did Vere recognize that his situation was one in which moral wrongdoing was inescapable? Did he feel as a person should feel in the face of such a situation? If no matter what he did he would violate a responsibility either to Billy or to the state, if in this sense he would unavoidably do something morally wrong, then regardless of his choice it would be appropriate for him to feel some form of moral distress about his action, some anguish about transgressing his responsibility to Billy or to the state as the case may be, even if in fact he acted for the best. What, then, did Vere feel?

The captain never had any doubt about what in the final analysis ought to be done. As soon as the surgeon declared Claggart dead, Vere exclaimed, "Struck dead by an angel of God! Yet the angel must hang!" (p. 101). He expressed this with such agitation that the surgeon wondered if he had become unhinged. But with these words, and this manner of expression, Vere was simply betraying the painful recognition of the moral complexity of his situation. During the trial itself Vere clearly acknowledged the presence of conflicting moral responsibilities. Still, in his argument that the court had an overriding responsibility to enforce the law, Vere drew away from the implications of this acknowledgment by disavowing any responsibility for their decision to execute Billy. By becoming officers, he said, we "ceased to be natural free agents," and for this reason "we are not responsible" for the law and "the rigor of it" (pp. 110–111). The force of this claim is that, since they had declared their loyalty to the king, they were no longer free and responsible agents: *They* were not executing Billy at all, *the king's law* was doing that. Because they were not really acting, we may also suppose they were not the ones who were violating the conflicting moral responsibility Vere had earlier recognized. This is perhaps why, though Vere spoke of compassion in these deliberations, it may be questioned whether he really spoke compassionately. In any case, Vere's position here is a manifest piece of deception. No declaration of loyalty, freely and accountably given, can eliminate an agent's responsibility for acts justified by that loyalty. Even if Vere's decision were correct, his way of defending his position was deeply flawed.

It is nonetheless possible that this argument was more a piece of rhetoric aimed at persuading the reluctant officers to make what Vere believed was the correct decision than it was an expression of his true feelings about the moral complexity of the case. Though Vere was not one to express his innermost emotions, it is important that, in describing Vere's visit to Billy to report the verdict, the narrator conjectures:

> Captain Vere in end may have developed the passion sometimes latent under an exterior stoical or indifferent. He was old enough to have been Billy's father. The austere devotee of military duty, letting himself melt back into what remains primeval in our formalized humanity, may in end have caught Billy to his heart, even as Abraham may have caught young Isaac on the brink of resolutely offering him up in obedience to the exacting behest (p. 115).

The reference to Abraham and Isaac is surely significant, not only as a reminder of the tragic conflict confronting Vere, but as an indication of the conflicting elements in his own moral nature. Perhaps the father in Vere was not, after all, completely repressed. A short time afterward, lying on his deathbed, Vere was heard to utter the words, "Billy Budd, Billy Budd," yet we are told that "these were not the accents of remorse" (p. 129). Vere did not feel remorse in the sense of feeling that he had made the wrong decision. Yet, by murmuring these words at this fateful moment, he was perhaps expressing his anguish that in doing what he confidently believed was morally best he nevertheless did something morally wrong. In the end, we are left to speculate about Vere's true state of mind. Melville's most fundamental intention in recounting this tale may have been to prompt our reflection on the proper affective response to a situation in which moral wrongdoing is inescapable.

VI. A Prospectus of Philosophical Issues

Most philosophers believe that moral wrongdoing may always be avoided. Though this position obviously does not entail an interpretation of *Billy Budd*, it does entail a view about the moral situation of Vere as Melville presented it. It requires these philosophers to maintain that there was some course of action open to Vere, in the aftermath of Billy's killing of Claggart, that would not in any way have involved moral wrongdoing. Many literary critics of *Billy Budd* appear to have shared this assumption. This view is compatible with differences of opinion both as to what the captain ought to have done and as to why it would have been free of wrongdoing. In the case of the critics, these differences have been substantial. These disagreements aside, it is a direct implication of the view of these philosophers and critics that, if Melville intended Vere to be in a situation in which moral wrongdoing is inescapable, then what Melville intended was something incoherent.

I will now put the interpretation of Melville aside and focus attention on the philosophical questions involved in the claim that Vere would have done something morally wrong no matter what as well as the counterclaim that there was something he could have done which would have involved no moral wrongdoing. In this way I will introduce some of the main philosophical issues that will concern me throughout the book.

Those philosophers who maintain that wrongdoing can always be avoided have not meant to deny that, at some level, moral reasons can conflict. They would probably grant that Vere had moral reasons both for and against executing Billy. What they have meant to deny is that moral conflict can in any meaningful sense survive the process of moral deliberation. I will argue that there is one respect in which these philosophers are correct: It would have been incoherent for Vere to determine, as the conclusion of moral deliberation about what, all things considered, he morally ought to do, that he both ought to execute Billy and ought not to execute him. To reach such a deliberative conclusion would be tantamount to deciding to perform incompatible actions, and this would clearly be irrational. Nonetheless, some proponents of the idea of inescapable wrongdoing have appeared to commit themselves to the idea that correct conclusions of moral deliberation may conflict, and much of the criticism of inescapable wrongdoing has gained plausibility by being directed against this latter idea. But I reject this idea *tout à fait*.

I have maintained that the moral reasons for showing Billy leniency were more compelling than the moral reasons for executing him, and thus that the correct conclusion of moral deliberation for Vere was to do the former. It is theoretically possible that the conflicting moral reasons here were equal in moral significance and hence were such that neither overrode the other. Even if this were the case, however, the correct deliberative conclusion for Vere would have been "Either I ought to execute him *or* I ought to show him leniency," leaving the decision as to which to do to be determined on the basis of nonmoral reasons or else arbitrarily. The correct conclusion would not have been "I ought to execute him *and* I ought to show him leniency." Or so I will argue.

Though conflicting moral reasons may be equal in weight, I see no ground for supposing they can be incomparable, meaning they are not equal and yet neither outweighs the other. It is sometimes held that the idea of inescapable moral wrongdoing involves the claim that conflicting moral reasons are incomparable. This makes it appear that legitimate criticism of incomparability also undermines my position. But I will argue that unavoidable moral wrongdoing does not require incomparability. Hence, objections to the latter are not objections to the former.

Once these clarifications are made, there remains a substantial issue about inescapable moral wrongdoing. My view is that, whatever Vere did, there is a sense in which he would have done something morally wrong. If I am right that the correct deliberative conclusion for Vere was that he ought to show Billy leniency, then there is an obvious sense in which he would have been wrong to execute him. But I am also claiming that he would have done something wrong *in some sense* if he had shown him leniency. Hence, he would have done something wrong no matter what. Most moral philosophers, though they might allow that Vere had conflicting moral reasons, would nonetheless reject this position. In their view, not only may correct conclusions of moral deliberation never conflict, so long as Vere acted on the correct conclusion he would have done nothing wrong *in any sense*.

The difference between these two positions may be understood as follows. On my view, the captain had both a moral responsibility to the king (and his country) to uphold the law and the order of the state, and a moral responsibility to Billy to be just and compassionate. Though deliberation can determine that one of these responsibilities is more compelling than the other, meaning that that responsibility is the one to be acted on, it does not thereby eliminate altogether the fact that there is another, conflicting responsibility. These different responsibilities are not unlimited in the sense of requiring any action at all for their respective beneficiaries. But each of them is fundamental, meaning that its moral demand does not simply disappear every time a more compelling moral consideration comes into conflict with it. A responsibility overridden in deliberation about what to do remains a responsibility. Hence, whatever Vere did, he would have failed to fulfill one of these responsibilities, and in this respect he would have done something morally wrong no matter what.

In opposition to this, the view that wrongdoing may always be avoided is committed to something like the following position. In a given situation, there is only one actual moral responsibility, and that is to do what moral deliberation determines in the final analysis ought to be done. Hence, the conclusion that Vere morally ought to take a particular course of action completely eliminates the validity of those moral reasons favoring incompatible courses of action. If the correct conclusion was that Vere ought to execute Billy, then it is simply not the case that in this situation there was a moral responsibility rooted in justice and compassion to be lenient. It only appeared that there was such a responsibility, and because deliberation established that this appearance was false, there is no sense at all in which it was wrong to execute Billy. Or, if the correct conclusion was that Vere ought to show Billy leniency, then it is not actually the case that in this circumstance there was a moral responsibility to enforce the law requiring execution. Once again, it only appeared that there was such a responsibility, and because deliberation showed that this appearance was false, there is not any respect at all in which it was wrong to show Billy leniency.

Between these two positions there is a fundamental difference in the understanding of morality. I will now give a brief indication of the way in which I will defend the claim that moral wrongdoing is sometimes inescapable. Many of the philosophers who have defended this claim have based their argument, at least in part, on an appeal to a specific emotional response to moral conflicts. They have claimed that in certain conflicts persons would or should feel regret, remorse, or perhaps guilt no matter what is done. There has been considerable debate about the precise nature of this feeling. Though this will require discussion later, for now I will simply state that the argument requires that it be some form of feeling extending from disquiet to anguish that involves a recognition that one has committed some moral transgression; for the argument goes on to claim that the best way to account for these feelings is to suppose that in these situations moral wrongdoing is inescapable.

I will refer to this line of reasoning (and variations on it) as "the phenomenological argument."[26] In my view, there is a fundamental insight in this argument: Our affective moral responses can be a source of moral understanding. But previous statements of the argument have been inadequate, both because they have not been sufficiently self-conscious methodologically and because they have been improperly formulated and developed. One of my principal aims is to remedy these deficiencies. My main suggestion is that the argument be understood as relying on a methodology I call "reflective intuitionism," a position I develop by making modifications in John Rawls's idea of reflective equilibrium. In brief, reflective intuitionism states that we begin with prima facie credible but fallible moral intuitions, and that we seek the best overall explanation of these intuitions. The best explanation may require us to reject some of our initial intuitions as unwarranted. In any case, whatever beliefs are required by the best explanation are justified.

The phenomenological argument as I will defend it begins with the claim that we have intuitions to the effect that there are moral conflicts in which it would be appropriate to feel some form of moral distress no matter what was done (what I will refer to as inescapable feelings of moral distress). For example, it would be appropriate for Vere to feel moral anguish whether he executed Billy or not. It is in order to ascertain our intuitions about these feelings that I believe it is necessary to reflect carefully on the particularities of moral conflicts such as that confronting Vere in *Billy Budd*. The fact that we have these intuitions, however, is not sufficient to establish that moral wrongdoing is inescapable. No direct inference of this kind would be valid. The method of reflective intuitionism requires an additional premise: that the best explanation of these intuitions is that moral wrongdoing is inescapable. Only from our intuitions about inescapable moral distress and this thesis about the best explanation of them may it be concluded that wrongdoing is sometimes inescapable.

This brief outline does not do justice to the complexities of my defense of the phenomenological argument. There are many difficult issues that need to be considered. The method of reflective intuitionism must be articulated and argued. The claim that we have prima facie credible intuitions about inescapable feelings of moral distress must be established. And the thesis that these intuitions are best explained by supposing that moral wrongdoing is sometimes inescapable must be shown. In my view, it is the last of these that requires the most attention, and I want to bring this introductory chapter to a close by saying more about it.

The heart of my explanation is an account of moral responsibilities. According to this account, an agent's moral responsibilities are based on a recognition of the intrinsic and unique value of the particular persons (or social entities) with whom the agent has, in various ways, established some connection. Hence, an agent's responsibilities are ultimately responsibilities to specific persons. The nature of these responsibilities is defined primarily by the agent's relationship with those persons to whom he or she is responsible and is not simply a function of the outcome of the agent's moral deliberations about what ought to be done in a given situation. For this reason, responsibilities to persons may conflict. When they do, the fact that deliberation of necessity directs the agent to fulfill his or her responsibility to at most one person does not mean that the responsibility to the other person has in this situation been eliminated. There will thus be occasions of conflicting moral responsibilities when, whatever the agent does, he or she will fail to fulfill at least one of these responsibilities. It is with respect to moral wrongdoing in the sense of not fulfilling a moral responsibility so defined that I believe moral wrongdoing is sometimes inescapable.

To return to *Billy Budd*, I argued that Vere had a moral responsibility to Billy to show leniency and a moral responsibility to the king to enforce the law and maintain order on the ship. Since these responsibilities conflicted, Vere could fulfill only one of them. Even if Vere had done what was morally for the best, he would still have failed to fulfill one of these responsibilities. I suggested that in this situation Vere's more compelling responsibility was to Billy. But this does not show that in this situation Vere had no responsibility to the king to enforce the law. That responsibility persisted, and even had Vere acted as he ought, he would nonetheless have done something wrong by violating this responsibility to the king. Likewise, if Vere had been correct in his decision to enforce the law, the responsibility to Billy would have remained and it would have been wrong to transgress it. Hence, moral wrongdoing was inescapable for Vere.

Those who reject this conclusion offer different explanations of inescapable feelings of moral distress. I will argue that these explanations are inadequate, in part because they do not give a good account of our moral feelings, but also because they have an unacceptable understanding of moral responsibilities. A principal though generally unstated reason why opponents of inescapable moral wrongdoing have resisted this idea is that they believe that our ultimate moral responsibility is not to specific persons at all, but to something that in comparison with concrete persons is an abstraction. On these accounts, to the extent that responsibilities regarding specific persons are recognized, they are thought of as secondary phenomena that are completely defined by the outcomes of moral deliberation in such a way that, properly understood, they never conflict. It is surprising how many otherwise diverse moral theories maintain this kind of position.

The most obvious example is utilitarianism. The utilitarian maintains that our ultimate moral responsibility is to maximize the sum of goodness in, as Mill puts it, "all mankind" and even "the whole sentient creation."[27] On the basis of this responsibility there may arise, in particular circumstances, secondary responsibilities to promote the well-being of particular persons. But these responsibilities are not so much responsibilities to specific persons as they are responsibilities with respect to these persons. Moreover, they are completely contingent on, and entirely defined by, the responsibility to maximize the sum of goodness in the world. They have, so to speak, no life of their own, and correctly understood they will never conflict. So long as an agent performs that action which maximizes the sum of goodness in the world, every actual moral responsibility will be fulfilled, and there will be no sense at all in which the agent will do anything morally wrong.

It is, of course, a common critique of utilitarianism that, in Rawls's oft-quoted words, it "does not take seriously the distinction between persons."[28] But other theories, including deontological theories, are also disposed to view moral responsibilities to specific persons as a secondary and contingent phenomenon. For example, though it might be thought that Kant, with his emphasis on respecting persons as ends in themselves, would be immune to this objection, he is quite clear that our ultimate moral responsibility is not to persons as such, but to the moral law. "Duty is the necessity of an action," Kant says, "executed from respect for law."[29] And, he says, "the only object of respect is the law. . . . All respect for a person is only respect for the law (of righteousness, etc.) of which the person provides an example."[30] It follows that, so long as we respect the moral law (and Kant insisted that the moral law cannot give rise to conflicting duties),[31] we will have fulfilled all our moral responsibilities and will not have done anything morally wrong.

My point is not that the methods of deliberation associated with utilitarian and Kantian moral theories are entirely wrong. It is compatible with what I am saying that one or both is partially correct in its account of how we should decide which action ought to be done. Rather, what is at issue is a conception of the object of moral responsibility assumed by these theories. They share the claim that our ultimate responsibility is not to particular persons as such, but to some abstraction such as "the whole sentient creation" or "the moral law."[32] In this respect, these theories improperly displace persons as direct objects of moral concern and thereby estrange us from the true nature of our lives as moral agents. Our lives are constituted by relationships with specific persons to whom we have moral responsibilities. By transforming these responsibilities into contingent and secondary manifestations of our responsibility to whatever abstraction is favored by the theory and by declaring our responsibility to this abstraction to be the only genuine responsibility we have, these theories distort our relationships with other persons.

It is thus not surprising that utilitarians and Kantians have been at the fore-front of those who have rejected the idea of inescapable moral wrongdoing.[33] For we can best make sense of this idea, I believe, by supposing that our moral responsibilities are ultimately responsibilities to specific persons and that when these responsibilities conflict, the fact that deliberation, of necessity, directs us to fulfill our responsibility to at most one of these persons does not mean that our responsibility to the other has in this circumstance been abolished. Since in our everyday lives we do understand our relationships and responsibilities in this way, it seems to us appropriate for an agent faced with conflicting responsibilities to feel moral distress no matter which course of action is taken. It is a reflection of the alienating character of the aforementioned theories that they are compelled to deny the appropriateness of these feelings and thereby promote a distortion in the nature of our moral lives.

A related indication of the estrangement engendered by these theories is the fact that they are committed to a reading of *Billy Budd* that eviscerates its tragic character. These theories entail that in this situation Vere's ultimate moral responsibility was not to either the king or Billy, and that his only contingent responsibility was to but one of these persons. Either Vere had no responsibility to the king to enforce the law or he had no responsibility to Billy to be just and compassionate through a show of leniency. Hence, so long as Vere correctly determined what was and was not his actual moral responsibility in this circumstance and acted in accordance with this conclusion, he would have done no wrong. He would have fulfilled his responsibility to that abstraction, whatever it might be, to which he as a moral agent owed his only true allegiance.

I have tried to show that this is an intuitively implausible reading of *Billy Budd*. For it fails to capture what is most compelling and disturbing in this tragic tale: that because he would have failed to fulfill his moral responsibility either to Billy or to the king, the captain would have done wrong no matter what. My aim in the remainder of this book is to give a philosophical defense of the position presupposed in this reading, that there are occasions in the lives of us all when we will do something morally wrong no matter what we do.

Notes

1. This reading of the Greek tragedians is developed in Nussbaum 1986. I discuss a concept of tragedy in chapter 9.

2. Some of the contributions to this debate have been collected in *Moral Dilemmas* (Gowans 1987).

3. For example, this is the main concern in Sinnott-Armstrong 1988.

4. Even Sinnott-Armstrong, who defends the thesis that there are conflicts among nonoverridden moral reasons, declines to describe such conflicts as situations in which wrongdoing is inescapable (see Sinnott-Armstrong 1988, p. 20). I discuss his understanding of "moral dilemmas" in chapter 3, sec. V.

5. For example, see Marcus 1980, pp. 130–33; Nussbaum 1986, p. 27; Phillips and Mounce 1970, pp. 100–101; Stocker 1990, p. 28; Walzer 1973, pp. 169–72; and Williams 1973a, pp. 172–75.

6. These expressions may be understood as having, as an approximate denotative definition, the views and debates in the essays collected in my aforementioned anthology and in other works that discuss these essays.

7. For some recent defenses of the value of reflection on literature in moral philosophy, see DePaul 1988; Nussbaum 1990; and Putnam 1979. For criticism of some uses of literary examples in moral philosophy, see O'Neill 1986.

8. Mumford 1929, p. 354.

9. Thompson 1952, p. 400.

10. Melville 1962. All references are to this edition (in parentheses).

11. For surveys of the literature on *Billy Budd*, see Melville 1962, pp. 24–27; Melville 1975, pp. xi–xiv; Milder 1989; and Sealts 1986, pp. 421–24. A bibliography accompanies each of these surveys. *Billy Budd* also attracted the attention of two prominent philosophers in the early sixties, with equally diverse results. For Hannah Arendt, the story endorses the thesis that compassion, being incapable of "argumentative speech," is irrelevant to political life (Arendt 1963, pp. 81–82). Thus Arendt sees Vere as a man of virtue, and this "virtue—which perhaps is less than goodness but still alone is capable 'of embod-

iment in lasting institutions'—must prevail at the expense of the good man" (p. 79). On the other hand, for Peter Winch, Vere was faced with "two conflicting sets of equally moral demands" (Winch 1965, p. 205). In resolving this conflict, Winch declares that he himself would "have found it morally impossible to condemn" Billy, but he denies that it is a logical consequence of his judgment, as proponents of the universalizability thesis maintain, that "Vere acted wrongly" (p. 208). It is not inconsistent, Winch argues, to say, about the same situation, that it would be wrong for me to hang Billy and that it would be right for Vere to do so. Finally, for an interpretation by a philosopher that relates to my own, see the very brief discussion of *Billy Budd* in Mallock 1967, pp. 176–78.

12. See Brodtkorb 1967.

13. See Melville 1975, pp. xiii-xiv and xlii-xliii.

14. Short 1946, p. xxxii.

15. Zink 1952, p. 134.

16. It has been pointed out that in several respects Vere's procedures and substantive arguments in the trial were in violation of the military law that actually governed the English navy in 1797 (see Ives 1962; Melville 1962, pp. 175–83 (notes on leaves 233, 245, 273 and 284); and Weisberg 1982, pp. 19–34). On the basis of this historical analysis, Vere has been criticized for disobeying the law (for example, by Ives and Weisberg). But I doubt that Melville expected his readers would be historians of military law. Moreover, the articles of war that governed the navy did state that striking an officer for any reason was punishable by death. Thus, according to actual law, Billy was subject to the death penalty, even though in the story the procedures of actual law were not correctly followed. It is true that at one point Vere appealed to "the Mutiny Act" (p. 112), which in fact applied to the army and not the navy. Hence, measured against actual law, it was extraordinary and outrageous for Vere to invoke the Mutiny Act. Yet neither the narrator nor any officer questioned this, though they did question Vere on several other points. I conclude that, within the universe of the story, the Mutiny Act did apply, and more generally, that the correctness of Vere's understanding and application of the law are to be doubted only insofar as there are grounds *within* the story for doing so (cf. Posner 1988, pp. 134–35 and 155–66, and Scalts 1986, pp. 418–19).

17. The perception of the danger of mutiny may explain the apparent contradiction in the appeal to "usage" by Vere and the surgeon: For Vere the situation is an extraordinary one, hence the relevant "usage" may differ from that of ordinary circumstances.

18. There is one possible exception to this. In an earlier phase of his plotting, Claggart had arranged for a sailor to approach Billy with a vague but sinister proposal, one perhaps intimating mutiny. This Billy flatly refused, though it never occurred to him to report the matter, as duty required. During the trial Billy was asked if he had any reason to suspect an incipient mutiny, and his answer was that he did not. Had the court become aware of this incident, it would have obtained further insight into the extent of Claggart's scheming, but it would also have seen another example of Billy's capacity to violate martial law, however innocent his intent. But on both these points the court already had some understanding.

19. Bolt 1962, p. 89.

20. Trotsky 1973, p. 36.

21. For a defense of a similar view of politics, see Walzer 1973, whose position I discuss in chapter 9.

22. There is an interesting passage by Melville that is relevant to this point. The passage was once thought to have been intended as a preface to the entire story (and was published as such), but it has been established that in fact Melville wrote it as part of Ch. 19 (just after Billy's killing of Claggart) and later deleted it from the text altogether (see

Melville 1962, pp. 9–10, 18–19, and 25). Because Melville discarded the passage, it would be a mistake to put much weight on it. But because there is no question that Melville did write it, it does have some relevance to his state of mind. About the French Revolution, the passage declares that it "involved rectification of the Old World's hereditary wrongs" but that "this was bloodily effected" and "straightway the Revolution itself became a wrongdoer." Nonetheless, the outcome of it all has "for some thinkers apparently" been "a political advance." About the mutinies at Spithead and the Nore, the passage claims that "something caught from the Revolutionary Spirit . . . emboldened the man-of-war's men to rise against real abuses, longstanding ones," and yet this involved "inordinate and aggressive demands." Still, "the Great Mutiny, though by Englishmen naturally deemed monstrous at the time, doubtless gave the first latent prompting to most important reforms in the British navy" (Melville 1956, p. 198). In both cases, I take the point to be the intertwinement of good and evil in the political workings of the world, in particular, the way in which worthy political ends are achieved through the instrument of evil means.

23. Bradley 1927, p. 220.

24. Though there are some fundamental disagreements between us, I nonetheless recommend the critiques of Vere in Adler 1976 and Zink 1952.

25. It is worth keeping in mind the narrator's remark at the end of the trial scene: "Forty years after a battle it is easy for a noncombatant to reason about how it ought to have been fought. It is another thing personally and under fire to have to direct the fighting while involved in the obscuring smoke of it. Much so with respect to other emergencies involving considerations both practical and moral, and when it is imperative promptly to act" (p. 114).

26. I am borrowing this expression from Santurri, who uses it to refer to some forms this argument (1987, pp. 47–60).

27. Mill 1957, ch. 2, par. 10.

28. Rawls 1971, p. 27.

29. Kant 1959, p. 16.

30. *Ibid.*, p. 18.

31. See Kant 1971, p. 23.

32. This phenomenon may also be exemplified in some theistic moral theories which maintain that our only ultimate moral responsibility is to God. On this view, our responsibility to God may give rise to secondary responsibilities regarding particular persons, but these responsibilities are entirely contingent upon and defined by what God requires of us. Hence, so long as we do what God requires—and it is often assumed that God's requirements, properly understood, do not conflict—we will have met every moral responsibility, and we will have done nothing wrong. In this connection, see Geach 1969, p. 128 and Santurri 1987. For a contrary view, see Niebuhr 1935 and Quinn 1989.

33. For an example of each, see Hare 1981, chs. 2 and 3, and Donagan 1984. I discuss these and other utilitarian and Kantian positions in chapters 7 and 8.

2

Methodological Issues: Reflective Intuitionism

Opposed views about "moral dilemmas" frequently reflect different methodologies of moral inquiry. Yet the debate about "moral dilemmas" has been conducted with little explicit consideration of methodological issues. This is surprising both because these issues are important for determining whether or not there are "moral dilemmas" and because contemporaneous with this debate there has been a significant discussion about methodology in moral philosophy. For the most part this discussion has not played a direct role in the debate about "moral dilemmas."[1] Though many arguments and objections concerning "moral dilemmas" have tacitly presupposed methodological positions, there has been little attempt to justify these positions in the context of the debate. My aim in this chapter is first to show the importance of methodological considerations for the question of "moral dilemmas" and second to develop and defend the methodology that informs my own approach.

Much of the recent concern about methodology has revolved around Rawls's method of reflective equilibrium and to a lesser extent the linguistic approach of R. M. Hare. Since these are incompatible, discussion has often concerned their respective merits. But there have also been critiques of assumptions they appear to hold in common.[2] I develop my own position through an examination of these discussions by and about Rawls and Hare. This approach has the advantage of allowing me to set forth my position with reference to familiar terrain. Of more importance, since the central issues about methodology apropos "moral dilemmas" are raised in these discussions, this approach enables me to confront these issues. In the end, I simply reject the method of Hare. With respect to Rawls, however, I argue in favor of a modified version of the method of reflective equilibrium, which I call "reflective intuitionism." Some of the departures I make from Rawls manifest the concerns of those who have been critical of the theoretical stance perceived as common to both Rawls and Hare. It is the methodology of reflective intuitionism that governs the arguments in the remainder of the book.

I. The Importance of Methodology

Proponents of the view that there are "moral dilemmas" have frequently relied on concrete, experiential observations in order to defend their position. This is evident in the prominent role assigned to various forms of the phenomenological argument and more generally in the widespread insistence on focusing attention on particular examples of moral conflicts. By contrast, opponents of this view have tended to dismiss the relevance of these concerns and have emphasized instead that there cannot be "moral dilemmas" on account of more rationalistic and abstract notions. Hence, the most common objection to the idea of "moral dilemmas" is that they would result in an inconsistency, a claim that is usually defended on the basis of some logical or conceptual principles such as those found in deontic logic. In rebuttal, proponents of the "moral dilemmas" view have generally been unimpressed by these inconsistency arguments and have often supposed that our moral experiences are more compelling than any of the a priori principles employed in these arguments.

It would be a mistake to suppose that every defense of the "moral dilemmas" view is experiential and that every critique of it is rationalistic. In citing this difference, I mean to refer to an important tendency of thought, not an essential connection. It is not the case that the real issues are all methodological, so that settling this dispute about method would automatically settle the question of "moral dilemmas." Still, in view of the aforementioned tendency and in view of the fact that it has not received much attention, it is important to become conscious of the role of methodology in arguments for and against "moral dilemmas." My aim is to defend a methodology that, though not neutral about methodological issues, is as much as possible neutral on questions pertaining to "moral dilemmas." Though the method of reflective intuitionism is not uncontroversial with respect to the debates about methodology, it does not beg the question in favor of the positions I defend regarding "moral dilemmas." In any case, it is important to emphasize the complexity of my views. I will argue that there is a methodological place for both experiential and theoretical concerns, and that there is a sense in which there are "moral dilemmas" and a sense in which there are not.

Before I begin, three preliminary points need to be made. First, it is customary among philosophers to distinguish between metaethics and normative ethics. Metaethics is said to consider basic questions about the meaning of moral terms and concepts, as well as epistemological and metaphysical issues about the possibility of objectivity and truth in morality, while normative ethics is thought to discuss substantive positions about what is good and bad, right and wrong, just and unjust, and so on, along with particular applications of positions on these subjects. This is a useful distinction that I do not dispute. But it is often tacitly supposed that metaethical questions and normative questions are independent of one another, as if it were logically possible to combine each metaethical position with each normative position. I doubt that this is generally true, though it is sometimes true that a given metaethical position (for example, noncognitivism) may be combined with various normative positions (for example, with either a consequentialist or a deontological theory).[3]

The debate about "moral dilemmas" has often been understood as a debate in metaethics, and sometimes it has been supposed that it can be resolved without making commitments to any particular normative position.[4] Up to a point, this attitude is correct: In many respects, the debate about "moral dilemmas" has concerned questions that are clearly metaethical rather than normative (for example, the correctness of principles of deontic logic). In fact, I will argue that certain theses about "moral dilemmas" can be judged on the basis of metaethical considerations that are independent of normative issues. Nevertheless, I will also argue that the specific thesis that moral wrongdoing is inescapable involves both metaethical and normative questions, and that it is not compatible with all normative positions. In particular, in the evaluation of the phenomenological argument, different explanations of inescapable feelings of moral distress are often associated with different normative accounts, and the explanation that I believe best explains these feelings—based on the responsibility to persons account—differs from the explanations of both utilitarian and Kantian theories. Hence, my defense of the view that moral wrongdoing may be inescapable is closely tied to a definite normative outlook, one that is incompatible with other commonly accepted outlooks. For this reason, I regard the debate about "moral dilemmas" as involving both metaethical and normative issues.[5]

In view of this, a methodology that is adequate to judging the "moral dilemmas" debate must be one that pertains to both metaethical and normative issues. In the case of Hare this would not be a problem. His methodology first establishes theses in metaethics and then on this basis establishes a position in normative ethics. But I will not be employing Hare's methodology. Rather, I will be following a modification of Rawls, and it may seem that there is a problem with this. For Rawls's method is clearly intended primarily if not exclusively for the discussion of normative issues. It is characteristic of his approach to eschew metaethical questions as much as possible. Hence, one of the revisions of the method of reflective equilibrium that I will make is to understand it as having broader scope than Rawls intends, so that it makes room for both metaethical and normative questions.

My second preliminary point concerns the definition of "moral dilemmas." As I noted in the last chapter, the standard definition of a "moral dilemma" (a person ought to do A and ought to do B, but cannot do both A and B) is ambiguous. It may refer to a situation in which (1) moral reasons conflict and there is no moral resolution of the conflict, (2) there are conflicting conclusions of moral deliberation, or (3) a person will do something morally wrong no matter what he or she does. Though these descriptions are quite different, for the purposes of this chapter these differences generally do not matter. Hence, I will usually speak of "moral dilemmas" without reference to these distinctions.

A final point: The methodological and epistemological issues I raise in this chapter are matters of great importance and controversy, and they deserve more extensive discussion than I can give them here. Since my concern is to discuss moral conflicts, I can only develop a brief account of methodology. Nonetheless, discussion of method is of the first importance. Methodological assumptions have been largely beneath the surface in the "moral dilemmas" debate. If progress is to be made in this debate, it is crucial to become conscious of these assumptions and to account for them. In this chapter, I hope to make my own methodological standpoint explicit and to give some indication of why it is correct.

I take my bearings from discussions concerning Hare and Rawls. There is an important reason for focusing on these figures in connection with "moral dilemmas." In significant ways they are representative of methodological tendencies that respectively oppose and favor the "moral dilemmas" view. Hare's rejection of any fundamental role for moral intuitions and his emphasis on the importance of logical and conceptual principles ally him with the rationalist tendency among opponents of the "moral dilemmas" view. On the other hand, Rawls's acceptance of an essential role for moral intuitions and his attempt to downplay the linguistic and logical concerns of the metaethical tradition make him an ally of the experiential tendency among proponents of the "moral dilemmas" view. I speak here of alliances rather than identities of positions, for Hare and Rawls are not fully representative of the methodological divisions in the "moral dilemmas" debate. Still, the ascendancy of Rawls's approach over that of Hare in the last two decades has been a substantial part of the reason for the increased interest in, and support for, the idea of "moral dilemmas."

II Hare's Linguistic Method

Hare's discussion of methodology[6] is based on a distinction between moral intuitions, which are beliefs about what morally ought to be done, and linguistic intuitions, which are beliefs about the logical properties of moral words. His central thesis is that moral intuitions have no legitimate place in arguments for moral theory, while linguistic intuitions are essential to these arguments. I discuss Hare's critique of moral intuitions in Section IV. Here I focus on his positive position. For Hare, the purpose of moral theory is the determination of rules for thinking rationally about morality. He takes these rules to be implicit in the meanings of moral words, of which 'ought' is the most important. The meaning of 'ought' is to be established on a strictly empirical basis: An account of this meaning is a description of what we, as speakers of English, mean when we use 'ought', of our linguistic intuitions concerning it. Hence, it must be tested against actual linguistic behavior.[7] Nonetheless, Hare believes the rules for moral thinking implied by the meaning of 'ought' logically commit us to a substantive normative theory (namely, utilitarianism).

An attractive feature of Hare's approach is that it holds the prospect of providing an objective basis for resolving the "moral dilemmas" debate. The method is not defined so as to beg the question for or against "moral dilemmas." Yet the application of it could provide empirical reasons for judging the issue, for some of the theories of meaning discussed by Hare have implications for the "moral dilemmas" thesis. Consider first the theory, rejected by Hare but defended by others, that some moral words such as 'kind' and 'cruel' have, inseparably, both descriptive and evaluative meaning.[8] That is, in virtue of their meaning, these words refer to empirically identifiable properties, the presence of which warrants their use, and at the same time they imply a moral evaluation of the action possessing these properties. They are, as Hare puts it, "*inherently motivative*" properties. For example, it might be said that an action is kind if and only if it has certain properties but to call an action kind is also to judge that it ought to be done, while an action is cruel if and only if it has certain properties but to call an action cruel is also to judge that it ought not to be done. Now, it seems possible that the same action could have a set of properties such that it was both kind and cruel.[9] For example, a situation might arise in which a person would have to agree with Hamlet that "I must be cruel only to be kind." In this case, it would follow from this theory that an action both ought to be done and ought not to be done. Here is an account of meaning, then, that provides prima facie support for one form of the thesis that there are "moral dilemmas."[10]

Consider next the theory of meaning, which Hare defends, according to which moral judgments of the form 'S ought to do X' are universalizable, prescriptive, and overriding. Each of these features may create a problem for the claim that there are "moral dilemmas," but I will discuss only one of them here. "To treat a principle as overriding," Hare says, "is to let it always override other principles when they conflict with it."[11] Now, suppose there is a "moral dilemma" in which a person ought to do A and ought to do B, but cannot do both A and B. Since these two moral principles conflict, it follows from Hare's account that each overrides the other. But this implies that each principle is ranked both above and below the other, and this seems absurd. Hence, Hare's account of the meaning of 'ought' provides a prima facie argument against the "moral dilemmas" thesis.[12]

If there were an empirical basis for assessing these theories, as Hare supposes, then the "moral dilemmas" debate might likewise admit of an objective resolution. However, there are serious difficulties with this linguistic approach, not the least of which is its purported empiricism. Hare claims to be giving an account of the meaning of 'ought' as revealed in the actual use of the word by speakers of English. But in fact, he does not offer any empirical evidence, such as a linguist would, to show that people do mean by 'ought' what he says they mean. Instead, he appears to have tested his account only against his own linguistic intuitions and then qualified it in response to objections raised by philosophers. Yet it is clear that many philosophers do not share Hare's linguistic intuitions, for they have rejected all or part of his account of the meaning of 'ought'. Hence, not only is empirical support for Hare's position lacking, there is some evidence against it.

It might be said that empirical evidence concerning people's actual linguistic behavior *would* establish that Hare's account is correct. But this is very unlikely. For example, it does not seem implausible to suppose that many people would agree with the statement, "Anyone who thinks there is nothing wrong with having sex with one's own children doesn't know the meaning of right and wrong." Yet if Hare's account were correct, people would not agree—or if they did, they would be confused or not know the meaning of 'wrong'. For this statement, by making incest part of the meaning of 'wrong', is committed to a form of descriptivism, which Hare rejects. It is possible that Hare could convince people that they should not agree with this statement, but then his account would not be a theory of what people do mean, but a theory of what they should mean. Hare insists, however, that he is not proposing a revision in linguistic usage. It does not follow from this that descriptivism is correct, but that no simple theory is likely to be correct. Though the everyday meaning of moral terms is not capricious, it is more a matter of family resemblances than of necessary and sufficient conditions, and it is subject to a fair measure of ambiguity, vagueness and indeterminacy.

A related objection to Hare's approach has been made by Richard B. Brandt.[13] He argues that any account such as Hare proposes would probably not be useful for philosophical inquiry. In ordinary language, Brandt says, moral words are vague and there is no reason to believe everyone uses these words with the same meaning. Moreover, ordinary language sometimes embodies confusing distinctions and leaves other, important distinctions unexpressed. For these reasons, Brandt claims, an account of the meaning of moral words based upon linguistic behavior is not likely to produce the definite and precise findings required to resolve philosophical issues. About this Brandt is surely correct: The mere fact that there has been so much controversy about the meaning of 'ought' among philosophers suggests that the word does not have a single, exact meaning in ordinary language. This does not mean that nothing can be said about the meaning of 'ought' as typically used by speakers of English. But it does mean that no account of this meaning is likely to establish the conclusive philosophical results envisioned by Hare.[14]

There is a final problem with Hare's methodology. Suppose many speakers of English typically used 'ought' with the meaning Hare attributes to it. It would seem to follow that for these persons there are no "moral dilemmas." But suppose some other speakers of English used 'ought' with a different meaning, one that allowed for the possibility of "moral dilemmas." For these persons it would seem that "moral dilemmas" are possible. If these suppositions were both true, then there would be a meaning of 'ought' used by some in which "moral dilemmas" are not possible and a meaning of 'ought' used by others in which they are possible. It might be thought that since these two groups of persons are using 'ought' with a different meaning, they are not talking about the same thing and so they are not really disagreeing with one another. But this need not be the case. There might be sufficient overlap in their understanding of 'ought' for there to be a meaningful sense in which they are talking about the same thing, even though their use of 'ought' also has different connotations in other respects. Moreover, their disagreement about "moral dilemmas" might make a difference in how they think, feel, and act in situations they would both agree are morally significant. There would thus be a pragmatic measure of their conflicting positions.

Under these circumstances, Hare's method would only be able to describe the differences between the meaning of 'ought' for these persons. For someone already determined to use 'ought' in one sense or the other, this would provide a resolution to the "moral dilemmas" issue in the sense of stating the implications of that use. But for someone trying to decide which sense of 'ought' to use, Hare's method is necessarily silent. Since it purports only to *describe* actual linguistic usage, it is not able to give reasons for *preferring* one way of speaking about morality, and hence about "moral dilemmas," over the other. In this deeper sense it cannot determine whether or not there are "moral dilemmas."

At one point Hare raises an objection similar to this. According to this objection, different groups of people might have different moral conceptual schemes and hence, on Hare's view, might have different methods of moral reasoning and in turn different substantive moral views. Hare acknowledges that it is possible to change our conceptual scheme. "I am not suggesting," he writes, "that we are tied to using words in the way that we do, or to having the conceptual scheme that we have." However, he says, "we come into moral philosophy asking certain moral questions, and the questions are posed in terms of certain concepts." If we are "to answer *those* questions, we are stuck with *those* concepts."[15] It is doubtful that this is generally true, for it may be that the best way to answer our questions involves modifying the concepts in terms of which they were originally formulated. In any case, Hare claims that these questions are important and that the concepts they presuppose are "serviceable."[16]

The difficulty with this response is that it completely alters the foundation of Hare's account. Once it is admitted that there are alternative conceptual schemes and that it is possible to abandon one and adopt another, then the crucial question is not "What conceptual scheme *do* we use?" but "What conceptual scheme *should* we use?" To declare that our conceptual scheme has "serviceable" concepts and allows us to ask questions we think are important does not establish that we should continue to use this scheme; for another conceptual scheme might employ more useful concepts or allow us to ask more important questions. Hare makes no attempt to justify the position that the conceptual scheme he takes to be ours is the one we should use. With the exception of his response to this objection, his argument throughout is implicitly that the fact that we use a concept provides sufficient reason for supposing we should use it. Since the possibility of alternative conceptual schemes shows that this is not a sufficient reason and since Hare has provided no other reason, his methodology is at bottom without justification.

There is a further consequence of this critique. Hare maintains that using 'ought' as he understands it commits us to a form of utilitarianism.[17] Suppose his argument for this implication is correct. It follows that by choosing to use 'ought' in this sense we are committing ourselves to a substantive normative theory. But since Hare gives no justification for this choice, he is in effect asserting the correctness of utilitarianism on the basis of a complicated but ultimately unjustified line of thought. It is hard to see how this procedure is superior to the direct appeal to moral intuitions that Hare finds so objectionable.[18]

My conclusion is that Hare's linguistic methodology is inadequate. Though it offers the promise of answering the question whether or not there are "moral dilemmas," this answer would in the final analysis be without foundation. It does not follow, however, that we need not pay any attention to the meaning of 'ought' and other moral terms. Indeed, one of the first issues that must be confronted concerns the meaning of 'ought' in the standard definition of "moral dilemmas." In considering this issue it may be worthwhile to consult our linguistic intuitions. But these intuitions do not have the privileged methodological status assigned to them by Hare. Even the presence of a clear and compelling linguistic intuition does not make it self-evident that a concept must be understood in a certain way. In the final analysis, we decide how to use our concepts, and a variety of considerations are relevant to the justification of this decision.

III. A Reformulation of Rawls:
From Reflective Equilibrium to Reflective Intuitionism

Rawls's methodology[19] was originally developed in connection with political philosophy, but it has been widely taken to have relevance for moral philosophy, an interpretation I share. By his methodology, I mean the conception Rawls refers to with the phrase "reflective equilibrium." His approach to methodology is in two important respects the exact opposite of that of Hare. On the one hand, he gives no special place to linguistic intuitions or, more generally, to the analysis of the meaning of moral terms.[20] On the other hand, he thinks appeal to moral intuitions cannot be avoided. "There is no reason," he says, "to suppose that we can avoid all appeals to intuition, of whatever kind, or that we should try to."[21] Reliance on moral intuitions lies at the heart of the method of reflective equilibrium.

Rawls begins by claiming that principles chosen by persons in the original position would be justified as principles of justice. This is the part of his account that corresponds to the social contract tradition. But this claim is embedded in a larger context, for the specification of the original position is not ethically neutral and the principles of justice chosen must match our "considered judgments" about justice. These are "those judgments in which our moral capacities are most likely to be displayed without distortion."[22] They exclude moral judgments that we are unsure about, that we make when we are upset, or that are clearly influenced by self-interest—criteria of exclusion, Rawls says, we would rely on in any area of concern in order to eliminate mistakes.

If the principles chosen in the original position have results that match our considered judgments, then we have achieved "reflective equilibrium." If they do not match, then we must revise our considered judgments or the specification of the original position (or both). The aim is to make whatever revisions are necessary to reach reflective equilibrium. Rawls's methodology is fallibilist through and through. There is no appeal at any point to self-evident and certain moral intuitions as in traditional intuitionist theories. According to Rawls, it is only when we have achieved reflective equilibrium that principles of justice are justified. He thus endorses a coherentist rather than a foundationalist account of justification for moral theory. Justification, Rawls says, "is a matter of the mutual support of many considerations, of everything fitting together into one coherent view."[23]

There is much that is attractive in Rawls's methodology, and I will employ a version of it in this book, albeit with some significant qualifications and extensions. These modifications are significant enough to warrant a new name for the resulting position. Hence, I will call it the method of "reflective intuitionism." In the next section I will offer a defense of this method. Here I outline my departures from Rawls. My aim is to use his familiar position as a reference point for developing a method suitable for discussion of "moral dilemmas." Though I take my approach to be close to the spirit of Rawls, no intrinsic importance is attached to being true to his actual intentions.

First, the selection of principles of justice in the original position is inessential to the method of reflective equilibrium per se. For Rawls, this hypothetical procedure expresses a substantive moral commitment, namely, that the right is prior to the good.[24] But there is nothing in the idea of reflective equilibrium itself that implies this or any other normative position. The only thing required by the concept of reflective equilibrium is that we bring into systematic coherence our considered judgments about relatively specific cases of justice and injustice, and some rather more abstract notions concerning justice that we find intuitively compelling. I emphasize this because the use I want to make of this method does not imply a commitment to the model of the original position or to the priority of the right over the good. My interest only concerns the idea of bringing into coherence intuitively plausible considerations.

Rawls regards the method of reflective equilibrium primarily as a means of evaluating normative rather than metaethical questions. Since the debate about "moral dilemmas" involves both kinds of questions, it is necessary to consider this method as relevant to metaethical as well as normative concerns. Here, however, there is an obvious problem. The method of reflective equilibrium seems to assume that there are no "moral dilemmas," for the very thing that constitutes a failure of equilibrium is a situation in which we have a considered judgment of the form 'A is required by justice' and an application of a principle of justice of the form 'B is required by justice', where A and B cannot both be done. As this looks to be a form of "moral dilemma," it would appear that the question is begged from the start.[25]

Although Rawls may have intended to deny that there are "moral dilemmas" in some sense, I suggest that his methodology may be modified in a way that is true to its underlying aim and at the same time leaves open the question whether there are "moral dilemmas." Its purpose is to develop an account that embodies moral intuitions in a logically consistent and systematic way. If it turns out that a "moral dilemma" implies a logical inconsistency, then the method would have as a result that there are no "moral dilemmas." But it is a matter of controversy whether a "moral dilemma" does imply a logical inconsistency. This depends partly on how "moral dilemmas" are understood and partly on whether we accept certain contested principles of deontic logic.[26] Hence, I propose to interpret the method as requiring the elimination of logical inconsistencies, where whether a "moral dilemma" implies an inconsistency is left as a question to be decided.

It might be said that the method of reflective equilibrium requires more than logical consistency, that it also requires what Ronald Dworkin calls "a coherent program of action."[27] Even if a "moral dilemma" did not imply an inconsistency, it might violate this condition. In the end, I will agree that a certain kind of "moral dilemma" is incompatible with a coherent program of action and is to be rejected for this reason (see Chapter 4). But the requirement that we have such a program should not be incorporated into the constraints of method per se. This is an issue to be settled by particular moral theories, not something to be imposed upon all theories from the start. Dworkin himself admits that his requirement is based on a substantive moral view, namely a "doctrine of responsibility" that requires public officials to act "on principle."[28] If a method is to be neutral among different moral positions, this doctrine of responsibility should not be included in the method.

In order to address metaethical questions, the method should include intuitions beyond the explicitly normative ones favored by Rawls. For example, there are intuitions of a linguistic or logical sort of the kind discussed by Hare that seem relevant to the debate about "moral dilemmas," such as the Kantian principle that 'ought' implies 'can'. There might also be intuitions about the nature of practical rationality, or even the nature of the person, that are significant. As in other cases, if such intuitions seem initially compelling, then there is reason to try to find a coherent place for them in the overall account, though it is always possible that in the final analysis it will prove best to revise or abandon them.[29] But they should not be given absolute priority over moral intuitions as Hare supposes.

There is also a special class of moral intuitions that it is important to include, those about how we ought to feel concerning what we have done, in particular about the appropriateness of such retrospective responses as guilt, remorse, compunction, regret, and the like.[30] One of the main arguments for "moral dilemmas" claims that in some moral conflicts it would be appropriate to experience such feelings no matter what was done, and that the best account of this phenomenon is that there are "moral dilemmas." By including intuitions about these feelings, it is possible to evaluate this argument from the standpoint of this method. Doing so provides no guarantee that the argument will receive a favorable evaluation. It still must be shown that our intuitions have the character claimed by the argument, that they should not be revised or rejected, and that they are best explained by supposing there are "moral dilemmas."

It might be thought that this emendation violates a central feature of Rawls's account, for he says explicitly that considered judgments exclude moral judgments "given when we are upset or frightened." These judgments are excluded because they "are likely to be erroneous."[31] This might be taken to imply that emotions generally tend to distort our moral judgments and that all moral judgments influenced by emotion should be disallowed. If so, the entire class of intuitions about retrospective moral feelings might be ruled out as being unavoidably tarnished by our emotions.

This would be a mistake. It may well be that an absolutely emotion-free state of mind is unobtainable. Moreover, some emotional states improve rather than distort our moral judgments. For example, being in a sympathetic or compassionate or caring state of mind can lead us to make more acute moral judgments than if we lacked these feelings. Rawls's main point in restricting the class of considered judgments is to include only judgments that manifest an accurate operation of our moral capacities. But if emotion-free judgments are impossible or if judgments influenced by certain emotions are especially perceptive, then this criterion need not be taken to exclude all moral judgments influenced by emotion.[32] On the other hand, in evaluating particular candidates for inclusion in the class of considered judgments, it is important to consider whether they are subject to distortion, either through the influence of emotion or in some other way. This is a burden that the aforementioned argument for "moral dilemmas" must meet in its claims about retrospective moral feelings.

When considering moral intuitions about particular cases, there is a danger of relying entirely on the thinly described examples so common in philosophical writing.[33] Highly simplified examples can be a way of eliciting intuitions for some purposes, such as examining the Kantian principle that 'ought' implies 'can'. In fact, it is sometimes precisely by being simplified that these examples are of value. But there are occasions when brief examples are unhelpful and potentially misleading. This is especially true with respect to examples of purported "moral dilemmas" intended to bring out our intuitions about retrospective feelings of moral distress. The problem with these minimally described examples is that they do not offer sufficient context and detail for adequate evaluation of moral judgments and emotional responses. Such evaluation may require an understanding of the personality and character of the persons involved, the relationships among these persons, their respective histories, the commitments and understandings they have made in the past, the social or institutional context in which they are acting, the immediate circumstances under which the situation under discussion has arisen, the expectations of each of the persons about future developments in one another's lives, and so forth. To the extent that such information is lacking, it may be unclear exactly what our intuitions are about. Moreover, part of the point of including intuitions about particular cases is that there is something to be learned from our engagement with specific circumstances that is not to be gained from reflection on more general and abstract ideas. Hence, we ought to consider a variety of cases with as much detail, context, and verisimilitude as possible. It was partly with this ideal in mind that I began with a discussion of the choice of Vere in *Billy Budd*. Of course, there are dangers here as well: The literary case imposes its own special problems and limitations, such as those having to do with the intentions of the author and the requirements of the narrative form.[34]

In this connection, it is worth commenting briefly on Martha Nussbaum's understanding of philosophical method.[35] Though there are some similarities in our approaches, I want to focus on what appears to be a major difference. Nussbaum maintains that certain philosophical positions can only, or best, be expressed in certain styles of writing. In particular, I take it that she believes that the claim that there are moral conflicts in which moral wrongdoing is inescapable is a claim that cannot be adequately expressed in the philosophical style common in Anglo-American philosophy and that requires for its proper expression the more "literary" style to which she herself aspires.

Though there are obviously relationships between style and content in writing, it is implausible to suppose that the thesis I am here advocating requires for its proper statement and defense the form of writing that Nussbaum prescribes. There is a place within moral philosophy for analysis of literary texts as a means of eliciting our moral intuitions. But reflection on these texts is only one phase in the development of a philosophical position, and it is an altogether different matter to claim that moral philosophy itself ought to be written in a style that in some respects emulates literary texts. My aim is to defend a view about inescapable moral wrongdoing in accordance with widely accepted standards of conceptual clarity, precise statement, explicit argument, and so on. My style of writing is dictated by these standards. I cannot see that the truth of the view I propose to defend would put these standards and this style into question. A perplexing feature of Nussbaum's account is that she regards Aristotle as a model for the method she advocates and practices, and also as a proponent of inescapable moral wrongdoing, and yet she rightly acknowledges that his style is not "literary."[36]

There is a final point to consider by way of elaboration of method. It is not enough to bring intuitively plausible judgments into a consistent or coherent account. The resultant account must also include an explanation of our considered judgments about particular cases.[37] Though an explanation involves logical relationships, it cannot be reduced to them. In general, an explanation answers the question "Why?" with respect to some phenomena. In the case at hand, we want to know why our considered judgments make sense (and also why considered judgments modified or rejected had appeared correct though in fact they are mistaken). An adequate explanation should include a plausible set of considerations that implies or makes probable the phenomena in question and thereby illuminates our understanding of the phenomena. Though the notions of plausibility and illumination are intuitively meaningful, it is difficult to give a formal, or even a useful informal, analysis of them. Nonetheless, it is of fundamental importance to achieve an explanation of our considered judgments about specific cases. We do not want to know merely that these judgments stand in certain logical relationships with other considerations, we want to understand why these judgments are reasonable.

In my examination of inescapable moral wrongdoing I will employ a "Rawlsian" method with the aforementioned provisos. Henceforth I will use the phrase "reflective intuitionism" to refer to this method.[38]

IV. A Defense of Reflective Intuitionism

The objections that have been raised against Rawls's method, and that by implication may be regarded as applying to my revision of this method, are mostly claims that intuitions brought into equilibrium cannot be regarded as justified. Before considering these objections, I will set aside in summary fashion two standpoints from which reflective intuitionism might immediately be rejected. First, if moral skepticism were correct, then we would not have the capacity to achieve understanding in morality, and no method would be adequate to justify moral beliefs. The possibility of moral skepticism should not be dismissed out of hand. Still, my interest is in evaluating arguments concerning "moral dilemmas." If moral skepticism were correct, these arguments would be pointless. But it is not obvious that moral skepticism is correct, however difficult it may be to show what is wrong with it. Given the importance of the issues raised in moral philosophy, we have a clear interest in doing what we can to achieve understanding of these issues even if no refutation of skepticism is available. Hence, I will assume that, to the extent that there is something to be known concerning morality, human beings have some capacity to know it.

Second, traditional foundationalism maintains that beliefs are justified if and only if they are either self-evident and certain, or can be inferred from other beliefs that are self-evident and certain. For the foundationalist, reflective intuitionism is obviously inadequate, since it explicitly rejects any appeal to self-evident and certain beliefs. But foundationalism is now almost universally rejected, at least in ethics, where it is thought implausible to suppose that some ethical beliefs are self-evident and certain.[39] I accept this consensus.

Most of the initial critics of Rawls's method were neither skeptics nor foundationalists. But they seemed to assume that some form of moral realism is true and that an adequate account of the justification of moral beliefs must establish a positive relationship between justified moral beliefs and mind-independent moral facts. They then interpreted the method of reflective equilibrium as a coherentist or subjectivist theory of justification that is appropriately judged by this standard, and they argued from this viewpoint that it is inadequate. Specifically, they claimed that there is no reason to think our moral intuitions accurately reflect moral reality, even when they are revised and placed into a coherent and systematic framework. Rawls's method would only be adequate, they supposed, if moral reality were in some way constituted by our moral beliefs.[40]

Rawls has now made it clear that he does not endorse moral realism.[41] For my purposes, an initial difficulty with this realism-based critique is that I understand reflective intuitionism to include the evaluation of metaethical issues, of which realism itself is surely preeminent. Thus it seems premature to claim that reflective intuitionism must be adequate to the demands of realism, for it is conceivable that the method will show realism to be false. Moreover, even if realism were true, our reasons for thinking it is true might depend on an application of this method. Many of the arguments for moral realism maintain that realism is the best explanation of our intuitions about the nature of our moral practices.[42] This problem may also be relevant to the "moral dilemmas" debate, for it has been argued that moral realists are committed to denying that there are "moral dilemmas" and contrariwise that there can be "moral dilemmas" only if moral realism is true.[43] If either of these claims were correct, then determining whether there are "moral dilemmas" would be directly related to the realism issue. Hence, for the method of reflective intuitionism to adjudicate the "moral dilemmas" debate, it would again be premature to assume from the start that moral realism is true.

On the other hand, we need to begin somewhere, even if provisionally. As my interest is in "moral dilemmas," I am mainly concerned with realism only insofar as it may have some bearing on this issue (see Chapter 6, sec. V). At the same time, I am assuming that there is something to be found out with respect to "moral dilemmas," and I am claiming that the method of reflective intuitionism is the best way to find it out. In some sense, then, I am presupposing a doctrine of realism with respect to these issues. The aforementioned realism-based critique is thus relevant to my concerns. For this reason, I propose to bracket the method's professed neutrality concerning moral realism and to respond to this critique as if realism were true. For the purpose of this discussion, I will understand moral realism in the strong sense that there are "moral facts" that are independent of our beliefs, values, desires, and the like.[44] It is reasonable to assume that less serious problems for the method are posed by weaker forms of moral realism, such as the view that moral facts are those moral beliefs that, within a given moral tradition, would be justified after critical evaluation in the long run.[45]

One of the main objections to the method of reflective intuitionism from the realist standpoint is essentially an application of the standard objection to coherence theories of justification.[46] According to this objection, though coherence may be necessary for justification, it cannot be sufficient, because there is no reason to suppose that a set of coherent beliefs must reflect reality. This point may be brought out in different ways. For example, it may be suggested that it is quite possible for there to be equally coherent but mutually incompatible sets of coherent beliefs. Since these sets are incompatible, one of them must depict reality incorrectly, but since they are equally coherent, coherence alone cannot tell us which depicts reality correctly and which does not. Or it might be pointed out that the fact that a set of beliefs is coherent does not ensure that these beliefs have any input from reality, since the justification of each belief is in terms of other beliefs. Once again, there is no reason to think that a coherent set of beliefs has anything to do with reality.[47]

It should be clear that this objection cannot be directly applied to the method of reflective intuitionism., for though this method involves coherence, it does not make justification depend solely upon coherence. This is because of the crucial role of moral intuitions (Rawls's "considered judgments"). On this account, a coherent set of beliefs would be justified only if it were the result of a process that begins with our moral intuitions. Since moral intuitions exclude judgments made under conditions likely to produce error, it might reasonably be supposed that moral beliefs brought into equilibrium would reflect moral reality, at least to some extent.

It is in response to this claim that a second objection to the method of reflective intuitionism may be brought forward. It states that our moral intuitions are variable and subjective, that they merely reflect our upbringing and cultural background, that they may well result from prejudice or custom, and so on. Hence, it is a mistake to think that these beliefs in any way reflect reality. As Brandt puts it, "the fact that a person has a firm normative conviction gives that belief a status no better than fiction."[48] But if moral intuitions are mere fictions, then (following the first objection) there is no reason to think that a coherent set of beliefs that results from a process beginning with these intuitions reflects reality.

The fact that moral intuitions are fallible does not establish that they have no credibility, since many fallible beliefs have evidential value (for example, perceptual beliefs). Of course, there is a danger that the moral intuitions to which we appeal are mere prejudices. But moral intuitions are not simply gut reactions. Though not the product of philosophical analysis, they are reflectively held. We are to look for those moral judgments made in cognitively favorable circumstances. Moreover, in speaking of our moral intuitions, we are not referring to the moral intuitions of just anyone, but of those persons we regard as morally exemplary. There is no point in appealing to the moral judgments of those we regard as morally corrupt or lax. These considerations do not eliminate the possibility of prejudicial judgments, but they do counteract it. In any case, the method does not suppose that the intuitions with which we begin will all survive the process of critical reflection. The point of that process is to determine which intuitions are ultimately untenable.

On the other hand, no account has been established that adequately explains the conditions under which moral judgments are and are not correct. In the absence of understanding the reliability conditions for moral judgments, it is not possible to say conclusively that the moral intuitions employed in the method of reflective intuitionism are likely to be true or not. This being the case, we have no choice but to proceed provisionally on the most reasonable hypothesis under this circumstance of inadequate knowledge. Given my assumption that human beings have some capacity for moral understanding, I think the most reasonable hypothesis is that our moral intuitions, with the aforementioned specifications, are likely to have something to do with the truth. This does not mean these judgments are certain, but it is enough to refute Brandt's claim that they have "a status no better than fiction."

Perhaps an adequate account of the reliability of moral judgments will eventually be established. This account might show that the hypothesis that our moral intuitions are connected with the truth requires revision or abandonment. It might turn out that the intuitions of people in Western cultures have very little to do with the truth. This might be the case for the intuitions of people in all cultures that have thus far developed. Or perhaps human beings simply do not have the capacity for moral knowledge. These are possibilities, and to the extent that one of them were shown to be true, the value of achieving equilibrium among our current moral intuitions would be diminished. But these possibilities should not deter us from attempts to develop an understanding that begins with our intuitions. As things now stand, we have some reason to think these judgments have something to do with the truth. Moreover, it may be that the only way we are likely to find out about the reliability of these judgments is by attempting to develop a systematic and coherent account of them.

Some might claim to have an account of the reliability of moral judgments and on this basis might argue that our moral intuitions are mostly or entirely unreliable. We can imagine such accounts being put forward, for example, by some Marxists, or religious fundamentalists, or act-utilitarians. But it cannot plausibly be said that any such account has been *established* in the sense of showing that it, and no competing account, is rationally compelling (meaning that it would be unreasonable for someone knowledgeable of the account to reject it). By contrast, we do have a pretty good understanding of the conditions under which perceptual judgments are and are not likely to be correct. For example, we know with some precision when vision or hearing may be expected to be faulty. No similar account has been established for the reliability of moral judgments. Though we have reason to think that some circumstances may render us prone to error in our moral judgments (for example, when our interests are at stake), our lack of understanding in this area is, by comparison, acute.

A second objection comes from the opposite direction. It might be said that there are widespread and deep conflicts among the moral judgments of people in the world and that there is no prospect of establishing that "our" judgments (whomever "we" may be) are superior to those of others. For this reason, it is presumptuous to assume that ours are likely to have some connection with the truth. The most reasonable hypothesis, then, cannot be that our moral intuitions have something to do with the truth.

This objection may be taken in two ways, depending on what hypothesis it is claiming *is* the most reasonable. On the one hand, it may be seen as an argument for moral skepticism: Irresolvable disagreements about morality make skepticism the most reasonable hypothesis. But I am making the assumption that we have some capacity for moral knowledge. On the other hand, if the objection is not taken in this way, then it would seem that it is claiming that there is a better place to begin than with our moral intuitions. The usual suggestion is that we should begin from a standpoint that does not itself include moral judgments at all. For example, we might begin with facts about human psychology, or with judgments about linguistic usage, or with the nature of rational agency.[49] It may be argued that premises from some such standpoint are well-established, and that they can serve as a basis for a valid argument to moral principles.

There is a well-known objection in principle to all proposals of this kind: that no argument from facts to values can be valid. But I do not want to endorse a general claim about a radical fact-value dichotomy in order to reject this proposal. My objection is an inductive one: that the various attempts to carry out this kind of program have thus far been unsuccessful. Though I cannot argue the point here, it is clear that these attempts have been extremely problematic. They typically rely on philosophical positions (such as naturalistic theories of meaning) or arguments (such as Hare's argument for utilitarianism or Gewirth's argument for the Principle of Generic Consistency) that are themselves far from rationally compelling. Moreover, I believe these programs have made progress in establishing substantive moral conclusions only by surreptitiously relying on moral intuitions and so do not constitute genuine alternatives to the method of reflective intuitionism. In view of this, it is implausible to maintain that it would be more reasonable to accept the moral judgments generated by such a program than it would be to accept the moral judgments that result from the method of reflective intuitionism.

A related objection to my position is suggested by Brandt's remark that "what we should aim to do is step outside our own tradition somehow, see it from the outside, and evaluate it, separating what is only the vestige of a possibly once useful moral tradition from what is justifiable at present." Brandt goes on to say that Rawls's method "in principle prohibits our doing this," for it may be no more than "a reshuffling of moral prejudices."[50] Now, from the realist standpoint, there is an obvious sense in which Brandt is right in saying that we should try to step outside our tradition: We want to know what is true, not merely what we happen to believe. It does not follow, however, that the method of reflective intuitionism is inadequate. The method *begins* with our judgments. But, on a realist interpretation, it *aims* at mind-independent truth. This is the point of beginning with judgments made under cognitively favorable circumstances, of being willing to revise these, of trying to achieve consistency, of striving for an explanation of particular judgments, and so on. These are recognized ways of gaining perspective on our tradition and evaluating it. Moreover, they may lead to substantial changes in our moral beliefs and hence may take us far from a mere reshuffling of our moral prejudices.

Perhaps Brandt means to imply that we should start from a standpoint independent of all moral traditions. But it is clear that this is simply not possible. Nor is it necessary. Objective understanding is acquired, when it can be acquired, not by replacing our present beliefs with those justified *sub specie aeternitatis*, but by subjecting beliefs we currently have reason to think are true to the processes of critical reflection. This is true of all attempts to achieve understanding. No one would suppose that in order to understand the American civil war we should "step outside" our tradition of historical understanding and begin from a standpoint independent of all our current beliefs about the war. Rather, we begin with these beliefs and subject them to analysis and critique. There is no reason to suppose that the same approach is inadequate for the development of moral understanding.

A similar response may be made to the common objection that the method of reflective intuitionism is "conservative," not (necessarily) in the sense of being allied with certain social and political beliefs, but in the sense of giving priority to those moral beliefs we happen now to hold. Of course, the method does begin with certain of our beliefs. But it may end up with a set of beliefs very far from the original ones.[51] It is possible, though not guaranteed, that over the long run persons starting out with very different considered judgments would be led to approximately the same place by pursuing the method of reflective intuitionism.

There is a final realism-based objection to the method of reflective intuitionism. It may be said that applying the method would not establish the truth because the method is indeterminate: It does not assure a single outcome, even when the original judgments are the same. It is easy to see why this is the case. Suppose it is recognized that two of our original judgments, J1 and J2, are inconsistent. The method says eliminate the inconsistency, but it says this can be done by rejecting either J1 or J2. Hence, the method is neutral between the set of judgments containing J1 but not J2 and the set of judgments containing J2 but not J1. Since these two sets of judgments are incompatible with one another, they cannot both be true. Therefore, the method of reflective intuitionism does not guarantee the truth.

This objection is, in effect, a restatement of the first realism-based objection—that coherence may have no relationship with the truth—reformulated so as to take into account the preceding discussion. The central contention of this objection is correct: Since the method of reflective intuitionism has different possible outcomes, it clearly does not guarantee the truth. It does not follow, however, that the method is inadequate, for it is doubtful whether any method can guarantee the truth (though traditional foundationalism may promise this). The point of justification is to bring us nearer to the truth, not to guarantee it. This is the standard by which the method of reflective intuitionism ought to be judged. Since the method requires more than mere consistency, there is reason to think its possible outcomes would be more limited than this objection suggests. The requirement to develop a consistent and systematic account that includes an explanation of particular moral intuitions may significantly narrow the field of possible results. Moreover, it is important to distinguish between the short and the long run. In the short run, different persons employing the method may well reach incompatible conclusions. But in the long run, the results of the method may tend to converge, at least over a large range of issues.

My conclusion is that there is no decisive objection to the method of reflective intuitionism from the standpoint of moral realism. In the chapters to come, I assume that there is some truth to be discovered about the issues raised in the "moral dilemmas" debate. But for the most part I do not consider in how robustly realist a sense this truth may be understood. To a large extent, my discussion is confined to the context of contemporary Anglo-American moral philosophy and to those figures in the history of Western philosophy, such as Mill and Kant, from which philosophers in this tradition draw inspiration. Both the moral intuitions I invoke and the possible explanations of these intuitions that I consider are largely drawn from this context. It may thus appear that my conclusions, to the extent that they are sound at all, would only be sound within this particular historical and cultural milieu. This may in fact be so. But it remains possible that these conclusions are true in a stronger realist sense. To establish this would require appeal to a much broader class of moral intuitions than those I rely upon and an evaluation of explanations of these intuitions from other moral traditions. My aims, however, are more modest.

Notes

1. For an exception, see Solomon 1985.
2. For example, see DePaul 1988; Nussbaum 1990; and Walker 1989. In addition, see the papers collected in Clarke and Simpson 1989.

3. For a brief critical discussion of the view that metaethical and normative concerns are independent, see Brink 1989, pp. 1–5.

4. I take this to be the view of Sinnott-Armstrong 1988. See esp. pp. 34–35.

5. Cf. MacIntyre 1990, p. 382.

6. I am relying primarily on Hare 1981, though I have also consulted Hare 1971 and 1975.

7. Hare proposes several empirical tests for evaluating a theory of meaning. See Hare 1971, pp. 121–22 and 125–26, and 1981, pp. 13–14, 65, and 80–81.

8. See Hare 1981, pp. 17–18 and 72–75.

9. This formulation assumes that the same action can have different descriptions. This is a common view, but it has been challenged in Goldman 1970. However, even if Goldman were right, this point could be restated in terms of his theory.

10. Cf. Platts 1979, pp. 245–46, whose position I discuss in chapter 6, sec. VI.

11. Hare 1981, p. 56. Hare's claim about overridingness is qualified, but this does not affect the present argument. See pp. 52–62.

12. I discuss Hare's full critique of the "moral dilemmas" thesis in chapter 7. For a somewhat different form of this argument, see Sinnott-Armstrong 1988, pp. 17–18. I discuss his argument in chapter 3, sec. V.

13. Brandt 1979, pp. 6–8.

14. Hare's response (1981, pp. 80–81) does not confront the fact that no procedure, however complex, can produce a single, precise account of the meaning of 'ought' as actually used if usage is vague, diverse, confusing, and so on.

15. Hare 1981, p. 18.

16. See Hare 1981, pp. 19 and 15, respectively.

17. See Hare 1981, ch. 6.

18. There is another way of seeing this objection. Suppose it were a consequence of our moral concepts that it would not make sense to take into account the experiences of animals in making moral judgments. Someone might say, "If our moral concepts imply that, then we should change our concepts." In response, Hare would have to justify continuing to use our moral concepts with this implication, or else justify changing them, and it is difficult to see how either justification could avoid confronting the moral intuitions of this critic. In fact, in what amounts to an elucidation of the concept of universalizability, Hare notes the suggestion of vegetarians that we consider the effects of our actions not just on people but on sentient beings, and he answers without comment "I am happy to accept this amendment" (Hare 1981, pp. 90–91). For criticism of Hare's attempt to rely only on linguistic rather than moral intuitions, see Dahl 1987, esp. pp. 416–18.

19. I am relying primarily on the discussions of methodology in Rawls 1971, esp. secs. 4, 9, and 87, but I have also consulted Rawls 1974–75, 1980, and 1985.

20. See Rawls 1971, pp. xi, 51–52, 130, and 579.

21. Rawls 1971, p. 44.

22. *Ibid.*, p. 47.

23. *Ibid.*, p. 21. This remark is repeated verbatim on p. 579. Rawls has since offered rather different accounts of the significance of reflective equilibrium. For example, see 1974–75, pp. 7–9; 1980, p. 570; and 1985, pp. 228–31.

24. See Rawls 1971, pp. 30–33; 1985, pp. 249–50; and 1988. For discussion of the relationship between the original position and the method of reflective equilibrium, see Daniels 1980; Dworkin 1975; and Lyons 1975.

25. This is implicit in Rawls. That a coherence theory precludes "moral dilemmas" is made explicit in Sayre-McCord, 1985 p. 171 and Solomon 1985, p. 53. However, this

point is not always recognized. For example, see Clarke 1987, pp. 239 and 242. Cf. also Goldman 1988, pp. 140–44.

26. I understand 'inconsistency' in the usual sense: Two statements are inconsistent if and only if they entail both the affirmation and the denial of some statement. 'A ought to be done' and 'It is not the case that A ought to be done' are obviously inconsistent in this sense. But an argument is needed to establish that the statements constituting a "moral dilemma"—'A ought to be done', 'B ought to be done', and 'A and B cannot both be done'—entail the affirmation and denial of some statement. In some cases, different concepts of consistency and inconsistency have been introduced. For example, see Marcus 1980, pp. 128–30, and Sinnott-Armstrong 1988, ch. 6. I discuss issues concerning consistency and "moral dilemmas" in several places, especially chapter 4, Secs. III–V, and chapter 6, Sec. V.

27. Dworkin 1975, p. 28.

28. *Ibid.*, p. 30.

29. Rawls himself may allow such a provision, but he has shown a tendency to exclude controversial philosophical assumptions as much as possible. See Rawls 1974–75 and 1985. For development of one form of the idea of wide reflective equilibrium, see Daniels 1979 and 1980.

30. Rawls briefly discusses the moral sentiments in 1971, ch. 8.

31. Rawls 1971, p. 47.

32. For helpful discussions of the cognitive significance of emotions in moral inquiry, see Blum 1980 and Nussbaum 1990, esp. pp. 40–42, 75–82, and 291–97.

33. Cf. O'Neill 1986 and Nussbaum 1990, esp. pp. 45–49.

34. Nussbaum, who places tremendous importance on the value of analysis of literary texts in moral inquiry, acknowledges that "stories too impose their own simplifications" (1990, p. 329).

35. See Nussbaum 1990, esp. chs. 1 and 6. For insightful analysis of Nussbaum, see Kalin 1992.

36. See Nussbaum 1990, pp. 18, 49, and 63–64 (cf. 1986, pp. 391–94). In fact, Nussbaum has found merit in expressions of views about "moral dilemmas" in such stylistically diverse writers as Sophocles, Aristotle, and Henry James. This suggests a more pluralistic view of the relationship between style and content than she allows.

37. Cf. Brink 1989, pp. 103 and 130–31; and Kagan 1989, pp. 13–14.

38. In selecting this name, I mean to emphasize continuity with Rawls and his stress on critical revision aiming for a coherent account, but also with traditional forms of intuitionism and their recognition of the importance of intuitive moral judgments (albeit without their claims about infallibility). I do not mean to embrace the descriptive theory of meaning Hare calls 'intuitionism'.

39. For a critique of moral foundationalism, see Brink 1989, pp. 100–122; for one defense, see Finnis 1980.

40. For examples of this kind of objection, see Brandt 1979, pp. 16–23; Lyons 1975; Nielsen 1977; and Singer 1974 (there is a more recent analysis of Rawls's methodology in Brandt 1990). These authors did not necessarily espouse moral realism, but their objections against Rawls seemed to presuppose some form of realism broadly construed. The same may be said about some of Hare's arguments against Rawls (see Hare 1975 and 1981, pp. 11–12), though Hare explicitly rejects realism as a form of "descriptivism" (see Hare 1985). Nonetheless, Hare's (now manifest) rationalist approach has made him an ally of realist critics of Rawls on this issue.

41. See Rawls 1980 and 1985.

42. For examples of this kind of argument, see Brink 1989, pp. 23–36; Dancy 1986; and Nagel 1986, p. 149.

43. See respectively Williams 1973a, p. 175 and 1973b, pp. 204–5; and Santurri 1987, p. 66.

44. Moral realism may be understood as the view that there are moral properties in the world that do not depend for their existence on being recognized by us. But it may also be understood in a more Kantian fashion as the view that there are reasons for action that bind every human being whether we recognize it or not. In my discussion, it will not matter which way moral realism is understood. In this connection, see Nagel 1986, pp. 139–40. For a typology of positions on the realism debate, see Sayre-McCord 1988.

45. For examples of mitigated moral realism, see Nussbaum 1990; Putnam 1981; and (perhaps) MacIntyre 1988.

46. For a useful statement of various forms of this objection, with reference to empirical justification, see Bonjour 1985, pp. 106–110.

47. For suggestions of arguments of this kind, see Brandt 1979, p. 20, and Lyons 1975, p. 146.

48. Brandt 1979, p. 20. Cf. Hare 1975, pp. 82–83, and 1981, pp. 11–12; Nielsen 1977, p. 40; and Singer 1974, p. 494. In this connection, see also Lukes 1974, pp. 182–85.

49. See, respectively, Brandt 1979, Hare 1981, and Gewirth 1978.

50. Brandt 1979, pp. 21–22.

51. It is sometimes said that it is possible that none of our initial considered judgments will survive the process of achieving reflective equilibrium. For example, see Brink 1989, p. 142. This appears overstated. Are we really to suppose that it could turn out that gratuitous cruelty against the innocent is morally obligatory?

3

Arguments for the Dilemmas Thesis

There is considerable controversy about the claim that there are moral conflicts in which wrongdoing is inescapable. For some it is obvious that wrongdoing may be inescapable, while for others it is equally obvious that this cannot be the case. Many may find themselves attracted to both positions. The fact of these conflicting intuitions is something that the method of reflective intuitionism ought to take into account. We ought to begin by accepting as significant input both the intuition that moral wrongdoing is sometimes inescapable and the intuition that it can never be inescapable. In the end we cannot conclude that both intuitions, taken in the same sense, are correct. Rather, we ought to aim for a consistent explanation of the fact that these conflicting intuitions are widely and deeply held. Such an explanation may take different forms. It may be said that one intuition is correct and that the other, though incorrect, is mistakenly held for reasons that the nature of morality, properly understood, makes intelligible and predictable. On this view, the conclusion is that one or the other intuition ought to be abandoned as untenable. Another approach would be to say that there is a sense of 'moral wrongdoing' such that it is sometimes inescapable and another sense such that it cannot be inescapable. On this view, the conclusion is that both intuitions, properly interpreted, should be retained.

My position follows the second form of explanation. I will argue that conclusions of moral deliberation cannot conflict and hence that wrongdoing in the sense of violating such a conclusion cannot be inescapable. But I will also maintain that moral responsibilities can conflict, and so wrongdoing in the sense of transgressing such a responsibility can be inescapable. This makes it look as if my view is an intermediate one—some kind of synthesis or compromise, finding partial truth on both sides of the debate. Though there is some validity in this portrayal, it is misleading to think of my position in this way. As I see it, I am much closer to those who have claimed that wrongdoing may be inescapable than to those who have denied this. Once explained, the sense in which wrongdoing cannot be inescapable is relatively obvious. By contrast, the argument for the claim that wrongdoing is sometimes inescapable is more controversial, and it captures much of the motivation of those who have defended inescapable moral wrongdoing. Or so it seems to me.

I first consider the question of conflicting conclusions of moral deliberation. In this chapter I show that arguments for the view that there can be such conflicts are inconclusive. In the next chapter I argue that there is a compelling reason to deny this view. Though my conclusion in this respect is a negative one, the issues raised in these chapters are of central importance for the "moral dilemmas" debate. Moreover, the points I make here clear the way for the defense of my positive thesis that there is a sense in which wrongdoing may be inescapable.

I. The Dilemmas Thesis

The questions with which I am concerned are usually thought to be a matter of whether there are "moral dilemmas," standardly defined as situations in which an agent morally ought to (and can) perform one action and morally ought to (and can) perform another action, even though the agent cannot perform both actions. As I pointed out earlier (chapter 1, Sec. I), the debate so defined has concerned both whether there are irresolvable moral conflicts and whether wrongdoing is sometimes inescapable, though these issues have not always been clearly distinguished. Since these issues concern the interpretation of moral conflicts, it is important to have a way of describing a moral conflict that does not prejudice the resolution of these questions, and in relationship to which different theses about moral conflicts may be defined. Moreover, for the purposes at hand, some precision is required, and it will help to make some simplifying assumptions. With these considerations in mind, I propose to use the following terminology.

First, suppose an agent is in a *deliberative situation*, that is, a situation in which the agent knows he or she can perform at least one of several alternative actions (or courses of action) and knows that some of these actions are potentially of moral significance. In addition, suppose the agent is committed to acting morally and deliberates about which of these actions, in the final analysis, morally ought to be done. In order to reach this conclusion, the agent will have to make use of premises that refer to what I will call the *morally relevant features* of these actions. Which features are morally relevant will depend on which normative outlook is correct. A morally relevant feature of an action may be the fact that it is an expression of a virtue or a vice, that it has a good or a bad consequence, that it fulfills or transgresses a moral duty, obligation, or right, that it meets or violates a moral responsibility, and so on. The terminology of morally relevant features is neutral on issues that divide normative accounts and also on the question whether morally relevant features should be given a realist interpretation (so as not to prejudice possible connections between "moral dilemmas" and moral realism).

There are two kinds of morally relevant features: positive-value features (PVs) and negative-value features (NVs). As examples, it might be said that Socrates's action of remaining in prison has 'obeying the law' as a PV, and Bru-

tus's action of slaying Caesar has 'harming a friend' as a NV. Features such as
these are essential to reasoning to conclusions about what, all things considered,
morally ought to be done. In particular, if a possible action X has a PV, then
that is a reason for the conclusion that X morally ought to be done (OX) and if a
possible action X has a NV, then that is a reason for the conclusion that X
morally ought not to be done (O~X)—where it is understood that these reasons
may be overridden.

Sometimes 'ought' is used to indicate the presence of a morally relevant feature, but I will restrict 'ought' to the expression of a conclusion of moral deliberation (indicating which action is morally required in view of all the morally
relevant features of available alternative actions and whatever priorities may be
thought to obtain among these). Also, the term 'prima facie ought' (duty, obligation, etc.) is sometimes employed to refer to morally relevant features. But in
view of the ambiguities in the use of this expression, I will avoid it altogether.

The "moral dilemmas" debate concerns the proper interpretation of moral
conflicts. For the time being, I will simplify and speak only of moral conflicts
involving positive-value features. In particular, let us say that a *moral conflict* is a
deliberative situation in which an agent faces two alternative actions, A and B,
each of which has a PV and no other morally relevant feature, and the agent can
perform A or can perform B, but cannot perform both A and B (and no other
alternative has an overriding PV). Actual moral conflicts are typically more
complicated than this and may take somewhat different forms.[1] However, the
issues at hand can be clarified by focusing on this simplified case. To allow that
there are moral conflicts is only to admit that there are circumstances in which
an agent has a reason for the conclusion OA and a reason for the conclusion OB,
when the agent cannot do both A and B. Taken by itself, this is an uncontroversial claim. Even Kant and Mill, who are prominent among opponents of the
view that there are "moral dilemmas," recognize that there can be conflicting
moral reasons. Kant says that it is possible that two "grounds [of obligation]
conflict with each other,"[2] while Mill states that all doctrines "believed by sane
persons" acknowledge "as a fact in morals the existence of conflicting considerations."[3] What is controversial is not whether there are moral conflicts, but how
they are to be understood.

Before turning to this topic, it is important to specify what it means to say
that an agent can and cannot perform an action (or conjunction of actions). To
say that an agent can perform an action implies that it is possible to perform the
action given the principles of logic and the laws of the physical universe. In
addition, it implies that the agent has, in the circumstance in question, both the
ability and the opportunity to perform the action. The reference of 'ability' and
'opportunity' is somewhat indeterminate here, but typical examples of moral
conflicts are not problematic in this respect. Finally, in order to avoid cases in
which an agent is deliberating in ignorance about what can and cannot be done,
it should be assumed as a matter of stipulation that an agent who can (cannot)
perform an action knows that he or she can (cannot) perform it. Hence, to say
that an agent can perform an action is to say that (1) it is logically and physically
possible for the agent to perform the action and (2) the agent has the ability and

opportunity to perform the action [and the agent knows (1) and (2)]; and to say that an agent cannot perform an action is to say that the conjunction of (1) and (2) is false (and the agent knows it is false).

With respect to conclusions of moral deliberation, two common and contrary interpretations of moral conflicts may now be defined. It might be supposed that:

> *The Dilemmas Thesis* (DT) There are moral conflicts in which the correct conclusion of moral deliberation includes both OA and OB.

On this view, not only may there be conflicting moral reasons, there may be conflicting conclusions of moral deliberation. It is this thesis which many defenders of "moral dilemmas" appear to accept and which many opponents of "moral dilemmas," such as Kant and Mill, appear to reject. In opposition to this, it might be claimed that:

> *The Options Thesis* (OT) For every moral conflict, the correct conclusion of moral deliberation includes exactly one of the following: (1) OA, (2) OB, or (3) ~OA & ~OB & O(A v B).

As will be seen later, for those cases in which advocates of DT argue that the correct conclusion is both OA and OB, advocates of OT argue that the correct conclusion is neither OA nor OB, but O(A v B).

DT is clearly relevant to the question whether moral wrongdoing is sometimes inescapable. For, if DT were true, then there would be situations in which an agent would violate a correct conclusion of moral deliberation no matter what, and wrongdoing in the sense of violating such a conclusion would sometimes be inescapable. But I will maintain in this chapter that arguments for DT are inconclusive, and I will claim in the next chapter that there is a convincing argument for rejecting DT in favor of OT. Hence, I will argue that wrongdoing in this sense cannot be inescapable.[4]

In the "moral dilemmas" literature, there are three prominent arguments for DT. Though they involve different considerations, each is substantially an experiential argument, for in each case the argument requires us to focus on particular examples of moral conflicts in order to appreciate its force. I will call these the equality argument, the incomparability argument, and the phenomenological argument. After criticizing these arguments, I will consider an approach to "moral dilemmas" that might be thought to circumvent some of my objections.

II. The Equality Argument

An agent who confronts a moral conflict needs to determine what, in the final analysis, morally ought to be done. In most cases, the agent will conclude that the PV of one of the actions overrides the PV of the other. Let us say that the PV of one action *overrides* the PV of another if, and only if, (1) the two actions

cannot both be done and (2) the first PV is greater with respect to moral deliberation than the second. To say that the PV of one action is greater with respect
to moral deliberation than the PV of another action is to say that, all things considered, it provides a morally stronger reason for performing that action in the
circumstance at hand than the other PV provides for performing the conflicting
action. Of course, just as normative outlooks differ in their accounts of what
qualifies as a moral reason, so they differ in their criteria for determining
morally stronger reasons. But any normative stance will have some understanding of what makes one PV morally stronger than another.[5]

When the PV of one action in a moral conflict overrides the PV of the other
action, it is clear that only the first action morally ought to be done. In such a
case, the correct conclusion of moral deliberation would be either OA or OB,
but not both OA and OB. Hence, if every moral conflict were such that the PV
of one action overrides the PV of the other action, then it would never be correct to conclude that both OA and OB, and so DT would be false. If DT is true,
then, it must be the case that:

(P1) There are moral conflicts in which neither PV overrides the other.

Two direct arguments may be given to support P1. One is based on the claim
that there are moral conflicts in which the PV of A and the PV of B are equal;
the other depends on the idea that there are moral conflicts in which the PV of
A and the PV of B are incomparable. I will consider the equality argument in
this section and the incomparability argument in the next. In my view, though
the first argument provides a reason for accepting P1, neither argument gives a
conclusive reason for accepting DT.

The equality argument begins by maintaining that there are moral conflicts
in which the PV of A and the PV of B are equal. That is, there are conflicts in
which the moral reason for doing A has the same moral strength overall as the
moral reason for doing B. It is generally thought that reflection on particular
examples is sufficient to show that there are such conflicts. Though the interpretation of examples may differ, I doubt that any plausible account would deny
that there are conflicts of this sort, or at least that they are possible. To see this,
consider the widely discussed example from William Styron's novel *Sophie's
Choice*.[6] In a concentration camp in World War II a Nazi doctor compels Sophie
to choose which of her two children, Jan and Eva, will be saved and which will
be sent to the gas chamber; if she declines to choose, both will be killed. In this
situation Sophie must choose one child or the other, but not both. Yet her
moral reason for choosing Jan and her moral reason for choosing Eva are
equally strong. It was partly in recognition of this equality that she screamed
over and over again "I can't choose." Of course, in a situation such as this there
might be a moral basis for choice. But there is no reason to suppose that, no
matter what the particulars of the case, it must turn out that one or the other
reason is morally stronger.[7]

The existence of moral conflicts in which the PV of A and the PV of B are
equal in moral strength does establish P1, for in such cases it is clear that neither

PV overrides the other. But what follows from this? According to the equality argument, in these situations the conclusion to be drawn is that both OA and OB. If this conclusion were correct, then of course DT would be true. However, this conclusion follows only if the following principle is accepted:

(P2) If A has a PV and B has a PV, then (1) OA *unless* the PV of A is over-ridden by the PV of B, and (2) OB *unless* the PV of B is overridden by the PV of A.

From this it does follow that, in moral conflicts in which the PV of A and the PV of B are equal in moral strength, both OA and OB. On this view, Sophie's conclusion should be that she morally ought to choose Jan and that she morally ought to choose Eva, even though she cannot do both.

However, it is not obvious that P2 is true, and proponents of OT have a plausible alternative to it. For it may be said that:

(P3) If A has a PV and B has a PV, then (1) OA *only if* the PV of A over-rides the PV of B, and (2) OB *only if* the PV of B overrides the PV of A.

From this, in moral conflicts in which the PV of A and the PV of B are equal in moral strength, it does not follow that both OA and OB. In fact, what follows is ~OA and ~OB. Accordingly, in order to account for moral conflicts in which the reasons have equal moral strength, advocates of OT commonly suppose that:

(P4) If (1) A has a PV and B has a PV and (2) neither PV overrides the other, then O(A v B).

In short, according to OT, in a moral conflict in which the PV of A and the PV of B are equal in moral strength, the conclusion to be drawn is ~OA and ~OB and O(A v B).[8] According to this view, Sophie's conclusion should be that she morally ought to choose Jan or Eva.

This second view does not resolve the conflict in the sense of providing a moral reason for choosing Jan rather than Eva or vice versa. But the first view does not resolve the conflict in this sense either. If the reasons for the two choices are really morally equal in strength, then no such resolution is possible on any view. Both views require that the choice between the two actions be made on the basis of some nonmoral reason (or else arbitrarily). Still, there is an important difference between these two positions. For the first view, the correct conclusion of moral deliberation is a pair of conflicting moral judgments, that is, judgments that cannot both be acted upon. A consequence of this view is that the agent will fail to fulfill a sound conclusion of moral deliberation no matter what, and in this sense will do something morally wrong no matter what. For the second view, on the other hand, the proper conclusion is that at least one of the two actions morally ought to be done, but (so far as deciding what to do is concerned) it does not matter morally which is done. There are no conflicting moral judgments in this conclusion. Hence, it does not make it inevitable that the agent will violate a sound deliberative conclusion. On this view, wrongdoing in the sense of violating such a conclusion is not inescapable.

There are thus two possible interpretations of the correct conclusion to be drawn in a moral conflict in which the PVs are equally strong. The first interpretation accepts P2 and thereby establishes DT. The second accepts P3 and P4 and provides no support for DT. The fact that there are moral conflicts in which the PVs have equal moral strength supplies no reason by itself for preferring one of these interpretations over the other. In order to establish DT, some further consideration beyond the fact of equally strong conflicting reasons is required. I conclude that, though the equality argument is correct in its claim that there are moral conflicts in which the PVs are equal in moral strength, it is mistaken in its claim that this fact by itself conclusively establishes DT.

III. The Incomparability Argument

Another approach to this issue common in discussions of "moral dilemmas" is based on the idea that there are moral conflicts in which the PV of A and the PV of B are "incommensurable." It might be supposed that, with respect to such cases, both P1 and P2 are correct (and not P3 and P4). If this were the case, then the incommensurability of conflicting moral reasons would establish DT. In order to assess this argument, it is necessary to consider what sense of 'incommensurable' is relevant, whether there are any situations in which conflicting moral reasons are incommensurable, and whether this fact would provide a basis for both P1 and P2, and hence for DT.

The argument requires more than that types of morally relevant features, such as justice and compassion, be incommensurable. It must be the case that the morally relevant features of particular alternative actions be incommensurable, for example, that the fact that action A promotes justice be incommensurable with the fact that action B exhibits compassion. In discussions of incommensurability and "moral dilemmas" it is not always clear what sense of 'incommensurability' is thought to be relevant. But I believe the most plausible and common interpretation of 'incommensurability' as something that might have bearing on DT is *incomparability:* the idea that morally relevant features of conflicting actions cannot be compared with one another in a way that is pertinent to moral deliberation.[9]

In general, to say that two actions are incomparable with respect to some mode of evaluation is to say that one is neither greater than, nor less than, nor equal to the other with respect to that mode of evaluation. DT has to do with moral deliberation in situations of moral conflict. Hence, the pertinent set of comparison claims is the set Q: with respect to moral deliberation, (1) the PV of A is greater than the PV of B; (2) the PV of A is less than the PV of B; and (3) the PV of A and the PV of B are equal. Actions A and B may be said to be *incomparable with respect to moral deliberation* if, and only if, no member of Q is true. Now, it might be supposed that:

The Incomparability Thesis (IT) There are moral conflicts in which actions A and B are incomparable with respect to moral deliberation.

It is the bearing of this thesis on DT that needs to be considered. However, in view of the varied use of 'incommensurability' in moral philosophy, it is important to first distinguish the concept of incomparability from other senses of 'incommensurability'.[10]

First, 'incommensurability' sometimes refers to the idea that it is not possible to make quantitative comparisons among instances of different values (such as that this action is twice as good as that one).[11] This is a weaker notion than incomparability. If comparisons are impossible, then so are quantitative comparisons. But comparisons may still be possible even if quantitative comparisons are not.

Second, 'incommensurability' is often taken to indicate the idea that tokens of different values do not always have in common a single, homogeneous characteristic on the basis of which comparative judgments of the overall value of these tokens may be made.[12] This thesis is independent of incomparability. First, the presence of a common, homogeneous characteristic does not guarantee that there can be comparisons: It may be a vague characteristic, such as sublimity, which is not always susceptible to comparative judgments. Second, the absence of such a characteristic does not mean that comparisons are impossible: One president may be greater in accomplishment than another, but this is not because each possesses the homogeneous characteristic of "presidential accomplishment." In the moral realm, one PV may be greater with respect to moral deliberation than another, but not because they have in common a homogeneous property such as "moral goodness."[13] Comparative judgments require that there be a basis for comparison, but this need not be a common, uniform characteristic; it may be a complex perspective involving priorities or weightings of different values.[14]

Finally, 'incommensurability' is occasionally used to refer to the claim that any amount of some value is always more (or less) valuable than any amount of some other value.[15] Incommensurability in this sense is incompatible with incomparability, for it presupposes that comparisons are possible: If any instance of one kind of morally relevant feature is always greater with respect to moral deliberation than any instance of another kind, then on any occasion when these features conflict, the PV of one action will be greater than the PV of the other.

In sum, the concept of incommensurability that is relevant to DT, if any is, is incomparability as articulated in IT. If quantitative comparisons are impossible, or if there is no homogeneous, common characteristic, it may still be that comparisons are possible; and the last sense of 'incommensurability' entails that comparisons are possible. But if comparisons are possible, it might be supposed, dilemmas of the form 'OA and OB' can be avoided. On the other hand, if comparisons are impossible, then it might be thought that such dilemmas cannot be avoided. Hence, IT is the thesis to consider in connection with DT.[16]

Arguments for IT typically involve some form of moral pluralism, the doctrine that there are distinct types of moral value. Usually these arguments invoke particular examples of moral conflicts in order to convince us that comparisons cannot always be made. I will consider two such arguments, one more general than the other. According to the first, there are moral conflicts in which the PV of A is of a different value type than the PV of B, and no tokens of these two types of value can be compared.[17] Thus, someone might claim that justice and utility are both morally relevant value types, but that tokens of justice cannot be compared with tokens of utility in a morally relevant way. For example, it may be said that the injustice of executing Billy Budd cannot be compared with the good consequences that are promoted by this execution. However, there is a strong objection to this argument. Even if sometimes a token of justice cannot be compared with a token of utility, sometimes it can (as when A promotes a great justice and B results in only a minor increase in utility). The problem is a widespread one: It is difficult to think of any two morally relevant value types such that every token of one type is morally incomparable with every conflicting token of the other type. Therefore, this argument for IT is intuitively implausible.

There is another argument for IT that avoids this difficulty. Walter Sinnott-Armstrong defends an account of "limited incomparability" that "admits that *some* particular requirements of one kind are comparable with *some* particular requirements of another kind, but still claims that *some* moral requirements of the first kind are incomparable with *some* moral requirements of the other kind."[18] Several explanations of limited incomparability are proposed by Sinnott-Armstrong, but he suggests that the best explanation is "the *inexactness* of moral rankings."[19] His example concerns a doctor who must decide whether or not to operate on a patient. Since the operation will probably save the life of the patient, there is a moral requirement to perform it, but since the patient would survive the operation only in a state of pain, there is a moral requirement not to perform it. In some cases, these requirements are comparable, because a little pain is clearly better than death. But in other cases, Sinnott-Armstrong argues, these requirements are incomparable: For some amounts of pain, it is not the case that death is better, or worse, or equal. It might be thought that, if death is neither better nor worse than some amount of pain, then it must be equal to it. But Sinnott-Armstrong claims that if death were equal to some exact amount of pain (say, 1000 units), then it must be better than a slightly greater amount (1001 units). Yet it might still be true that death is neither better nor worse than 1001 units of pain. Since death cannot be equal to both 1000 and 1001 units of pain and since there is no reason to think it is equal to one amount instead of the other, it must be incomparable to these amounts.

Since this argument supposes that conflicting moral requirements are incomparable only in a limited number of special cases, it is more plausible than the first argument. Nonetheless, I am not convinced that it establishes that there are any situations in which moral requirements are incomparable. In reference to his example, it is true that there may be more than one exact amount of pain where it seems correct to say that death is neither better than nor worse than that amount. But there is another explanation of this besides incomparability: It may be that death is equal to some exact amount, but we do not know what that amount is. According to this explanation, because we are ignorant of the exact amount, several different amounts may appear as likely candidates for equality and hence as amounts for which death is neither better nor worse. Sinnott-Armstrong says that it begs the question to insist that there must be some such unknown exact equation. But it also begs the question to insist on incomparability unless it can be established that incomparability is clearly the better explanation. I cannot see any basis in Sinnott-Armstrong's argument for preferring the incomparability explanation to the unknown equality explanation, especially since it is acknowledged that in some cases death and pain are comparable. Hence, I cannot see any reason to think that death must be incomparable with some amounts of pain.[20]

In general, for any purported example of incomparable positive-value features, it is always possible that there is a comparison between the features that is unknown to us. Unless there is a way to clearly tell the difference between these two cases, there is no way to be confident that there are cases of incomparability. Since I cannot see that there is a sure way to establish this difference, I am not convinced that IT is true. On the other hand, I do not have an argument against IT. Since it is often supposed that IT is true, it will be worthwhile to consider its bearing on DT. Let us suppose for the sake of argument, then, that there are moral conflicts in which the PV of A and the PV of B are incomparable with respect to moral deliberation. What consequences would this have for DT?

It is clear that P1 would follow. If the PV of A and the PV of B are incomparable, then neither overrides the other. But P1 is also established by the relatively uncontroversial fact that there are moral conflicts in which the PV of A and the PV of B are equal. Hence, so far as P1 is concerned, IT does not advance the case for DT any further than the equality argument did. The more important issue is whether IT provides any basis for accepting P2 rather than P3 and P4. DT requires both P1 and P2, but equality cases by themselves provide no reason to accept P2. If it could be shown that incomparability cases give support to P2, then IT would provide an argument for DT. And it might be thought that the incomparability of morally relevant features would provide such support.

For DT, when the PV of A and the PV of B do not override one another, the conclusion to be drawn is both OA and OB. On the other hand, for OT, the conclusion to be drawn in such a situation is neither OA nor OB, but O(A v B). A proponent of DT might argue as follows: To say that O(A v B) implies that it does not make any moral difference whether one does A or does B. But if the PV of A and the PV of B were incomparable, then it would make a difference, since both are morally valuable, but in incomparably different ways. Hence, when A and B are incomparable, the conclusion to be drawn is not O(A v B), but OA and OB.[21] If this were correct, then IT would be sufficient for DT. Moreover, the argument might continue, if the PV of A and the PV of B were equal, then it would not make any moral difference whether one did A or did B, since the moral value of each would be exactly the same. Thus the proper conclusion would be O(A v B) and not OA and OB. In equality cases, then, the correct principles would be P3 and P4 rather than P2, so equality would not support

DT. This would establish that IT is not only sufficient for DT, but necessary as well (unless something independent of incomparability could be shown to support DT).[22]

It is important to recognize that in both incomparability and equality cases it makes a difference what one does. If A fulfills a promise and B increases utility (assuming these are incomparable), then there is an important difference between doing A and doing B: Different people may be affected, and in different ways. But consider a case in which the PVs of two actions are equal. Suppose A keeps a promise to one person and B keeps an equally binding promise to someone else. As with incomparability, it makes a significant difference whether A or B is done: Different people may be affected, and in different ways. Do these respective differences have different effects on reasoning about what morally ought to be done?

It is hard to see that they do. Whether we accept P2, as opposed to P3 and P4, will depend on whether we accept the thesis that a nonoverridden PV in some action X is sufficient for the conclusion OX. There is no reason to think that incomparability, and only incomparability, supports this thesis. To see this, compare the following two moral conflicts. In the first, Katherine can either marry Greg (action A) and thereby fulfill a promise to him, or marry Peter (action B) and thereby make her parents enormously happy, since they are enthralled with Peter but indifferent to Greg. In the second conflict, Katherine's first choice is the same, A, but the alternative is not B. Rather it is to marry Michael (action C) and thereby fulfill a promise to him.[23] Assume that keeping the promise and increasing happiness are incomparable, and that keeping the two promises are equal (and to simplify, that there are no other morally relevant features in either case).

According to the view that incomparability supports P2 but equality does not, in the first case the fact that A keeps a promise is sufficient for the conclusion OA (because the alternative to A is incomparable), while in the second case the fact that A keeps the same promise is not sufficient for the conclusion OA (because the alternative to A is equal). This is implausible. In the first case, the fact that A keeps the promise does not override the PV of B. Hence, since the conclusion OA cannot be based on the PV of A overriding the PV of B, this conclusion must depend on something intrinsic to the fact that A keeps a promise, for example, that promise-keeping is of such moral importance that promises must always be kept in the absence of overriding considerations. But if this is true, the conclusion in the second case will also be OA, since in this case A keeps the same promise, and this is not overridden by the PV of C. What is needed to justify the conclusion that a non-overridden PV in some action X is sufficient for the conclusion OX, and thereby to support DT, is some consideration beyond both incomparability and equality, a consideration to the effect that in some moral conflicts morally relevant features provide, as Thomas Nagel puts it, "decisive and sufficient" reasons when "either choice will mean acting against some reasons without being able to claim that they are *outweighed*."[24] Hence, the foregoing argument does not show that IT is either sufficient or necessary for DT.[25]

In sum, there is no good reason to think there are moral conflicts in which the positive value features of the two actions are incomparable, and even if there were such conflicts, this would not show that in these cases the correct conclusion of moral deliberation must be that both actions ought to be done. The incomparability argument for DT does not succeed.

IV. The Phenomenological Argument

I have argued that there are moral conflicts in which neither PV overrides the other, but that no convincing reason has been given so far for inferring DT from this. The best argument for this additional step is a version of the phenomenological argument. Though I will here reject this as an argument for DT, I will later employ its central premise in an argument for my own position. Hence I regard the considerations brought forth in this argument as being of fundamental importance.

As applied to DT, the phenomenological argument begins with the claim that in some moral conflicts in which neither PV overrides the other, the agent would appropriately feel some form of moral distress such as guilt, or remorse, or at least regret, whichever course of action is taken. This claim is generally regarded as intuitively evident on the basis of reflection on particular examples. If, as OT maintains, the correct conclusion in these cases is O(A v B), then whichever of these actions the agent performs, he or she does what ought to be done and does nothing that ought not to be done (in this situation). Hence, if OT were correct, it would seem that, as long as the agent does A or does B, there is no reason for the agent to feel any form of moral distress. Such feelings would not be inescapable. On the other hand, if, as DT maintains, both OA and OB are the correct conclusions in these cases, then whatever the agent does, he or she will fail to do something that ought to be done, and this will justify moral distress. Hence, moral distress cannot be avoided. In short, DT rather than OT must be accepted in order to explain our intuitions that there are moral conflicts in which appropriate moral distress is inescapable.[26]

One objection to this argument is to deny that there are any moral conflicts in which it would be appropriate for an agent to feel moral distress no matter what. In my view, however, this argument should be interpreted in terms of the method of reflective intuitionism. In accordance with this, I believe its first premise, properly understood, should be accepted: We do have (fallible) intuitions to the effect that there are moral conflicts in which appropriate moral distress is inevitable,[27] and we should attempt to develop a coherent position that explains these intuitions. This version of the phenomenological argument maintains that DT offers the best explanation of these intuitions. My objection is that there is a better explanation available, one that accepts OT and rejects DT, and yet makes sense of our intuitions. The full development of this response will require the remainder of the book. For now, I will give a brief outline of my position and indicate in a preliminary way several of its advantages.

First, the argument for DT supposes that, if the proper conclusion of moral deliberation is O(A v B), then so long as the agent performs one of these actions, he or she will have no reason for feeling moral distress. But it may be that there are grounds for feeling moral distress besides the violation of a conclusion of moral deliberation. In particular, there may be what I will call a moral responsibility to perform an action that is distinct from the conclusion that the action morally ought to be done. On this view, there are situations in which there is a moral responsibility to do A and a moral responsibility to do B, even though A and B cannot both be done. In these situations, the correct conclusion of moral deliberation conforms to the requirements of OT, but an agent who acts in accordance with this conclusion, whatever it is, still inevitably fails to fulfill some moral responsibility (either to do A or to do B), and this is a reason for feeling moral distress. If this account can be defended, then another explanation of intuitions concerning inescapable moral distress will be available.[28]

Second, the claim of the present version of the phenomenological argument that DT provides the best explanation requires that DT be an otherwise acceptable thesis. This is implicit in the method of reflective intuitionism: The best explanation ought to cohere with other positions it is reasonable to hold. In the next chapter I will argue that there is a strong objection to DT based on the prescriptivity of conclusions of moral deliberation, and I will argue later that this objection does not apply to the explanation just described, since moral responsibilities are not prescriptive in the same way as conclusions of deliberation. Hence, in this respect at least, the explanation relying on moral responsibilities is a superior one.

Finally, there are two additional advantages of this position over the explanation based on DT. First, this explanation would provide a way of avoiding the charge often made against proponents of DT that they mistakenly suppose that the inevitable moral distress warranted in conflict situations is the same kind of moral distress that is warranted in nonconflict situations when a person does not do what ought to be done, say because of *akrasia* (or "weakness of will") or improper deliberation.[29] By distinguishing the violation of a conclusion of moral deliberation from the violation of a moral responsibility, this explanation provides a conceptual basis for distinguishing distinct forms of moral distress appropriate to each case.

Moreover, this explanation gives a reason for saying, what proponents of "moral dilemmas" frequently and plausibly do say, that justified moral distress may be inevitable even in moral conflicts where one PV overrides the other.[30] For there may be conflict situations in which there is a moral responsibility to do A, but the correct conclusion of moral deliberation is OB. In these cases, a person who does B would do what ought to be done but would not fulfill the moral responsibility to do A, and this would be a reason for moral distress (and of course failing to do B would also be a reason for moral distress). Though DT does not deny that moral distress may be warranted in these cases, it provides no account of it either. Hence, the explanation based on moral responsibilities has broader scope than DT.

For these reasons, expressed here in preliminary form, I believe there is a better explanation of intuitions concerning inescapable moral distress in moral conflicts than that provided by DT. Hence, I reject the phenomenological argument for DT.

V. Sinnott-Armstrong's Understanding of "Moral Dilemmas"

It might be thought that some of my objections to these arguments for DT are circumvented by Sinnott-Armstrong's understanding of "moral dilemmas."[31] He begins by stating that a moral dilemma involves a conflict between a class of moral reasons he calls "requirements." "A moral reason to adopt an alternative is a moral requirement," he says, "if and only if it would be morally wrong not to adopt that alternative if there were no moral justification for not adopting it."[32] But he claims that not every conflict between moral requirements is a moral dilemma. This is because some moral requirements override other moral requirements. Hence we need to distinguish conflicts between (a) (possibly overridden) moral requirements, (b) overriding moral requirements, and (c) nonoverridden moral requirements. Sinnott-Armstrong then argues as follows.

If a moral dilemma were defined as a conflict between (a) (possibly overridden) moral requirements, then a conflict between moral requirements in which one requirement overrides the other would count as a moral dilemma. However, he says, though there are such conflicts, it is not conflicts of this kind that have been at issue in the moral dilemmas debate. That is, those who reject moral dilemmas have not typically denied that there are conflicts between moral requirements in which one requirement overrides the other, and those who accept moral dilemmas have usually claimed something more than that there are such conflicts.

On the other hand, Sinnott-Armstrong argues, if a moral dilemma were defined as a conflict between (b) overriding moral requirements, then there would be a moral dilemma only if there were a conflict between moral requirements each of which overrides the other. But this, he says, is "clearly impossible." For, "if one requirement overrides another, and the other also overrides the former, then the former must override itself."[33] However, he does not think this shows that moral dilemmas are impossible, because "philosophers who defend the possibility of moral dilemmas do not define moral dilemmas" as conflicts between overriding moral requirements.[34]

For these reasons, Sinnott-Armstrong defines a moral dilemma as a conflict between (c) nonoverridden moral requirements. In other words, a moral dilemma is a situation in which "moral requirements conflict but neither is overridden by the other (or by any other moral reason)."[35] This definition, he says, is what "most defenders of the possibility of moral dilemmas have in mind."[36] Moreover, while the first definition is "too weak to be controversial" and the second is "so strong that it is absurd," this definition is "precise enough to make sense of the complex issues that surround moral dilemmas."[37] With this definition in hand, Sinnott-Armstrong goes on to argue, often with considerable plausibility, both that there are good reasons for thinking there are moral dilemmas and that various objections to moral dilemmas (from the standpoint of norma-tive theories as well as deontic logic) are unfounded.

In effect, Sinnott-Armstrong defines the thesis that there are moral dilem-mas as the claim that P1 is true. What I have been calling a PV is, at least approximately, the same as what Sinnott-Armstrong calls a moral requirement, and P1 states that there are moral conflicts in which neither PV overrides the other. Since I have already granted that the equality argument establishes P1, I agree that there are moral dilemmas as Sinnott-Armstrong understands them.[38] In this respect, then, there is no substantial difference between our positions. Nonetheless, though Sinnott-Armstrong has done much to clarify some of the central issues in the "moral dilemmas" debate, I do not think his approach is the best way to reveal the most fundamental and significant disagreements among participants in this debate. It is important to see why this is so.

Sinnott-Armstrong is correct in claiming that there is no dispute about the assertion that there are moral conflicts in which one (and only one) moral requirement overrides the other. No one denies that there are such conflicts, and proponents of the claim that there are "moral dilemmas" clearly mean to main-tain something more than, or other than, this. On the other hand, there are sub-stantial disputes about the status of overridden moral requirements. In particular, there is the question whether an agent who acts in accordance with the overrid-ing moral requirement in a moral conflict of this kind ever has good reason to feel moral distress on account of not acting in accordance with the overridden moral requirement. Proponents of "moral dilemmas" have often argued that there sometimes is reason to feel some such sentiment in this circumstance,[39] and opponents of "moral dilemmas" have typically denied this. In my view, this dis-pute is at the heart of the "moral dilemmas" debate, for these two positions reveal a significant divergence in conceptions of morality. By focusing attention on moral conflicts in which neither moral requirement overrides the other, both Sinnott-Armstrong and DT obscure the importance of this issue.

Sinnott-Armstrong is also correct to maintain that there cannot be conflicts between overriding moral requirements. For this would mean that each require-ment is both morally stronger and morally weaker than the other, and this is clearly impossible. In addition, he is right to hold that there can be conflicts between nonoverridden moral requirements. But I am not convinced that it is the existence of this kind of conflict per se that has been the central issue in the debate about "moral dilemmas." In particular, I doubt that those who have argued against "moral dilemmas" would deny that there are conflicts between non-overridden moral requirements, and I think that many of those who have argued in favor of "moral dilemmas" have meant to claim something consider-ably stronger than that there are such conflicts. I will consider each of these points in turn.

Sinnott-Armstrong regards it as sufficient to establish his position that there be situations, such as in *Sophie's Choice*, where there is "no morally relevant differ-ence" between conflicting moral requirements.[40] Because Sophie has the same moral reason to save one child as she has to save the other, and because she can-not save both, she has a conflict between moral requirements neither of which overrides the other. It is hard to see why anyone would deny that this could happen. To do so would mean insisting either (1) that there is no moral requirement to save at least one of the children, or (2) that there is a stronger moral reason to save one child rather than the other. Given Sinnott-Armstrong's definition of a moral requirement, to maintain (1) would be to deny, with respect to at least one of the children, that it would be morally wrong not to save that child without justification. Though, as Sinnott-Armstrong notes, there is a kind of justification for not saving Jan in this circumstance (since Eva has an equal and conflicting claim to be saved), the fact remains that it would be wrong not to save Jan without justification. The same can be said for Eva. Hence, there is a moral requirement to save each child. In order to establish (2) it would have to be shown that, no matter what the specific facts of the case, it must turn out that there is a stronger moral reason to save one child rather than the other. But for any plausible moral reason that might be advanced as a basis for giving preference to one child, it is surely possible that circumstances be such that the reason applies equally to both children. For example, if it were thought that one child would have a better chance of survival than the other, it might have been the case that each child would have an equal chance for survival. Hence, it cannot be guaranteed that some morally relevant consideration will favor one child rather than the other, though exact equality may in fact be rare.

Moreover, opponents of "moral dilemmas" have not been concerned to establish (1) or (2). Alan Donagan, for example, who argued vigorously against "moral dilemmas," specifically addresses the claim that there are conflicts between equally strong moral requirements—for example, when a fireman can save some but not all persons in a burning building.[41] With respect to (1), Donagan grants that there is a "ground" of obligation to save each life, and he admits that this ground "would give rise to a moral obligation" in other circumstances. Hence, it is clear that he thinks it would be wrong, with respect to each life, not to save that life in circumstances where there would be a moral obligation to save it—in other words, in circumstances where there was no justification for not saving it. This is tantamount to saying there is a moral requirement to save each life in Sinnott-Armstrong's sense of the term. As for (2), Donagan says explicitly that the conflicting grounds have "the same force." He makes no attempt at all to establish that one of them must be morally stronger than the others. In sum, Donagan clearly admits that there are moral dilemmas as Sinnott-Armstrong defines them.[42] I believe the same can be said of many other prominent opponents of "moral dilemmas."[43]

On the other hand, there is reason to think that many of those who have defended "moral dilemmas" have had in mind a position much stronger than Sinnott-Armstrong's. For example, Bernard Williams speaks of "tragic" moral conflicts in which "an agent can justifiably think that whatever he does will be wrong," conflicts in which "whatever he does, the agent will have reason to feel regret at the deepest level."[44] And in his essay on dirty hands, Michael Walzer argues that there are moral dilemmas, understood as situations in which an agent "must choose between two courses of action both of which it would be wrong for him to undertake."[45] Walzer's suggestion is that in a moral dilemma, whatever the agent does, the agent will do something that is morally wrong, something that would make it appropriate for the agent to feel guilt.

From the fact that an agent faces a conflict between nonoverridden moral requirements, as defined by Sinnott-Armstrong, it does not follow that, no matter what the agent does, he or she will do something morally wrong or will have reason to feel deep regret or guilt. These claims about wrongness and moral distress clearly involve considerations that either go beyond, or are simply different from, the unexceptionable thesis that there are conflicting requirements that do not override one another;[46] for a conflict of this kind may be interpreted in different ways. It may be said that in such a conflict the only obligation is to perform one action or the other and that so long as the agent does this he or she will do nothing morally wrong in any sense. Indeed, this often is said by opponents of "moral dilemmas." Argument is required to establish that these conflicts are tragic, that they make moral wrongdoing inescapable, or that they engender unavoidable guilt. It is these contentions that have been at the heart of the controversy over "moral dilemmas."[47] This is why the issues raised by the phenomenological argument are of fundamental importance. Though Sinnott-Armstrong may be right that some advocates of "moral dilemmas" have meant to argue only for dilemmas in his sense, it is clear that most of these advocates have intended something that involves a good deal more than this minimal claim. What this "more" might be is one of the central topics of this book.

Notes

1. Two other simple forms of moral conflict are (1) situations in which A has a PV and A has a NV (and no other morally relevant feature) and (2) situations in which there are two alternative actions, A and B, each of which has a NV and no other morally relevant feature, and the agent must perform either A or B. The latter is given special attention in Greenspan 1983 and Vallentyne 1987 and 1989. In my view, similar points can be made, *mutatis mutandis*, for these other forms of moral conflict as for the form I discuss.

2. Kant 1971, p. 23.

3. Mill 1957, ch. 2 par. 25.

4. It is sometimes said that there cannot be "moral dilemmas" except in those moral conflicts that result from prior wrongdoing on the part of the agent (for example, see Donagan 1984, pp. 305–6). With respect to the theses at hand, this might be interpreted as the claim that OT is true of all moral conflicts unless they result from the agent's prior wrongdoing, in which case DT is true. In my view, though it is clear that some moral conflicts result from previous wrongdoing and some do not, this distinction is not relevant to the truth or falsity of DT. Hence, my argument against DT will concern all moral conflicts, whether or not they result from previous wrongdoing. I discuss the issue of prior wrongdoing and "moral dilemmas" further in chapter 8, sec. IV and chapter 9, sec. I.

5. Some might object to defining 'overriding' in terms of morally stronger reasons, preferring to speak of the evaluation of conflicting reasons without the metaphor of strength. But my intention is that the understanding of 'overriding' be neutral with respect to different normative accounts.

6. Styron 1980, p. 589.

7. Some might argue that there is a superior choice in this case, namely to choose

neither child, since choosing one or the other would be to cooperate in the evil project of another. However, there are other examples which are not open to this objection, as when a mother can save one but not both of her drowning children who have accidentally fallen into a lake.

8. I take 'O(A v B)' to mean that at least one of the two actions, A and B, ought to be done, but it is morally optional which action ought to be done. Opponents of "moral dilemmas" of various normative persuasions commonly argue, in effect, that though P1 is true, we should accept P3 and P4 rather than P2. In this connection, see Conee 1989; Donagan 1984, p. 307; Feldman 1986, p. 201; Odegard 1987; and Santurri 1987, p. 123 (however, cf. p. 83).

9. This is most explicit in Foot 1983; Guttenplan 1979–80; Raz 1986, ch. 13; and Sinnott-Armstrong 1988, pp. 58–71.

10. For a good survey of different senses of 'incommensurability' among values, see Griffin, 1986 chs. 5 and 6.

11. Different kinds of quantitative comparison are distinguished in Griffin 1986, ch. 6. See also Finnis 1980, pp. 112–15 and 1983, pp. 86–90; Griffin 1977, pp. 47–55; Nussbaum 1986, pp. 106–17 and 1990, chs. 2 and 3; and Rescher 1987, pp. 55–71.

12. This is perhaps the most frequent meaning assigned to 'incommensurability'. See Finnis 1980, pp. 112–15 and 1983, pp. 86–90; Nagel 1979c, pp. 131–34; Nussbaum 1986, pp. 106–17 and 1990, chs. 2 and 3; Rescher 1987, pp. 59–66; and Williams 1981c.

13. Cf. Santurri 1987, pp. 74–75.

14. See in this connection, Rescher 1987, pp. 71–79, and Stocker 1990, pp. 151–55, 175–78, and 214–15.

15. For example, see Griffin 1986, pp. 83 and 85, and Ross 1988, p. 150. Cf. Barry 1984, pp. 307–8.

16. It is important to recognize that IT is a metaphysical and not an epistemological thesis. It claims that there are moral conflicts in which no member of Q is true, not that it is not known which member of Q is true. As such, IT might be understood in two ways: as (1) the noncognitivist thesis that the members of Q have no truth-value, and hence do not have the truth-value "true," or (2) the cognitivist thesis that the members of Q do have truth-value, but in each case it is the truth-value "false." Either or both of these might be incompatible with moral realism, depending on how that doctrine is defined. On the relationship between incommensurability and moral realism, see Foot 1983, pp. 397–98; Guttenplan 1979–80, p. 71; MacIntyre 1981, pp. 8, 68–69 and 133–34; and Wiggins 1987, pp. 123–37.

17. Cf. De Sousa 1974, p. 547, and Finnis 1980, p. 115.

18. Sinnott-Armstrong 1988, p. 62.

19. *Ibid.*, p. 66.

20. For another response, see Sorensen 1991, pp. 297–98.

21. Another possibility, suggested to me by Terrance McConnell, is to suppose that, when A and B are incomparable, no conclusion at all can be made about which action ought to be done [that is, there would be no basis for accepting OA, OB, or O(A v B)]. This would be a disturbing consequence of incomparability. However, if this were implied by incomparability, then IT would not provide a reason for accepting DT, and that is the issue I am concerned with here. In this connection, see Conee 1989, pp. 139–40, and Foot 1983, pp. 395–96.

22. For a proponent of "moral dilemmas" who stresses the importance of the difference between incomparability and equality in moral deliberation, see Nagel 1979c, pp. 128–29.

23. We may suppose that Katherine first made her promise to Greg and later was

notified that he had been killed in an avalanche while mountain climbing in the Himalayas. She then made her promise to Michael, and after a short while Greg unexpectedly returned.

24. Nagel 1979c, p. 129. What Nagel does not seem to see is that both incomparability and equality result in situations in which it is necessary to act against reasons that are not outweighed.

25. Cf. Conee 1989, pp. 139–40.

26. For examples of those who believe that there are moral conflicts in which some form of moral distress is sometimes justified no matter what the agent does and who accept some form of the "moral dilemmas" view at least partly in order to account for this, see Marcus 1980, pp. 126–27 and 130–33; Nussbaum 1986, pp. 32–47; Phillips and Mounce 1970, pp. 100–101; Rescher 1987, pp. 39–40; Sinnott-Armstrong 1988, pp. 44–53; Stocker 1990, ch. 1; Trigg 1971; van Fraassen 1973; Walzer 1973; and Williams 1973a.

27. I defend this claim in chapter 5.

28. I develop this conception of moral responsibilities in chapter 6.

29. For an example of this objection, see Levi 1986, p. 25.

30. For example, see Marcus 1980, pp. 130–33; Nussbaum 1986, p. 27; Phillips and Mounce 1970, pp. 100–101; Stocker 1990, p. 28; Walzer 1973, pp. 169–72; and Williams 1973a, pp. 172–75. Cf. Ross, 1988 p. 28 .

31. For additional discussion of his book, see Gowans 1992.

32. Sinnott-Armstrong 1988, p. 12. A more precise version of this definition is given in the next passage.

33. Sinnott-Armstrong 1988, pp. 17–18.

34. *Ibid.*, p. 18.

35. *Ibid.*, p. 20. For his final statement of this definition, see p. 29.

36. *Ibid.*, p. 19.

37. *Ibid.*

38. His concept of a moral requirement is actually somewhat stronger than my concept of a positive value feature. Nonetheless, I allow that the equality argument shows that there are conflicting moral requirements that do not override each other.

39. Sinnott-Armstrong himself holds a form of this view (1988, p. 53).

40. Sinnott-Armstrong 1988, p. 54. He also argues for his position on the ground that there are conflicts between incomparable moral requirements.

41. Donagan 1984, pp. 307–8 .

42. Donagan goes on to say that in such a situation "the fireman's only duty or obligation is to act on as many of [the grounds] as possible, it does not matter which." (1984, pp. 307–8) In a similar way, Sinnott-Armstrong is willing to admit that there is a "*disjunctive* moral requirement for Sophie to choose either one child or the other" (p. 56). However, Sinnott-Armstrong holds that this disjunctive requirement does not override either of the nondisjunctive requirements to save each child "because it does not conflict with them." There may be some disagreement lurking between Donagan and Sinnott-Armstrong here, but it does not change the fact that Donagan accepts moral dilemmas as Sinnott-Armstrong defines them.

43. For example, see Conee 1989. Conee states that "someone may be subject to what Sinnott-Armstrong calls incompatible non-overridden moral requirements without being in anything that is plausibly regarded as a moral dilemma." He adds that "such requirements could not constitute the philosophically controversial sort of dilemma" (p. 134).

44. Williams 1981c, p. 74.

45. Walzer 1973, p. 160.

46. Walzer does not think these claims have anything to do with conflicts between nonoverridden moral requirements, for both his examples of moral dilemmas are cases in which he argues that one requirement does override the other (see 1973, pp. 164–68). His main thesis is that an agent who follows the overriding requirement in these cases has nonetheless done something morally wrong on account of not following the overridden requirement. Williams allows that in "tragic" conflicts neither requirement overrides the other, though he also insists that there are conflicts of obligations in which one obligation outweighs the other. In these latter conflicts, Williams claims, an agent acting on the stronger obligation may owe an apology or some other form of compensation to the person to whom the weaker obligation was owed (see 1981c, p. 74).

47. One indication of the nature of Sinnott-Armstrong's concerns is his statement that in a moral dilemma "there is an adequate moral justification for violating either moral requirement," and hence that in a dilemma "it is not morally wrong to violate either moral requirement" (1988, p. 20). This last remark is followed by the stipulation, "since I reserve 'wrong' for the strongest possible criticism in the relevant kind of situation." I am not sure what "strongest" means here, but it is clear that, in arguing for moral dilemmas as he defines them, Sinnott-Armstrong is not concerned to establish a thesis about inescapable moral wrongdoing. In correspondence, however, Sinnott-Armstrong has said that the term 'wrong' has different uses, and that violations of moral requirements or of nonoverridden requirements could be described as wrong. This makes it look as if the claims about inescapable moral wrongdoing that have been made by proponents of "moral dilemmas" are largely matters of stipulation. In my view, whether these claims are sound depends on considerations that go beyond Sinnott-Armstrong's thesis and that cannot be adjudicated simply by stipulating how 'wrong' is to be used.

4

A Prescriptivist Argument against the Dilemmas Thesis

In the last chapter I found inconclusive the three most prominent arguments in favor of DT. In this chapter I defend an argument against this thesis. Thus I conclude that DT is false and that OT is true, and hence that wrongdoing in the sense of transgressing deliberative conclusions cannot be inescapable. So understood, the intuition that wrongdoing can always be avoided may be preserved. On the other hand, the apparently contrary intuition, that wrongdoing sometimes is inescapable, should also be retained, for there is a sense of 'moral wrongdoing' for which this intuition is correct. My arguments here make way for my defense of this position, beginning in the next chapter.

Arguments against "moral dilemmas" typically take one of two forms. As applied to DT, the first tries to show that, when A and B cannot both be done, there is always a way to avoid the conclusion that both OA and OB. These arguments usually defend some normative system in which there is a guarantee that in a moral conflict the correct conclusion of deliberation will be, as OT claims, exactly one of the following: (1) OA, (2) OB, or (3) ~OA & ~OB & O(A v B). This approach, common among utilitarians and Kantians, requires a commitment both to a particular normative system and to the prior idea that moral deliberation should proceed on the basis of some normative system.[1] But acceptance of OT rather than DT does not entail these commitments, for it is possible to maintain that the outcome of deliberation must conform to the requirements of OT while claiming that it is a mistake to think moral deliberation must be based on a normative *system* at all. This was the position of W. D. Ross. Though he clearly accepted OT rather than DT, he held that there is a set of possibly conflicting moral considerations ("prima facie duties") and that in a particular case when these conflict it is a matter of perception what morally ought to be done. In any case, I do not give an argument of this first kind. My objection to DT depends on considerations that are metaethical and are not tied to any particular normative system, or even to the claim that deliberation requires such a system.

The second kind of argument against "moral dilemmas" takes a stronger position: It maintains that there is something about the idea of "moral dilemmas" that is irrational, incoherent, impossible, or absurd. At the heart of these arguments is the claim that a "moral dilemma" implies something inconsistent in a sense of 'inconsistent' that is deeply objectionable.[2] If an argument of this form is sound, then whatever the correct normative viewpoint turns out to be, it will have to preclude "moral dilemmas." These inconsistency arguments are not based solely on considerations of "pure logic." By itself a "moral dilemma" does not entail a logical inconsistency (via the rules of standard systems of propositional, predicate, and modal logic). This result obtains only if certain metaethical principles are assumed, such as those found in traditional deontic logics. But these principles are controversial, not only with regard to whether they should be accepted but also with regard to why they should be accepted. Hence, inconsistency arguments against "moral dilemmas" may be based on quite different considerations even if they have the same formal structure.

In this chapter I present an argument of this second type against DT. Though it bears some relationship to one of the inconsistency arguments common in the "moral dilemmas" literature, its ultimate basis is a form of prescriptivism. In brief, I argue that conclusions of moral deliberation are prescriptive, in a sense to be explained, and that it is implausible, given some views about the rationality of intending, to think there are conflicts among prescriptive judgments. It is only from this prescriptivist standpoint that I think arguments relying on traditional deontic principles should be accepted. There has been some discussion of the significance of prescriptivism for the "moral dilemmas" issue.[3] But there has not been widespread appreciation of the central role that prescriptivism should play in evaluating this issue. Once this is appreciated, it is possible to see the debate about "moral dilemmas" in a different and more revealing light; for it will then be possible to disentangle, from the myriad of conflicting and sometimes dubious claims made in this debate, the true and important thesis that many advocates of "moral dilemmas" have defended: that there is a sense in which moral wrongdoing may be inescapable. For the time being, however, I confine myself to the refutation of DT.

I. Prescriptivism and the Dilemmas Thesis

The term 'prescriptivism' has been used to refer to a variety of positions, and I will not consider all the views which have been expressed under this label. In general, it refers to the idea that moral judgments are prescriptive, meaning that they are action-guiding. The preeminent defender of prescriptivism, Hare, understands this as a linguistic thesis about the meaning of moral words. But I do not regard prescriptivism as a theory of meaning, resting solely on linguistic intuitions. In my view, it is based more broadly on a recognition of the role of morality in our lives. Since for us morality is a practical and not purely theoretical concern, there must be some moral judgments that are action-guiding in some sense. Though it may be logically possible to accept moral judgments and never have any motivation to act on them, someone with this disposition would adhere to but a theoretical shadow of morality. Hence, I will assume that the agents under consideration are committed to morality as something having practical force in their lives. This does not beg the question against the "moral dilemmas" view, for this is presented as a view about which moral judgments are correct for agents in certain conflict situations. It is not restricted to a special and unusual class of agents who regard morality as having no bearing on their motivations to act. To the contrary, "moral dilemmas" are often attributed to persons, such as Antigone, who are strongly devoted to morality as being efficacious in their lives. Moreover, it is hard to make sense of the phenomenological argument without presupposing that morality is practical since moral distress is said to be inescapable because, no matter what the agent does, he or she fails to perform an action positively evaluated by some moral judgment. If moral judgments are not regarded as having some relevance to action, it is hard to see why it should be distressing that the action is not performed.[4]

The recognition that morality is practical requires that some moral judgments be, in some respect, action-guiding. The paradigm cases of these judgments are conclusions of moral deliberation. Since the aim of deliberation is to determine what ought to be done, all things considered, conclusions of deliberation are the moral judgments that are most evidently made with a view to action. They mark the point where moral deliberation ends and action is to begin. It does not follow from this, and I do not claim, that all moral judgments are directly action-guiding. There are other moral judgments, including judgments that are employed *in* deliberation, that are at most only indirectly related to action. For example, the judgment that an action has a PV provides a reason for action, but since it may be overridden it is not itself action-guiding in any straightforward sense.[5] It is also clear that there are nonmoral judgments that are action-guiding. In the discussion that follows, however, I will assume that moral judgments are regarded as always having priority over conflicting nonmoral practical judgments. Later I will consider the view that nonmoral practical judgments sometimes have priority over conflicting moral judgments, and I will show that this would not refute my argument about the incompatibility of DT and prescriptivism.

With these preliminaries in mind, let us suppose that an agent S, committed to morality as practical, is in a deliberative situation and reaches the conclusion that, all things considered, S morally ought to do an action X. Prescriptivism asserts that there is an important connection between S's accepting this moral judgment and S's doing X. According to a common but very strong form of this doctrine:

> *Action-Prescriptivism* If an agent S sincerely believes that S morally ought to do an action X, then S does X.

For the purpose of my argument, it is necessary to assume only that this conditional states a thesis that would be falsified by a case in which the antecedent were true and the consequent false (the same will hold for my revised version of prescriptivism). According to action-prescriptivism, if S does not do some action A, then S does not sincerely believe that S morally ought to do A. On this view, there can be no gap between acceptance of a deliberative conclusion and performance of the action required by it.

It is obvious that action-prescriptivism creates a problem for DT. If DT were true, then there would be deliberative situations in which an agent S would correctly conclude that S ought to do A and S ought to do B even though S cannot do both A and B. By action-prescriptivism it follows from S's acceptance of these two moral judgments that S does A and that S does B. But if S does A and does B, then it is not the case that S cannot do both A and B. In fact, any form of prescriptivism that asserts an inescapable connection between the sincere acceptance of a moral judgment and action (for example, that of Hare[6]) will create a problem for the claim that there are "moral dilemmas" consisting of these judgments.

There is, however, a well-known objection to this strong form of prescriptivism. *Akrasia* shows that it is possible for an agent S to sincerely believe S morally ought to perform some action A (here and now) and at the same time voluntarily and intentionally perform an action S knows to be incompatible with A. Hence, if action-prescriptivism were true, it would be possible for an agent both to do A and to do something incompatible with A. Since this is not possible, action-prescriptivism must be false.

The subject of *akrasia* is a matter of controversy at several levels (as to what the phenomenon is, whether it is possible, and how it is possible), and it is not my purpose to offer a resolution of these problems here. But I am convinced that *akrasia* as just described is possible, and hence that this is a sound objection. Therefore, I will propose a weaker form of prescriptivism that circumvents it. In this I make a significant departure from the approach of Hare.[7] According to this view:

> *Intention-Prescriptivism* If an agent S sincerely believes that S morally ought to do an action X, then S intends to do X.[8]

On this account, if S does not intend to do some action A, then S does not sincerely believe that S morally ought to do A. To say that an agent intends to do something is to say more than that the agent wants to do it. It is possible to want to do something and yet have no intention of doing it (for example, to travel to China). Intending takes an agent closer to action than merely wanting. To say that an agent intends to do something is to say that the agent has a plan of action to do it.[9] On the other hand, it is possible to intend to do something and yet not do it. One might forget, change one's mind, find it too difficult, and so on. Moreover, as in the case of *akrasia*, it is even possible for an agent S to intend to do some action A (here and now) and at the same time voluntarily and intentionally perform an action S knows to be incompatible with A. No doubt there is a sense in which this is irrational, but *akrasia* is a form of irrational behavior. Such behavior may be perplexing, but it is not impossible.[10] Therefore, intention-prescriptivism is immune to the *akrasia* objection.

Intention-prescriptivism asserts a connection between acceptance of a moral judgment and action, but the connection is not inevitable, as in action-prescriptivism. There can be a gap between acceptance of a deliberative conclusion and performance of the action required by it. For this reason, intention-prescriptivism does not create a problem for DT in the straightforward way stated earlier. Nonetheless, it is implausible to maintain both positions. DT asserts that there are deliberative situations in which an agent S would be correct to conclude that S ought to do A and ought to do B while knowing that S cannot do both A and B. By intention-prescriptivism it follows from S's acceptance of these two moral judgments that S intends to do A and intends to do B while knowing that S cannot do both A and B. This is not impossible, but it is irrational.

To see this, consider a nonmoral case of conflicting intentions. John intends to drive to his dance lesson on Tuesday, as he does every Tuesday, and also intends to have his car repaired on the same day, since it needs a tune-up. It turns out that he cannot fulfill both intentions. Once John realizes this, it would clearly be irrational for him to continue to maintain both intentions. In this circumstance, it would not be unreasonable for John both to want to go to his lesson and to want to have his car repaired. But it would be unreasonable for him both to intend to do the one and to intend to do the other.

The irrationality of knowingly having conflicting intentions may be explicated by reference to two principles of rational intending. It is worth making these principles explicit, as they are analogous to the deontic principles used in the most common inconsistency argument against DT (see sec. III). I take these principles to be based on the teleology of intending, specifically, on the fact that an intention is a plan to act, and that a plan to act is rational only if it is believed to be realizable in one's life. According to the first principle:

(PRI1) If an agent S knows S cannot do an action X, then it would be irrational for S to intend to do X.[11]

For example, if an agent knows she cannot travel to China next week, say because she does not have a passport, it would be irrational for her to intend to travel to China next week. In this respect, intending differs from wanting. It is not irrational to want to travel to China while knowing one cannot. But to intend is to do more than to want. To intend is to plan to act: It is to orient oneself, at least psychologically, toward the performance of the action. Though not every intention culminates in action, the point of every intention is action, and so it would be irrational to intend to do something one knows one cannot do. According to the second principle:

(PRI2) If an agent S intends to do an action X and intends to do an action Y, then it would be irrational for S not to intend to do both X and Y.[12]

In this respect, intending differs once again from wanting. A man may want to marry this woman and want to marry that woman, yet he would not be irrational if he did not want to marry both women. But if he intends to marry this woman and intends to marry that woman, then he clearly would be irrational if he did not intend to marry both women. An agent intending rationally must regard separate intentions as conjoined into a unified intention; for an intention is a plan to act, and a particular action must take place in conjunction with other actions one performs. Hence, a rational agent will combine intentions into a single conjunctive intention in order to determine the feasibility of fulfilling the entire set of intentions.

In sum, DT claims that there are deliberative situations in which an agent S would be correct to conclude that S ought to do A and ought to do B while knowing that S cannot do both A and B. According to intention-prescriptivism, it follows from S's acceptance of these judgments that S intends to do A and intends to do B while knowing that S cannot do both A and B. Yet by PRI2, if S intends to do A and S intends to do B, then it would be irrational for S not to intend to do both A and B; while by PRI1, if S knows that S cannot do both A and B, then it would be irrational for S to intend to do both A and B. Since S must either intend or not intend to do both A and B, a consequence of DT is that S, though judging correctly, will be irrational no matter what. In view of this, DT should be rejected. Moreover, since none of the conclusions sanctioned by OT would result in conflicting intentions, these difficulties do not arise for OT [in particular, it is not irrational to conclude that O(A v B)]. Therefore, OT is more plausible than DT.

Three objections might be raised against this argument. According to the first, it is not always irrational to knowingly have conflicting intentions. For example, a person might set out with the intention of doing several chores over spring vacation knowing that she cannot possibly do them all, but believing that by intending to do them all she will do more of them than she would if she set out with a realistic set of intentions. It might be claimed that this is a rational policy and hence that it is not always the case that having intentions one knows cannot all be fulfilled is irrational. In response, I would say that such a person does not actually intend to do all the chores over spring vacation. Rather, she intends to do as many of them as she can and believes that by acting as if she intends to do them all, she will do as many as she can (and thus fulfill her actual intention). But acting as if one intends to do something is not the same as actually intending to do it. Therefore, though such a policy might be a rational one, it does not involve actually having conflicting intentions.

The second objection maintains that there is a different reason why it is not always irrational to knowingly have conflicting intentions. This objection is based on situations addressed by the principle of double effect (though not on the principle itself). Suppose an agent in wartime (1) intends to destroy a munitions factory, (2) knows that he cannot both destroy the factory and not harm innocent civilians, and yet (3) intends to not harm innocent civilians. Surely, it may be said, this agent is not irrational. Yet it follows from PRI1 and PRI2 that

this agent is irrational. From (2) it follows by PRI1 that the agent would be irrational to intend to both destroy the factory and to not harm innocent civilians.
But from (1) and (3) it follows by PRI2 that the agent would be irrational not to
intend to both destroy the factory and to not harm innocent civilians. Since the
agent must either intend or not intend to do both of these things, the agent is
irrational no matter what.

My response is to insist that this agent is irrational. However, an agent in a
somewhat different position would not be irrational, and it may be that confusion between these two cases underlies the apparent plausibility of this objection. An agent would not be irrational who (1) intends to destroy a munitions
factory, (2) knows that he cannot both destroy the factory and not harm innocent civilians, and yet (4) does not intend to harm innocent civilians. PRI1 and
PRI2 cannot be used to show that this agent is irrational [since (1) and (4) do not
conform to the conjunction required by the antecedent of PRI2]. What is
important here is the distinction between intending to not do something and
not intending to do it. An agent who intends to do X and knows that he cannot
both do X and not do Y would be irrational if he intended to not do Y, but
would not be irrational if he simply did not intend to do Y. Once this distinction
is recognized, the preceding objection loses its force.

According to the final objection, it is no more irrational to have conflicting
intentions than it is to intend to perform an action and at the same time do
something one knows to be incompatible with this action (that is, *akrasia*). Since
I have acknowledged that the latter is possible, the former must be as well. This
objection is not to the point. What is at issue here is not whether it is possible to
have conflicting intentions, but whether it is plausible to accept DT if intention-
prescriptivism and the principles of rational intending are true. If, as I have
argued, a consequence of the conjunction of these positions is that agents are
sometimes correct to behave irrationally, then, assuming that intention-prescriptivism, PRI1, and PRI2 are true, there is good reason not to accept DT. A
philosophical position that justifies irrational behavior (as opposed to explaining
its possibility) should not be accepted.

II. Attempts to Reconcile the Dilemmas Thesis
and Intention-Prescriptivism

A proponent of DT with prescriptivist proclivities might suggest that intention-
prescriptivism is basically correct but should be modified in such a way as to
make it compatible with DT. I will consider two forms of this proposal, and I
will argue that neither offers a promising line of defense for DT.

Earlier I made the assumption that conclusions of moral deliberation always
have priority over conflicting nonmoral practical judgments. If this assumption
were denied, then intention-prescriptivism would need to be qualified, and this
might be thought to have bearing on its incompatibility with DT. Though it is a
matter of controversy whether what Williams calls "the necessary supremacy of

the moral"[13] should be denied, it is worth considering the consequences of doing so for the issues raised in this chapter.

The story of Abraham and Isaac (Genesis 22) provides a possible ground for such a denial, and it will be convenient to explore this topic by reference to it. Abraham, we may suppose, sincerely believes that he morally ought to refrain from killing his son Isaac under any circumstance, and ordinarily it follows from this that he intends to refrain from killing Isaac. But in the extraordinary circumstance where God commands that Abraham kill Isaac, Abraham accepts the moral judgment "I morally ought to refrain from killing Isaac" but regards this moral judgment as not overriding God's command, where this command is understood as constituting a conflicting nonmoral reason. To say that the moral judgment does not override God's command means that it is overridden by it, that it is equal to it, or that it is incomparable with it (it does not matter which for the issue at hand). Finally, let us suppose that Abraham intends to kill Isaac because, though he accepts the moral judgment, he also accepts God's command and does not believe it is overridden by the moral judgment. So understood,[14] the story of Abraham and Isaac provides a case in which an agent believes he morally ought to do something but does not intend to do it, and this is a counter-example to intention-prescriptivism.

If there are such cases, intention-prescriptivism would have to be qualified as follows: If an agent S sincerely believes that S morally ought to do an action X, then S intends to do X *unless* S believes there is an action Y such that X and Y cannot both be done and there is a nonmoral reason to do Y that is not overridden by the moral reason to do X. This modified form of intention-prescriptivism asserts a connection between the acceptance of a moral judgment and the intention to act on it, but the connection is contingent upon the agent not recognizing a conflicting nonmoral reason that is not overridden by the moral reason. Hence, it is compatible with the moral judgment and intention of Abraham.

This qualified form of intention-prescriptivism does not affect my argument against DT. DT concerns cases in which there is a conflict between reasons both of which are moral. A nonmoral reason has no role in the description of the conflict. But if no nonmoral reason is recognized, then the "unless" clause is false, and there is a direct implication from acceptance of the moral judgment to the intention to act on it. This implication is all that is needed for my argument.

In view of this, it is clear that a rather different modification of intention-prescriptivism is required if it is to be reconciled with DT. A proponent of DT might naturally suggest the following: If an agent S sincerely believes that S morally ought to do an action X, then S intends to do X *unless* S believes there is an action Y such that X and Y cannot both be done and there is a moral reason to do Y that is not overridden by the moral reason to do X. If conclusions of moral deliberation were prescriptive only in this weaker sense, then DT would be immune to my argument; for DT claims that there are dilemmas in precisely those cases in which A and B cannot both be done and the PV of A and the PV of B are not overridden. But then an agent S who accepted (as applying to S) the two moral judgments in a dilemma, OA and OB, would correctly believe with respect to each judgment that there is a conflicting action for which there is a nonoverridden moral reason, and hence from the acceptance of neither judgment would it follow that S has an intention to do the action. Without this implication from moral judgment to intention my argument fails.

There is an immediate problem with this approach. It has the apparent result that an agent who accepts the judgments in a dilemma need have no intention at all regarding the two actions. In particular, it seems possible on this account that S could believe S ought to do A and ought to do B, and yet intend to do neither A nor B. This is surely an unacceptable result for any form of intention-prescriptivism.

A more plausible approach is suggested by OT and intention-prescriptivism unmodified. According to OT, in a moral conflict in which neither PV overrides the other, the conclusion to be drawn is ~OA and ~OB and O(A v B). By intention-prescriptivism, if S accepts this conclusion, it does not follow that S intends to do A or that S intends to do B, but it does follow that S intends to do A or B. Given this disjunctive intention, S would need to form a more specific intention, either to do A or to do B (though not both), on the basis of nonmoral considerations, or else arbitrarily. This is surely the result that is to be expected from an intention-prescriptivist perspective.

A proponent of DT might attempt to accommodate this expectation by modifying DT so that the correct conclusion in a moral conflict in which neither PV overrides the other is OA, OB, *and* O(A v B).[15] This, together with the qualified form of intention-prescriptivism, would have the result that, if S accepts these three judgments, then it does not follow that S intends to do A or that S intends to do B, since with respect to each of these actions S believes there is a conflicting action for which there is a non-overridden moral reason. But it does follow that S intends to do (A v B) since (we may suppose) S does not believe there is an action C such that (A v B) and C cannot both be done and there is a moral reason to do C that is not overridden by the moral reason to do (A v B).[16] By modifying DT and intention-prescriptivism in these ways, it is possible to reconcile them.

At first sight this proposal appears to provide the correct prescriptivist analysis of a moral conflict in which neither PV overrides the other. For on this view, the only judgment of the three—OA, OB, and O(A v B)—that has prescriptive force in the sense of implying an unconditional intention to act is O(A v B), the judgment regarded as correct on all sides (that is, by both OT and this revision of DT). According to this proposal, the acceptance of O(A v B) is sufficient to form an intention to do A or B. The acceptance of the judgments about which DT and OT disagree, OA and OB, results in no modification of this intention; and without O(A v B) they would result in no direct intention at all. Herein lies the difficulty. On this view, the judgments affirmed in a dilemma have no more prescriptive force than it might be supposed the initial judgments that A has a PV and B has a PV have: They are in general relevant to deliberation about what to do but in this circumstance imply no intention to act. But then the acceptance of OA and OB cannot be regarded as conclusions of moral deliberation in the same sense as the acceptance of O(A v B).

This last point makes clear the inadequacy of this modification of intention-prescriptivism. For the intention-prescriptivist, the purpose of moral deliberation is to evaluate the morally relevant features of alternatives and on this basis form an intention to act.[17] The recognition that A and B have PVs establishes that these alternatives are weakly prescriptive. In some situations the presence of these PVs would be the basis of an intention to act. The aim of deliberation is to move *from* this recognition *to* a conclusion sufficient to establish an intention to act in this situation. From this perspective, the acceptance of O(A v B) achieves the end of moral deliberation, but the acceptance of OA and OB (on this proposal) does not. The latter takes the agent no closer to action than the premises that A has a PV and B has a PV. To regard deliberative conclusions as prescriptive only in this limited sense is to undermine the prescriptivist understanding of moral deliberation.

III. Intention-Prescriptivism and a Common Argument Against the Dilemmas Thesis

I believe intention-prescriptivism is fundamental to the evaluation of DT. An important indication of this is the relationship between the foregoing prescriptivist argument against DT and the most common inconsistency argument against "moral dilemmas," as applied to DT. As I noted earlier, the two principles of rational intending are analogous to the two deontic principles used in this inconsistency argument. For the first deontic principle:

The Kantian Principle[18] If an agent ought to perform an action X, then the agent can perform X.

The second deontic principles states that:

The Agglomeration Principle If an agent ought to perform an action X and ought to perform an action Y, then the agent ought to perform both X and Y.)

According to the inconsistency argument, if an agent S ought to do A and ought to do B, then S ought to do both A and B (by the agglomeration principle), and if S ought to do both A and B, then S can do both A and B (by the Kantian principle). But then it is not possible, as DT maintains, that there are situations in which S ought to do A and ought to do B, but cannot do both. Since this argument is plainly valid, its soundness depends upon the acceptability of the two deontic principles. Proponents of the argument have claimed that these principles are true,[19] while defenders of "moral dilemmas" have felt little compunction in rejecting one or the other of them.[20]

Intention-prescriptivism and the principles of rational intending give us a basis for judging the dispute about these deontic principles, understood as applying to conclusions of moral deliberation. The deontic principles pertain to conditions under which these conclusions are true or false, while the principles of rational intending pertain to conditions under which certain intentions are rational or irrational. Given this difference, it is nonetheless clear that there is a structural similarity between the contrapositive form of the Kantian principle and PRI1, and between the agglomeration principle and PRI2. It does not follow that intention-prescriptivism makes it possible to deduce the deontic principles from the principles of rational intending. Still, the similarity is an instructive one, for it suggests that the plausibility of the deontic principles is closely related to prescriptivism.

This is especially true in the case of the Kantian principle. If this principle were denied, then it would sometimes be correct for an agent S to believe S ought to do A even though S knows S cannot do A.[21] But by intention-prescriptivism, if S believes S ought to do A, then S intends to do A, and by PRI1, this intention is irrational if S knows S cannot do A. Hence, the denial of the Kantian principle entails that there are cases in which S's correctly believing that S ought to do A would result in S having an irrational intention—on the assumption that intention-prescriptivism and PRI1 are true. Therefore, if they are true, it is implausible to deny the Kantian principle.

With respect to the agglomeration principle, it is not clear that there is any point to denying it if intention-prescriptivism and PRI2 are true. If the agglomeration principle were accepted, and S believes S ought to do A and S ought to do B, then, assuming S acts rationally, S would believe S ought to do both A and B; and by intention-prescriptivism it follows that S would intend to do both A and B. But given intention-prescriptivism and PRI2, a rational agent S who believes S ought to do A and S ought to do B would form this same intention even if the agglomeration principle were denied; for by intention-prescriptivism it follows from these beliefs that S intends to do A and S intends to do B, and a consequence of this, by PRI2, is that S would be irrational not to intend to do both A and B. Hence, assuming S behaves rationally, S's belief that S ought to do A and S ought to do B will result in S intending to do both A and B. Since a rational agent in this circumstance would intend to do both A and B with or without the agglomeration principle, it is difficult to see the point of denying this deontic principle.

In short, if intention-prescriptivism and the two principles of rational intending are accepted, then, with respect to moral judgments that are conclusions of moral deliberation, it is implausible to deny the Kantian principle and it is pointless to deny the agglomeration principle. Intention-prescriptivism and these principles of rational intending thus provide a prima facie justification for these deontic principles and hence for the inconsistency argument against DT based upon them.

These deontic principles have nonetheless been a matter of considerable controversy. Since the intention-prescriptivist outlook has provided a reason for accepting them, it is important to consider the objections that have been raised against them in order to determine whether these objections cast doubt on this outlook. I do this in the next two sections. In general, I maintain that, though there are versions of both the Kantian principle and the agglomeration principle that are false, no objection has been raised that calls into question the forms of these principles that are supported by the intention-prescriptivist outlook and that are necessary for the form of the inconsistency argument against DT stated earlier.[22]

IV. The Kantian Principle

There is a substantial literature pertaining to the Kantian principle.[23] Though various arguments have been given in support of this principle, my argument is based only on intention-prescriptivism and PRI1. But this argument may be seen as an expression of a familiar, intuitive idea. Since the purpose of moral deliberation is to decide, from a moral perspective, what action ought to be done, a necessary condition of successful deliberation is that the action that one decides to do can be done. It would be incoherent to decide to do something that cannot be done. Suppose, for example, that a person who does not know how to swim sees someone drowning in the middle of a lake. If the person is trying to decide what she ought to do and she reaches the conclusion that all things considered she ought to swim to the middle of the lake and save the person, her deliberation has clearly failed. The reason it has failed is because she cannot swim. But this can be the reason only if the 'ought' that expresses a conclusion of moral deliberation implies 'can'.[24]

This argument does not depend on other considerations commonly brought forward in favor of the Kantian principle, such as the unfairness of blaming someone for failing to do what cannot be done. This contention has been criticized, perhaps rightly, on the ground that blameworthiness has considerable independence from the concept of 'ought'.[25] But objections of this kind have no bearing on my position. What potentially does have bearing is a set of purported counterexamples to the Kantian principle. One complication in discussions of these examples is that there are different interpretations of the meaning of the key terms in the principle. In particular, there is a wide range of moral senses of 'ought', and there is no doubt that some of these senses are such that 'ought' does not imply 'can'. No one who has seriously considered the Kantian principle has denied this. Hence, the question is not whether every moral sense of 'ought' implies 'can', but whether any well-recognized moral sense of 'ought' implies 'can'.

The form of the principle I mean to defend is as follows: If (1) an agent S morally ought to do an action X (where this is understood as an "all things considered" conclusion of moral deliberation), then (2) it is logically and physically possible for S to perform X, and S has the ability and opportunity to perform X. For simplicity, I will assume that S knows the truth-values of (1) and (2), and that these truth-values are at the same time (unless otherwise noted). Though these are not trivial assumptions, they do not beg the question with respect to the argument against DT. My contention is that none of the purported counterexamples to various versions of the Kantian principle is a genuine counterexample to this version of the principle.[26]

Three kinds of counterexample require only brief mention. First, 'ought' is occasionally used to indicate what would be a good state of affairs ("Young children ought not to die in natural disasters"). Second, 'ought' is often used to express standing social or institutional duties ("Fathers ought to attend their children's high school graduations"). Finally, 'ought' is sometimes employed to state a worthy goal or ideal ("Nuclear weapons ought to be eliminated"). In each case, it is not plausible to suppose that 'ought' implies 'can'. But the 'ought' in these statements does not itself express a conclusion of moral deliberation, though it may express a consideration relevant to establishing such a conclusion ("Given our goal, I ought to vote against so-and-so").

Brief consideration is also sufficient for cases concerning unfulfilled past obligations ("I ought to have attended her wedding yesterday"). Here 'ought' does not imply 'can'. But the 'ought' is clearly not expressing a conclusion of moral deliberation about what to do, because it concerns a past action. Of course, the statement may be taken to imply that two days ago "I ought to go to the wedding tomorrow" would have been a correct deliberative conclusion. But presumably it was true at that time that the person could go, and so the 'ought' in this deliberative conclusion does imply 'can'.

The more significant counterexamples involve a sense of 'ought' that is more closely related to that in my version of the Kantian principle. In these examples, it is claimed that an agent who ought to do something nonetheless cannot do it on account of, respectively, psychological inability, external constraint of ability or opportunity, or self-imposed constraint of ability or opportunity.

Psychological Inability

Suppose a person suffers from an extreme psychological compulsion such that sometimes she cannot help but steal things. If the Kantian principle were true, it would follow that it is not always the case that the person ought to refrain from stealing. But surely the person ought not to steal, psychological compulsion or not. A related form of this objection concerns cases where a person ought to feel something such as sympathy with regard to the plight of another. These feelings are said to be beyond our control. An unsympathetic person cannot feel sympathy even though he ought to feel it. Once again, psychological inability shows that 'ought' does not imply 'can'.

I doubt that it is generally true that our feelings are beyond our control. But I grant that there are cases in which, due to psychological inability, a person cannot feel something that (in some sense) the person morally ought to feel. Moreover, psychological inability sometimes renders a person unable to do something that (in some sense) the person morally ought to do. Hence, these examples do refute the Kantian principle for some sense of 'ought'. But what sense?

When a person S genuinely cannot do (or feel) some X on account of psychological inability, S is incapable of deliberating about whether or not to do X. If psychological factors preclude doing X, then S can make no decision concerning this. This is what psychological inability means: No decision is possible. But if no decision is possible, then there is no conclusion of moral deliberation regarding S's doing X that is true or false. For a conclusion of moral delibera-tion is a decision to act. Still, several truths may be expressed by saying that S ought to do X: that it would be a good state of affairs for S to do X, that S's doing X is something we have reason to encourage, that S's doing X is some-thing regarding which, were S able to decide, S would be correct to decide to do, and so on. But none of these judgments provides a counterexample to the Kantian principle as I am defending it.

External Constraint

Oftentimes a person S morally ought to do some X but circumstances then develop for which S is neither responsible nor negligent in failing to anticipate, but which prevent S from doing X. Sometimes, it may be claimed, it remains the case that S ought to do X even though S cannot do it. For example, a teacher ought to be on time for class, and this is still true when through no fault of his own he gets stuck in an elevator and cannot make it on time. In this circum-stance, he has a good excuse for being late, and hence it seems unjustified to blame him for being late. But it is still the case that he ought to be on time. Hence, 'ought' does not imply 'can'.

The issue here turns on the sense of 'ought' for which it is true that the teacher ought to be on time. There is a standing institutional duty to be on time. However, though an 'ought' used to express such a duty does not imply 'can', the statement of this duty does not itself express a conclusion of moral deliberation. It is also true that, prior to being stuck on the elevator, the correct conclusion of moral deliberation would have been "I ought to be in class on time." But at that time, we may presume, it was still possible to be on time. On the other hand, once the teacher was stuck on the elevator and could not be on time, the correct conclusion surely would not be "I ought to be in class on time." Rather, it would be something such as "I ought to get word to them by the emergency phone," or "I ought to schedule a make-up class." Thus, there is no time at which an 'ought' expressing a conclusion of moral deliberation is true and the corresponding 'can' is false.

Self-imposed Constraint

Perhaps the most frequent and important purported counterexample to the Kantian principle concerns a case related to, but significantly different from, the previous one. Suppose a teacher could not make it to class on time because, knowing it would make him late, he had a leisurely breakfast before leaving home. Here there is more than a standing institutional duty to be on time, for none of the implicit factors that might override or cancel this duty are present. Hence, there is a significant sense of 'ought' for which, right up to the time the class is scheduled to begin, the teacher ought to be there on time. This judg-ment remains true even after the time has passed when he can still make it on time. Otherwise, it would be possible to avoid failing to do what ought to be done by putting oneself in a position where one could not do it. As this is obviously unacceptable, from the fact that at some point in time it is false that the teacher can be on time, it does not follow that from that time on it is false that he ought to be on time. Therefore, 'ought' does not imply 'can'.

Though the contentions in the previous paragraph are correct, it is possible to maintain this without denying my version of the Kantian principle. First, what was said regarding the previous example may also be said here: There is a standing institutional duty to be on time; as long as it is still possible to be on time the correct deliberative conclusion would be "I ought to be there on time," but after this time the correct conclusion would be something else such as "I ought to call to say I will be late." So there is no time at which the correct conclusion of moral deliberation would be "I ought to do X" even though X cannot be done. It follows that it is not true, say, at the beginning of class, that the correct deliberative conclusion is "I ought to be there now." Yet there certainly is a significant sense of 'ought' for which it is true, at this time, that the teacher ought to be there. Indeed he himself would be correct to think at this time "I ought to be there now." Hence, he would in one sense be correct and in another sense incorrect to think "I ought to be there now." Some explanation of this apparent incongruity is required.

Let us refer to the sense of 'ought' in which this judgment would be correct as 'ought$_c$', and the sense in which it would be incorrect (a conclusion of moral deliberation) as 'ought$_d$'. What needs to be explained is how it is possible for the teacher to correctly affirm at time t1 (the beginning of class), "I ought$_c$ to be there at t1," and correctly deny at t1, "I ought$_d$ to be there at t1." The explanation is that "I ought$_c$ to be there at t1" is true if, and only if, (1) there was a time t0, before t1, when the judgment "I ought$_d$ to be there at t1" was true, and (2) nothing has happened since t0 to cancel or override this judgment. But the truth at t1 of "I ought$_c$ to be there at t1" does not entail the truth *at* t1 of "I ought$_d$ to be there at t1." Hence, there is no contradiction in affirming the former and denying the latter at t1. In the example at hand, there was a time (before breakfast) when it was correct for the teacher to judge, "I ought$_d$ to be in class on time." Since nothing has happened to cancel or override this judgment, at the beginning of class it is correct for the teacher to judge, "I ought$_c$ to be in class now," even though at this point it is incorrect for him to judge, "I ought$_d$ to be in class now."

The judgment expressed at the beginning of class, "I ought$_c$ to be in class now," is a way of referring to the fact that a correct deliberative conclusion that has not been canceled or overridden requires him to be in class now. This ought$_c$ judgment does not entail 'can'. But a consequence of the foregoing explanation is that an ought$_c$ judgment does entail 'can or could have'; for on this account an ought$_c$ judgment entails that there was a time at which an ought$_d$ judgment was true, and an ought$_d$ judgment does entail 'can'. With respect to ought$_c$ judgments, then, the suggestion sometimes made that 'ought' implies 'can or could have' is correct.

Sinnott-Armstrong argues that there are cases that run counter to this explanation.[27] For example, suppose I promise to introduce you to Madonna at lunch tomorrow, knowing full well that I cannot do this because I have never met her myself. Surely it follows from this promise that I ought$_c$ to introduce you to Madonna tomorrow even though there was never a time when I could do this, and hence (on my analysis) there was never a time when I was correct to judge, "I ought$_d$ to introduce you to Madonna tomorrow." If this were the case, then my explanation would fail.

Because I knew I could not keep the promise, I would say that I was wrong to make it and owe you an apology, but that it is not binding on me, and so I do no *additional* wrong by not keeping it.[28] Hence, there is no time at which I either ought$_c$ or ought$_d$ to introduce you to Madonna at lunch tomorrow. You are thus entitled to chastise me for making an unfulfillable promise and thereby getting you unnecessarily _____ about tomorrow's lunch (you fill in the blank). But you are not entitled to chastise me for breaking a promise.

V. The Agglomeration Principle

The agglomeration principle is less controversial than the Kantian principle, and discussion of it is mainly confined to contexts where "moral dilemmas" are at issue.[29] Though there are formulations of the agglomeration principle that are false, none of the arguments that have been offered against it compel rejection of the version employed in the argument against DT. According to this version, if an agent ought to perform one action and ought to perform another action, then the agent ought to perform both actions (where 'ought' is used to express a conclusion of moral deliberation). I argued that intention-prescriptivism and PRI2 make it pointless to deny this principle. Of course, this does not establish that it is true. But I think it is true, and it would be an oddity of my position if there were counterexamples to it. Sometimes the agglomeration principle is rejected simply on the ground that there are "moral dilemmas." Beyond this, several independent reasons for rejecting the principle have been proposed.

Williams suggests an argument by analogy against the principle.[30] He claims that there are many evaluations of actions where agglomeration is not true. For example, "it may be *desirable*, or *advisable*, or *sensible*, or *prudent*, to do *a*, and again desirable or advisable etc. to do *b*, but not desirable etc. to do both *a* and *b*." Though Williams acknowledges that this is not a "knock-down disproof of the agglomeration principle," he thinks it shows that the principle "is not a self-evident datum of the logic of *ought*." And since rejecting it allows for dilemmas, and hence for "a more realistic picture of moral thought," he believes it should be rejected.

Williams is right in saying that an agglomeration principle is not true of the evaluative concepts he mentions. But it is illegitimate to infer from this that other evaluative concepts, in particular 'ought' as used in the expression of conclusions of moral deliberation, are not governed by an agglomeration principle. Such inferences are clearly not justified in other families of concepts. For example, with respect to modal concepts, agglomeration holds for necessity but not for possibility. Again, with respect to epistemic concepts, it holds for certainty (taken as implying truth) but not for probability. The lesson to be drawn here is that, even within families of concepts, for some concepts an agglomeration principle holds and for some it does not. This is an area where arguments by analogy are especially perilous. There can be no substitute for a specific analysis of the particular concept in question.

Torbjörn Tännsjö thinks that moral realism implies the falsity of the agglomeration principle.[31] "If moral realism is true," he writes, "then . . . rightness, wrongness, and obligatoriness are *de re*, they are possessed by *concrete* actions." But an agglomeration principle does not generally hold for properties of concrete actions. For example, if doing A has the property of taking ten minutes and doing B has the property of taking ten minutes, it does not follow that doing both A and B has the property of taking ten minutes. In a similar way, assuming that obligatoriness is a property of concrete actions, if doing A is obligatory and doing B is obligatory, it does not follow that doing both A and B is obligatory. Tännsjö concludes that if norms are understood *de re*, it is "self-evident" that the agglomeration principle is false.

It is obvious that an agglomeration principle is not true of all kinds of properties of actions. On the other hand, it is true of some kinds. For example, if A is performed by Marie and B is performed by Marie, then both A and B are performed by Marie. Again, if A is done before Tuesday and B is done before Tuesday, then both A and B are done before Tuesday. These are properties of actions for which an agglomeration principle holds. Since properties of action may thus be partitioned into those for which an agglomeration principle does and does not hold, even if obligatoriness were understood along realist lines as a property of concrete actions, it would not follow that the agglomeration principle is false for obligatoriness.

S. L. Hurley suggests that the agglomeration principle may be true in some contexts but not in others.[32] In particular, it may hold within but not across various kinds of reasons. For example, Hurley says, "if justice requires that p and justice requires that q, then justice requires that p and q; but if justice requires that p and kindness requires that q, there may not be any reason requiring that p and q." If this were the case, Hurley argues, it would be possible to maintain that there are moral conflicts across different kinds of reasons such as justice and kindness.

Hurley's point is to show how moral reasons can conflict, but it might be thought that her position could be extended to establish how conclusions of moral deliberation can conflict. Thus it might be said that if justice requires that p and kindness requires that q, and it is not possible to do both p and q, and neither reason is overridden, then the correct conclusion of moral deliberation is that p ought to be done and q ought to be done (as DT would maintain). But since in this case there is no reason that requires p and q, it is not the case that p and q ought to be done. So the agglomeration principle is false.

It is not clear why the agglomeration principle should not hold in situations where there are different kinds of reasons since the fact that deliberative conclusions are based on justice and kindness does not mitigate against the practical rationale for agglomerating these conclusions.[33] Moreover, even if the principle did not hold in these situations, this would not be sufficient to defend DT in all cases: A single moral principle such as 'protect the lives of your children' can result in a conflict between nonoverridden moral reasons. If in these cases we accept the agglomeration principle and hence reject DT, then it is not clear why, in conflicts between nonoverridden moral reasons that involve different moral principles, we should reject the agglomeration principle so that we can accept DT. If OT is an adequate position for moral conflicts generated by a single moral principle, then it is hard to see why it is an inadequate account for moral conflicts generated by different moral principles (see Chapter 3, sec. III).

A final argument against the agglomeration principle is proposed by Sinnott-Armstrong.[34] It is based on the fact that two actions performed together may have an altogether different significance than when each is performed separately. For example, it might be that a woman ought to take her husband out to dinner tonight, because it is his birthday, and that she ought to take her sister out to dinner tonight, because it is also her birthday. But since her husband and her sister detest one another, it would make for an extremely unpleasant evening if the three of them had dinner together. So it is not the case that she ought to take both her husband and her sister out to dinner tonight.

This example does show that an agglomeration principle does not hold for positive-value features of actions.[35] Taking her husband out has a PV and taking her sister out has a PV, but taking them both out may have no PV. But this is not sufficient to reject the agglomeration principle for conclusions of moral deliberation. For this, it would have to be shown that she would be correct to conclude that, all things considered, (1) she ought to take her husband out to dinner tonight, (2) she ought to take her sister out to dinner tonight, and (3) it is not the case that she ought to take both her husband and her sister out to dinner tonight.

Since it would be unpleasant for the three of them to have dinner together, the woman presumably would be correct to reach a conclusion that includes (3). But for the same reason, it would be a mistake for her to reach a conclusion that includes both (1) and (2). The problem is not exactly that she cannot do what is required by (1) and (2) together; it is that she can do both only in such a way that the reason for doing either would thereby be frustrated. She has a moral reason to give her husband a pleasant evening, but her sister's presence would spoil it (and vice versa). By acting on both reasons the woman would satisfy neither. Hence, whatever conclusion is correct here, it is not a conclusion that includes both (1) and (2).

VI. The Significance of the Argument against the Dilemmas Thesis

This brings to a close my argument against DT and in favor of OT. It is important to emphasize that, though I have defended one form of an inconsistency argument against DT,[36] there is a significant respect in which this argument differs from other defenses of inconsistency arguments against DT. It is often supposed that these arguments show that there are features specific to morality that preclude "moral dilemmas."[37] But my argument has nothing essentially to do with morality per se. Rather, it is based on features specific to deliberation, of which moral deliberation is but one species. To see this, suppose there are two plays I want to see, but I can only see one because tonight is the last performance of each. Assume no moral considerations are relevant to my deliberation. I would argue, for the kinds of reasons I have developed in this chapter, that it would be irrational for me to conclude that, all things considered, I ought to see the one play and ought to see the other. It would be irrational because (assuming no competing considerations come into play) a consequence of these conclusions would be that I intend to see the one and intend to see the other, knowing that I cannot see both. In general, since conclusions of any deliberation, moral or nonmoral, may be prescriptive in the sense of implying intentions to act, and since according to the principles of rational intending, incompatible intentions are irrational, any conclusion of deliberation that results in intentions the agent knows cannot both be fulfilled is irrational. It is because DT countenances such conclusions that DT is inadequate.

It is often supposed that inconsistency arguments against "moral dilemmas" establish more than this. In particular, it is frequently thought that inconsistency arguments show that, at bottom, genuine conflict in morality is an illusion, an illusion that is revealed and corrected through sound moral deliberation. On this view, though there are moral conflicts in the sense that it may appear initially that there is a moral reason for doing A and a moral reason for doing B (when both cannot be done), in the final analysis it must turn out that at least one of these apparent reasons was not in this circumstance a genuine moral reason at all. Moral deliberation properly conducted will thus not only guide action, it will expose at least one of these apparent reasons as a kind of moral mirage—something that, had our moral vision been perspicuous in the first place, would not have seemed to us to be a genuine moral reason.

Nothing in my argument against DT has these implications. Though moral conflict cannot persist at the level of conclusions of moral deliberation, it may well have a significant role elsewhere in the moral infrastructure of our lives. The earlier example of nonmoral deliberation provides a useful analogy here. The fact that I cannot rationally conclude that I ought to see this play and that I ought to see that one does not imply that there is no actual conflict of desires in this circumstance: The constraints of deliberation do not eliminate the fact that I really do want to see each of them. In a similar way, when A has a PV and B has a PV and I cannot do both, the fact that I cannot rationally conclude that I ought to do A and that I ought to do B does not imply that there is no actual moral conflict in the situation: The constraints of moral deliberation need not eliminate the fact that there really are genuine moral considerations that favor A and that favor B. This is a fact that may be important to us in a variety of ways.

If DT were true, then moral wrongdoing in the sense of violating a correct conclusion of moral deliberation would sometimes be inescapable. Since I have rejected DT, I agree that wrongdoing in this sense cannot be inescapable. In this respect, the intuition that there are no "moral dilemmas" is sound. But the rejection of DT leaves open the question whether or not a significant form of genuine moral conflict can remain once conflict in the form of conflicting conclusions of moral deliberation has been shown to be irrational. If so, then it may still be the case that moral wrongdoing in another sense is sometimes inescapable, and that the intuition that there are "moral dilemmas" in this sense is sound. It is to these topics that I turn in the next chapter.

Notes

1. For example, see Hare 1981, chs. 2 and 3; and Donagan 1977, chs. 5 and 6, and 1984. For critical discussion of several such arguments, see Sinnott-Armstrong 1988, ch. 3.

2. For example, see McConnell 1978, and Conee 1982. For a detailed evaluation of such arguments, see Sinnott-Armstrong 1988, chs. 4, 5, and 6.

3. For example, see Castañeda 1966 and 1982, pp. 195–201; Ladd 1958; Santurri 1987, pp. 9–10, 31–32, 37–38 and 42–43; Sinnott-Armstrong 1988, pp. 182–88; Steiner 1973; Stocker 1990, chs. 1 and 4; and Trigg 1971.

4. It may be thought that I am assuming internalism, the view that an agent who accepts a moral judgment necessarily has some motivation to act on it, rather than externalism, the view that it is possible for an agent to accept a moral judgment and have no motivation to act on it. To avoid making this assumption, I am simply restricting attention to those agents who as a matter of fact do regard morality as having motivational force.

5. Hence, I do not dissent from Stocker's claim that "there are important act-evaluations which are not action-guiding" (1990, p. 95). Indeed, I will later maintain that there are judgments pertaining to our moral responsibilities that are not directly action-guiding.

6. According to Hare, moral judgments are prescriptive in the following sense: "We say something prescriptive if and only if, for some act A, some situation S and some person P, if P were to assent (orally) to what we say, and not, in S, do A, he logically must be assenting insincerely" (1981, p. 21; for earlier formulations, see 1952, p. 20 and 1963, p. 79).

7. For Hare's responses to this problem, see 1952, pp. 168–70; 1963, pp. 67–85; and 1981, pp. 52–60.

8. Cf. Castañeda 1982 and Sellars 1963; 1966; and 1968, ch. 7.

9. For someone who emphasizes the connection between intentions and plans, see Bratman 1987.

10. This position is not uncontroversial. For a brief discussion, see Mele 1987, pp. 18–20.

11. Cf. Baier 1970, p. 649; Meiland 1970, pp. 45–47; and Harman 1986, pp. 82–83. Here and in the discussion of the Kantian principle below, I understand 'can' and 'cannot' as defined in chapter 3, sec. I.

12. Cf. Bratman 1987, pp. 134–38, and Castañeda 1982, pp. 175 and 279. A counterexample to this principle is proposed in Donagan 1987, pp. 103–5. Even if this example forced modification of PRI2, standard cases of moral conflicts would not be affected.

13. 1973a, p. 185.

14. For the purpose of this discussion, I am following the Kierkegaardian reading of the story, which sees it as a conflict, not between moral reasons, but between a moral and a nonmoral, religious reason, and does not assume that the moral reason overrides the religious one. In this connection, see Mooney 1986 and Quinn 1986.

15. If we accept the deontic principle that logical consequences of what ought to be done, ought to be done, then DT as originally stated entails this modification. But this

principle is not without its problems. For discussion of these, see Sayre-McCord 1986 and Sinnott-Armstrong 1988, pp. 141–46.

16. Since an agent can do A and (A v B), and can do B and (A v B), neither A nor B is incompatible with (A v B).

17. Leaving aside the qualification that would be required if there were cases such as that of Abraham.

18. So named in honor of Kant, who attached great importance to the principle. See his 1929, p. 637; 1956, p. 38; and 1971, p. 37.

19. For defenses of some form of this argument, see Donagan 1984, pp. 296–302; Feldman 1986, p. 199; Hare 1981, pp. 27–28; and McConnell 1978.

20. For defenses of a version of the "moral dilemmas" position that depend on the rejection or qualification of the Kantian principle, see Brown 1977; Larmore 1987, ch. 6; Lemmon 1962; Nagel 1979a; Rescher 1987, ch. 2; Stocker 1990, ch. 1; and Trigg 1971. For defenses of a form of the "moral dilemmas" view that involve rejection or modification of the agglomeration principle, see Hurley 1985–86; Marcus 1980; Tännsjö 1985; van Fraassen 1973; and Williams 1973a. Sinnott-Armstrong 1988 (ch. 4) defends a weak form of the "moral dilemmas" view (discussed in chapter 3, sec. V) by modifying the agglomeration principle and substantially rejecting the Kantian principle.

21. I again assume that agents know what they can and cannot do.

22. In chapter 6, sec. V, I reject versions of these principles pertaining to our moral responsibilities.

23. I have found the following discussions especially helpful: Dahl 1974; Frankena 1950; Hare 1963, ch. 4; Henderson 1966; Stocker 1971; White 1975, pp. 147–57; and Zimmerman 1987. See also the references concerning the Kantian principle in note 20.

24. Cf. Hare 1963, pp. 51–61.

25. For example, see Brown 1977.

26. Since most of the counterexamples are discussed by several authors, I will usually not attribute each one to a specific source. In general, see the pertinent references in notes 20 and 23.

27. Sinnott-Armstrong 1988, pp. 118–19.

28. This does not beg the question against the Kantian principle. For there are other cases, having nothing to do with what can be done, where the act of promising does not create a binding obligation. For example, suppose I promise to do in your rival in love or career. Here too it was wrong to make the promise, but it is not binding, and I do no additional wrong by letting your competitor be. It would be extraordinary to say that, having made the promise, I ought to keep it, or even that I have an overridden moral reason to keep it.

29. Most of those who accept the agglomeration principle regard it as obvious and make use of it without further ado. For those who oppose it, see the relevant references in note 20.

30. Williams 1973a, pp. 181–82.

31. Tännsjö 1985, pp. 116–17. Tännsjö's main concern is with the converse of the agglomeration principle. But he explicitly states that he means his argument to apply to the agglomeration principle as well.

32. Hurley 1985–86, p. 26.

33. There is also the difficulty of specifying what counts as a different kind of reason, for there are different kinds of justice, different kinds of distributive justice, and so on.

34. Sinnott-Armstrong 1988, pp. 129–34.

35. Sinnott-Armstrong claims that examples of this sort refute the agglomeration

principle for moral reasons and for nonoverridden moral reasons. He accepts the principle for overriding moral reasons.

36. There is a second rather common deontic argument, which I have not discussed. It depends on the following deontic principles: (1) [OX & ~C(X & Y)] → O~Y (where 'C' stands for 'can be done'); (2) OX → PX (where 'P' stands for 'is morally permitted'); and (3) PX → ~O~X. Taking a moral dilemma to be a case in which OA, OB, and ~C(A & B) are all true, the argument proceeds as follows: From OA and ~C(A & B) it follows by (1) that O~B; from OB it follows by (2) that PB; and from PB it follows by (3) that ~O~B. Therefore, by these principles a moral dilemma entails that O~B and ~O~B. Since this is impossible, moral dilemmas are impossible. (For a detailed examination of this argument, see Sinnott-Armstrong 1988, ch. 5.) This argument is clearly valid, so its soundness depends on the truth of the three deontic principles. It may be that intention-prescriptivism and some plausible principles of rational intending (in addition to PRI1 and PRI2) could also be used to support these principles and hence to show the soundness of this argument. But I have not undertaken this enterprise here because what I have already said is sufficient to refute DT, and because doing so would involve considerations similar to those already discussed plus further complications. In chapter 6, sec. V, I reject a form of this argument concerning conflicting moral responsibilities.

37. For example, see Donagan 1984, pp. 296–302.

5

The Phenomenological Argument
for the Remainders Thesis

In this chapter I begin my argument for the central positive thesis of the book: that there are moral conflicts in which moral wrongdoing in some sense is inescapable. DT would obviously support this thesis, but I have rejected DT. Hence, the first step in defending my position is to explain the difference between it and DT. My claim is that in situations where an agent cannot do both A and B, though the correct conclusion of moral deliberation could not be that both OA and OB, nonetheless in some of these situations an agent would do something morally wrong no matter what he or she did. I call this position the Remainders Thesis, because it maintains that deliberation may leave a "moral remainder" that renders an action morally wrong, in some sense, even if performing the action fulfills what is required by the deliberative conclusion in that situation.

I regard the main argument in favor of the Remainders Thesis to be a version of the phenomenological argument considered earlier in connection with DT. My contention is that a form of this argument, understood in the context of the method of reflective intuitionism, is sufficient to justify the Remainders Thesis. In this chapter I clarify the nature of the argument and respond to some common objections to it. It will become evident that the key issue in evaluating this argument is the assessment of competing explanations of inescapable feelings of moral distress in the wake of moral conflicts. In the next chapter I present what I believe is the best explanation of these feelings, an explanation that supports the Remainders Thesis on the basis of a normative account I call "responsibilities to persons." In the chapters that follow I consider alternative explanations of these feelings that reject the Remainders Thesis, based respectively on utilitarian and Kantian approaches, and I argue that these explanations are less adequate than that provided by the responsibilities to persons account.

I. The Remainders Thesis

As I observed in chapter 1, in the recent debate about "moral dilemmas," two distinct issues have been discussed. The first concerns the possibility of irresolvable moral conflicts. With respect to this issue, I have argued that conflicting moral reasons may be equally strong, but when they are, the correct conclusion of moral deliberation is not that each action ought to be done, but that one or the other ought to be done (that is, OT rather than DT). The second issue concerns the possibility of inescapable moral wrongdoing. Many proponents of the claim that there are "moral dilemmas" have intended to suggest by this, not merely—or even necessarily—that some moral conflicts are irresolvable, but that there are circumstances in which, whatever an agent does, he or she will do something morally wrong.[1] This is the position I propose to defend.

The two issues are not entirely unrelated. For if DT were true, there would be a straightforward sense in which moral wrongdoing is sometimes inescapable: Agents would sometimes violate a correct conclusion of moral deliberation no matter what. Some of those who have accepted the idea of inescapable moral wrongdoing may have done so because they held DT. But since I have argued against DT, it is obvious that I cannot take this stand. It might seem, however, that moral wrongdoing could be inescapable in moral conflicts *only if* DT were true. If 'moral wrongdoing' means failing to fulfill a sound deliberative conclusion, this might be true. In any case, since I agree that it is always possible to avoid moral wrongdoing in this sense, it is necessary for me to identify a sense of 'moral wrongdoing' in which an agent who does everything that is required by the correct conclusion of moral deliberation may nonetheless do something morally wrong.

There is an additional reason for specifying this sense of 'moral wrongdoing'. Many proponents of the possibility of inescapable moral wrongdoing have claimed, correctly in my view, that moral wrongdoing may be unavoidable even in moral conflicts in which one PV clearly overrides the other.[2] That is, they have claimed, in effect, that there are moral conflicts in which, on the one hand, the correct conclusion of moral deliberation is OA and not OB, and yet on the other hand, not only will an agent who does B rather than A do something morally wrong (in the sense of failing to fulfill the correct conclusion of deliberation), but an agent who does A rather than B will also do something morally wrong (in some sense). Hence, the agent will commit some form of moral wrongdoing no matter what.

It is clear, then, that the issue of inescapable moral wrongdoing should not be regarded as identical with the issue of irresolvable moral conflicts. In my view, unavoidable moral wrongdoing may occur in moral conflicts in which neither PV overrides the other, and in those in which (exactly) one PV overrides the other. Cases of the first kind are rather infrequent since these are situations in which the PV of each conflicting action is exactly equal in strength. The more common cases of inescapable moral wrongdoing are likely to be those in which one PV overrides the other. For this reason, though the moral conflicts

relevant to the question of inescapable moral wrongdoing will coincide to some
extent with those conflicts relevant to the issue of irresolvable moral conflicts,
discussion of the former will concern a larger class of cases than will discussion
of the latter.

It is therefore essential to the defense of my position to identify a sense of
'moral wrongdoing' that is not equivalent to failing to fulfill the correct conclusion of moral deliberation. Ordinary usage suggests that there is moral wrongdoing whenever some moral value such as a law or principle or rule is transgressed or violated. To say that moral wrongdoing is inescapable is to say that
some such value will be infringed upon no matter what. It might be supposed
that a condition of adequacy on an account of moral values is that what is
required by these values must coincide with correct conclusions of moral deliberation. Given the rejection of DT in favor of OT, it would follow from this
condition that it could never be the case that a genuine moral value will be violated no matter what. But it is merely an assumption that there is something in
the logic of the concept of moral value which imposes this condition. It is neither self-evidently true nor supported by common usage. It must be established
that moral values properly understood cannot impose conflicting requirements.
Whether or not this is so is precisely what is at issue in the debate about
inescapable moral wrongdoing.

The doctrine that wrongdoing is sometimes inescapable may thus be taken
to mean that there are occasions when some moral value will be transgressed no
matter what the agent does. Different versions of this doctrine are possible,
based on different accounts of moral values. Assuming that DT is false, all of
them reject the aforementioned condition and suppose that moral values have
some independence from deliberative conclusions: The practical necessity of
conflict-free conclusions is not taken to entail that there can be no conflicts
among the requirements of moral values properly understood. My aim is to
defend a particular form of this doctrine, based on an understanding of moral
responsibilities to persons. According to this account (which I develop in the
next chapter), we have moral responsibilities to persons that it is wrong to violate, and these responsibilities sometimes conflict. Hence, to say that moral
wrongdoing is sometimes inescapable is to say that infringement upon some
moral value, in particular a moral responsibility to someone, may be inescapable.

With these preliminary points in mind, the issue about inescapable moral
wrongdoing may be formulated as follows. With respect to the question of irresolvable moral conflicts, I now assume the debate between DT and OT to be
settled in favor of the latter. The remaining question concerns inescapable
moral wrongdoing, both in moral conflicts in which one PV overrides the other
and in those in which neither PV overrides the other. Those who have defended
the idea of inescapable moral wrongdoing have sometimes expressed this idea by
claiming that there are "moral remainders." The suggestion is that there is
something that remains of a moral conflict after the process of moral deliberation and that thereby explains the presence of wrongdoing even when the correct conclusion of deliberation has been followed. Thus it is maintained that in a
moral conflict in which, say, deliberation establishes that all things considered A

ought to be done, the PV of the conflicting action B persists as a moral remainder that renders failing to do B morally wrong in some sense. By contrast, those who believe moral wrongdoing is always avoidable maintain, in effect, that there are no such moral remainders, since to establish through deliberation that, say, A ought to be done is tantamount to establishing that B makes no genuine moral claim at all in this case (even though it may have appeared to do so at the outset of deliberation). On this view, deliberation eliminates any moral remainder that would make moral wrongdoing inescapable.

Though I do not mean to endorse everything that has been defended under the heading of "moral remainders," I will employ this convenient terminology to describe the debate about inescapable moral wrongdoing as a debate between those who think there are moral remainders and those who think any such alleged remainders are eliminated by deliberation. According to the first view:

> *The Remainders Thesis* (RT) OT is true, but there are moral conflicts in which, whatever the agent does, he or she will do something which is morally wrong in the sense of transgressing some moral value.

By contrast, on the second view:

> *The Elimination Thesis* (ET) OT is true, and there are no moral conflicts in which, whatever the agent does, he or she will do something which is, in any sense, morally wrong.

RT does not maintain that moral wrongdoing is inescapable in every moral conflict. It only claims that it is inescapable in some moral conflicts. Hence, a defense of RT will require an account of which conflicts have this feature and which do not. In any case, RT clearly differs from ET, which maintains that moral wrongdoing is inescapable in no moral conflicts.[3]

With respect to this issue, it is not always evident how to interpret the position of those who have rejected DT and accepted OT.[4] It is reasonable to think that some of these persons endorse RT while others embrace ET. In many cases, however, this may be unclear. Some do not address the dispute between RT and ET. Others maintain that doing what all things considered ought to be done may have "moral costs," or violate "prima facie duties." These latter positions might entail a version of RT, depending on how these expressions are understood (in particular, whether a form of wrongdoing is involved in an action that has moral costs or violates a prima facie duty). For the most part, my main concern is not to identify the specific position of particular persons. But I do suppose that many objections that have been made against various versions of "moral dilemmas" and the phenomenological argument are potentially relevant to my defense of RT, irrespective of whether this was their precise, intended target.

It might seem that a proponent of ET and a proponent of RT could entirely agree on the correct conclusions of moral deliberation, disagreeing only as to whether or not acting in accordance with these conclusions could involve some form of wrongdoing. But this is true only insofar as we confine our attention to

the choice between the two actions A and B. As will be seen, it can make a difference in the broader deliberative context whether or not acting so as to fulfill
the correct conclusion regarding A and B is thought to involve wrongdoing. For
example, a supporter of RT is likely to claim that, when wrongdoing is
inescapable, even though OA, an agent who does A nonetheless ought to apologize for not doing B, something that is not likely to be accepted by an adherent
of ET. Hence, proponents of RT and ET may disagree about further deliberative conclusions even if they agree about the specific choice between A and B.

This draws attention to the fact that RT and ET have been defined with
respect to a simple and narrowly drawn form of moral conflict (see chapter 3,
sec. I). This simplification was helpful with respect to the issues discussed in the
last two chapters, and I have defined RT and ET in this way in order to coordinate them with the debate about DT and OT. But for the issues to come, such
simplification is less necessary, and it is more important to recognize that actual
moral conflicts often have greater complexity, by involving more conflicting factors, by offering more choices, by being situated in a larger moral context, and
the like. For this reason, I will sometimes speak of "the remainders view" as a
way of referring to the central idea in RT—that, though deliberative conclusions may not conflict, wrongdoing in the sense of transgressing some moral
value may be inescapable—with respect to moral conflicts that may have greater
complexity than the simple form earlier defined (and similarly for the expression
"the elimination view").

There is one final clarification worth noting at this stage. Proponents of
"moral dilemmas" have sometimes argued against the claim that conflicts among
moral values may be resolved on the basis of some general procedure, such as
establishing a hierarchy or set of priority principles among these values, or perhaps by drawing up lists of exception clauses within them. It is often said that it
is not possible to carry out these procedures, either because of the complexities
of life or on account of the fact that the values in question are "incommensurable." As an alternative, it is usually proposed that in resolving a conflict
between values we must rely on an "intuition," or "judgment," or "perception"
of each particular case.[5] By contrast, opponents of "moral dilemmas" have typically been critical of this proposal and have supposed that some general structural feature established by the correct normative theory would guarantee a
resolution of all moral conflicts, and hence would render otiose the reliance on
intuition and the like (which in any case they have regarded with suspicion).[6]

Whatever might be said about this debate, the issues it raises do not directly
concern the question of inescapable moral wrongdoing. This debate pertains to
the proper *means* of moral deliberation, whether we must apply a general
method or rely on intuition. Both sides may well agree that there is a resolution
to be discovered by moral deliberation (however it be carried out), and hence
they may both endorse OT rather than DT as the correct account of the possible outcomes of deliberation.[7] Moreover, the difference between these views
about the correct mode of deliberation does not have a direct bearing on the
disagreement between RT and ET. There is nothing in the generalist approach
per se that rules out RT. Even if there were a general procedure for determining

what, all things considered, morally ought to be done, it might still be the case that an agent who does everything that ought to be done would transgress some genuine moral value. Conversely, from the fact that the conclusion of deliberation in a moral conflict could only be established via intuition, it would not follow that an agent who acts in accordance with this conclusion would violate a genuine moral value. In short, however deliberation proceeds, it is a further question whether in doing what, as the conclusion of deliberation, morally ought to be done, an agent will nonetheless do something morally wrong in some sense.

Nonetheless, it is not simply as a result of a mistake or a coincidence that proponents and opponents of "moral dilemmas" have lined up in the way they have on the question of the proper means of deliberation. Though there is no direct connection between these issues, there is an indirect one. This will emerge in the evaluation of the phenomenological argument. It turns out that explanations of inescapable moral distress that support RT are associated with normative accounts favoring a particularist deliberative approach, while explanations that support ET are associated with normative theories favoring a generalist approach. Hence, in examining the phenomenological argument, it is necessary to consider these different explanations and the various normative theories connected with them. In this way, the debate about modes of deliberation does have relevance to the question of inescapable moral wrongdoing.

II. The Phenomenological Argument Revisited

The phenomenological argument has been widely discussed in the literature on "moral dilemmas." In fact, various forms of this argument, and of inconsistency objections such as the one considered in the last chapter, have been the two main foci of discussion in the debate about "moral dilemmas." Proponents of "moral dilemmas" have relied rather heavily on the phenomenological argument in defending their position. By contrast, their opponents have frequently argued that this position entails an inconsistency, given some abstract and purportedly obvious principles of deontic logic. As I noted earlier, this disagreement is indicative of an implicit methodological difference that commonly divides proponents and opponents of "moral dilemmas." Proponents have usually been relatively impressed with the epistemological value of our moral experiences and relatively unimpressed with the credentials of the abstract principles underlying the various inconsistency arguments; they have claimed that our moral experiences may give us reason to modify or abandon some of these principles. For example, part of the reason Williams thinks we should reject the agglomeration principle is because doing so allows for "a more realistic picture of moral thought," a picture revealed to us in moral conflicts in which we would feel regret no matter what.[8] Opponents of "moral dilemmas," on the other hand, have usually had it the other way around. They have generally assigned a high epistemological status to one or another abstract principle, in comparison with the cognitive value of our moral experiences, and they have argued from this standpoint that there are no "moral dilemmas" and that moral experiences that seem to suggest otherwise should be either reinterpreted or corrected. For example, Donagan argues on the basis of what he calls a "rationalist" moral theory that both the Kantian principle and the agglomeration principle are correct, and hence that "moral dilemmas" are inconsistent. For this reason, he claims that, when a person is morally justified in breaking a promise, there is no obligation to keep the promise, and hence it would be "irrational guilt" to feel morally distressed about doing so.[9]

My response to this methodological divide was outlined in my discussion of the method of reflective intuitionism. In general, it is a mistake to give methodological priority either to moral experiences or to abstract principles. The correct approach is to suppose that our intuitions concerning both moral experiences and abstract principles have some initial credibility, and to strive to develop a coherent account of these intuitions—an account that may require modification or rejection of some of them and that includes an explanation of intuitions pertaining to particular cases. It is from this perspective that I propose to evaluate and defend a form of the phenomenological argument, understood as an argument specifically for the remainders view. As I interpret it, the argument should be seen as an application of the method of reflective intuitionism. Hence, I share with many proponents of "moral dilemmas" the view that intuitions about our moral experiences are of fundamental methodological importance: Moral philosophy should not start from a standpoint altogether outside moral experience. But I reject the view, implicit in some discussions, that these intuitions should be accepted at face value; for they must be reconciled with other intuitions, and more important, they must be given an adequate explanation.

In the remainder of this chapter, I develop this interpretation of the phenomenological argument and clarify and defend some of its claims. Since nearly all discussions of the argument make reference to its original statement by Williams, it will be helpful to begin with his formulation.[10] He constructs the argument in terms of a comparison of moral conflicts with conflicts of beliefs and conflicts of desires. When we discover that two factual beliefs conflict (meaning that in the circumstance they cannot both be true), Williams says, the discovery tends to weaken at least one of the beliefs. Moreover, the determination that one of these beliefs is true requires us to abandon the other belief. By contrast, when we discover that two desires conflict (meaning that in the circumstance they cannot both be satisfied), the discovery need not weaken either desire: The desire for each thing may be as strong as ever. In addition, the decision to act on one of these desires does not require us to abandon the other: In particular, the unfulfilled desire "may reappear in the form of *regret* for what was missed."[11] According to Williams, in both the aforementioned respects, moral conflicts are more like conflicts of desires than they are like conflicts of beliefs. That is, when we discover that *oughts* conflict (meaning that in the circumstance they cannot both be acted on), the discovery need not weaken either of them. Moreover, the decision to act on one of the conflicting *oughts* does not require us to abandon the other: This too may show itself in a form of regret for what was not done (though not the same form as in the desire case). Williams says the *ought* that was not acted on "may find a new object, and I may try, for instance, to 'make up' to people involved for the claim that was neglected." Moreover, he says, these feelings do not depend "on whether I am convinced that in the choice I made I acted for the best; I can be convinced of this, yet have these regrets, ineffectual or possibly effective, for what I did not do."[12]

On this basis, Williams argues that it is a mistake to think "that in a conflict situation one of the conflicting *ought's* must be totally rejected." The fact that both *oughts* cannot be acted on, he says, "does not mean that they do not both (actually) *apply* to the situation; or that I was in some way mistaken in thinking that these were both things that I ought to do."[13] He maintains that it is "a fundamental criticism of many ethical theories that their accounts of moral conflict and its resolution do not do justice to the facts of regret and related considerations: basically because they eliminate from the scene the *ought* that is not acted upon."[14] What the phenomenon of regret shows, Williams concludes, is that moral conflicts are not "all soluble without remainder."[15]

Williams might be interpreted as arguing for DT or RT, depending on what is meant by saying that conflicting *oughts* cannot be eliminated.[16] But my concern is not to determine exactly what Williams meant. My aim is to use his presentation as a starting point for developing a defensible argument for the remainders view. Hence, I take the argument to conclude that, though deliberative conclusions may not conflict, there are moral conflicts in which wrongdoing in the sense of transgressing some moral value is inescapable.[17]

On any interpretation, the heart of the phenomenological argument is a claim about our moral experiences in circumstances of moral conflict. Williams maintains that in some of these circumstances an agent would feel "regret" no matter what he did, even if he "acted for the best." It is important to consider the nature of this feeling. Others with sympathy for the phenomenological argument, or at least for the idea of inescapable moral wrongdoing, have employed terms in this connection that are apparently stronger in their connotations than 'regret'. For example, Ruth Barcan Marcus speaks of inescapable "guilt,"[18] and D. Z. Phillips and H. O. Mounce refer to unavoidable "remorse."[19] Opponents of the idea of unavoidable moral wrongdoing have tended to see a significant difference between regret on the one hand, and guilt and remorse on the other: The former but not the latter may be inescapable, they have commonly argued, but there would be unavoidable moral wrongdoing only if the latter were inescapable.[20] There is very little agreement, however, about the meaning and reference of these various terms. 'Guilt' in particular is a word latent with connotations that are both mysterious and potentially misleading in this context. It would be helpful to have a full phenomenology of the experiences referred to by these words.[21] In the absence of this, it is still possible to give an account of the feeling that is typically intended by proponents of the phenomenological argument and that in any case is required for a defensible form of the argument. Rather than engaging in a fruitless debate about whether this feeling is correctly thought of as regret, guilt, remorse, or something else, I will set these terms aside and speak of the feeling I define as being "morally distressed" or "morally disturbed" (terms I will use interchangeably).[22]

To begin, the feeling is one of distress: It is painful or at least in some manner unpleasant. The degree of this distress may vary depending on the circumstances. In some cases it may merely be mild disquiet, in others intense anguish. There is a range of possibilities between these. In addition, the feeling has a moral dimension to it. It is not, for example, mere disappointment in the wake of unfulfilled desire. The focus is on a moral deficiency. But this may be understood in two different ways. On the one hand, a person might be morally pained by the fact that there is a moral deficiency in the world, as when one reads in the newspaper about a morally admirable person who has fallen victim to disease or some senseless criminal act. Here the object of the feeling has no connection with anything the person having the feeling has done. One is simply morally pained to hear that this virtuous person has suffered at the hands of indifferent natural forces or vicious actions. It is clear that this is not the sort of feeling that is pertinent to the phenomenological argument. The argument requires that the focus of the moral distress be on something the person experiencing the feeling has done. In this case, the person feels morally distressed, not simply because something morally lamentable has happened to someone in the world, but because he or she has done something morally wrong. But 'morally wrong' in what sense?

Moral wrongdoing in one sense means violating the correct conclusion of moral deliberation. But since the moral wrongdoing RT maintains is inescapable is not that of failing to do what, as the conclusion of deliberation, morally ought to be done, it cannot be the feeling of moral wrongdoing in this sense that is required by the phenomenological argument. For the same reason, the feeling need not include the thought, "I have made a mistake, I should have done something else," perhaps accompanied by the resolution "I should act differently in the future." This would be an appropriate thought in the face of knowledge that one had failed to do what was required by moral deliberation (through ignorance, faulty reasoning, weakness of will, etc.). But since for RT an agent may do something morally wrong even when the agent knows that he or she has made no such mistake, this cannot be the feeling referred to in the phenomenological argument.

In defenses of the phenomenological argument, it is not always clear in exactly what sense the agent is supposed to be distressed about his or her moral wrongdoing. Williams, for example, does not say much positively about the status of the *oughts* he thinks cannot be eliminated. In accordance with what I said earlier, it may be said that the feeling is focused on having transgressed some moral value. But since I will be defending a particular form of the remainders view based on conflicting moral responsibilities, I will suppose, more specifically, that the feeling is a response to the fact that one has failed to fulfill a moral responsibility to some person (or persons)—a responsibility that is thought to persist even if its fulfillment has not been judged of highest importance in the deliberative process. Since detractors of the phenomenological argument have questioned the cogency of this sense of moral wrongdoing, more needs to be said to explain its significance. This I will do in the next chapter. For the time being I am only trying to identify, in terms that are meaningful to our moral experience, the nature of the feeling required by the argument. All that is necessary at this stage is that we have an intuitive understanding of what it would be like for someone to feel disturbed about failing to meet a moral responsibility to a person while at the same time recognizing that he or she acted morally for the best.[23] And we do have this understanding. We may well imagine, for example, reflecting back on *Billy Budd*, that Captain Vere, although confidently believing he made the correct decision all things considered, was nevertheless deeply pained by his execution of the essentially undeserving Billy. Though he acted in accordance with the law and for the greater good of his country as he understood it, he may still have supposed himself to have failed morally in his responsibilities to this unfortunate young man "innocent before God." In this circumstance, distress focused precisely on this failure is not difficult to comprehend (even if we ultimately go on to judge it mistaken or incoherent).

There is a further aspect to the feeling of moral distress invoked by the phenomenological argument. The morally distressed agent is not only pained at having failed to fulfill a moral responsibility to someone. The agent also feels a sense of culpability, or blameworthiness, for this failure. This feeling is different, of course, from the sense of culpability that arises from the recognition of having failed to do what, all things considered, ought to have been done (on account of maliciousness, weakness, negligence, and the like). But it is a feeling of culpability nonetheless.[24] In extreme cases, it may take the form of regarding oneself as deserving of censure or even punishment, though I will later express some skepticism about the warrant for this. More commonly, and more constructively, it consists in the felt need to apologize, or to compensate in some way, for the failure of responsibility. As Williams says, the agent might try "to 'make up' to people involved for the claim that was neglected."[25] On some occasions, an adequate apology or compensation may not be possible, as surely was the case for Vere. But possible or not, the agent feels the need to somehow make up for the failure of responsibility.

To sum up, when I speak henceforth of agents being "morally distressed" or "morally disturbed," I will mean that they are feeling some measure of mental pain in response to the recognition that they have done something morally wrong—not necessarily in the sense of having violated the correct conclusion of moral deliberation but in the sense of having transgressed some moral value, in particular a moral responsibility to someone—and that they feel the need to in some way apologize or compensate to the person for this wrongdoing. I leave aside the question whether this feeling is properly thought of as guilt, remorse, regret, or what have you.

The first premise of the phenomenological argument is a claim about people's moral experience: namely, that there are moral conflicts in which persons would feel morally distressed no matter which course of action they followed. In order to evaluate this claim, it is essential that it be judged with reference to examples of moral conflicts that are realistic, both with respect to their veracity to actual human lives and in terms of their degree of detail. Oftentimes in discussions of the phenomenological argument, this claim is considered in connection

with the most sketchily described examples. In order to rectify this, it is important to introduce moral conflicts with more depth. To some extent it will suffice
to refer back to my discussion of *Billy Budd.* But it would be a mistake to rely on
a single example. Hence, I will introduce two additional moral conflicts by which
the claim about inescapable moral distress may be examined.

The Plight of Craig

Craig and a younger acquaintance from work, Roberto, were hiking in a rather
remote area of a state forest in Pennsylvania on a weekday in early November.
After lunch, they became separated from one another, and Craig was unable to
find Roberto. Moreover, while frantically looking for him, Craig lost his way
and then fell and broke his arm. Though injured and exhausted, he managed to
keep moving, and eventually he came upon a deserted picnic area. He had no
idea where Roberto was, or for that matter where he was. There was no phone
in sight, only a few picnic tables in a state of disrepair. A dirt road appeared to
go down the valley, but it could be miles before it reached civilization, and Craig
was too fatigued to go any farther. So he waited, hoping that someone—
Roberto, or help from the outside world, or both—would arrive soon. Several
hours passed and no one came. The afternoon began turning to evening.
Finally, and it seemed miraculously, a car came up the road. It stopped and two
teen-age girls got out, laughing, a six-pack of beer in hand. Craig approached
them and tried to explain the situation. But they were frightened by his
disheveled appearance and desperate demeanor. They refused to help and hur-
riedly headed back towards the car. It was clear they were leaving.

Craig was uncertain whether or not they would send someone to help. They
did not seem to believe him and appeared more scared than concerned. Moreover, he felt that if they did not send help, it could be a very long time, perhaps
days, before someone else would come along. The prospect of this did not strike
Craig as exactly life-threatening. After all, he was somewhat knowledgeable in
the ways of wilderness survival. On the other hand, he was injured, perhaps
more seriously than he realized, and the nights were beginning to get very cold.
Moreover, he had no idea where Roberto was, and as it seemed that Roberto
had agreed only with reluctance to go hiking in the first place, he was unsure
about *his* ability to take care of himself in the wilderness. Who knows what
might happen to the two of them? As all this passed through his mind, Craig
realized that, if he acted quickly, he could probably grab the girl with the car
keys, forcibly take them from her, steal the car, and go and get help. Though he
felt it would be wrong to treat the girls in this way, he also felt it would be
wrong to fail to help Roberto as well as himself.

The Plight of Jennifer

Jennifer, a divorced mother living in a large city on the east coast, has always
been extremely devoted to her sixteen-year-old son John, her only child. She has
regarded the nurture and protection of him as her chief responsibility in life.

And he in turn has grown into a son equally devoted to his mother and responsive to her needs. At the same time, Jennifer has long been concerned about the fact that John is terribly vengeful and short-tempered (in large part, she believes, because of the verbal and physical abuse he suffered as a boy at the hands of his father). She has tried to deal with this, but to no avail, and she has now come to realize that his quick temper has led John to attack and injure a man, though he has not been and is not likely to be apprehended for the crime. Moreover, she recognizes that it is probably only a matter of time before his violence will erupt again. And next time the consequences could be much more serious.

Jennifer believes she has a responsibility to her community to confront violence and antisocial behavior, and she has no doubt that for this reason she should inform the authorities of criminal activities, including the action of her son John. But she also knows that, if she were to turn him in, he not only might spend some time in jail, where he would suffer horribly and probably become even more prone to crime, but he would feel betrayed by her and would be incapable of ever again maintaining the same relationship with her. To this Jennifer sees only one alternative. She has an opportunity to move across the country to Wyoming, where her father and sister now live and where her employment prospects are good. By beginning life anew in this small-town environment, free from the frustrations and tensions endemic to their present urban existence, and with the support of her family, she feels that there is a real possibility that John would overcome his propensity for violent revenge. But she knows she could be wrong. She might simply be taking an incurably dangerous person away from justice and permitting him to strike again someplace else. Jennifer feels that she must act promptly and choose one of these two alternatives.

As applied to these two examples, the phenomenological argument claims that Craig and Jennifer, as morally sensitive persons, would feel moral distress no matter which course of action they chose. Thus, Craig would feel morally distressed whether or not he stole the car, and Jennifer would feel morally disturbed whether she turned her son in or took him to Wyoming. According to the argument, we are to infer from this that Craig and Jennifer would each do something morally wrong in the sense of transgressing some moral value no matter what they did. Moreover, the argument may be generalized: Since there are numerous moral conflicts in which moral distress is inescapable, we may conclude that there are many situations in which agents would do something morally wrong in this sense no matter what.

The issue here does not pertain to the correct resolution of these conflicts. Different views about this are possible, but I am not concerned with these disputes here. Since I am assuming the truth of OT, I do suppose that Craig and Jennifer can each do everything that, as the correct conclusion of moral deliberation, he and she ought to do. Let us suppose, then, that each of them promptly comes to know what the correct resolution of his or her conflict is (whatever that may be). If they act contrary to this resolution, there is an obvious sense in which they will do something morally wrong. But the point of the phenomenological argument is that since they will feel morally distressed no matter what, there is also a sense in which they will do something morally wrong even if they act in accordance with the correct resolution. Hence, whatever they do, they will engage in a form of moral wrongdoing.

III. The Phenomenological Argument and the Method of Reflective Intuitionism

When the phenomenological argument is expressed in this way, it must be acknowledged that it is subject to a serious objection. This is suggested by Philippa Foot in her critique of Williams. Foot grants that feelings may be "propositional," so that to feel regret is "to feel *as if* something in some way *bad* has happened." However, she says, "it does not follow that it has happened." For example, people often feel guilty about giving away the belongings of a deceased person. But "it would obviously be wrong to conclude from the fact—the normality almost—of such feelings that there was indeed some element of wrongdoing involved." In general, Foot argues, "it is impossible to move from the existence of the feeling to the truth of the proposition conceptually connected with it." She concludes that it is incorrect "to think that the existence of feelings of regret could show anything about a remainder in cases of moral conflict."[26]

Foot is clearly right that it does not immediately follow from the fact that people naturally feel moral distress that there really is something morally distressing. People's feelings, even when natural, may be irrational or mistaken. Hence, insofar as the phenomenological argument makes this direct inference, there is a lacuna in the argument. On the other hand, in response to this, it might be supposed that the first premise says, not that moral distress is natural, but that it is rational or appropriate.[27] But if the argument is understood in this way, then it would seem that it begs the question. For surely, as Foot says, "the feelings are rational feelings only if it is reasonable to think that in a given conflict situation there *is* something regrettable or distressing even in a choice that is clearly right."[28] In short, the phenomenological argument appears subject to the following dilemma. The first premise claims that there are moral conflicts in which inescapable moral distress is either natural or appropriate for agents. If the claim is that these feelings are natural, the premise may well be true, but it is invalid to infer from this that moral wrongdoing is inescapable. But if the claim is that these feelings are appropriate, then the inference is valid, but the argument begs the question. So the argument is unpersuasive on either interpretation.

My response to this objection is complex. First, I do insist both that in some moral conflicts inescapable feelings of moral distress are natural, and that this fact is important, albeit not sufficient, for the argument for inescapable moral wrongdoing. Craig's feeling moral distress whether he forcibly took the keys from the girls and stole their car in order to get help or he let them go and risked harm to himself and his friend Roberto is a natural human response. Something similar may be said about Jennifer and Captain Vere. In saying that these are natural responses I do not mean that every human being necessarily would have these feelings. Since our feelings are subject to variation on account of education, accidental circumstance, individual difference, and the like, none of them can be said to be universal and necessary. Nevertheless, this evident fact of psychology should not prevent us from recognizing that some emotional responses are deeply rooted in our nature. It is in this sense natural that a person mourns the death of a friend, that a parent loves his or her child, and that someone on the wrong road feels grateful for the spontaneous help of a stranger. Not everyone has these feelings. But people commonly have them, and they do so on account of the kind of beings we humans are. For this reason, it goes against the grain to try to discourage these feelings in people. It is in this sense of 'natural', then, that I maintain that there are moral conflicts in which it is natural for people to feel moral distress no matter what they do.

Not only are these feelings natural for us, it is important for the phenomenological argument that they be natural. We are interested in a morality that is appropriate for human beings and for the forms of social relationships that we are able to sustain. Hence, we need to know what capacities for moral response to one another we have. If a certain form of feeling were completely alien to us, no philosophical argument could establish that it would be appropriate for us to feel in that way. Even those doctrines that aim to effect a radical transformation in our lives must, and typically do, assert a potentiality for this transformation deep within our nature. Without this potentiality, these doctrines could not have normative force for us. To see this, imagine that we encountered a species of beings rather like ourselves in many respects, except that they showed no inclination to form particular attachments to one another. Suppose these beings were far more altruistic in their behavior than we are, but that each related to the other on precisely the same basis, neither as friend, nor as enemy, nor as stranger. Suppose further that these beings lived a life of such harmony and well-being that we were strongly tempted to emulate them. There is no question that there is much that we might learn from these creatures. But it is inconceivable that we could decide to stop relating to ourselves in terms of particular attachments as a means of achieving this way of life. Even if it could be established that in many respects our lives would be better if we abandoned these attachments, this would not show that this mode of relationship is appropriate for us. For it is not in our nature to relate to one another with this kind of indifference. In thinking about morality we need to pay close attention to the type of beings we are and to the forms of moral responses we are capable of having.

The fact, then, that there are situations in which persons would commonly feel moral distress no matter what they did is an important fact about us. Still, it does not directly follow that these feelings are appropriate, or rational, or something we should cultivate and encourage. Nor does it immediately follow that the situations in which these feelings are natural are situations in which some form of moral wrongdoing is inescapable. Our feelings, even when natural, may be irrational or unjustified. Some of them may be pointless and even harmful (such as the desire for revenge). In these cases, we should be careful about inferring truths concerning the moral life from these feelings, and perhaps we should discourage or at least not encourage their development.

Therefore, though it is significant that inescapable feelings of moral distress

are natural, this is not sufficient to establish that moral wrongdoing is sometimes inescapable. The first horn of the aforementioned dilemma is correct. But
the second may be challenged. To say, simply, that there is inescapable moral
wrongdoing because these feelings are appropriate would seem to beg the question. Nonetheless, a more complex form of argument may be developed here,
one that is not circular in this simple way and that conforms to the method of
reflective intuitionism. We may suppose that the argument begins with a class of
prima facie credible, but fallible, intuitions to the effect that inescapable feelings
of moral distress are not only natural but appropriate in certain moral conflicts.
It then claims that there is a coherent account of these intuitions that establishes
as the best explanation of them that they are, at least commonly, responses to
situations in which moral wrongdoing in some sense cannot be avoided. On the
basis of these considerations, it concludes that moral wrongdoing in this sense is
sometimes inescapable.[29]

The fact that we find inescapable feelings of moral distress natural does not
necessarily mean that we also find them appropriate. It is quite possible to find an
emotional response natural, even irresistible, and yet regard it as inappropriate
(as in the case of jealousy for example). Still, in the absence of some contrary consideration, we typically do regard our natural responses as appropriate ones. For
the most part, then, morally sensitive persons would regard inescapable feelings
of moral distress in certain moral conflicts as both natural and appropriate.
Hence, we may imagine that Jennifer not only finds herself compelled to feel, but
regards it as reasonable to feel, that she would in some sense do something
morally wrong whether she took her son John across country or turned him into
the authorities. For she feels that she has both a responsibility to her son to nurture and protect him and a responsibility to her community to promote justice
and protect it from violence, and that in this circumstance she cannot fulfill both
of these responsibilities. Hence, it would make sense to her to feel moral distress
no matter what she did, even if she thought she was acting for the best.

The intuition that inescapable feelings of moral distress are appropriate in
some moral conflicts is quite widespread. Of course, there can be no decisive
demonstration of this. We can only reflect on how morally perceptive persons
would feel, and would find it reasonable to feel, in realistic examples of conflict
situations. Most persons would agree, for instance, regarding Craig's situation,
that if the danger to him and his companion were great enough (if, for example,
on account of the cold they would probably die if they spent a night or two in
the woods), then the correct conclusion of moral deliberation would be that he
ought to steal the car and get help. Agreeing with this, Craig grabs the arm of
the girl with the keys, forcibly takes them from her, and fights her off when she
tries to prevent him from getting into the car. We may well expect that, while
doing this, Craig would feel, and would find it appropriate to feel, that he is in
some way doing something wrong to her, and that he ought to find a way to
make up for this wrongdoing, if only to apologize. After all, she has no
antecedent responsibility for their plight, she was naturally frightened by him in
the first place, and it is possible that she would have sent for help had he let her
go. Hence, she can hardly be said to deserve this treatment.[30]

IV. The Status of Intuitions about Inescapable Moral Distress

There have been attempts to question whether people generally would find inescapable feelings of moral distress appropriate in the kinds of moral conflicts brought forth in defenses of the phenomenological argument. For example, Foot describes a case in which a person fails to keep a promise to meet someone because he must take someone else to the hospital. She then supposes that the promisee is not at all annoyed and in fact, while waiting, is offered a job or meets his future beloved. Foot finds it incredible that "in the general rejoicing there should be an element of distress (moral distress) because after all a promise was broken and that is something bad." It would be "rather foolish" to feel moral distress about the broken promise, she says, unless it had bad consequences, or was done out of wickedness.[31]

Though the phenomenological argument is not committed to saying that every moral conflict makes inescapable moral distress appropriate, it is not clear that such distress would be inappropriate even in this case. The plausibility of her interpretation rests on a conflation of cases in which a sentiment is inappropriate because it is an improper response to a particular feature of a situation and cases in which it is inappropriate because some other feature of the situation overshadows the first feature. If I have just been promoted to vice-president, this is reason to celebrate. But if I then hear that my competitor for the job committed suicide on account of this setback, this news would diminish the propriety of celebration, not because celebrating is not, in itself, a proper response to being promoted, but because my promotion is overshadowed by the suicide of my co-worker. In a similar way, distress about the broken promise in Foot's case is overshadowed by other considerations, but this does not mean that breaking a promise is not in itself moral distressing.

A promise broken with good intentions and good results surely can occasion appropriate moral distress. Suppose that, in order to secure passage of a piece of legislation authorizing funds, a presidential aide promises Congress that the money will be used for X and not for Y. On the basis of this promise, Congress passes the bill, but circumstances then develop that lead the aide to suppose that the public good will be served only if the money is used for Y rather than X. For this reason she decides, with "the best of intentions," to spend the money on Y and thereby break her promise to Congress. It then turns out, for reasons no one anticipated, that this expenditure has what everyone agrees are very positive results. Here moral distress would still be appropriate, because breaking promises made to Congress violates what should be one of the constitutive features of the relationship between Congress and the president.

The structure of Foot's example is rather unusual, and this may give rise to different intuitions about what it would be appropriate to feel in such a case. But precisely because it is unusual, this example cannot be used to show that, in general, people do not have the intuitions the phenomenological argument supposes they have. In any case, challenges to this argument have not, for the most part, taken the form of denying that people commonly believe there are moral conflicts in which, no matter what was done, moral distress would be appropriate. Rather, they have argued that the best explanation of these beliefs does not require the assertion that moral wrongdoing is inescapable (or some form of the "moral dilemmas" view). I will consider these alternative explanations in due course. My point here is that this concession suggests that the intuitions about the appropriateness of inescapable moral distress are widely and deeply held.[32]

Still, the method of reflective intuitionism requires that these intuitions be formed in circumstances that are unlikely to produce error. The fact that these intuitions concern our emotional reactions should not by itself render them cognitively suspect. But it might be supposed that this, in combination with the fact that they are responses to conflicting moral considerations, does have this effect. In particular, it might be maintained that intuitions about what it would be appropriate for us to feel are likely to be unreliable whenever we consider situations in which apparently compelling moral reasons conflict and in which serious harm will or may come to somebody whatever we do. For these are situations in which we are likely to experience some confusion about what to do and in which it makes a great deal of difference to the well-being of people how we act. It might be said that this is a cognitively disadvantageous state to be in, and for this reason, these intuitions do not qualify for the method of reflective intuitionism.

This is potentially a serious objection, for there certainly are cases in which persons confronting a moral conflict are so confused about what to do, and are so overwhelmed by the harms that will result from their various alternatives, that their intuitions about what it would be appropriate for them to feel should not be taken as a reliable indication of the moral realities of the situation. To be effective, however, this objection must not merely challenge this or that suspect intuition but raise doubts about the entire class of intuitions concerning the appropriateness of inescapable moral distress in conflict situations. This it cannot do.

First, the moral conflicts in which persons feel moral distress would be appropriate no matter what need not be conflicts in which there is any confusion at all about what, in the final analysis, morally ought to be done. Though they may be situations in which the conflicting moral considerations seem equally strong, they may also be ones in which it is obvious that one consideration is more important than the other. Confusion about what to do is not an intrinsic feature of these cases. Moreover, even if a person were confused about what to do, the person might be quite sure that each of the conflicting alternatives would be morally distressing—not because whatever was done he or she would lack certainty about having taken the best action, but because each action has morally distressing features. Analogous to this, I might be uncertain which of two plays to see when I cannot see both and know that no matter which I see I will be disappointed to have missed the other. I may know this not because I think that whatever I do I will wonder if I made the best choice, but simply because I really do want to see both plays. Throughout the practical realm, confusion about which alternative is best is compatible with confidence about the fact that each alternative is desirable, good, right, and so on.

Second, though moral conflicts in which inescapable moral distress seems appropriate will typically be circumstances in which someone will or may be harmed no matter what, it need not be the case that the harms are substantial or irreparable. Examples brought forward in support of the phenomenological argument do tend to be situations in which great harms are in question. There is a good reason for this: These examples are a poignant means of focusing attention on the issue, and they demonstrate that inescapable moral wrongdoing, were it real, would not be a trivial matter. But such examples are misleading insofar as they suggest that all cases in which moral wrongdoing cannot be avoided must involve significant harms. Even as there are ordinary cases of avoidable moral wrongdoing in which the harm is not serious (as when a person fails to keep an appointment because it is inconvenient), so may there be cases of inescapable moral wrongdoing where one or both of the harms is minor (as when someone can keep an appointment only by failing to return something when promised). There is no reason to think that persons who feel inescapable moral distress would be appropriate must be bewildered by the agony of having to cause somebody a great harm. Though this might sometimes be true, it is not an intrinsic feature of these cases. Moreover, even when the harms are significant, it need not be supposed that agents will typically be driven to distraction. The person may be rare who confronts these conflicts with aplomb, but between this and utter bafflement are a range of more or less cognitively acute states into which most of us fall.

It is also important to note that intuitions about unavoidable moral distress may be formed by reflecting on conflicts that are hypothetical, either by being purely fictional or by being actual for some person but supposititious for us. In either case, we may imaginatively place ourselves in a situation and consider how we would act and feel in those circumstances. Even if this were a situation in which the conflicting considerations seem evenly balanced and the harms associated with each alternative are serious, the fact that our intuition is based on an imaginative exercise gives us a measure of detachment and critical perspective that may overcome whatever cognitive deficiencies would attend an actual encounter with the conflict. Hence, to the extent that this objection has force, it is diminished with respect to intuitions formed by reflection on hypothetical conflicts.

Moral conflicts in which moral distress seems inescapable are somewhat unusual situations: They are typically not the routine moral transactions of everyday life. This might also seem to cast doubt on our intuitions concerning them. It is true, of course, that we should be careful about drawing inferences from exceptional cases. But the unwonted nature of these cases is a double-edged sword. Not only may beliefs generated by the ordinary moral affairs of daily life be dulled into unreflective prejudice, but the striking event may provide an opportunity for insight into a previously unnoticed feature of the moral landscape. The fact that the moral conflicts in question are not routine may thus be seen as a reason for paying special attention to our intuitive responses to them.

In short, there is no reason to think these intuitions are as a whole more prone to error than other moral intuitions. I will henceforth assume, then, that there is a body of widely and deeply held—albeit fallible—intuitions to the effect that in some moral conflicts it would be not only natural but appropriate for agents to feel moral distress no matter what was done. As I understand it, the phenomenological argument for the remainders view claims that there is a coherent account of these intuitions that establishes as the best explanation of them that, at least typically, they are responses to moral conflicts in which persons would transgress some moral value (in particular, as I will claim, a moral responsibility) no matter what. It then concludes that there are moral conflicts in which moral wrongdoing in the sense of violating these values is inescapable.

This claim about the best explanation of intuitions concerning inescapable moral distress has been widely questioned. Though the distinction between DT and RT has not always been recognized, many have maintained that these intuitions may be explained without supposing that there are "moral dilemmas." These contentions are clearly potential challenges to the phenomenological argument interpreted as supporting the remainders view, for they suggest a variety of alternative explanations of intuitions about inescapable moral distress.[33] What needs to be considered is whether or not the *best* explanation of these intuitions is one (or perhaps a conjunction of several) that does *not* involve the idea of inescapable moral wrongdoing. The assertion that this is the case I take to be the most important objection to the phenomenological argument. But since this objection takes many forms, extensive discussion is required to respond to it. I conclude this chapter by briefly considering several common but less serious versions of this objection. In the next chapter, I defend what I believe is the correct explanation, one based on an understanding of human relationships and moral responsibilities in which moral wrongdoing in the sense of violating these responsibilities is sometimes unavoidable. I then argue, in the chapters that follow, that this explanation is superior to the most substantial alternative explanations, those rooted respectively in utilitarian and Kantian moral theories.

V. Some Common Explanations of Inescapable Moral Distress

It might be said that intuitions about the appropriateness of inescapable moral distress are irrational. We know they are irrational, on this explanation, because it would be appropriate to feel moral distress no matter what only if we would actually do something morally wrong no matter what, and it flies in the face of reason to suppose this could ever happen. Of course, we may be able to provide a psychological account of why people are irrational in this particular way. But such an account would only exhibit the psychological mechanism generating the irrational response. It would not show that, deep down, the response has a justification.

In the absence of an argument as to why it is unreasonable to suppose moral wrongdoing cannot always be avoided, this explanation is in danger of begging the question. Moreover, we should be suspicious of the immediate attribution of irrationality to thoughts and feelings and actions that initially perplex us. This is particularly true when our behavior is natural, in the sense of 'natural' described earlier. For example, in a catastrophe in which many lives are lost, it is natural for the sole survivor to feel guilty and to regard this feeling as appropriate, even though he or she was not in any ordinary way responsible for what happened (both for the calamity itself and for being the only one to escape death). The temptation is to say that this reaction, though perhaps "understandable," is irrational, since rational guilt requires a belief in responsibility. But we should not immediately give in to this temptation. Perhaps in the end this response will prove irrational, but it is more likely that there are ways in which it can be seen as reasonable.[34] We should assume that natural human reactions have a rational basis until we have compelling reason to think otherwise. In the present case, this would mean showing that all explanations attributing rationality fail.

Most critics of the phenomenological argument have tried to show why intuitions about the appropriateness of inescapable moral distress are rational even though moral wrongdoing can always be avoided. Thus, it has been suggested that persons with these intuitions may accept a moral code in which principles sometimes conflict. When this happens, these persons believe they will violate one of their principles no matter what, so they believe they will appropriately feel moral distress no matter what. These beliefs may be rational, since it may be rational to accept the moral code in the first place and since it is rational to feel moral distress when violating a moral principle one accepts. But it does not follow from the rationality of these beliefs that the correct set of moral principles would result in conflicts which make moral wrongdoing inescapable; for it is possible to be rational in accepting a moral code which is false, and in fact the moral code accepted by these people is false, since the correct code would preclude unavoidable moral wrongdoing.[35]

This is only a slight improvement over the irrationality explanation, because it attributes a fundamental mistake to persons without showing why it is a mistake and without explaining why persons who are nonetheless rational in accepting a moral code are prone to make it. The explanation correctly supposes that a person may be rational in believing something that is in fact false. On this view, we are rational in believing what we have been brought up to accept, what we have found no reason to question, what has withstood our critical scrutiny, and so on. Yet some of our beliefs may pass all these tests and turn out to be wrong. So far the explanation is on a sound footing. But why suppose that the rationally accepted moral codes of persons with intuitions about inescapable moral distress are false? Why suppose that people with these intuitions have made this mistake? In the absence of an answer to these questions, this explanation is also in danger of begging the question. In order for this to be the best explanation, there must be an account both of why moral wrongdoing can always be avoided and of why persons with rationally acceptable moral codes have mistakenly thought otherwise. Without such an account, this explanation is mere speculation.[36]

There is another approach to explaining intuitions about inescapable moral distress that allows that they are rational while denying that inescapable moral wrongdoing is possible. It may be said that, when acting in the face of conflicting moral considerations, there is typically a measure of uncertainty about whether or not, all things considered, the correct choice has been made. Hence, no matter which choice is made, an agent will commonly have the thought, "Perhaps I have made a mistake, and I should have gone the other way." This thought can itself be a reasonable source of a form of moral distress. Though it is not the same as believing that one has actually done something wrong, it can be deeply distressing, from a moral point of view, to believe one might very well have done something wrong. For this reason, agents are likely to believe that they would feel, and would find it appropriate to feel, moral distress no matter which course of action they took in a moral conflict. But it does not follow that they actually would do something morally wrong whatever they did. In fact, agents with this belief might very well acknowledge this. They might think there is exactly one course of action that is right, and in no way wrong, and go on to attribute their belief about inescapable moral distress to the fact that, no matter what they did, they would be uncertain as to whether they chose this right action. On this explanation, then, intuitions about inescapable moral distress should be understood as reasonable responses to uncertainty in the face of moral conflict, and not as perceptions of inescapable moral wrongdoing.[37]

Part of what makes this explanation seem compelling is that it describes a phenomenon that does sometimes occur. There are moral conflicts in which we feel so uncertain about which action is morally best that, no matter what we do, we are left with the thought, "Maybe I should have performed the other action," and we are naturally distressed by this. But as an attempt to give the best overall explanation of our intuitions about inescapable moral distress, this approach is inadequate. Two points mentioned earlier are relevant here.

First, the moral conflicts in which it is claimed that moral wrongdoing is inescapable need not be conflicts in which there is any uncertainty about which choice is best. We may presume that this explanation does not assume that moral agents are so consumed by doubt that, in the face any choice whatsoever, they are plagued with the thought, "I might have made a mistake." Rather, it requires that there be some real basis for uncertainty. Though there clearly are some cases in which there is such a basis, this is not typically true of those conflicts in which moral wrongdoing is purported to be inescapable.

Second, even where there is uncertainty, it is quite possible for us to disentangle the distress occasioned by worry over what may have been an erroneous decision from the distress resulting from the recognition that each choice is morally problematic. We can see our ability for this discrimination in other practical conflicts. For example, when desires conflict we can know that either choice would have resulted in disappointment, irrespective of the degree of our confidence in having made the better choice. Likewise in the moral conflicts under consideration: With or without certainty about having made the right decision, there may be a sure grasp of the wrongness of each action.

There is a final difficulty with this explanation. It introduces a feeling that is related to, but nonetheless distinct from, the feeling described in the phenomenological argument, and it then claims that what people believe is that it would be appropriate to have this other feeling no matter what. This done, it is easy to explain the inescapability of this new feeling without recourse to inescapable moral wrongdoing. The feeling introduced in this explanation centers on the thought, "Perhaps I made a mistake." But the moral distress referred to in the phenomenological argument is quite independent of this thought. In effect, this explanation changes the subject.

Another explanation that is also open to this objection depends on a distinction between the things that happen to a person and what a person does in response to these things. On this explanation, what happens to a person can be extremely bad since it might leave a person with no option but to do something horrible. When something this bad happens to us, we will naturally and appropriately feel enormously distressed, no matter how we act. Yet what we will be distressed about is not anything we do, but the fact that the world in which we are situated is this bad. Terrance McConnell writes, "one can regret being in a situation where only bad alternatives are open to one." He explains that it may make sense to "regret having to live in a world where such cases arise."[38] On the other hand, it may be claimed, when we focus our thought on what we do, in contrast to the way the world is, there is no basis for inescapable moral distress, for no matter how bad the world may be, there will always be a way to respond to it which is in no way wrong. In sum, what is inescapably distressing has to do with the way the world is, not with anything we do.[39]

The problem with this explanation is that the moral distress in the phenomenological argument focuses not merely on the badness of the world, but on something the agent experiencing the distress does in the world. One way of seeing this is to compare the difference between the first- and third-person perspective. When an uninvolved observer reflects on Craig's situation, he or she may be distressed by the fact that the world is such that Craig had to either steal the car or else risk the lives of himself and his friend. And Craig too may be so distressed. But there is no sense in which the outside observer can be distressed about anything he or she has done with respect to this situation. For Craig, on the other hand, he most certainly is distressed by his actions. It is, in fact, primarily what he must do that seems morally disturbing to him.

It may also be wondered why, if what makes the world bad is the fact that it can force me to do something horrible, there is nothing wrong with my doing something horrible. If the world does not force me to do something wrong, then why suppose it bad in the first place? The answer is likely to be that it is bad because it makes it inevitable that some people will suffer. In other words, these situations are bad in just the way natural disasters are bad: They cause human suffering, but this suffering cannot be regarded as the moral responsibility of anyone.[40] But this merely reaffirms the fact that for this explanation, the focus of distress is on the way the world is and not on what anyone does. Like the previous explanation, this changes the subject.

The explanation that is perhaps the most common response to the phenomenological argument is also open to this objection, though it brings us closer to the subject. It is frequently claimed that the distress that is inescapable has to do with the belief that our action or its outcome is bad or harmful. According to this explanation, the fact that our action has this undesirable feature must be distinguished from the fact that our action is morally wrong. Being undesirable in this way does not entail moral wrongness. Hence, though there are situations in which it is inescapable that we will do something that is bad or harmful, it does not follow, and it is not the case, that there are situations in which it is inescapable that we will do something morally wrong.

There are several versions of this explanation, and it is worth noting some of their specific formulations. McConnell writes that regret "is appropriate if some good has been lost, or if some bad, even if unavoidable, has obtained." However, "doing the least evil act is surely the most rational thing to do, and one cannot regret having done the most rational thing."[41] Earl Conee says that a person can reasonably feel regret for the "harmful results" of his or her actions. However, Conee says, in reference to Agamemnon's killing of his innocent daughter, there is "no need for him even to *think* that he was obligated *not* to do that"; for "it is regrettable enough that he *was* obligated to do something that bad, and that he could do nothing better."[42] According to Fred Feldman, "it would be appropriate for the young man in Sartre's story to feel genuine guilt no matter which of the two alternatives he selects"; for whatever he does, "he will be directly responsible for the occurrence of a bad state of affairs." But Feldman claims that "there is a big difference between feeling guilt because you have caused something bad to happen, and feeling guilt because you have failed to do something you morally ought to have done." If "one chooses the lesser of two great evils, one neverthe-less chooses an evil," and that, Feldman says, is sufficient for guilt in the former, though not the latter, sense.[43] Finally, for Edmund Santurri, there may be moral regret for the loss of a moral value or good involved in one's action. However, "the loss of a moral value or a moral good does not entail the violation of a moral obligation or a moral requirement." Santurri adds that, "to assume that it does is to confuse the categories of the moral good and the moral right."[44]

Each of these accounts acknowledges that there are situations in which it is inescapable that an agent would appropriately feel a kind of distress on account of doing something that is (or has a consequence that is) harmful, bad, or evil, or at least involves a loss of goodness or value. Moreover, I take it that it is not being denied that in some circumstances an action having this undesirable fea-ture would for that reason be morally wrong. Thus, on some occasions it would be wrong for Agamemnon to kill his innocent daughter and for Sartre's student to leave his ailing mother. Nonetheless, interpreted as an objection to my posi-tion, the claim is that when in different circumstances these actions are morally better than any available alternative, they are not in any sense morally wrong. In these circumstances, there may appropriately be distress for the undesirable fea-ture of the action, but not for its moral wrongness.[45]

Insofar as this account purports to explain how people actually feel, we need to consider whether in fact the inescapable distress that people find appropriate is focused exclusively on the badness of their actions and has nothing to do with the wrongness of these actions. To assert that this is an accurate account of peo-ple's feelings is, on the face of it, an implausible claim. Indeed, to suppose that a morally sensitive agent would be prepared to admit that there are circumstances in which there would be *nothing at all wrong* with killing his innocent daughter or abandoning his ailing mother seems extraordinary. Again, it is hard to believe that Craig would feel that stealing the girl's car is in no way wrong, that Jennifer would see no wrong in sending her son to jail, or that Vere would find nothing wrong in executing the undeserving Billy. This being the case, this explanation fails to address what people actually feel. In effect, it maintains that people who believe there are moral conflicts in which, no matter what was done, it would be appropriate to feel moral distress (in the sense I have described it) are mistaken.

This may in fact be the point of this explanation: To argue that people tend to confuse badness and wrongness, and so they fail to recognize that the inescapability of the former does not entail the inescapability of the latter. But if this is a confusion, then we need an account of why it is. I have already granted—and indeed insisted—that it cannot be inescapable that an agent will do something morally wrong where this means an agent cannot avoid violating the correct conclusion of moral deliberation. The question is whether there is any other sense of moral wrongdoing in which wrongdoing is inescapable. In order to avoid saying that there is, this explanation would have to maintain that an action can be bad, harmful, evil and the like, and still not be morally wrong *in any sense*. Only then could it be said that the inescapable distress that is appropriately felt by Agamemnon and Sartre's student is a response to the badness of their actions and not to their wrongness. What needs to be shown is why an action that is manifestly bad, and that would in other circumstances clearly violate the correct conclusion of moral deliberation, is not in these circumstances in any way wrong. The point is far from obvious, and nothing will be solved by merely stipulating that 'moral wrongness' refers only to the violation of the correct conclusion of moral deliberation.

This explanation is more concessionary to the remainders view than those I considered earlier, since it allows that a kind of appropriate distress may be unavoidable because there are situations in which a person will do something bad no matter what. The final explanation I will consider in this chapter is more concessionary yet. In fact, though it is aimed at undermining the possibility of "moral dilemmas," it comes close to endorsing the remainders view—so close, in fact, that it is unclear how it can withhold this endorsement. According to this explanation, in a moral conflict in which, say, A is morally better than B, the correct conclusion of moral deliberation is a conjunction: (1) A ought to be done, and (2) something—call it C—ought to be done to make up for the fact that B was not done, such as an apology, or some kind of compensation. What explains the thought that moral distress is inescapable is the twofold belief that failing to do A would be wrong (and so distressing), and that even when doing A, the failure to do B leaves something morally important undone (and so is distressing), which omission must then be made up for by doing C. Nevertheless, on this account, it would be a mistake to conclude from this that moral wrongdoing is inescapable, because in this situation it is possible for the agent to do both A and C, and if the agent does do both he or she will not have done anything morally wrong in any sense.

This point is usually expressed with respect to an obligation to keep a promise that is overridden by some other moral consideration (another promise, the need to help someone in distress, etc.). For example, Santurri allows that in such a case there may be "residual obligations" to the promisee such as "apologizing" for the failure to keep the promise or "compensating any loss sustained by the promisee as a result of the failure." In such a case, he writes, "the agent's conviction that he has incurred residual obligations may be explained as the consequence of his recognition that he has brought evil into the world through his failure." But Santurri insists that "we may speak of these residual obligations as the outcome of agent contribution to the loss of moral value signified by the broken promise without implying thereby that a moral wrong has been committed."[46] Sometimes this idea is expressed by suggesting that the overridden obligation, by being overridden, is transformed into the new obligation to make amends. Isaac Levi says that "an obligation to make amends may remain as a trace of an obligation no longer in force."[47] David Mallock claims that when a person correctly fails to keep an appointment in order to help someone in distress, the right of the person with whom he was to meet "has, as it were, been transmuted into other and perhaps lesser rights," for example, the right to an explanation or an apology or some compensation. In this way, not keeping the appointment, though right, "gives rise to trailing obligations" that it would be wrong to violate.[48] Each of these authors, however, introduces these secondary obligations to make up for something as means of rejecting the thesis that there are "moral dilemmas."[49]

As applied to the remainders view, the central idea in this explanation is that a person can have a moral obligation to apologize or compensate for doing something, or failing to do something, which act or omission was not in itself morally wrong. On the face of it, this is a perplexing idea. Ordinarily when we speak in moral contexts of it being obligatory to render an apology or to pay compensation, we assume that what is being apologized and compensated for is a moral wrong. It is precisely because there has been wrongdoing that these remedial actions are thought necessary. If this is so, then it must have been in some way wrong to break the overridden promise; and if it was wrong, then wrongdoing was inescapable. Hence, this explanation requires an account of why apologizing and compensating can be obligatory when there has been no wrongdoing. The passage from Santurri suggests that the agent is required to make up for having "brought evil into the world." But this merely reverts to the previous explanation. We still need to know why a person who has brought evil into the world, and who is thereby obliged to apologize and compensate for this, has nonetheless done nothing wrong in any sense.[50]

It is also unclear whether this explanation can account for our intuitions about the inescapability of appropriate moral distress. If the agent does both of the required actions—that is, the action overriding the promise, and the action of making up for breaking the promise—then on this account the agent has done everything that is morally required in this situation. Hence, it would seem that an agent who accepted this account would find nothing morally distressing about his or her actions, and so appropriate moral distress would no longer be inescapable. Perhaps the idea is that the agent would appropriately feel moral distress before fulfilling the obligation to apologize and compensate, though not after. But this would not be an accurate account of our intuitions. In some cases at least, we can well imagine that an agent would go on feeling some moral distress, and reasonably so, beyond any efforts to make up for the broken promise (suppose, for example, it was a promise to marry). It might be said that an agent would continue to be distressed because breaking the promise was a bad thing to do, even though it was not in any sense wrong. This again reverts to the previous explanation. Or it might be said that in order to sincerely apologize a person must feel morally distressed. But distressed in what sense? Presumably not, on this account, for doing something wrong. Once again, it would seem that it must be for doing something that was bad but in no way wrong.[51]

It is hard to see, then, how this account provides an advance over the last one in explaining the inescapability of appropriate moral distress. Moreover, it faces the additional burden of showing why, as Levi says, "making amends does not entail an acknowledgment that one has done wrong."[52] In view of this, it seems that there must be some more fundamental consideration underlying this explanation. Once it is acknowledged that an agent who acts for the best nonetheless has reason to apologize, it is difficult to see why it would not be further acknowledged that in acting for the best he or she still did something in some way wrong—unless there were an independent ground for regarding this latter idea as incoherent. But it has yet to be shown, in this or the previous explanations, why it is incoherent.

The conclusion to be drawn is that, without further development, none of these explanations provides an adequate account of intuitions about inescapable moral distress, in the sense of 'distress' defined earlier. If there is a way to explain these intuitions that does not involve a commitment to inescapable moral wrongdoing, it will have to go beyond the considerations that have been brought forth here. As I will explain in the next chapter, such an explanation will have to be based on the elaboration of the structure of some specific normative viewpoint, such as utilitarianism or Kantianism.

Notes

1. For example, see Nagel 1979a, pp. 73–74; Phillips and Mounce 1970, p. 103; Walzer 1973, p. 160; and Williams 1981c, p. 74.

2. For example, see Marcus 1980, pp. 130–33; Nussbaum 1986, p. 27; Stocker 1990, p. 28; Walzer 1973, pp. 169–72; and Williams 1973a, pp. 172–75.

3. Some maintain that moral wrongdoing is avoidable except as a result of previous, avoidable wrongdoing. I discuss this position in chapter 8, sec. IV and chapter 9, sec. I. For the time being, I take the inescapable moral wrongdoing affirmed by RT and denied by ET to be wrongdoing that need not result from previous wrongdoing.

4. Likewise, those who have accepted DT may have different views about whether wrongdoing can be inescapable in moral conflicts where one PV overrides the other.

5. For an example of this approach, see Nagel 1979c.

6. For one statement of this kind of analysis, see Donagan 1984.

7. Generalists virtually always reject DT, compatible deliberative conclusions typically being regarded as a sine qua non of an adequate method. But those who reject a general procedure may also reject DT, as in the case of Ross, for whom Aristotelian perception is thought to determine the "comparative stringency" of conflicting prima facie

obligations (Ross 1988, pp. 41–42. An incommensurability argument against a general method might be associated with a thesis about "moral dilemmas," but this need not entail a claim about the importance of intuition and the like. It may be said that incommensurable moral conflicts show a limitation in the generalist approach but do not point to a need for intuition (in fact, if 'incommensurable' means incomparable, there cannot be an intuition of the comparative value of the conflicting actions).

8. Williams 1973a, p. 182.

9. Donagan 1984, p. 304. Donagan clearly means to reject DT and RT. Though Donagan and I both reject DT, and apparently on partially similar grounds—an inconsistency argument involving the agglomeration principle and the Kantian principle—at a deeper level our views regarding DT are quite different, since intention-prescriptivism is essential to my position, but not to Donagan's. In any case, there is a basic disagreement between us concerning RT. I discuss Donagan's position in chapter 8.

10. See Williams 1973a.

11. *Ibid.*, p. 170.

12. *Ibid.*, p. 172.

13. *Ibid.*, pp. 183–84.

14. *Ibid.*, p. 175. Williams goes on to say that it is realist theories in particular that make this mistake. I discuss this aspect of his position in chapter 6, sec. V.

15. *Ibid.*, p. 179.

16. Since he explicitly distinguishes the sense of *ought* in which conflicting *oughts* cannot be eliminated from what he calls the "deliberative *ought*" (p. 184), it might be thought that Williams is arguing for some form of RT. But the point is not obvious, in part because he does not make a clear distinction between DT and RT.

17. Since I have reserved the term 'ought' for expressing conclusions of moral deliberation, I do not describe RT in terms of conflicting *oughts*.

18. Marcus 1980, pp. 132–33.

19. Phillips and Mounce 1970, pp. 99–103.

20. For example, see Goldman 1988, p. 143; Halfon 1989, pp. 106–7; Herman 1990, pp. 325–26; McConnell 1978, pp. 277–78; Odegard 1987, p. 82; and Santurri 1987, p. 53.

21. For an interesting attempt at this, see Taylor 1985.

22. My assumption, and the assumption of virtually all discussions of the phenomenological argument, is that these feelings have as a component an evaluative belief on the basis of which they may or may not be appropriate in a particular circumstance. I take 'appropriate' here to mean 'cognitively correct' (at least in relationship to the normative outlook of the agent), and not merely 'understandable' or 'to be expected' on the part of morally well-educated persons, or 'on the whole beneficial' for someone or another (as, for example, in a critique to be discussed later in Hare 1981, pp. 28–31). Of course, the exact form and extent of the feeling that is appropriate will depend on the particular circumstances of a given case. All that can be considered at this point is the general shape of these feelings.

23. In speaking of what is "morally for the best," no particular understanding of how this is determined should be assumed. I use this expression to refer to what is required by the correct conclusion of moral deliberation, without commitment to a specific account of deliberation.

24. In this connection, there are two possible misunderstandings I would like to avert. First, Levi says that Williams and others who defend the phenomenological argument "seem to think that the guilt or regret generated by breaking a promise [so as to keep another promise] in this dilemma must be the same as in the case of breaking a promise due to weakness of will, for in both cases the agent has disobeyed a moral injunc-

tion which is in force" (Levi 1986, p. 25). Whether or not this is an accurate criticism of others, it should be clear that I do not think the moral distress (as well as wrongdoing) that is inescapable is just the same as the distress (and wrongdoing) that is found in cases of weakness of will. Moreover, they may be different even if in both cases a moral injunction which is in force has been disobeyed. Second, Philippa Foot writes that "there is some notion of *fault* which is such that no one can be at fault both if he does *a* and if he doesn't do *a*," except, she says, when the fault results from one's prior action (Foot 1983, p. 388). Foot may well be right that there is such a notion of fault. But it does not follow from this that there is no other notion of fault, and this is the issue raised by RT.

25. Williams 1973a, p. 172.

26. Foot 1983, p. 382. Cf. Santurri 1987, pp. 54–55.

27. In this connection, see Sinnott-Armstrong 1988, pp. 44–53 (esp. p. 46).

28. Foot 1983, p. 382. A similar point is made in McConnell 1978, p. 278.

29. When the argument is understood in this way, intuitions about our moral feelings are regarded as fallible sources of understanding that require confirmation by an analysis of their underlying beliefs. It may be objected that on this interpretation it becomes irrelevant whether people actually have these feelings. The only thing that matters is whether or not there is an account that would make sense of them in terms of inescapable moral wrongdoing. But this objection fails to appreciate the import of the methodology employed by the phenomenological argument. It is a significant fact that these emotional reactions are natural for us. This tells us something about our capacity for moral response to one another. Though it is essential that we consider whether these reactions make sense, it is also important that we do naturally have these reactions.

30. For those who reject this deliberative conclusion, the same point may be made in reverse.

31. Foot 1983, p. 387.

32. Foot herself goes on to give an example in which she thinks some form of inescapable moral distress might be appropriate. She concludes that "the area seems to be one of uncertainty" and suggests that "perhaps this very fact makes the argument from feelings to 'remainder' in the solution of moral conflicts a bad one" (1983, p. 387). A related response is given in Morris 1992. He maintains that for any moral conflict where inescapable moral distress is appropriate for some person, we can imagine another person in the same situation for whom such distress is not appropriate (his example is Sophie's choice). Thus he concludes that the evidence of moral experience is "mixed," and cannot decisively support the thesis that there are "ultimate moral conflicts" (which in any case look to be closer to what is affirmed by DT than RT). I am not convinced that there is great uncertainty concerning our intuitions about inescapable moral distress as I have defined this. But I have allowed that, without clarification, there are conflicting intuitions about inescapable moral wrongdoing, and I have suggested an account of this in terms of the distinction between DT and RT. Both Foot and Morris interpret the phenomenological argument as moving directly from intuitions about moral feelings to a conclusion about moral conflicts. I agree that without an account of the best explanation of these feelings the argument is unconvincing. Finally, for those who think our intuitions about these feelings are uncertain, the method of reflective intuitionism might still be employed to resolve this uncertainty in favor of the idea of unavoidable moral wrongdoing (cf. Rawls 1971, p. 19); for the account I will put forward to explain intuitions about inescapable moral distress might be sufficient to show that there is unavoidable moral wrongdoing even in the absence of these intuitions, and so it might resolve what uncertainties there are. But this is not the argument I am making.

33. Generally speaking, these explanations have been normative rather than natural-

istic. The usual assumption on both sides of the "moral dilemmas" debate is that these intuitions should be explained in some broadly moral framework rather than that of naturalistic psychology.

34. In this connection, see Morris 1987, esp. pp. 232–37.

35. For one statement of this kind of objection, see Conee 1982, pp. 90–92.

36. In chapter 7 I consider an explanation that purports to meet these conditions (that of Hare). In the article cited in the previous note, Conee also suggest answers to these questions. I will consider these in due course. My point here is to establish that these conditions would have to be met in order for this explanation to be compelling.

37. For an expression of this kind of explanation, see Santurri 1987, p. 51. The presence of uncertainty in confronting moral conflicts is stressed in Levi 1986, ch. 2 and 1992; MacIntyre 1990, pp. 375–79; and McConnell 1978, pp. 280–85. The importance of this explanation has been emphasized to me by Jonathan Adler.

38. McConnell 1978, pp. 277–78.

39. McConnell does not explicitly state the objection in this form, but I take his quoted remarks, offered in a critique of the phenomenological argument, to be suggestive of it.

40. It is not uncommon in these discussions to compare moral conflicts to natural disasters, thereby suggesting that what is disturbing is not anything involving human agency. For example, see Foot 1983, p. 387 and Santurri 1987, p. 59.

41. McConnell 1978, p. 277.

42. Conee 1982, p. 90.

43. Feldman 1986, p. 203. Feldman is referring to Sartre's story about the student who must choose between staying with his mother and fighting against Germany in World War II (see Sartre 1975).

44. Santurri 1987, p. 53.

45. The aforementioned authors were arguing against "moral dilemmas," but I am considering the objection as relevant specifically to RT.

46. Santurri 1987, pp. 55–56.

47. Levi 1986, p. 27. See also 1992, pp. 826–27.

48. Mallock 1967, p. 168.

49. Feldman makes a similar point with respect to conflicting promises to meet for lunch, where neither promise overrides the other. In this case, Feldman maintains, "the promisor owes each promisee this: either to show up or to apologize" (1986, p. 206). Hence, there is no categorical obligation to have lunch with either person. Rather, there is only a disjunctive obligation to each person, and since these two disjunctive obligations can both be fulfilled, Feldman thinks it is possible to avoid wrongdoing. An odd consequence of this view is that both obligations are fulfilled by having lunch with neither person and apologizing to both. Perhaps what Feldman intends is that the person has an obligation to have lunch with one person and to apologize to the other. A similar position is given in Donagan 1984, p. 304.

50. In this connection, see Stocker 1990, pp. 35 and 112.

51. If it were claimed that the secondary obligation to the promisee is to explain what happened, but *not* to apologize or compensate, then there clearly would be no basis for accounting for inescapable moral distress. The obligation to explain something does not by itself warrant moral distress.

52. Levi 1992, p. 827.

6

Responsibilities to Persons: An Explanation of Inescapable Moral Distress

The detractors of the idea of "moral dilemmas" rightly suppose, as I argued in chapter 4, that it is incoherent to think correct conclusions of an agent's moral deliberation about what to do could conflict with one another. For this reason, it is a mistake to think that there are situations in which an agent would violate a correct conclusion of moral deliberation no matter what. In this sense, moral wrongdoing cannot be inescapable. But it is a further question, as I argued in the last chapter, whether or not moral wrongdoing in any other sense is sometimes inescapable. With regard to this question, the remainders view asserts that there are moral conflicts in which, whatever the agent does, he or she will do something that is morally wrong in the sense of transgressing some moral value. On the other hand, the elimination view denies this: It maintains that there is no sense of 'moral wrongdoing' in which an agent will do something morally wrong no matter what. It is the debate between these two views with which I am presently concerned.

The best argument for the remainders view is the phenomenological argument. In the last chapter I developed an interpretation of this argument and began my defense of it by considering some common objections to it. My aim in this chapter is to continue this defense by developing a normative outlook that explains inescapable feelings of moral distress as appropriate responses to situations in which moral wrongdoing in the sense of violating moral responsibilities cannot be avoided.

I. Normative Issues in the Debate about the Remainders Thesis

As I understand the phenomenological argument, It begins with the claim that people commonly believe there are moral conflicts in which it would be both

117

natural and appropriate to feel moral distress no matter which course of action
was taken. To say that a person feels moral distress means that the person experiences some degree of mental pain in recognition of having done something
wrong, in the sense of transgressing some moral value, and of needing to somehow apologize or compensate for this wrong. The argument claims that beliefs
about inescapable moral distress have some credibility, and it maintains that
there is a coherent account of these beliefs that establishes as the best explanation of them that they are, at least typically, responses to moral conflicts in
which moral wrongdoing in some sense is inescapable. On this basis of these
considerations, it concludes that RT is true and ET false.

The most important objection to the phenomenological argument is the
claim that beliefs about inescapable moral distress may be best explained in a
way that does not involve unavoidable moral wrongdoing. In the last chapter, I
considered several versions of this objection, and I argued that each is unconvincing. A principal reason for this is that these explanations were presented
from a standpoint independent of any particular normative outlook. At least in
the form I considered them, none of these explanations was connected in any
important and direct way with the approach of a particular normative perspective. Yet to understand the full significance of RT and to determine whether or
not it is true, it is necessary to consider specific normative outlooks. The most
compelling explanations of inescapable feelings of moral distress—those offered
both for and against RT—are rooted in determinate normative accounts. Moreover, the particular form of the remainders view that I will defend is committed
to a definite and distinctive understanding of the moral life, and it is an understanding that is at odds with the philosophical theories of morality that have
been most influential in recent years. In order to evaluate RT, then, we need to
bring these diverse normative perspectives to the fore.[1]

In this chapter I outline a normative position based on the concept of
responsibilities to persons that explains people's unavoidable feelings of moral
distress as reasonable responses to circumstances in which moral wrongdoing in
the sense of transgressing these responsibilities cannot be escaped. I argue that
this position provides a good explanation of (at least many of) these feelings. In
saying this, I mean that this account captures important features of people's
understanding of morality, that people often have the feelings referred to in the
phenomenological argument because they accept this account (or something
close to it), and that this account is a reasonable one. On the basis of these
claims, I maintain that we have some reason for thinking moral wrongdoing in
this sense is sometimes inescapable. Of course, the phenomenological argument
requires not merely that this be a good explanation of inescapable feelings of
moral distress, but that it be a better explanation of these feelings than those
explanations which deny inescapable moral wrongdoing. For this reason, I
argue in the next two chapters that it is a better explanation than those critiques
of the remainders view and the phenomenological argument rooted in the two
most prominent traditions in contemporary Anglo-American moral philosophy—utilitarianism and Kantianism. In the end, I will claim that, at least with
respect to the contemporary debate, the best explanation of these feelings

involves inescapable moral wrongdoing, and thus that there is inescapable moral wrongdoing.

Before beginning, it will help to make a general observation about the way in which the understanding of normative systems has influenced the evaluation of RT. For many philosophers the idea of inescapable moral wrongdoing appears mistaken, indeed deeply and obviously mistaken. This is why there have been so many attempts to explain why people have moral feelings that (on this view, incorrectly) seem to imply that one might do something wrong no matter what. One source for this almost instinctive rejection of RT is the fact that many philosophers accept a model of what morality, and in particular moral theory, consists of that effectively precludes the possibility of inescapable moral wrongdoing, or of any genuine moral conflict at all. Borrowing a term from the philosophy of science, I will refer to this as the "covering law model."[2] This model clearly has a powerful appeal for many moral philosophers, especially those in the utilitarian and Kantian traditions, and in the grip of this model it can seem nearly impossible to understand how inescapable moral wrongdoing could make sense.

The covering law model supposes that the primary concern of morality and moral theory is the determination and justification of conclusions of moral deliberation, those action-guiding judgments about what in the final analysis morally ought to be done by a person in a particular situation.[3] It correctly assumes that sound deliberation cannot produce conflict among these judgments. The distinctive feature of the model is that it requires the justification of these judgments to take the form of an inference from a first moral principle as applied to the facts of the case. In particular, it is typically thought that there is a single, abstract, universal, moral principle that cannot be derived from other moral considerations.[4] Some uses of the categorical imperative and the greatest happiness principle are examples of such principles. According to the covering law model, moral deliberation properly understood consists in applying the first principle to particular situations in order to determine what morally ought to be done. By some process of deductive reasoning from the first principle and the relevant facts of the case, a conclusion is reached about what in the final analysis the agent in that situation morally ought to do.[5] The model allows that there may be a plurality of secondary moral principles that have a role to play in this process, either as strict corollaries of the first principle or as "rules of thumb" for correctly carrying out the reasoning. But these other principles are clearly understood to have a subordinate status: The basic structure is the application of the first principle to particular cases.

The covering law model assumes that the first principle must be formulated in such a way that no application of it can result in conflicting conclusions. The absence of conflict is thus an a priori requirement imposed by the model. But it is acknowledged, and indeed frequently claimed, that conflict may *appear* among the secondary principles, and consequently among deliberative conclusions. If these secondary principles are understood as strict corollaries, it is assumed that once properly formulated they will not conflict. On the other hand, if they are understood as "rules of thumb," it may be admitted that they can occasionally conflict, but it is claimed that this does not show that there is a real moral conflict or that moral wrongdoing is inescapable; for these "rules of thumb" are merely approximate guidelines to what morally ought to be done. They have no moral force in themselves. Where they conflict, the ultimate measure of right and wrong is the derivation of deliberative conclusions from the first principle, and here there can be no conflict.

My account of the covering law model is quite simple and general. Nonetheless, it provides a reference point for a familiar range of widely accepted positions, of which some versions of utilitarianism and Kantianism are prominent examples. With elaboration and qualification, the model could be shown to encompass many important theories on the landscape of contemporary moral philosophy. My point in sketching an outline of the model is this. If the covering law model is accepted, the suggestion that sometimes moral wrongdoing is inescapable will naturally be met with disbelief. For on this model, it cannot be the case that an agent would do something morally wrong no matter what. The only way in which wrongdoing could occur would be for someone to violate a correct conclusion of deliberation, and these conclusions cannot conflict. Moreover, the covering law model suggests an account of why it might appear that wrongdoing is inescapable, and also why this appearance is mistaken: Conflicting secondary principles might create the impression that wrongdoing cannot be avoided even though properly understood these principles do not carry this implication. In this way, the model suggests a powerful critique of the phenomenological argument: Inescapable feelings of moral distress may be explained as being a result of this mistaken impression.[6]

A normative position that defends the remainders view will have to present a different understanding of morality than the one suggested by the covering law model. Previous defenses of the phenomenological argument have not paid sufficient attention to articulating such a position. They have tended to put too much emphasis on eliciting intuitions about inescapable moral distress and too little on developing an account of morality that explains these intuitions. The absence of such an account, in combination with the predominance of the covering law model, has made it easy to suppose that these intuitions must be mistaken.

In this chapter, I describe and defend a normative position which supports the remainders view. Though other defenses of this view may be made, based on different normative positions, I believe this account is most adequate in explaining intuitions about inescapable moral distress.[7] There may be historical antecedents of this account, but I make no attempt to consider these here. My aim is to describe a way of thinking about the moral life that makes sense of a form of inescapable moral wrongdoing and to argue that inescapable feelings of moral distress may be explained in terms of this approach. This aim is best accomplished by focusing attention on the position itself, unencumbered by questions of historical scholarship. What is most important is to see that there is available a reasonable alternative to the covering law model as well as allied utilitarian and Kantian approaches.

I call this position "the responsibilities to persons" account. In the next two sections I describe various aspects of this account. I then show how it explains inescapable moral distress in terms of inescapable moral wrongdoing. In the last two sections, I consider various objections that may be raised from foes as well as friends of the idea of "moral dilemmas."

II. Responsibilities to Persons

In order to defend RT, it is necessary to identify a sense of 'moral wrongdoing' that is not equivalent to violating conclusions of moral deliberation and that can allow for inescapable moral wrongdoing. It might seem that this is merely a verbal issue, with no substantial philosophical question at stake. For example, in the final two objections to the phenomenological argument in chapter 5, it was acknowledged that sometimes an agent will do something morally bad no matter what, and that on account of this an agent who chooses the lesser of two evils ought to apologize or compensate for doing that evil. It may be unclear what difference it makes whether or not we go on to say that an agent may do something morally wrong no matter what (especially when it is understood that 'morally wrong' does not necessarily mean violating a correct conclusion of moral deliberation). Not all those who argue against inescapable moral wrongdoing make these concessions, of course, but the fact that several do might be taken to indicate that the difference between affirming and denying RT is not as significant as it has seemed to those on both sides of the debate.[8] What, we may ask, is conveyed by the expression 'morally wrong' that has led so many to think it important to justify one position or another concerning the possibility of inescapable moral wrongdoing?

It is consistent with common usage to speak of moral wrongdoing whenever there is a transgression or violation of some moral value, such as a law, principle, rule, or the like. Since the statement of moral values need not coincide with conclusions of moral deliberation, it is consonant with ordinary usage to suppose that these values may actually conflict and that wrongdoing in the sense of violating one of these values may be inescapable. I will now introduce a particular category of moral value I call "responsibilities to persons," and I will argue both that these responsibilities may conflict and that it is morally wrong to violate them even when they do conflict. It is in the specific sense of transgressing moral responsibilities that I maintain that moral wrongdoing is sometimes inescapable. It should become clear that endorsing or rejecting this position is not merely a matter of semantics.

The responsibilities to persons account should not be taken as a complete theory of morality. There are moral values such as virtues and ideals that cannot be fully understood in terms of this account. For example, the virtue of generosity, though it may sometimes be involved in responsibilities to persons, cannot plausibly be reduced to some set of these responsibilities. Moreover, some conflicts involving such values, as when one can be generous to this person or that person but not both, need not be thought to occasion inescapable moral wrongdoing. Though generosity requires being generous to some persons some of the time, it may not require being generous to a particular person on some specific occasion. Hence, someone may do nothing wrong by being generous to this person rather than that one. By so acting there is no transgression of the virtue of generosity. It will be recalled that RT does not say that every moral conflict makes wrongdoing inescapable, only that some do. My claim is that it is conflicts of moral responsibilities in particular that have this result. Though other moral values are important, I make no attempt to discuss them here.

The covering law model begins with an abstract first principle, usually conceived as embodying a conception of impartiality, from which we are to derive particular deliberative conclusions. The responsibilities to persons account begins instead with a paradigm, one that focuses on considerations of partiality. We are to start with reflection on what is involved in our particular, concrete relationships with persons with whom we are to a greater or lesser extent, and in various ways, intimate, especially relations of kinship, friendship, and love. It is mainly in the context of such relationships that we first come to employ and understand moral considerations. Responsibilities situated in intimate relations form an exemplar on the basis of which moral responsibilities in other circumstances ought to be understood via analogical reasoning from comparisons and contrasts.

Regarding these responsibilities as paradigmatic challenges a familiar order of thought often associated with the covering law model. On that view, we first understand moral relations that may obtain among any two human beings, even strangers, and then consider as a special (and possibly problematic) case the moral relations among intimates. On the responsibilities to persons account, we begin with moral relations among intimates, and then consider other moral relations, such as those with relative strangers and social entities. This might be thought to undermine the aspiration to universality widely believed to be constitutive of the moral point of view. But in one respect this aspiration is fully accommodated by this approach. For there is nothing more universal than the primacy accorded to moral responsibilities of partial relationships.

This procedure is consonant with the method of reflective intuitionism. For among our intuitions is the recognition of the fundamental importance of moral responsibilities to intimates. Taking these responsibilities as paradigmatic means regarding them as a central source of insight. It does not mean accepting them uncritically.[9] As we move from the paradigm to other contexts, pressure may be exerted to revise our original understanding. The method's fallibilism and demand for coherence preclude thinking of beliefs about responsibilities to intimates as a traditional "foundation" of moral knowledge.

Intimate relationships, then, are the paradigmatic location of moral responsibilities as I will understand them. All of us suppose that we have, with respect to various particular persons with whom we are so related, a set of more or less well-defined specific moral responsibilities. For example, Jennifer supposes that she has several responsibilities of this kind to her son John, such as the responsibility to nurture and protect him. Reflection on such relationships draws our attention to the importance of responding in ways appropriate to particular human beings. This is the underlying thought that the responsibilities to persons account aims to articulate.

Our responsibilities to intimates are rooted in two kinds of consideration. The first is the perception that each of these persons has intrinsic and unique value. The second is the recognition that some connection or another obtains between oneself and these intimates. Thus, it is because Jennifer regards John as intrinsically and uniquely valuable, and because she knows he is her son and the person whom she has raised, that she understands herself to have these responsibilities. These considerations require some explanation.

To say that persons are valuable in themselves means that they are valuable, but not only as a means to some further valued end and not only by being a part of some valued whole. Even if persons were not valued in these ways (which, of course, they often are), they would still be valuable. Individual persons are valuable in and of themselves. Various reasons may be given as to why this is so: for example, that persons are rational, free, can act according to norms, have a subjective standpoint, are capable of affective interaction, and the like. For my purposes, it is not necessary to develop a full rationale for the idea of intrinsic value. It is sufficient to observe that it is a fundamental feature of moral experience that individuals are regarded as valuable in themselves. This is, in any case, a familiar idea in moral philosophy. It is related to Kant's notion of respecting persons as ends in themselves. By emphasizing this notion, Kant glimpsed an important characteristic of morality, one that the utilitarian tradition is famously unable to recognize in any deep way. In this respect, the responsibilities to persons account is closer to Kant than to utilitarianism.

Nonetheless, the idea that persons are valuable in themselves, as understood here, is not equivalent to Kant's conception. There are at least two important differences between them.[10] First, for Kant it is only the noumenal person, the person as a rational and free agent, that is regarded as an end in itself. On the responsibilities to persons account it is, so to speak, the whole person that is so regarded. The whole person may include rationality and autonomy, on some understanding of these terms, but it also includes much about a person that Kant would regard as being merely "empirical" and hence of no moral significance in this regard—for example, a person's capacity for emotional response, a person's physical comportment in the world, and various features associated with a person's particular history.[11] In general, there is no commitment on this account to the metaphysics presupposed by Kant's noumenal-phenomenal distinction.

Second, Kant regards respect for persons as ends in themselves as a manifestation of respect for the moral law dictated by pure practical reason. This aspect of Kant's enterprise, which is related to the covering law model, is not endorsed here. On the responsibilities to persons account, we do not regard an intimate as intrinsically valuable by application of an a priori moral law, but through the experience of concrete interaction. In the context of our particular relations with the person, the empirically embodied and conditioned person, we come to perceive him or her in this way. Moreover, as we come to have a general view of all human beings as valuable in themselves, this is determined inductively from particular cases, and not as a result of an a priori apprehension of rational nature. Once again, there is a good deal associated with Kant's insightful notion of respect for persons that is not being maintained here.

To say that persons, taken individually, are uniquely valuable is a less familiar idea, at least in the mainstream of the Western philosophical tradition. In both

the Kantian and utilitarian perspectives, the unique value of individual persons is
either denied or regarded as morally insignificant (and sometimes as morally
harmful). Hence, there has been little discussion of this idea among contemporary moral philosophers.[12] On this view, a person is not only intrinsically valuable, but has an intrinsic value which is different from that of everyone else. By
contrast, for Kant, what makes persons ends in themselves is a property shared
equally by all: rationality and autonomy. Since only this property is morally fundamental, nothing about persons that distinguishes them from one another is of
deep moral relevance. Persons are intrinsically valuable, but equally so. In the
utilitarian tradition, persons are neither intrinsically valuable nor uniquely valuable. According to Bentham's famous and oft-quoted slogan, in calculating the
goodness of the consequences of our actions, "everybody [is] to count for one,
nobody for more than one."[13] Once again, a concept of the moral equality of persons is the fundamental doctrine. In both the Kantian and utilitarian traditions,
the central thought is that persons are of equal moral value (though, of course,
this is not understood in the same way). For both, whatever may be unique about
individual persons cannot be of basic moral significance. Persons cannot be
uniquely valuable in a way that makes a difference to morality.

It might be supposed that the only alternative to regarding persons as
morally equal is to regard some as morally more valuable than others (historically such hierarchical conceptions were the principal target of egalitarian doctrines). The assumption that this is the case is what makes moral equality seem
such an attractive, indeed almost irresistible, idea. But there is another alternative: Persons may be uniquely valuable. That is, each person may have value, but
in a way that is distinctive, different from everyone else. To say this is to claim
that, in an important respect, the value of each person is "incommensurable"
with that of every other, meaning that we should decline to judge that, for any
two persons, either one is worth more than the other or else they are worth the
same amount.[14] This is not to deny that, in some contexts and for some purposes, a concept of moral equality has an important role to play. For example,
we think that persons should be equal in the eyes of the law and hence should
have the same rights in criminal proceedings. Again, we suppose that citizens
should be equal in their relations with the state and so should be equally entitled
to vote.[15] But to acknowledge the significance of a concept of equality in these
special situations, important as they are, is not the same as asserting, what both
the Kantian and utilitarian traditions assert, that some notion of moral equality
is constitutive of the first moral principle in such a way that the unique value of
persons has no basic moral significance.

That persons have unique value is a deep feature of our moral experience. It
is revealed most poignantly in our attitudes toward the death of a loved one.
When such a person dies there is an irreplaceable loss. We regard the deceased
person as uniquely valuable, and hence as someone who cannot be fully replaced
by another person (or anything else), no matter how valuable he or she may be.
When Ismene objects to Creon's plan to execute Antigone, the fiancée of his
son Haimon, Creon responds by declaring abruptly and crudely, "there are
other furrows for his plow." To this Ismene rightly exclaims, "but where the

closeness that has bound these two?"[16] To think that there are other women who could adequately replace Antigone as Haimon's bride, as Creon thinks, is to seriously misunderstand the value of the person he loves. Even if Haimon had lived and gone on to marry another women after Antigone's death, he would have suffered a permanent loss on account of her death—namely, the loss of Antigone and his loving relationship with her. No other woman, no matter how wonderful, could have fully made up for this loss. This is not because no other woman would have been as valuable as Antigone, as if she were more valuable than anyone else. Rather, it is because no other woman would have been the particular person who was Antigone. It was in recognition of this that Haimon, in desperation upon the discovery of Antigone's body, took his own life. While most of us find a way to live with the loss of a loved one, we understand and appreciate what in the pain of this loss drove Haimon to his final act.

By contrast, if your television stops working and the warranty provides you with a new one, then you have been fully compensated for your loss. Televisions, unlike persons, can be replaced without loss of value. Kant, of course, insists on the fundamental moral difference between persons and things. But it is not enough to capture this difference to regard the value of persons simply in terms of being free and rational beings, a property shared equally by all. Haimon is not distressed merely because *a* free and rational being is now gone. If that were the case, then another such being could make up for the loss. Rather, his distress is focused on the fact that *the person who was Antigone* is now gone. Another women would not fully compensate for this loss. We can only understand this by supposing that each person has a unique value.

As we take persons to be uniquely valuable, we suppose them to have unique properties. Of course, there are many respects in which some people do have the same properties, or at least quite similar ones. Persons are obviously not unique in every respect. Partly for this reason, another woman could *partially* compensate for the death of Antigone. But if the valued characteristics of a person were exhausted by characteristics all of which could be found in another person, then in principle one person could be fully replaced, without any loss of value, by another person. Yet it is one of the most important features of our practical lives that we do not regard human beings as replaceable in this way.[17] To focus attention exclusively on similarities of value is thus to miss something of fundamental importance: the unique and hence irreplaceable value of each person. Any plausible account of morality must make this a central consideration.

It may be objected that focusing attention on the unique value of each person is nothing but a recipe for prejudice. But this will be so only if we already think that the only alternative to regarding persons as equally important is to regard some as more important than others. To respond to whom a person uniquely is, and hence to respond to different persons differently, need not be a form of unwarranted prejudice. Differential treatment will be seen as prejudicial only if the standard is sameness. Moreover, those who are prejudiced in the ordinary, pejorative sense of the term are certainly not attempting to respond to the unique value of each person. To the contrary, they regard some repeatable feature of the person—race, sex, ethnicity, religion, etc.—as the determining factor in all relations with the person, even when it is quite irrelevant. This feature is regarded as a sufficient basis for negative assessments of each member of the class of persons possessing it, irrespective of his or her individual value. The prejudiced person is thus blinded to the unique value of these persons. Far from encouraging such prejudicial attitudes, this account proscribes them.

It may also be said that, even if persons are uniquely valuable, it is nonetheless often necessary for practical reasons to set this fact aside and regard them as equally valuable; for in situations where people's claims compete, we have to act one way rather than another, and this imposes on us the alternatives of regarding these people as equally valuable or of regarding some as more valuable than others. To regard each person as uniquely valuable, and hence as having no relation of comparative value to any other person, cannot be a basis for choice. Hence, for the purpose of deciding what to do, there is no alternative but to assume that people are equally valuable (since it is untenable to regard some as more valuable than others).

This objection gains plausibility from the covering law model. For it regards all moral value as a function of what can count as correct conclusions of moral deliberation. It is precisely this assumption about moral value that should be rejected. In making decisions about what to do we sometimes have to make judgments about the comparative importance of people in that situation. But it does not follow from this constraint on deliberation about action that our conception of what our moral responsibilities are must be defined solely in terms of what it is possible to do in every situation. In deciding what in the final analysis ought to be done in some circumstance, the Kantian principle that 'ought' implies 'can' governs. Yet in determining what in the first place our moral responsibilities are (on the basis of which we then decide what ought to be done), we should not focus on what in every circumstance can be done, but on the ways in which the unique and intrinsic value of individual persons requires response. On this view, our responsibilities are established by our various concrete responses to distinct individuals, not by a deduction from first principle to deliberative conclusion. To say that we have to act does not entail that our moral responsibilities to one another are exhaustively defined in terms of our ability to act.

Even in deciding what to do, various factors are relevant. It makes considerable difference how we are related to the persons involved. The women who saves her husband from drowning before saving another passenger on the ship is making a comparative assessment with respect to that action. She is judging that it is more important for her to save her husband than to save the other passenger. But she need not be taken as judging that her husband is more valuable than the passenger simply speaking. She can acknowledge that that person is also an intrinsically and uniquely valuable being, albeit one for whom she does not have the same responsibilities as for her husband. Likewise, a military commander might say, "This military objective is worth this many lives." This could be a sound military judgment and a morally defensible one. But it need not be taken as denying that there is nothing that is worth those lives, in the sense of fully making up for their loss. The necessity of acting, and of acting on the basis of reasonable judgments, should not lead us to repudiate our understanding of the ways in which persons are valuable.

It is also important to emphasize that the uniqueness of persons can play different roles in deliberation. In some cases (for example, that of familial or romantic love), the specific ways in which a particular person is unique are vitally important: We strive to respond to what is uniquely valuable about *that* person. In other cases, especially as we move away from the paradigm of intimate relations, we are in less of a position to understand or appreciate much of what is uniquely valuable in a person. There is a wide range of possibilities here. In the extreme case, that of the virtual stranger, we can hardly respond to anything specific about the person at all. Here we assume that the person is uniquely valuable and we respond not so much to what is uniquely valuable per se as to the fact of unique value. We try to respond as one should respond to any uniquely and intrinsically valuable person. In this respect, of course, there is a kind of equality. We suppose that each person is uniquely and intrinsically valuable. Yet precisely because each person is uniquely valuable, this notion of equality does not take us far in understanding our moral relations with one another.[18]

That we regard persons as being intrinsically and uniquely valuable is one of the most significant features of our understanding of ourselves. Because we regard persons in this way, we suppose that they are in various respects deserving, in and of themselves and irrespective of circumstances. For example, a child suffering from malnutrition is deserving of food, simply by being an intrinsically and uniquely valuable creature with this vital need, and quite independent of whatever factors give rise to, or inhibit the alleviation of, the lack of nutrition. Still, to say that a person is deserving in this sense does not immediately entail that anyone has any moral responsibilities to this person. Which persons have responsibilities to feed this deserving child depends upon a variety of circumstances.

Being intrinsically and uniquely valuable creates the potentiality for responsibility: It establishes that this is a kind of being for whom one can have moral responsibilities. It does not by itself establish that someone, indeed that anyone, has responsibilities. These only arise when some connection is established between persons—for example, through family relation, friendship, love, nationality, ethnicity, agreement, proximity, knowledge, common background, commitment, interest, and the like. On the basis of one or more of these various forms of connection, and typically (but not always) the mutual recognition of the unique and intrinsic value of one another, a relationship between persons may be formed. Constitutive of such relationships is an understanding of some form of responsibility by each person for the well-being of the other, though the nature and scope of these responsibilities, as well as the extent of their symmetry and the degree to which they are well-defined, varies with the nature of the relationship.

Two points need to be emphasized about the formation of these relationships. First, there is a great deal of diversity in the ways in which connections among us come about. Much of this diversity results from the fact that our relationships depend upon social institutions that are both complex and variable across history and cultures. How we can come to be related to persons is substantially determined by the possibilities of our particular social world.[19] As a consequence, there is considerable variety among the moral responsibilities that arise from these various relationships. Second, relationships typically arise through a combination of choice and unchosen circumstance. In some cases, there is no element of choice at all, as in responsibilities children have to parents. Often relationships come about through choice in the context of circumstances that are unchosen and contingent. In part, these circumstances are the possibilities of relationship in our specific social world. In part, they are simply a matter of chance. In the modern, Western world we choose our spouses. But the kind of marriage that is possible depends upon social institutions such as the expectations and opportunities for men and women in the workplace, the resources for child care, and the like. And though spouses are chosen, they are chosen from the limited number of persons one happens, largely by chance, to encounter in the world.[20]

In sum, moral responsibilities have a twofold origin: first, in the belief that because persons are intrinsically and uniquely valuable, they are beings who are in various ways deserving and as such are beings for whom we can have responsibilities; and second, in the diverse ways in which particular persons come to be connected with one another, whether through choice or unchosen circumstance, and thereby establish a relationship of which specific responsibilities are a constitutive part.

III. More on Responsibilities

Statements of our responsibilities to persons are principal among the premises we appeal to in determining what, in the final analysis, we morally ought to do. Yet these statements should not be confused with the secondary principles of the covering law model. Moral responsibilities are neither corollaries of a first moral principle nor "rules of thumb" for determining sound deliberative conclusions. They have no natural place in the covering law model. Moral responsibilities are a product of the multiplicity of relationships with particular persons that make up our lives. We cannot plausibly be thought to enter into these relationships, and thereby acquire their responsibilities, by deliberating about what to do on the basis of a general, abstract principle as applied to the circumstances of our lives.[21] Rather, it is through the specific, concrete experience of encountering this person in these circumstances, or of being connected in these ways, and also of recognizing the intrinsic and unique value of this person, that a relationship is formed in which responsibilities are recognized. This is not to say that no reflection is involved in their formation or development. Surely it is, but the concrete perception of the value of the person is crucial, and reflection is not inference from an abstract first principle.

In this connection, it is worth returning to a point raised earlier (chapter 5, sec. II). I noted that proponents and opponents of "moral dilemmas" are commonly divided over a deeper methodological question: Proponents tend to be impressed by the epistemological credentials of moral experiences, while opponents generally give more epistemological weight to abstract principles such as those found in deontic logic. When we examine normative accounts employed to explain feelings of inescapable moral distress, we discover a related division. Those who reject the idea of inescapable moral wrongdoing tend to accept forms of the covering law model. They understand morality as founded on a single, abstract, first principle from which conclusions about what ought to be done are derived. By contrast, those who accept this idea frequently reject this approach in favor of a normative account in which a plurality of relatively less abstract moral values is taken as basic. Later I will distinguish my position from some of these pluralistic accounts. But it should now be clear that the doctrine of responsibilities to persons has some affiliation with this latter approach, for I have been arguing that a plurality of concrete responsibilities to persons is fundamental.

In the justification of responsibilities, concrete experiences are crucial. For example, the perception of the value of this particular person with whom I am connected in these specific ways plays an essential role in establishing my responsibilities for this person. But these experiences should not be understood as a source of self-evident or infallible truths, nor as independent of influence by "theory." Thus my experience of the value of a new acquaintance may be affected by my conception of the value of persons in general. There is clearly a place for general considerations in moral thought. We interpret particular experiences in terms of these considerations. Conversely, general considerations are themselves interpreted and revised on the basis of particular experiences. Such reciprocity is what the method of reflective intuitionism would lead us to expect.

I have taken the paradigm of moral responsibilities to be those associated with relatively intimate relationships. It is these relationships and their concomitant responsibilities that are central to what makes our lives worthwhile, and it is within such relationships that we come to best understand what is involved in the notion of responsibility. But we clearly have responsibilities in other contexts and of other kinds as well. For example, a momentary encounter with a person looking for the right road may be sufficient to generate a sense of responsibility, say to give directions, limited and fleeting though this may be. As we move away from the paradigm of responsibilities to persons in intimate relationships, we encounter possibilities for responsibility in a variety of directions: responsibilities to strangers within our community, to persons in foreign countries, to human beings on the edges of life such as fetuses or those in an irreversible coma, to generations past and future, to animals, to the environment, to a deity, and so on. In striving to understand such responsibilities we need to examine their similarities and dissimilarities with the paradigm case. Though it is beyond the scope of this discussion to consider all such possibilities, one form of responsibility is so common in the debate about "moral dilemmas" that it requires brief elaboration.

We have responsibilities not only to individual persons, but to social entities, which consist of persons brought together through some common interest, purpose, origin, need, belief, aspiration, hope, and the like. Thus there may be responsibilities to one's community, nation, government, ethnic group, race, family, clan, tribe, religious institution, university, company, profession, labor union, political party or movement, and so on. In one respect these social entities differ radically from persons. There is nothing that constitutes a person as persons constitute social entities. Yet, though not indivisible in this way, social entities have a life of their own that transcends the persons who make them up. This is due in part to the fact that these collectivities often have as their raison d'être some concern that transcends the needs of any specific individuals (for example, a university's commitment to education and research, or a community's devotion to a way of life). The existence of these entities typically does not depend upon the membership of any particular persons. For this reason, our relationships with these groups and our responsibilities to them are not reducible to our relationships with and responsibilities to some list of persons. At the same time, our responsibilities to these organizations are ordinarily understood to benefit some more or less specifiable group of human beings. Moreover, if human beings were not valued as they are, most of these organizations would lose their point. The importance of these social entities is thus parasitic upon the value of individual persons. Our responsibilities to a social entity should be thought of, not as responsibilities to something which is not a person, but to something which consists of persons united in some human interest.[22]

These social relationships and concomitant responsibilities play an important part in human life. Though social entities differ in many ways from individual persons, it does not seem misplaced to regard some of them as having a unique value the loss of which would be irreplaceable. They can certainly inspire their own forms of intimacy and passion. There are obvious dangers of glorifying these collectivities: They can mistakenly come to be seen as ends that have no relation to and override other vital human concerns. This is one reason why social entities are associated with so much of the evil and oppression in the world. But they are also the source of much of what makes our lives valuable. Human flourishing requires more than individual relationships. It requires participation in collective forms of human activity. Moreover, many relationships with individual persons are possible only within the context of these collectivities.

Finally, it is important to recognize that the nature, scope, and importance of our responsibilities to persons and social entities varies considerably, depending on the characteristics of the relationship in question. Some responsibilities are attached to virtually any relationship. Others are quite specialized in that they occur only in certain kinds of relationships, as for example in those between husband and wife, parent and child, lawyer and client, therapist and patient, mayor and citizen, and the like. In all cases, our responsibilities are not unlimited: We do not regard ourselves as prepared to do anything at all, to anyone, at any time for the person or group with whom we are related. A given relationship implies an understanding of the features of the responsibilities that are constitutive of it. These features depend on a variety of factors: the nature of the persons or social entities involved, the nature of the relationship, various circumstances of people's lives (history, health, finances, talents, opportunities, etc.), other relationships, and a sense of what is realistically possible in human life generally and specifically for the particular persons involved. Relationships and their accompanying responsibilities are a function of the potentialities in the concrete circumstances of people's lives. In addition, they have a temporal dimension that is crucial to their proper understanding: They develop over time, sometimes growing, or just altering, sometimes declining, and sometimes ending altogether.

For these reasons, we have an ongoing but open-ended sense of the general shape of our moral responsibilities, of their nature, scope, and importance. Though we can certainly discuss these responsibilities, there is no reason to suppose we can be fully articulate about them. Nor is there any reason to think they can be expressed in a set of more or less simple rules. This is not to say that the moral rules that are a commonplace in discussions of many moral philosophers have no place in our understanding of our responsibilities. They clearly do. But their function is to provide us with a set of guidelines for determining what, in a given situation, our specific responsibilities to a person are, and beyond this, for determining what to do. This is in part because of the complexity of life, but it is also because of the unique qualities of the persons involved. These factors make it impossible to render our moral responsibilities in a set of fully explicit rules, simple or complex. In a particular situation, it may be obvious what our responsibility is: No conscious deliberation is needed, though perhaps reasons could be given. In other situations, conscious reflection may be required to determine what in that circumstance is called for. In sum, we are neither completely in the dark, nor fully articulate in advance, about the nature of our moral responsibilities.[23]

IV. Conflicting Responsibilities and Inescapable Moral Distress

It is now possible to consider what is of primary importance for my concern here: that our moral responsibilities may conflict with one another, and that these conflicts explain many of those cases in which moral distress is inescapable. It is essential to see both what it means to say that responsibilities may conflict and why this is so. In paradigm cases, our relationships and responsibilities are established on the basis of our perception of the intrinsic and unique value of persons with whom we are connected in various ways. For a variety of reasons, responsibilities to a given person are not unlimited. Our lives are more worthwhile to the extent that they include different forms of relationship, and one of the defining features of these different forms is the diverse nature and scope of their constitutive responsibilities. In addition, the value of autonomy limits the ways in which we can be responsible to a person. Having responsibilities to someone does not mean taking over his or her life. Moreover, a life that included unlimited responsibilities to several persons would be, practically speaking, impossible. Hence, there is a reason to seek a life in which conflicts are not commonplace and constant. The value of the relationships that establish our responsibilities depends on our being able to fulfill these responsibilities a good deal of the time. It would be self-defeating to enter into a set of relationships knowing that it will not be possible to fulfill most of the responsibilities.

Still, to acknowledge that we have a reason to avoid a life of unremitting conflict does not entail that we have an overriding reason to avoid conflict altogether. Our desire to avoid conflicting responsibilities is one concern among others. If it were our only or our highest concern, our best hope of fulfilling it would be to take on as few responsibilities as possible. This would also be self-defeating: It is, among other things, the relationships constituting these responsibilities that make life worthwhile in the first place. Though we have a reason to avoid a life in which responsibilities are constantly conflicting, we also have a reason to eschew a life in which by radical reduction of responsibilities conflict cannot possibly arise.

The principal reason we sometimes have conflicting responsibilities is that these responsibilities originate in responses to the intrinsic and unique value of each of the particular persons with whom we are connected. It is the recognition of the value of, and hence the appropriateness of our specific response to, each of these persons that generates our various moral responsibilities. Though these responsibilities arise in the context of conditions that preclude taking on unlimited responsibilities, they are nonetheless driven primarily by the perception of the value of each particular person with whom we are related. It is because they develop out of these separate responses to distinct persons that conflict cannot plausibly be eliminated.

In many cases, reflection about responsibilities to a given person in a specific situation focuses on the person, and the relationship with the person, within a general understanding about how this relationship fits into one's overall life. In these cases, responsibilities to other persons may not directly come into consideration at all. But when it becomes clear that there is a conflict between responsibilities to this person and responsibilities to that person, it is necessary to move to a broader perspective in order to determine what, all things considered, is the best thing to do under the circumstances. I doubt that there is a general form to which this deliberative process must conform in every case. The way to proceed will depend on the particularities of the relationships and circumstances in question. But it will rarely if ever be the case that the correct procedure is to invoke the most general perspective possible and to resolve the conflict by reference, say, to how we stand with respect to the sentient universe as a whole, or to any human being we might encounter. In any event, my aim here is not to develop an account of moral decision-making. RT is concerned, not with the nature of deliberation per se, but with whether or not conclusions of deliberation can leave moral remainders.

Whatever the process of deliberation, it can have different outcomes. Sometimes it will lead us to realize that we have misunderstood the nature of our relationships and their concomitant responsibilities. One possibility in deliberating about what is best to do when responsibilities appear to conflict is to reach the conclusion that, properly understood, they do not really conflict. But this is only one possibility, for reflection on conflict may not reveal any reason for altering our relationships or their responsibilities. It may in fact reinforce our original understanding and make it all the more evident that in this situation these responsibilities conflict. For example, a recently married woman who discovers that her widowed mother has suddenly and unexpectedly become disabled may well find that no amount of reflection reveals that she was mistaken in supposing herself to have certain responsibilities to her husband and her mother. The fact that these now conflict is not an occasion for determining that her relationship with one or the other of these persons must now be sharply curtailed. Rather, it is a time for determining how best to fulfill as many of the responsibilities to each as she continues to regard herself as having.

It might be objected that knowledge of conflict necessitates changing our understanding of our responsibilities. It may be said that we cannot always know in advance the full implications of our responsibilities as we conceive them. Hence, we may take ourselves to have responsibilities that, unknown to us, will come into conflict. But once we discover that they do conflict, we have no choice but to modify our understanding of them. This may be painful, because we thought we could be responsible in ways which we cannot. But there is no choice but to revise. On this view, deciding what is best to do is tantamount to making such a revision.

This argument assumes that avoidance of conflicting responsibilities is an overriding consideration. I have argued that avoidance of conflicting conclusions of deliberation is an overriding consideration, for these conclusions are intentions to act, and it is irrational to knowingly have conflicting intentions to act. But to acknowledge a responsibility to a person is not itself a specific intention to act. Hence, the discovery that responsibilities conflict does not compel a revision of these responsibilities in the way that the discovery that deliberative conclusions conflict compels a revision of those conclusions. Though moral responsibilities are obviously connected with a concern for action in a general way, and thus are prescriptive in the sense of being relevant to action, they are motivated primarily by the aforementioned separate responses to the value of individual persons with whom one is connected. The discovery of conflict need not lead to the conclusion that there was something defective in those separate responses.

There is another way of putting this. Our relationships and concomitant responsibilities are as much ways of being as they are ways of doing or acting. As such, they are in one way less and in another way more than specific intentions to act. On the one hand, moral responsibilities are not themselves direct intentions to act, though they are concerned with action. For this reason we consider our responsibilities in deciding what morally ought to be done. On the other hand, responsibilities are ways of being that cannot be reduced to a collection of required acts. Much more is involved in responsibilities than action. There are beliefs about the kind of person we are, about the value of the person with whom we are related, and about the bond between us. There are also feelings that are the affective expression of these beliefs. Our responsibilities to a person are manifestations of these beliefs and feelings. It is obviously an exaggeration to say that every change of responsibility entails a change of relationship. But it is often difficult to change the former without changing the latter. This is why when responsibilities conflict we resist the option of simply abandoning or abridging some of them. We can only do what we can do. Yet even in the face of conflict, one of the things we can do is to acknowledge to ourselves the persistence of unfulfillable responsibilities and to seek to express this acknowledgment to the persons involved. Such expression is an affirmation of the particular value of these persons and of our standing with them.[24] In some cases this may be more symbolic than substantive, but it is no less meaningful and vital for the relationship for that. Often what is "merely symbolic" is of the greatest significance.

On the responsibilities to persons account, then, our responses to particular persons are primary. Moral responsibilities are not implications of an abstract, first principle about how we ought to relate to persons in general, where there is an a priori constraint against conflicting responsibilities. Rather, they arise from our perceptions of the value of separate and distinct persons with whom we are connected, and there is no reason to deny that these responsibilities may conflict. On this view, our aim as moral agents is not simply to act for the best, but to respond appropriately to each of the persons with whom we are related and for whom we have a sense of responsibility.

This account provides a compelling explanation of the phenomenon of inescapable moral distress referred to in the phenomenological argument. Consider first the example of Craig, who is faced with the choice between letting himself and his lost friend Roberto endure the potentially life-threatening danger of remaining in the wilderness and forcibly taking the keys from the teenage girls in order to steal their car and get help. According to the phenomenological argument, (1) Craig would feel, and would find it natural and appropriate to feel, moral distress no matter what he did, and (2) the best explanation of (1) is that there is a sense in which Craig would do something morally wrong no matter what he did. I have already argued for the truth of (1). The responsibility to persons account gives a convincing explanation of (1) and thus provides the beginning of an argument for (2).

Craig has at least two responsibilities: to help Roberto in this threatening situation, and to not steal the car from the girls. There is no reason to suppose that determining what is morally best in this situation will establish that Craig was mistaken in thinking that he has both of these responsibilities. Each is based on an appreciation of the distinct value of the persons involved. It is because of the value of his friend Roberto, and the fact that he is his friend, that Craig has a responsibility to protect him from danger. With respect to the two girls, though they are not acquaintances, Craig nonetheless has the basic responsibilities to them which are owed to any human being. Among these is the responsibility not to forcibly take their possessions (and, in the process, to terrify them). As persons with intrinsic and unique value, they do not deserve such treatment, and in this chance encounter he has a responsibility to respect this. Hence, whatever Craig does in this situation he will violate one of these responsibilities, and in this regard he will do something morally wrong.

Since wrongdoing in this sense is unavoidable for Craig, it is reasonable for him to feel moral distress no matter what. The moral distress in question has two elements: mental pain in response to the recognition that he has done something wrong in this sense, and the felt need to apologize or in some way to make up to the person for this wrong. Since Craig will violate a responsibility to someone no matter what, it is inescapable that he will have reason to feel pained by violating this responsibility. Feeling such pain is part of his recognition of the continuing reality of the responsibility, even if in this circumstance doing what is morally best prevented him from fulfilling it. It is also inevitable that he will have reason to feel the need to apologize or make up to someone. Even when acting for the best, such compensatory actions are expressions of his recognition of the enduring validity of the responsibility to the person he has neglected or harmed by so acting. In both cases, these feelings are part of his affirmation of the value of this person. They are manifestations of the belief that this person did not deserve to be neglected or injured by him in these ways.

That Craig finds it natural and appropriate to feel moral distress is thus explained by the fact that it *is* natural and appropriate. These feelings are not based on a mistaken understanding of his situation. Similar things may be said about other examples referred to in the phenomenological argument. Jennifer confronts the choice between turning her son John into the legal authorities for his criminal act and moving to another state, where she hopes a better environment will curb his quick temper and propensity for violence. She has a responsibility to John to provide for and protect him. But she also has a responsibility to her community to promote justice and prevent violence. Each of these responsibilities is grounded in the separate value of, respectively, her son and her community, and in her relationship to them. Since they conflict, whatever Jennifer does she will violate one of them, and for this reason she will have reason to feel moral distress no matter what.

Suppose she concludes that it is morally best to turn her son into the authorities. In so acting she is not abdicating her responsibility to him, but she is working directly against that responsibility. She has reason to be pained by failing to nurture and protect him on this crucial occasion, and to express that pain to him by way of apology or compensatory action. In a situation in which her relationship with him may well be in danger of collapse, these feelings and their expression are especially important forms of reaffirming that relationship. On the other hand, if she concludes that she ought to try to help her son by moving to another state, she is violating her responsibility to her old community to promote justice, and she is in jeopardy of violating her responsibility to her new community to prevent violence. These failures of social responsibility would also be cause for moral distress. These communities are not deserving of injustice and violence, and as a member of them Jennifer has responsibilities to prevent these things. Failing to act on these responsibilities is a reasonable basis for moral distress.

V. Wrongdoing and Objectivity

The "moral dilemmas" literature suggests a variety of critiques that might be made of this account. In this section I consider those objections that are likely to be prominent among those who reject RT. In the next section I look at some issues that may be raised by those who are sympathetic with it.

The first objection could be made by proponents of either ET or DT. They might agree that wrongdoing would be inescapable only if there were conflicting conclusions of moral deliberation and might go on to argue that there is nothing wrong per se with violating moral responsibilities as I understand them, and hence that I have not shown that wrongdoing in any sense is inescapable. Conee has expressed the intuition that gives force to this objection. What is at issue in the debate about "moral dilemmas," he says, is whether or not there are actions that "are both absolutely, unconditionally, and not merely prima facie morally obligatory, and absolutely, unconditionally, and not merely prima facie morally impermissible."[25] The implication is that there are only two categories that are relevant to the "moral dilemmas" debate: duties or obligations that are unconditional and absolute and those that are "merely prima facie." It would be wrong to violate an absolute and unconditional duty. But a prima facie duty is merely a claim "to be something that matters" morally.[26] Surely, it may be supposed, it cannot be wrong to violate this. Bringing this distinction to bear on the responsibilities to persons account, absolute and unconditional duties would correspond to conclusions of moral deliberation. The only thing moral responsibilities could correspond to are prima facie duties. Hence, there can be nothing wrong with violating a moral responsibility per se.[27]

The import of the responsibilities to persons account is to challenge the validity and usefulness of this exhaustive dichotomy. Conclusions of moral deliberation cannot conflict, and hence wrongdoing with respect to these is not inescapable. But moral responsibilities, though they are moral reasons for action, are not merely prima facie duties. Nor are they "rules of thumb" for the determination of actual duties. Moral responsibilities provide premises for deliberative conclusions, but their significance is not exhausted by their contribution to the deliberative process. In particular, a moral responsibility is not merely an appearance, which may or may not be veridical, of a sound deliberative conclusion. Even if, all things considered, the correct conclusion is to do an action A, it may remain the case, all things considered, that there is a responsibility to do a conflicting action B. There is nothing prima facie about the fact of this latter responsibility, and it is wrong to violate it.[28]

In ordinary usage, moral wrongdoing refers to a transgression or violation of some moral value. Since a moral responsibility constitutes a moral value, it is consistent with common usage to say that it is wrong to violate a moral responsibility. It is also consonant with the more specific notion that in wrongdoing there is someone or something wronged: A violation of a responsibility is typically a violation of a responsibility to some person or social entity. The claim that *only* a violation of a correct conclusion of moral deliberation is wrong *in any sense* is not a self-evident conceptual truth. It is an assumption of certain philosophical theories about morality. For these theories, if moral responsibilities are spoken of at all, either they are prima facie moral considerations that it is not per se wrong to violate, or else they coincide with sound conclusions of moral deliberation and so cannot conflict. The responsibilities to persons account questions the assumptions of these theories.

I will discuss some of these theories in the next two chapters. Here I want to focus on another way in which this objection may be expressed.[29] It might be said that there are several important connotations of 'wrongdoing' that are inappropriate with respect to the violation of a moral responsibility (at least when this does not coincide with a sound deliberative conclusion), and that for this reason it is misleading to speak of wrongdoing in this connection. In particular, there are many ordinary second- and third-person attitudes towards wrongdoing having to do with indignation, blame, and punishment that appear misplaced, if not outrageous, where wrongdoing is inescapable.[30] My response to this objection is twofold. First, even in the absence of moral conflict, wrongdoing in the sense of violating a deliberative conclusion does not necessarily justify these attitudes. Second, I am not claiming that every sense of 'wrongdoing' is inescapable. Nonetheless, with respect to inescapable transgressions of moral responsibilities, some of these attitudes are sometimes appropriate and some are not. But enough of them are appropriate that there is nothing untoward about speaking of wrongdoing in connection with these transgressions.

We think a person who has been wronged is typically justified in feeling indignation or outrage towards the person who has inflicted the wrong. But if what I have done is morally best, would the person who has been harmed or neglected by my action be justified in feeling indignation toward me? Oftentimes this person would have reason to feel that he or she did not deserve the harm or neglect, and it is neither unnatural nor unreasonable to feel anger towards the person who brought this undeserved outcome about. Such might be the case with both Roberto and the two girls in the example concerning Craig. In other cases, the harm or neglect may be deserved in itself, but not as inflicted by the person in question. Jennifer's son could hardly object to the fact that someone turned him into the authorities, but he might have reason to be angered by the fact that it was his mother who did. It is also important to recognize that in cases of wrongdoing where there is no moral conflict, we do not suppose indignation is always justified. Or we might say it is justified, but a more magnanimous person would not feel it. Moreover, even when it is justified, there may be reasons why it is not justified to express it. Various mitigating factors might lead us to withhold indignation, or its expression, when wronged—for example, if the wrongdoer had been abused, or had acted under great stress or grief, or had been well-intentioned but misguided. The fact that the wrongdoing was inescapable may itself be one such factor.

It is often said that persons who act wrongly deserve blame, either by those wronged or by knowledgeable third parties. Again, if what I have done is morally best, would others be justified in blaming me for failing to fulfill one of my responsibilities? It is widely supposed that more than wrongdoing is required for blame to be appropriate. For example, it is often said that there must also be reference to deficiencies in the person's character, motives or desires.[31] If in doing what is best I nonetheless violate some responsibility, it need not be the case that I have acted out of corrupt motives or evil desires. Insofar as blame requires this, it may not be justified. But the same may be said of transgressions of deliberative conclusions in the absence of moral conflict. Where appropriate psychological states are lacking, blame may not be warranted in these cases either.

Blame is typically taken to express some form of criticism for what a person has done. Sometimes the criticism is to the effect that the person should have acted otherwise. Such criticism is often appropriate when someone violates a correct deliberative conclusion, but it would obviously be inappropriate to think or say this of someone who violates a moral responsibility while doing what is morally best. Still, other forms of criticism may be appropriate in these cases, criticism having less to do with the action itself than with the attitude towards it. For example, it might be appropriate to expect me to take responsibility for what I have done, that is, to recognize that this action was *my* action and that it did violate one of *my* responsibilities. These are things I ought to acknowledge, and others may reasonably expect this of me. In addition, since I might have reason to apologize or make up to the person to whom I did not fulfill my responsibility, others might be justified in expecting such a response from me. In the case of Craig, he might be criticized if he justifiably stole the car and then took the attitude that the harm suffered by the girls was of no particular concern to him (or of no more concern than anyone else who knew about it), or if he failed to acknowledge the fact that he caused this harm, that they did not deserve it, that he regretted having to do it, and the like. Mitigating factors might lead us to withhold these judgments, or the expression of them. But this is true of all cases of wrongdoing, even those where there is no conflict.

Finally, it is sometimes said that wrongdoing warrants punishment. Does this mean that an unavoidable violation of moral responsibility would justify punishment no matter what? Some proponents of inescapable wrongdoing have claimed that there are extreme cases in which it would be justified to punish someone who does what is morally best.[32] This can easily seem incredible. But in some cases of civil disobedience, it might reasonably be said that someone who broke an unjust law did what is morally best (as a means of getting it changed, etc.) and yet ought to be punished because after all there is a moral and legal responsibility not to break the law. In fact, some who practice civil disobedience might be willing to accept this judgment (and perhaps also that, had they not broken the law, they would have been all the more deserving of punishment, say, by God). Likewise, we can imagine someone in Vere's situation who judged it morally best to set Billy free and yet accepted as justified his own punishment for dereliction of duty in doing so. Thus it does not seem inconceivable that punishment could be justified for those who do what is morally best.

Nonetheless, at least in the realm of personal morality, it is hard to see what the point or justification would be for punishing someone no matter which responsibility was violated. It seems both unfair and counterproductive to subject the person to such strictures, at least where these are understood to go beyond the pain the person would appropriately feel for being unable to fulfill a responsibility to someone. It is bad enough that the person would do something morally wrong no matter what. Why compound this by inflicting additional harm upon the person? However, it is again worthwhile to reflect on other cases of wrongdoing. Wrongdoing is a necessary condition for punishment, but it is not a sufficient one. In fact, it is only in rather special cases that we think in terms of punishing wrongdoers at all. If we know someone who tends to be unreliable, we do not typically look for ways to punish the person (of course, we may try to avoid him, but this is not the same as punishment).

In sum, where a person who does what is morally best nonetheless violates a moral responsibility, some of the typical implications of 'wrong' are appropriate and some are not. This is just what is to be expected from the responsibilities to persons account, for I have claimed that there is a sense of 'wrong' for which wrongdoing may be inescapable, but also that there is a sense of 'wrong' for which this is not possible. The two senses have overlapping meanings, but there is no reason to suppose they have exactly the same implications.

A very different critique of the responsibilities to persons account is suggested by the large number of arguments in the "moral dilemmas" literature to the effect that there cannot be genuine moral conflicts because morality would then lack objectivity. I will consider three versions of this objection. The most prominent and, if successful, most serious is the claim that moral conflicts render morality logically inconsistent. A set of statements is logically inconsistent when it implies both the affirmation and denial of the same thing. The responsibilities to persons account maintains that there are situations in which a person S has a responsibility to do A and a responsibility to do B even though S cannot do both A and B (hereafter a "conflict of responsibilities"). Taken by itself, there is nothing that such a conflict both affirms and denies. To show that it entails an inconsistency, it is necessary to invoke some additional principles, typically drawn from classical accounts of deontic logic.

The most common inconsistency argument depends upon versions of the agglomeration principle and the Kantian principle. I have already endorsed this argument with respect to conclusions of moral deliberation.[33] The question here is whether a sound version of the argument can be employed against the claim that there are conflicts of responsibilities. In this context, the agglomeration principle would state that, if S has a responsibility to do X and a responsibility to do Y, then S has a responsibility to do both X and Y. The Kantian principle would state that, if S has a responsibility to do X, then S can do X (where 'can' is defined as before). If these two principles were accepted, then a conflict of responsibilities would entail an inconsistency. But both should be rejected.

Consider the agglomeration principle first. If Katherine promises to marry Greg, she has a responsibility to do so. Suppose that Greg then disappears while mountain climbing and is presumed dead. Later Katherine promises to Michael, and hence she has a responsibility to marry him. Then, the week of the wedding, Greg returns (having been rescued and brought back to health over a long period of time by natives of the Himalayas).[34] In a situation such as this Katherine might well have a responsibility to marry each person. Each would have compelling reason to feel that he was entitled to this. But for any number of reasons it would not follow that she would have a responsibility to marry both (for example, her conception of marriage might exclude polygamy, so that to "marry" both would be to marry neither).[35]

With respect to the Kantian principle, it is one of the basic features of the responsibilities to persons account that we cannot always fulfill our responsibilities. It is true that a person's responsibilities can generally be fulfilled, that they are the sort of thing that human beings typically can do and that this particular person ordinarily can do. Our capacities are one of the conditions by reference to which we come to have responsibilities in the first place. But it does not follow that what is needed to fulfill a responsibility can be done on each and every occasion. It is not necessary to consider moral conflicts to see this. There are numerous cases, common in the literature, that give reason to reject the Kantian principle as applied to moral responsibilities. For example, I may have a responsibility to make my car payment but be unable to do so because I have been laid off from work. Or through forgetfulness I may put myself in a position where I am unable to return something when promised. In cases such as these, the responsibility may well remain even though I cannot fulfill it.[36]

Similar responses may be made to versions of the inconsistency objection employing other principles. I will briefly consider one more prominent example. In its usual formulation, this argument employs two principles concerning some purported logical implications of 'ought'.[37] As applied to moral responsibilities, the first principle would state that, if S has a responsibility to do X and S cannot do both X and Y, then S has a responsibility not to do Y. The second principle would state that, if S has a responsibility to do X, then it is false that S has a responsibility not to do X. If these principles were accepted, then a conflict of responsibilities would entail an inconsistency. From the fact that S has a responsibility to do A and S cannot do both A and B, it follows by the first principle that S has a responsibility not to do B. But if S has a responsibility to do B, then according to the second principle, it is false that S has a responsibility not to do B. Hence, it is both affirmed and denied that S has a responsibility to do B. Since the argument is valid, the question is whether or not to accept the principles entailing this conclusion.

The first principle has some odd results, but I will not challenge it here.[38] It is sufficient to see that the second principle should be rejected. To see why, return to the example of Katherine's two promises to marry. According to this principle, if she has a responsibility to marry Michael, then it is false that she has a responsibility not to marry him. However, when Greg returns, he might reasonably say, "You promised to marry me, and that means you have a responsibility not to marry anyone else." So she does have a responsibility not to marry Michael. Therefore, it cannot be a logical implication of her responsibility to marry him that it is false that she has a responsibility not to do so.

It may be objected that here and earlier this example begs the question because it involves an alleged case of conflicting responsibilities. Instead of rejecting these principles, it might be claimed, we should reject conflicts of responsibilities because we already have reason to accept these principles. But these principles do not come to us with a warranty saying "valid a priori." Nor does the fact that they may be valid with respect to other moral concepts, such as 'ought' in conclusions of moral deliberation, show that they are valid here. As is the case with many deontic principles, whatever reason we have for accepting or rejecting them depends on their intuitive plausibility as applied to particular cases. For both principles (the one just considered and agglomeration), the relevant cases to consider naturally include those that have at least the potential for conflict. If, as I have argued, we have reason to think moral responsibilities can conflict, then that may provide us with a reason for rejecting these principles. These are the sorts of considerations upon which such principles are to be judged.

There is no convincing reason, then, to think that a conflict of responsibilities entails a logical inconsistency, for there is reason to reject the principles that are required to show this. Still, a conflict of responsibilities does constitute a practical inconsistency, meaning simply that the responsibilities cannot both be fulfilled.[39] It might be thought that, even in the absence of logical inconsistency, there is something problematic about moral values which are practically inconsistent. But this is a different kind of objection, one not directly concerned with objectivity. I will return to it in chapter 9.

The second form of the objectivity critique is the claim that genuine moral conflicts are incompatible with moral realism. This claim is not always presented as an objection. Indeed, for Williams, whose arguments are the focal point of most discussion of this issue, moral realism is rejected because it cannot account for moral conflicts.[40] But for the friends of realism, if a doctrine concerning moral conflicts were incompatible with realism, then that would constitute an objection to that doctrine. In any case, my aim here is not to argue for or against moral realism, but to consider whether the thesis that there are conflicts of responsibilities is compatible with it. I will argue that there is no reason to think it is not.[41]

For the purpose of this discussion, I will understand moral realism to be the view that there are mind-independent moral facts in virtue of which each moral judgment is either true or false (and not both). What needs to be considered, then, is whether when a person cannot do both A and B, the judgments that the person has a responsibility to do A and a responsibility to do B are precluded from both being true in this realist sense.[42] It is hard to see what basis there is for supposing this, at least once it is recognized that these judgments are distinct from conclusions of moral deliberation and that they are logically consistent.

After stating the phenomenological argument, Williams declares that realist theories cannot "do justice to the facts of regret" since "they eliminate from the scene the *ought* that is not acted upon." For these theories, Williams says, "since it is just a question of which of the conflicting *ought* statements is true, and they cannot both be true, to decide correctly for one of them must be to be rid of error with respect to the other."[43] In a companion essay, he says that for the moral realist, "moral judgments being straightforwardly assertions, two inconsistent moral judgements cannot both be true," and so "one of them must be rejected."[44] It is not clear why Williams thinks that, for the realist, the conflicting *ought* statements "cannot both be true." If these statements entailed a *logical* inconsistency, then the realist would hold that at least one must be false. But Williams rejects the agglomeration principle precisely in order to avoid the objection that conflicting *ought* statements entail a logical inconsistency, and in the second essay he defines the relevant notion of inconsistency as practical inconsistency. Hence he appears committed to the view that moral conflict must be interpreted in such a way as to avoid logical inconsistency. Since this is equivalent to showing why both *ought* statements can be true, it is difficult to see why Williams supposes his position is incompatible with realism. As he interprets moral conflict, it would seem that the realist would have no reason to reject it.[45]

The consideration underlying Williams's claim is his comparison of conflicting moral statements with conflicts of factual belief and conflicts of desire. The reason the realist cannot account for regret, he says, is because "a structure appropriate to conflicts of belief is projected on to the moral case."[46] Williams had argued that, whereas the resolution of conflicting beliefs requires the abandonment of one of the beliefs, the resolution of both conflicting desires and conflicting *oughts* does not require the abandonment of one element of the conflict: The desire or *ought* that is not acted upon may persist as a "remainder." It may be that his thought is that, since realism is the correct account of factual beliefs but is not the correct account of desires, this comparison provides a reason for rejecting realism in the moral case.

Support for this interpretation may be found in a related argument in the companion essay. This argument is based on the distinction between theoretical and practical discourse, and the contrasting roles played by the relevant concept of consistency in each. Williams takes theoretical discourse to aim at statements that "fit the world." For this reason, there is an overriding requirement that these statements be logically consistent, since the world cannot contain inconsistent states of affairs. But for practical discourse, the goal is the opposite: It aims for statements (in particular, imperatives) "which the world has to fit." In this case, practical consistency is "a general requirement," but its justification is "pragmatic" (having to do with the need for action) and may "admit of exceptions."[47] Hence, while in practical discourse practically inconsistent statements can be supported by "the best possible reasons," in theoretical discourse logically inconsistent statements cannot be supported by such reasons. In the former case, we have to decide what to do, but this decision does not entail a rejection of one of the conflicting statements. These may continue as a remainder. For Williams, the mistake of the moral realist is to assimilate practical discourse to theoretical discourse, and the evidence of this mistake is the inability to account for remainders.

In these arguments, Williams is right to emphasize the distinctions between theoretical discourse and practical discourse, between factual beliefs on the one hand and desires and *oughts* on the other.[48] These distinctions are relevant to the issue of remainders. But they are not relevant in a way that bears directly on the question of moral realism. In theoretical reasoning we strive for conclusions that are logically consistent because our goal is to understand the world and we suppose the world cannot contain logically inconsistent states of affairs. Logical consistency is an exceptionless requirement of theoretical reasoning.[49] In practical reasoning, moral or otherwise, we seek conclusions that are practically consistent because we cannot perform incompatible actions. Insofar as we are aiming at conclusions that constitute intentions to act, there are no exceptions to this requirement either. So far, these differences have no bearing on the question of remainders.

The remainders issue arises because of the following further difference between theoretical and practical reasoning. The former aims at understanding the world, and (except insofar as it is taken to be subservient to practical interests) it has no other concern. Hence, once we have reached correct theoretical conclusions, they will be logically consistent, and there will be no room left for conflicting factual beliefs. In theoretical reasoning, the resolution of conflicting beliefs does not leave behind any level of residual conflict: The rejected belief is declared *tout à fait* false.[50] On the other hand, in practical reasoning our aim is to do what is best, but this is not our only concern. Striving to do what is best presupposes a prior commitment to what I will refer to, with intentional vagueness, as value. Hence, our primary concern is the promotion of value. On this basis we try to do what is best. This distinction does not entail remainders, but it makes them possible.

The example of desires suggests one area in which practical reason can leave remainders. Here our first concern is to fulfill our desires, and on this basis we decide what is best to do. But what is best to do may not fulfill all our desires. Hence, though conclusions of practical reason must be practically consistent, the determination of these conclusions leaves room for a residual layer of conflict: In doing what is best there may remain desires that are unfulfilled. Statements of what we desire may be practically inconsistent, both with each other and with conclusions about what is best to do. Even here, however, remainders are not guaranteed. We may suppose the Stoic to desire only what can be achieved: The prior concern to fulfill desire is defined by reference to the possibility of its achievement.

Whether there are remainders in the moral case, and how they are understood, will depend on our conception of moral value. On any account, our primary concern is to achieve moral value, and on this basis we determine what is morally best to do. If doing what is best can infringe upon some of what is morally valuable, this will be because moral value is conceived independent of the possibility of its achievement. The responsibilities to persons account is an example of such a view. On this account, though conclusions of moral deliberation must be practically consistent, statements of our moral responsibilities may be practically inconsistent, both with one another and with deliberative conclusions. On the other hand, if (analogous to the aforementioned Stoic) moral value is defined by reference to the possibility of its achievement, so that there is nothing of moral value that cannot be achieved, then moral remainders are ruled out. Some normative theories appear to understand moral value in this way.

While theoretical reason excludes the possibility of remainders, practical reason leaves it open. Whether there are remainders in a given domain of practical reason will depend upon the understanding of value relevant to that domain. But this issue is separate from the question whether value should be given a realist interpretation. There is nothing in realism per se that excludes a conception of value such that what is valuable cannot always be fulfilled or respected. Statements of value that are prior to conclusions of practical reason may be practically inconsistent and still be given a realist interpretation. On the other hand, the antirealist is not compelled to embrace such a conception. Though Williams correctly emphasizes the difference between the theoretical and the practical with respect to remainders, he incorrectly connects this difference with realism. The moral realist need not mistakenly assimilate practical rationality to theoretical rationality. Moreover, even if we accept a realist account of factual beliefs and an anti-realist account of desires, the fact that there are remainders in the latter but not the former would not establish that, since there are remainders in moral judgments, we must give an antirealist account of them.

The final form of the objectivity critique concerns the nature of moral deliberation. It might be said that on the responsibilities to persons account deliberation is subjective, is made a matter of intuition or feeling, or is in some way lacking in rationality. This objection may be motivated by my rejection of the covering law model or by the fact that I have emphasized the particularity of moral responsibilities and have expressed skepticism about our ability to articulate these responsibilities in rules or principles. To some extent, I am prepared to acknowledge those "nonobjective" features that this critique attributes to my position, and to deny that these features are defects. If the covering law model is taken as definitive for moral rationality, then the responsibilities to persons account will appear defective. More generally, if it is supposed that moral deliberation must conform to an explicit decision-procedure or algorithm, then this approach is going to seem rather fuzzy. Still, there are several points worth making here in response.

First, the remainders view is not itself a thesis about how deliberation should proceed. On the other hand, there is an indirect connection between inescapable wrongdoing and deliberation since explanations of inescapable moral distress are typically associated with accounts of deliberation. While the covering law model presents an understanding of deliberation that effectively precludes inescapable wrongdoing, the responsibilities to persons account allows for inescapable wrongdoing, but suggests a very different picture of deliberation. Still, in developing this account, I was not attempting to give an explanation of how we should undertake moral deliberation. Rather, I was trying to sketch a way of thinking about morality that makes it possible to speak of inescapable moral wrongdoing while acknowledging that conclusions of deliberation cannot conflict. My primary concern was to show how moral responsibilities could have a life of their own, independent of conclusions of deliberation, such that the impossibility of conflict in the latter does not preclude the reality of conflict in the former.

Given what I have said, it is to a great extent a further question how deliberation should proceed on this approach. The rejection of the covering law model rules some things out, but many possibilities are left open. On the responsibilities to persons account, the aim of deliberation is first to determine what our responsibilities are and second to determine how best to fulfill them. I have urged that these may be complex issues, but that does not mean that deliberation is nothing more than some mysterious "intuition" about what to do. Though moral responsibilities cannot be fully articulated in general rules, it does not follow that there is no place in deliberation for general considerations. The method of reflective intuitionism itself imposes the constraint of logical consistency on moral reasoning. Moreover, there is nothing in this approach that suggests that some moral values are incomparable. It is compatible with this account that there are some kinds of actions that, as conclusions of deliberation, ought always or never to be done. It is also compatible with it that sometimes deliberative conclusions should be based on consequentialist reasoning. How "objective" deliberation might be on the responsibilities to persons account is thus a large question, one that a complete defense of this account would address. But it is not a question that I have attempted to deal with here.[51]

VI. Pluralism and Incomparability

So far I have considered objections that may be anticipated mainly from those who reject the idea inescapable moral wrongdoing. There are also objections that may be forthcoming from those who accept this idea. In particular, there are two theses that have been commonplace in defenses of "moral dilemmas" but have played no role in my argument: the claim that there is a plurality of kinds of moral values, and the claim that these values are sometimes incomparable. In my view, neither of these claims is necessary for inescapable moral wrongdoing. But I see no reason to deny the first claim, though it is sometimes interpreted in a way that I find unacceptable. On the other hand, as I have already argued, I see no reason to accept the second claim. Yet there is another concept, which I will refer to as "inconvertibility," that is necessary for inescapable wrongdoing and might be confused with incomparability.

The idea that some form of "moral dilemmas" is based on moral pluralism is quite widespread.[52] Moral conflicts in which wrongdoing is inescapable obviously require a plurality of something, since without plurality there can be no conflict. But the claim here goes beyond this truism. Moral pluralism, as ordinarily understood, is the view that there is a plurality of *kinds* of moral values that cannot be reduced to a single value. So understood, it is contrasted with moral monism, which claims that there is one ultimate moral value to which whatever apparent diversity of moral values there is may be reduced. Though there are many varieties of moral pluralism on the scene (concerning duties, obligations, rights, virtues, goods, ideals, etc.), the suggestion in these arguments is that different kinds of values may conflict, and that as a result some form of wrongdoing may be inescapable.

There are two issues here: whether moral pluralism is necessary for inescapable moral wrongdoing, and whether it is sufficient. Mark Platts has expressed one form of the argument for the common assumption that it is both necessary and sufficient. For monism, such as the view that the only moral property is goodness, it is hard to see how there could be real dilemmas. For on this view, "the only problem-case is that in which each of two possible actions shares to the same extent the property of being good." But these cases, Platts says, "are not true dilemmas." For pluralism, on the other hand, "there are *many* distinct ethical properties" such as loyalty and honesty, and these may conflict in "tortuous" or "deep" ways. Such conflicts are true dilemmas. Therefore, "moral dilemmas" can arise if and only if pluralism rather than monism is true.[53]

This argument is apparently plausible to many. In view of this and the frequent association of pluralism with defenses of "moral dilemmas," it is not surprising that some opponents of dilemmas have regarded it as important to criticize pluralism.[54] But pluralism is not necessary for inescapable moral wrong-doing as I understand it. It is possible for there to be a monist view in which there are conflicting responsibilities, because a single principle might generate conflicts when applied to different persons.[55] Platts's argument seems to acknowledge this but claims such a conflict would not be a "true dilemma." Whatever this might mean, conflicts generated by a single principle could support RT. For example, the principle to aid one's friends when in need could generate the responsibility to help this friend and the responsibility to help that friend when it is not possible to do both. Wrongdoing might then be inescapable, but the conflicting responsibilities would be based on the same moral principle. Moral pluralism is thus not required for inescapable moral wrongdoing in the sense of violating a moral responsibility no matter what.

It is true that my examples have typically involved a variety of moral values. By itself, this does not entail a commitment to pluralism, since a monist might argue that they can all be reduced to a single value. But I am skeptical of such monist arguments,[56] and I am prepared to grant that conflicting responsibilities often do involve irreducibly distinct kinds of moral values. Still, it is important to see that on my account it is not the fact that conflicting responsibilities involve distinct kinds of value that makes wrongdoing inescapable. Rather, it is the fact that they involve distinct responsibilities (which may or may not be of the same kind), responsibilities which are ordinarily to separate persons or social entities.[57]

It might be supposed that, even if moral pluralism is not necessary for inescapable moral wrongdoing, it does give an additional argument for inescapable wrongdoing (or perhaps supports a different form of inescapable wrongdoing). For example, suppose I were in a situation in which whatever I did I would either be dishonest or be disloyal. A moral pluralist might argue that whatever I do I will do something wrong, not necessarily or so much because I will violate a responsibility to some person, but simply because I will violate some kind of moral value, namely honesty or loyalty. On this account, the focus of wrongdoing is not on failing to fulfill responsibilities to persons, but on transgressing moral values.

In my view, this position is mistaken, though it is somewhat difficult to explain why. There is no problem speaking of values such as honesty and loyalty. These are useful general terms. The question is whether or not we should understand them, so to speak, in a "Platonic" or an "Aristotelian" way.[58] On the Platonic interpretation, being dishonest is wrong because it violates the value of honesty. It is not wrong, primarily if at all, because it violates a responsibility to some particular person. By contrast, on the Aristotelian interpretation, being dishonest is wrong only insofar as it violates a responsibility to some particular person. There is no value of honesty over and above our particular responsibilities to specific persons to be honest.

The responsibilities to persons account is Aristotelian in this sense. Wrongdoing, inescapable or otherwise, always involves a violation of a moral responsibility *to* some particular person, social entity, or what have you. Moral pluralism can be given an Aristotelian interpretation, and so understood I have no objection to it. But moral pluralism often seems to be taken in the Platonic way.

Moreover, the aforementioned argument for inescapable moral wrongdoing requires this reading. In order to be an argument for inescapable wrongdoing that is different than, or goes beyond, the argument I have given, wrongdoing must be understood Platonically—as transgressions of a value over and above violations of responsibilities to particular persons and the like.

This is a possible position, and it would support a doctrine of inescapable moral wrongdoing. But it is not my position. My objection to the Platonic view is similar to my objection to many of the views that reject inescapable moral wrongdoing altogether: It is an account of morality in which the central object of moral concern is some abstraction (in this case, a plurality of abstractions), and it thereby has the effect of displacing particular persons as objects of moral concern.[59] On the Platonic view, our main concern is to be true to the various moral values of honesty, loyalty, sincerity, and so on. Being true to these values has implications for how we deal with particular persons, of course. But our primary concern is to conform our lives to these values. We are concerned with specific persons only insofar as we are concerned with these values. In the language of responsibility, our immediate responsibility is to live up to these values. We have responsibilities to persons only indirectly, as a function of this.[60]

On the responsibilities to persons account, particular persons are our immediate objects of concern, and our only moral responsibilities are responsibilities to persons (and social entities, etc.). These responsibilities may conflict, and when they do wrongdoing in the sense of violation of responsibility is inescapable. Often the conflicting responsibilities will be of different kinds. But this has no special bearing on the issue of inescapable moral wrongdoing. It may be wrong to break a promise to a person whether this is done in order to help another person in need or simply to fulfill a promise to someone else.

There is another aspect to this issue. Moral pluralism is often combined with a thesis about incomparability: It is claimed that there is a plurality of moral values that are incomparable. Moreover, it is argued that it is the incomparability of these values that generates "moral dilemmas." For example, Nagel contrasts a conflict in which there is an "even balance" of "comparable quantities" with a "conflict between values which are incomparable." The former, he says, is "merely a difficult decision." But cases of the latter are "genuine dilemmas."[61] The suggestion is that it is not pluralism per se, but incomparability, that produces dilemmas.

I have already rejected arguments for incomparability as well as arguments for DT based on incomparability (see chapter, 3 sec. III). There may be types of values that are incomparable in the sense that it is not true that every token of one type bears the same comparison to every token of another type. But I am not convinced that there are conflicts between two particular responsibilities that are incomparable with respect to moral deliberation; for this would mean that in this situation, with reference to deciding what is morally best, it is true neither that the first is greater than the second, nor that the second is greater than the first, nor that they are equal. It may sometimes be difficult to know which of these is true, but that is different from saying that none of them is true. At any rate, my defense of inescapable moral wrongdoing does not depend on

an incomparability thesis of this sort. On my view, even if, say, the first responsibility is greater than the second, there may still be a sense in which it is wrong
to violate the second.

There is, however, another concept that is relevant to inescapable moral
wrongdoing—what I call "inconvertibility."[62] This is not the same as incomparability, though they may be confused with one another. To see this, first consider
two nonmoral examples. Suppose I have a choice between two investments. One
gives a return of $50,000 and the other gives a return of $100,000. In all other
respects (security, liquidity, etc.) they are the same. The second investment is
obviously the better choice. Not only is it the better choice, it is a choice that
gives me everything the first investment would ($50,000) and more (another
$50,000). Now suppose my investments have paid off and I am redecorating my
apartment. There is a space above the couch that needs to be filled, and two
paintings at Christie's have caught my eye, a Degas and a Kandinsky. Either
would be perfect for the room, but in entirely different ways. (The cost looks to
be about the same, and I do not regard paintings as investments, so the only
considerations are aesthetic.) Here too there may well be a better choice, the
Kandinsky let's say. Yet, unlike the first example, the Kandinsky does not give
me everything the Degas would, and more. Each painting creates an altogether
different room.

In each example, there is a better choice, and hence with respect to deciding
what to do, there is comparability. But what the first example has that the second lacks is convertibility. Choices are convertible when the better choice
results in no loss, when it provides everything that the poorer choice would have
provided, plus some. When choices are convertible, regret does not make sense
if one believes the best choice has been made (I cannot regret not having the
$50,000 from the first investment; in effect, I have that $50,000, plus $50,000
more).[63] By contrast, choices are inconvertible when the better choice still
results in a loss, when there is something that the poorer choice would have provided that is not provided by the better choice (Degas-pleasure, if you like).
When choices are inconvertible, it is possible to have regret without having any
doubt that one made the better choice. I may think, "I'm glad I took the
Kandinsky, but it's painful to think I let the Degas go."

On the responsibilities to persons account, moral choices in which wrongdoing is inescapable are analogous to the choice of paintings. They are choices in
which there is comparability but not convertibility. Suppose Craig decides to
steal the car in order to get help for his friend. He may have no doubt that this is
the better choice. Even afterward he may think, "I would do it again if need be."
Still, it is not the case that this choice does everything that the poorer choice
would have done, plus some. This choice involves stealing the car from the girls.
His other choice, to wait, would not have involved stealing the car at all. Hence,
the better choice does not fulfill all the responsibilities that the poorer choice
would have fulfilled and others besides. By fulfilling one responsibility, it violates another that would not have been violated had the poorer choice been
taken. For this reason, it is possible to feel moral distress even though there is

no doubt about having made the better choice. Craig can reasonably feel moral distress about stealing the car.[64]

Inescapable moral wrongdoing does require a doctrine of inconvertibility. But this should not be confused with incomparability. Insofar as defenses of inescapable moral wrongdoing have relied upon inconvertibility they are on sound footing. They do not need to claim that moral conflicts are incomparable, and in my view, there is no good reason to claim this. It may be objected that inconvertibility and incomparability go together, that if there is loss no matter what, then there can be no better choice (or even an evenly balanced choice). But the painting example—and a very large number of choices we make in life—shows that this is not so. There is no reason to deny that the Kandinsky may be the better choice, even though it fails to provide everything the Degas would have provided. For much that we value in life, it is reasonable to make comparative, practical judgments while acknowledging that the better choice involves some loss of value relative to the poorer choice.

It may also be objected that inconvertibility requires pluralism, and hence that inescapable moral wrongdoing requires moral pluralism. Inconvertibility does require a plurality of something, but it need not be a plurality of types. In the painting example, the choice might be between two paintings of the same type—two abstract works, two Kandinsky's, two Kandinsky's of his Bauhaus period, etc.— and inconvertibility would still be possible. In the moral case, a choice between conflicting responsibilities of the same type, say promises to two persons, may also be inconvertible: Keeping the promise to one person, even though the better choice, need not do everything that the poorer choice would have done, for it may do nothing to fulfill the promise to the other person. In moral conflicts, inconvertibility requires a plurality of responsibilities, but it does not require a plurality of types of responsibilities.

Notes

1. Much of the debate about "moral dilemmas" has concerned conceptual issues, or principles of deontic logic, where it has been assumed that the debate could be resolved without making commitments to specific normative outlooks. With respect to DT, this attitude is correct: At any rate, my prescriptivist argument against DT did not presuppose any particular normative position. But in order to make progress in the debate between RT and ET, normative accounts must be considered. In this connection, see Sayre-McCord 1986 and MacIntyre 1990.

2. There are, of course, many differences between the account of scientific explanation to which this term ordinarily refers and the model of moral theory I am about to describe. In particular, whereas in the former there is an inference from empirical law and particular empirical facts to a statement about what did or will happen (the explanandum), in the latter there is an inference from moral principle and particular empirical facts to a statement about what ought to be, or to have been, done (a deliberative moral conclusion). Nonetheless, there are sufficient similarities between the two to warrant the appropriation of the term 'covering law model' in this context.

3. For effective criticism of this preoccupation, see Stocker 1990, ch. 4.

4. The principle might be regarded as self-evident, as derived from nonmoral considerations, as implied by the nature of practical rationality, or even as an unjustified assertion. The covering law model includes all these approaches.

5. Though the reasoning from first principle and relevant facts to deliberative conclusion is generally thought to be deductive, it is acknowledged that the determination of the facts of the case and their relevance is not a matter of deduction but requires an empirical procedure and perhaps some form of "judgment."

6. In the last chapter I suggested that generalist accounts of moral deliberation, though not necessarily committed to the denial of RT, were nonetheless associated with critiques of the phenomenological argument that do reject RT. The covering law model is indicative of this association, though the point in the previous note about the role of judgment raises questions as to the extent to which the covering law model can avoid the reliance on intuition connected with particularist accounts.

7. I do not mean to preclude the possibility that other defenses of inescapable moral wrongdoing are viable, though I will be critical of one prominent defense in the last section of this chapter.

8. Insofar as those who make these concessions are merely stipulating that 'wrongdoing' only applies to a transgression of a correct conclusion of moral deliberation, the substance of their position may in fact not be far from RT. But I take it that they typically mean to say more than that RT is unsound by such stipulation.

9. In this connection, see Friedman 1991.

10. I discuss these issues in more detail in chapter 8, sec. III.

11. In this connection, see the discussion of the "concrete other" in Benhabib 1987.

12. However, I have benefited from the following discussions: Badhwar 1987; Blustein 1991, ch. 17; Nozick 1981, pp. 452–57; Nussbaum 1986, esp. ch. 6, and 1990, esp. ch. 13; and Vlastos 1973.

13. I discuss this in chapter 7, sec. V.

14. The issue here is different from that in my earlier discussion of the idea of incommensurability (see chapter 3, sec. III). There I was concerned with determining which action morally ought to be done. Here I am concerned with the more fundamental question of the way in which we take persons to be valuable.

15. Even in these situations, determination of the relevance of the concept of equality is a complex question. In the United States, persons from states with small populations have much more political power in the Senate than persons from states with large populations (since each state elects two senators regardless of size). Again, on account of the electoral college system, it is possible for the presidential candidate with a majority of the popular vote in the country to lose the election. Yet these phenomena are not widely believed to violate the principle of "one person, one vote."

16. Sophocles 1973, lines 568–70.

17. For this reason, from the perspective of moral experience it is incomprehensible to us that perfect duplicates could be made of persons. However possible this might seem theoretically, it is rejected out of hand from the practical standpoint. On the other hand, if there actually were duplicates of us, then we would be compelled to change our view about the replaceability of persons. This would make an enormous difference in our lives. But as things now stand, there is no reason to think this is possible. Interesting metaphysical questions are raised by this conception of a person. On the one hand, we do not want to say that a person is valuable merely in virtue of repeatable properties (otherwise the person would be replaceable). On the other hand, it would be a mistake to say that a person's

properties are irrelevant to the value of a person, or that what we value in a person is a "bare particular." Perhaps we should say that what we value in each person is that person's individual essence, the complex configuration of properties that constitutes the person, which configuration may never be instantiated elsewhere, though of course in various respects other persons may resemble it. In this connection, cf Plantinga 1974, ch. 5.

18. It might be supposed that it will take us some distance in understanding moral relations with complete strangers. Perhaps, but the idea of the "complete stranger" is really a limiting concept: No one with whom we have moral relations is truly a complete stranger, since there can be no moral relations with persons unless there is some connection with them. As long as there is some connection, the door is open to begin appreciating their unique value.

19. Of course, we may seek to change the possibilities of our social world, and sometimes we ought to. I do not mean to suggest an uncritical attitude towards social and political institutions. Still, the need and responsibility for such change, and the probability of success, is itself an unchosen feature of our social world. Moreover, no society can make possible every conceivable kind of human relationship. On this last point, see Hampshire 1983b.

20. What I call "chance" might be regarded by others as fate or providence. These are alternative interpretations of the large role of unchosen circumstance in human life. However interpreted, our relationships and concomitant responsibilities depend to a substantial extent on factors that are not a matter of choice.

21. Whether variations of the covering law model could adequately account for responsibilities to persons is considered in the next two chapters.

22. This would have to be qualified in the case of some social entities, such as organizations devoted to the preservation of wildlife or religious institutions in which the main point of the institution is worship of or service to a transcendent, nonhuman reality. In these cases, the social entity is united around a human interest, but it is an interest in something beyond human beings per se.

23. For congenial accounts of the role of rules in moral deliberation see Jonsen and Toulmin 1988; and Nussbaum 1990.

24. In this connection, cf. Bishop 1987, esp. pp. 11–16.

25. Conee 1982, p. 87. A similar point is made in 1989, p. 134.

26. Conee 1982, p. 89.

27. Arguments of this kind may be expressed in different ways. Thus it may be said, in a metaethical spirit, that real moral judgments have certain logical properties, such as prescriptivity, and that it is only wrong to violate judgments of this kind. Since statements of moral responsibility lack these properties, they are at best pseudo moral judgments and so it is not wrong to violate them. Or it might be said, in a Kantian vein, that genuine moral duties "necessitate" or "obligate." Only violations of these duties are wrong. Any other moral value, such as a moral responsibility, is a mere claim for consideration as a duty. This lacks practical necessitation, and hence there is nothing wrong with violating it. In this connection, cf. respectively Levi 1992, p. 824; and Herman 1990, pp. 312 and 315. My response to these arguments is that they are based on narrow conceptions of what counts as a "real" moral judgment or as "genuine" wrongdoing, conceptions we need not accept. I have already indicated the senses in which moral responsibilities are and are not prescriptive. I discuss Herman's position in chapter 8, sec V.

28. It is worth observing how conflicts between moral responsibilities relate to Sinnott-Armstrong's understanding of the "moral dilemmas" debate (see chapter 3, sec. V). They are clearly neither conflicts between his "overriding moral requirements" (which he

rightly regards as incoherent) nor conflicts between his "nonoverridden moral requirements" (since one responsibility may override another without precluding inescapable
moral wrongdoing). It might be supposed that they are simply conflicts between his
"(possibly overridden) moral requirements." Some of what he says about these conflicts
suggest that this is the correct interpretation. But he also says that the possibility of these
conflicts is relatively uncontroversial (1988, pp. 17 and 19), while I take conflicts of moral
responsibilities to be controversial, at least with respect to commonly accepted philosophical theories. Moreover, Sinnott-Armstrong defines a moral requirement in such a
way that an agent who violates one without justification or excuse is "liable to punishment" (1988, p. 13). I doubt whether this is always true of moral responsibilities, and I
have not defined them in this way. Conversely, I have said much about moral responsibilities that he does not say about moral requirements. Hence, conflicts of moral responsibilities have no precise equivalent in his typology of moral conflicts.

29. I am indebted to Jonathan Adler for emphasizing the importance of this form of
the objection.

30. The objection might be put this way: These attitudes are correlates of first person moral distress, and since they are unjustified, so too is this distress.

31. See Brandt 1958.

32. See Walzer 1973, pp. 178–80; and Nussbaum 1986, p. 41.

33. See chapter 4, secs. III—V. References to relevant literature may be found there
(see notes 19, 20, and 23). My acceptance of this argument as applied to DT was closely
related to intention-prescriptivism, the thesis that conclusions of moral deliberation
imply intentions to act. Since moral responsibilities are not prescriptive in this sense, this
argument as applied to conflicts of responsibilities can draw no direct support from my
claims in chapter 4.

34. This is a return engagement for Katherine et al. (see chapter 3, sec. III). The
example is not as improbable as it may seem. Many wives of MIAs in Vietnam later
remarried without being certain their husbands were dead.

35. I am here accepting the kind of counterexample to the agglomeration principle,
with respect to moral responsibilities, that I earlier rejected with respect to conclusions of
moral deliberation (see the final argument of chapter 4, sec. V).

36. I am again accepting the kind of counterexample to the Kantian principle, with
respect to moral responsibilities, that I earlier rejected with respect to conclusions of
moral deliberation (see the counterexamples concerning constraint in chapter 4, sec. IV).
Some of these cases might be construed as moral conflicts (thus it may be said that I can
either steal some money or miss the car payment). But this is not true in all cases. For
example, if a snowstorm prevents me from being best man in your wedding, there is no
moral conflict, but I cannot fulfill a moral responsibility nonetheless. In a case of this
kind, wrongdoing may be inescapable, but the wrong is not chosen. By contrast, in the
cases I have been concerned with, I choose to do something that is wrong, in the sense of
violating some moral responsibility, and I could have chosen to do something else that
would not have violated that responsibility, although it would have violated another. In
the wedding case, the wrong that is inescapable is not chosen at all. Rather, that wrong
will be committed no matter what I choose.

37. I mentioned a form of the argument in chapter 4, note 36.

38. For discussion of these, see Sinnott-Armstrong 1988, pp. 146–55.

39. Sinnott-Armstrong uses the terms "truth-inconsistency" and "act-inconsistency"
to mark a similar distinction (1988, pp. 170–78).

40. Williams's position is developed in 1973a and 1973b. For critical responses to

the anti-realist arguments in these essays see Foot 1983; Guttenplan 1979–80; Harrison 1979; Hurley 1985–86; Sinnott-Armstrong 1988, pp. 196–200; and Tännsjö 1985. Also in this connection see DeCew 1990; De Sousa 1974; Goldman 1988, pp. 140–44; Railton 1992, pp. 738–40; and Taylor 1989, ch. 3.

41. Santurri turns the argument around and claims that moral dilemmas *require* moral realism. The phenomenological argument, he says, "presupposes that the experiences in question have some normative foundation," and hence that the dilemmas view "will need at its foundation some form of moral realism" (1987, p. 66). His point is that a moral conflict would not be experienced as something making moral distress inescapable unless each side of the conflict were perceived as grounded in moral reality. Indeed, more recently Williams has written that "insofar as it is features of our moral experience that draw us towards ideas of the objectivity of ethics, the experience of moral conflict is precisely one that conveys most strongly such an idea" (1981c, p. 75). Nonetheless, Williams resists the realist intimations of this experience, and he is right to do so. If someone believes that whatever she does, she will violate a moral value to which she is deeply committed, this will be sufficient for her to have reason to feel moral distress no matter what. She need not accept moral realism. Firm personal commitment to the value could be enough. On Santurri's view, it seems that only persons who take themselves to be moral realists would have reason to feel guilt in any circumstance. This is implausible.

42. Of course, there might be reasons unrelated to conflict why these judgments cannot be true in a realist sense. My concern here is only with the question whether the fact that they can conflict speaks against realism.

43. Williams 1973a, p. 175.

44. Williams 1973b, p. 204.

45. Cf. Foot 1983, p. 391.

46. Williams 1973a, p. 175.

47. Williams 1973b, p. 203.

48. Levi, following Dewey's contention that the practical-theoretical distinction is untenable, argues that Williams's insistence on moral conflict "cuts off the possibility of inquiry" (1992, p. 826). It should be clear that my position, which concerns inescapable moral wrongdoing and not irresolvable moral conflicts, is not open to this charge.

49. Insofar as we regard our theoretical conclusions as provisional we may tolerate inconsistency. But we recognize that these conclusions cannot all be correct if they are inconsistent.

50. Harrison and Guttenplan challenge Williams by making room for, respectively, inconsistency and remainders among theoretical beliefs. In my view, these strategies are mistaken, and are not necessary to respond to Williams's claim that moral conflicts preclude realism.

51. For possible lines of development, see Jonsen and Toulmin 1988, ch. 13; and Nussbaum 1990, ch. 2. However, I do not completely endorse these approaches. For example, according to Nussbaum, "good deliberation is like theatrical or musical improvisation, where what counts is flexibility, responsiveness, and openness to the external; to rely on an algorithm here is not only insufficient, it is a sign of immaturity and weakness" (1990, p. 74). Though I see the point of this comparison, there are limitations to artistic improvisation as a model for moral deliberation. In part, this is because improvisation does not typically involve the degree and kind of intellectual reflection which is often appropriate in deliberation, but it is also because we are usually prepared to allow that a wide variety of very different improvisations of the same work may be done quite well, whereas we frequently think of moral deliberation as seeking *the* best course of action.

52. For example, see DeCew 1990; Hook 1974; Lemmon 1962; MacIntyre 1981, chs. 11 and 15; Nagel 1979c; Nussbaum 1986 and 1990; Paske 1990; Platts 1979, ch. 10; Taylor 1989, ch. 3; and Williams 1981c.

53. Platts 1979, p. 246. The second part of the argument requires not merely pluralism but the (plausible) assumption that different kinds of values do sometimes conflict.

54. For example, see Santurri 1987, pp. 66–76 and 100–101.

55. A similar point is made in Marcus 1980, p. 125.

56. For criticism of some of these arguments, see Stocker 1990, esp. chs. 6–8.

57. It is possible that they are to the same person. Suppose that I promised to be at your house by six o'clock and that I promised to prepare charlotte aux marrons glacés for dessert. If I could do one of these things, but not both, it might be said that I have conflicting moral responsibilities to the same person. (The possibility of such an example was pointed out to me by Paolo Annino.)

58. I am referring here to the (commonly assumed) difference between Plato and Aristotle on the ontology required for general terms. I do not mean to invoke other differences concerning their moral philosophies.

59. I discuss this objection more in the next two chapters.

60. In a sympathetic exposition of Aristotle, Nussbaum writes, "each friend is to be cherished for his or her sake, not simply as an instantiation of the universal value, friendship" (1990, p. 82). This seems right, but even here the implication is that there is a value, friendship, to which we ought to be true, over and above the value of particular friends and friendships. It is this surplus value of friendship which I question. In this connection, cf. Stocker 1976.

61. Nagel 1979c, p. 128.

62. This is similar to the second sense of 'incommensurability' distinguished in chapter 3, sec. III.

63. Of course, I may regret not being able to find an investment with a $150,000 return, but that is not regret with respect to my choice relative to the options available to me.

64. When comparable choices are equal in value, there can also be inconvertibility: Whatever one does there will be some loss relative to the other possibility.

7

Utilitarian Critiques of
the Phenomenological Argument

In the last chapter I argued that the responsibilities to persons account shows how inescapable feelings of moral distress can be reasonable responses to situations in which a form of moral wrongdoing is inescapable. My argument was that this account provides a good explanation of these feelings, and hence that it gives us a good reason to accept the remainders view. But the phenomenological argument also requires that this be a better explanation than alternatives, in particular those that purport to give a good account of these feelings while denying the possibility of inescapable moral wrongdoing. Most of these explanations are rooted in the utilitarian or Kantian traditions.[1] I consider utilitarian critiques in this chapter and Kantian ones in the next. In each case, I argue that these critiques are unconvincing, both in their theoretical understanding of moral obligation and moral conflict and in their explanation of inescapable feelings of moral distress. I also suggest that, different as these traditions are, there are some similarities in the ways they go wrong.

I. Utilitarian and Kantian Explanations
of Inescapable Moral Distress

It will help to begin with some general and intuitive observations about the utilitarian and Kantian approaches. Both are associated with the covering law model. Utilitarians and Kantians commonly suppose that there is an abstract, first principle—such as the greatest happiness principle or the categorical imperative—which, in conjunction with factual premises, entails particular conclusions of moral deliberation, conclusions that cannot conflict. It would obviously be a mistake to say that every utilitarian and Kantian moral philosopher accepts this model as I have defined it. But many do accept it, or accept something close to it, and it provides a helpful reference point for beginning discussion and drawing attention to pertinent issues.

The claim of the covering law model that conclusions of moral deliberation cannot conflict—that is, that DT is false—is not what is here in question. RT acknowledges that these conclusions cannot conflict. The issue lies elsewhere. What RT claims is that, though these conclusions cannot conflict, there is nonetheless a significant form of moral conflict such that wrongdoing in some sense may be inescapable. On my account, there are responsibilities to persons which may conflict. When they do, deliberation establishes what all things considered is morally best to do. But this conflict-free conclusion does not necessarily eliminate the overridden responsibility. This responsibility may persist, and when it does failure to fulfill it is wrong.

The covering law model declares that there are no genuine moral conflicts and hence that there is no sense in which wrongdoing may be inescapable. It is often claimed that there is a place for secondary moral principles that are intermediate between the first principle and deliberative conclusions, and it is allowed that these secondary principles may create the appearance of moral conflict. But these principles are interpreted in such a way that there is only appearance. For example, they are regarded as guidelines for applying the first principle, guidelines that may conflict but that have no moral force in themselves. Or they are thought of as corollaries of the first principle, which improperly formulated may conflict but which correctly formulated may not. In these and other ways, both utilitarian and Kantian theories attempt to account for the appearance of moral conflict while denying its reality. Moreover, this appearance is often instrumental in critiques of the phenomenological argument: It is the appearance of conflict that is said to explain inescapable moral distress. As a result, such distress is often regarded as involving a mistake. This line of thought is a persistent theme in utilitarian and Kantian critiques.

It is important to observe at the outset how this contrasts with the responsibilities to persons account. On the covering law model, the primary concern is to establish a conflict-free deliberative conclusion on the basis of the first principle. To the extent that conflict enters this picture, it is in the form of an appearance in the intermediate zone between first principle and deliberative conclusion. On the responsibilities to persons account, we start with responsibilities that have the potential for conflict. These responsibilities are not some epiphenomena that may surface in the deliberative process. They are the substance of ethical life. When they conflict, deliberation is required to determine what is morally best to do, and this deliberation must result in a conflict-free conclusion. But the aim of such deliberation is to determine how best to fulfill these responsibilities. It does not assume that one of them is really just an appearance. Hence, the fact that one responsibility is overridden in deliberation is not taken to mean that it is not a responsibility at all.

The logic of the covering law model leads us to suppose that there is really only one moral responsibility: to act on the conclusion of moral deliberation. This precludes genuine moral conflict. But it does so at a price, for this understanding of responsibility makes responsibilities to persons at best a secondary phenomenon. Our primary responsibility is to act as the first principle directs. Insofar as this principle requires us to treat a particular person in a certain way, we might be said to have a responsibility to that person, but not otherwise. Responsibilities to persons have no life of their own. This conception of moral responsibility is a recurrent feature of both utilitarian and Kantian moral theories.

It would obviously be incorrect to say that these theories do not require us to be concerned with persons. What is correct to say is that, in different ways, they have a tendency to displace persons as direct objects of moral concern. On the responsibilities to persons account, what is primary is that we have a plurality of responsibilities to concrete persons (social entities and the like) with whom we are connected. But on these theories we have only one responsibility, to act as the first principle directs, and this responsibility is not to specific persons as such but to something else that, by comparison with actual human beings, is an abstraction—an abstract entity or a law, for example. For utilitarians we are to act for the maximization of the goodness of, as Mill puts it, "the whole sentient creation," while on the Kantian view we are to act out of respect for "the moral law." Our fundamental moral relation is, respectively, with the sentient universe and with the moral law. It is not with particular persons. Our only real moral responsibility is to maximize the good of sentient creation or to act out of respect for the moral law.

Of course, these theories do not deny that there is a sense in which we have moral responsibilities to persons. But these person-directed responsibilities are derivative and contingent phenomena: Correctly understood, they can be reduced to our only actual moral responsibility, which is to act on the basis of the first principle. In a given case, my moral responsibility to this person turns out to be nothing more than what is required to fulfill my moral responsibility to sentient creation or to act out of respect for the moral law. My primary concern is to fulfill this latter responsibility.

The displacement of persons in these theories goes hand in hand with the rejection of moral conflict. The same procedure is at work in both considerations. By supposing our one and only moral responsibility to be the responsibility with regard to sentient creation or the moral law, to be the responsibility to act as directed by the first principle enunciating these abstract requirements, at one and the same time moral conflict is precluded and persons are displaced as direct objects of moral concern.

It may be objected that these theories are not directing us to be responsible to some abstraction that is not a person. Rather, they are giving us an account in terms of this abstraction of what our responsibilities to persons should be. There is a sense in which this is true. Yet, as an account of what our responsibilities should be, these theories are inadequate. Our responsibilities have their basis in our concrete relationships with particular persons, not in our relationship with the whole of sentient creation or the moral law. It might be supposed that, though our responsibilities have their origin in these concrete relationships, they should nonetheless be constrained by the more fundamental requirements of one or the other of these theories. But since these theories assume genuine moral conflict to be impossible, the effect of such constraints is to substantially simplify and reduce our responsibilities to persons, and thereby to truncate our relationships with them. We will have no reason to accept such constraints unless we regard our primary responsibility as being to something such as sentient creation or the moral law. In other words, these constraints are reasonable only if we endorse a perspective from which persons are displaced as direct objects of moral concern.[2]

This critique does not imply that these theories have no value as methods of deliberation. RT grants that deliberative conclusions cannot conflict and does not by itself imply a definite method of deliberation for establishing these conclusions. The responsibilities to persons account is more determinate and is suspicious of the idea that there is a single, general method of moral deliberation. But this is compatible with acknowledging that there are aspects of these theories, taken as strategies of deliberation, that may be accepted. In particular, some dimensions of Kantian moral theory, with its emphasis on respect for persons as ends in themselves, have a natural affinity with the responsibilities to persons account.

In the last chapter I noted that, though moral pluralism is often associated with defenses of inescapable moral wrongdoing, it is not playing a part in my defense of the remainders view. The other side of this point is that the fact that utilitarian and Kantian theories (as typically understood) are forms of moral monism is not the reason they are problematic. Monism per se does not preclude moral conflict, and it is not the monist aspect of these theories by itself that makes wrongdoing avoidable. Moreover, the feature of these theories to which I have objected, their tendency to displace persons as direct objects of moral concern, is also a feature of some pluralist theories and is no less objectionable there. My critique of utilitarianism and Kantianism does not directly concern the pluralism-monism debate. Rather, it concerns the particular form of monism exhibited by these theories.

I now turn to a detailed discussion first of utilitarianism and then of Kantianism. In each case, I argue that there are theoretical difficulties centering on the displacement of persons as objects of direct moral concern as well as related phenomenological inadequacies resulting from the attempt to explain inescapable moral distress in terms of moral conflicts that have the status of mere appearance. Yet there is a difference in my response to these two theories. While utilitarianism is fundamentally flawed, there is a dimension of truth in Kant.

II. The Act-Utilitarian Rejection of Inescapable Moral Wrongdoing

Utilitarians who have discussed "moral dilemmas" have almost always argued against the idea of inescapable moral wrongdoing. This is not surprising. The utilitarian understanding of morality is essentially at odds with the normative outlook suggested by the remainders view, and especially with the responsibilities to persons account of this view. To see this, it is helpful to begin with the act-utilitarian thesis according to which the moral rightness of an action requires the maximization of the overall goodness of persons, where the good of each person counts equally. Though most utilitarians defend a more complex theory than this, act-utilitarianism is nonetheless the benchmark by reference to which these theories are developed. On this account, it may be said that an action X is morally wrong if and only if there is an available alternative action Y that has better overall consequences for persons than X. For the act-utilitarian, in order for wrongdoing to be inescapable, it would have to be the case that, whatever the agent did, he or she could have done something else with better consequences. But this is impossible, since there is always some action the agent could take such that no available alternative action would have better consequences.[3] There could be two or more conflicting actions, each of which had equally good consequences and each of which did not have an available alternative action with better consequences. But in this case, so long as the agent did at least one of these actions, the agent would do nothing wrong (since there would be no available alternative action with better consequences).[4] Therefore, moral wrongdoing cannot be inescapable.

It is important to recognize what it is about act-utilitarianism that generates this conclusion, for several of the most important features of act-utilitarianism are not sufficient by themselves to eliminate the possibility of inescapable moral wrongdoing. In particular, consequentialism, maximization, and impartiality are each compatible, and indeed are collectively compatible, with a form of inescapable moral wrongdoing. Consider, for example, the claim that moral rightness requires the maximization, not of the good of persons as a whole, but of the good of each person taken individually (where it is equally important to maximize the good of each person). In other words, for each person, we are morally required to do everything possible to maximize the good of that person. On this view, an action X is morally wrong if and only if there is an available alternative action Y which has better consequences *for someone* than X does. Since it will virtually always be the case that, no matter what is done, an agent could have done something else with better consequences for someone, this doctrine makes moral wrongdoing nearly always inescapable. So it is not act-utilitarianism's consequentialist, maximizing, or impartial features per se that rule out inescapable moral wrongdoing.

What does rule it out is act-utilitarianism's additional commitment to the idea that it is the good of persons as a whole, and of nothing else, that is to be maximized. According to the act-utilitarian, we have one and only one moral responsibility: to maximize the good of all human beings taken collectively. It is because act-utilitarianism makes the good of the aggregate of individual persons the only object of responsibility that wrongdoing can always be avoided. Since there is only one thing—the good of the whole—to maximize and since there is always some available action such that no other available action would result in a greater good for the whole, no conflicting requirements can be derived from the act-utilitarian principle. Any form of inescapable moral wrongdoing is precluded.[5] Moreover, this same feature of act-utilitarianism results in the displacement of persons as direct objects of moral concern. Since our responsibility is only to maximize the good of the whole, we do not have responsibilities to particular persons as such. It is true that, in order to maximize the good of the whole, we will typically be required to benefit this or that person. But this does

not mean we have a responsibility to the person in question. It means that bene-
fiting this person is the best means in the current situation of fulfilling our
responsibility to the aggregate of persons to maximize its good. We do not have
responsibilities to specific persons. We have responsibilities with respect to specific persons. And even these latter responsibilities are completely derivative and
contingent phenomena. They can be reduced without loss to the responsibility
to maximize the good of the whole. In comparison with our concrete experience
of particular persons, the aggregate of persons is an abstraction. For the act-utilitarian our only moral responsibility is to maximize the good of this abstraction.

Though the normative outlook of act-utilitarianism is fundamentally
opposed to that needed for inescapable moral wrongdoing as I understand it,[6]
this outlook does not by itself provide a critique of the phenomenological argument for RT, since it does not explain our intuitions about inescapable moral
distress. In fact, act-utilitarianism is in so many respects so far removed from the
ordinary understanding of morality that it has little hope of explaining many of
our moral intuitions. Virtually no one approaches each choice with the aspiration to act so as to produce the maximum goodness in human beings taken in
the aggregate. For this reason, act-utilitarianism is regarded by some, not as giving an account of ordinary moral thought, but as offering a radical critique of it.
This is one source of the suspicion, so frequent among utilitarians, of any
methodology that gives epistemic value to moral intuitions.

On the other hand, though nearly all those in the utilitarian tradition propose some reforms of commonsense morality, many have not regarded utilitarianism as radically undermining that morality. They have argued instead that a
utilitarian moral theory, usually with more complexity than act-utilitarianism
but with recognizable connections to it, can account for much of the shape of
the ordinary understanding of morality while providing a basis for reforming
certain aspects of that understanding. Utilitarians engaged in this enterprise
have been extraordinarily resourceful in attempting to show how, despite
appearances to the contrary, some formulation of utilitarianism can account for
the intuitive features of ordinary moral thought. The premier classical contribution to this project is Mill's *Utilitarianism*. In recent years the project has been
carried forward with renewed vigor in Hare's *Moral Thinking*. Each of them
suggests a critique of the phenomenological argument. That is, each proposes
an account that explains why, given the truth of utilitarianism, the idea of
inescapable moral wrongdoing is likely to appear correct even though it is in fact
mistaken. In this way, utilitarianism purports to better explain intuitions about
inescapable moral distress than RT does and thereby to refute the phenomenological argument.

In the remainder of this chapter, I evaluate the arguments of Mill and Hare.
With respect to the issue at hand, these two figures are especially important. In
addition to being central representatives of the utilitarian tradition, through
their attempt to reconcile utilitarianism with ordinary moral life, they each
directly address questions pertaining to moral conflicts and the topic of
inescapable moral wrongdoing. More so than other classical utilitarians, Mill is
especially sensitive to the issue of conflict in morality. Among contemporary

utilitarians, Hare engages the "moral dilemmas" debate in greater depth and detail than anyone else. Though their approaches differ from one another in several respects, there is a common theme in their critiques of the phenomenological argument. I proceed by first explaining their positions separately, and then evaluating them together.

III. Mill's Critique of the Phenomenological Argument

Writing more than a century and a quarter ago, Mill was not in a position to speak about "moral dilemmas" precisely in the terms of the recent debate. In his discussions of moral conflicts, it is the nineteenth-century intuitionists with whom he is mainly concerned—and concerned to oppose. Yet much of what Mill says about moral conflicts is surprisingly relevant to contemporary discussions. Indeed, it is possible to reconstruct from his remarks a response to the phenomenological argument.

There has been considerable controversy among scholars of Mill about the proper understanding of his utilitarianism. Much of this controversy has concerned the place of moral rules in Mill's account, and in particular the question whether he is best read as an act-utilitarian or a rule-utilitarian.[7] My own view is that he is most plausibly understood as accepting a form of rule-utilitarianism.[8] But to some extent it is a matter of convenience that I present Mill in this way. For much of what is important in my discussion is compatible, *mutatis mutandis*, with other interpretations. In any case, it is beyond the scope of my present concerns to defend a complete interpretation of Mill, and I hope as much as possible to circumvent points of interpretation about which there is dispute. My main interest is in evaluating the position suggested by Mill's comments on moral conflicts. It is a further question whether this position can be reconciled with other statements made by Mill.[9]

There is no doubt that Mill asserted the following theses in *Utilitarianism*: There are rules stating our moral obligations; the justification of these rules must be based, in some way, on the principle of utility (and nothing else); in most cases morality requires us to simply follow these rules, but these rules may conflict with one another, and when this happens, the resolution of the conflict must be based, in some way, on the principle of utility (and nothing else); finally, to say that a person's action is morally wrong implies that the person ought to be punished. The interpretation of each of these theses has occasioned disagreement. But my main concern is with what Mill says about conflicts of moral rules and the relationship between wrongness and punishment.

Mill makes a point of insisting that, in some sense, there are moral conflicts. Every moral doctrine that has been accepted by "sane persons," he says, acknowledges "as a fact in morals the existence of conflicting considerations." There is no moral system, he continues, in "which there do not arise unequivocal cases of conflicting obligation."[10] Indeed, *Utilitarianism* is replete with discussions of moral conflicts.[11] The question for Mill is how these conflicts are to be understood. His central claim is that one of the main advantages of utilitarianism over intuitionism is that, by making the greatest happiness principle the foundation of morality, it provides "an ultimate standard to which conflicting rights and duties can be referred."[12] Mill declares this principle to be "that actions are right in proportion as they tend to promote happiness; wrong as they tend to produce the reverse of happiness,"[13] and he makes it clear that what counts is the happiness, not only of persons, where the happiness of each counts equally, but of "the whole of sentient creation."[14]

According to Mill, "if utility is the ultimate source of moral obligations, utility may be invoked to decide between them when their demands are incompatible."[15] He offers the following example.[16] Adherence to the rule that we ought not to lie has great utility. But "even this rule, sacred as it is, admits of possible exceptions." We ought to lie "when the withholding of some fact . . . would save an individual . . . from great and unmerited evil, and when the withholding can only be affected by denial." The suggestion is that there is an obligation not to lie and an obligation to protect persons from substantial undeserved harm, each obligation being justified by utility.[17] When these obligations conflict, one of them must admit of an exception, in this case the former. This resolution is itself to be determined on utilitarian grounds. "If the principle of utility is good for anything," Mill concludes, "it must be good for weighing these conflicting utilities against one another and marking out the region within which one or the other preponderates."

In short, for Mill rules (or obligations) are an essential part of morality. These rules are warranted by utility, and when they conflict, this is to be resolved by utility.[18] It is reasonable to suppose that Mill believes every conflict can be so resolved and hence that he rejects DT. This is the tacit assumption in his polemic against intuitionism. It is less straightforward to ascertain Mill's position with respect to RT. Whether he believes there are conflicts of obligations in which, whatever the agent does, the agent will do something morally wrong in some sense, depends on what he thinks about an obligation that conflicts with and is overridden by another obligation. If for Mill the overridden obligation remains in force, then the way may be open for an endorsement of RT. On the other hand, if he believes that the overridden obligation does not remain in force, that when it is overridden it is not a genuine obligation, then he is effectively rejecting RT. According to L. W. Sumner, Mill's position regarding the resolution of conflicting obligations is that, "in resorting to the principle of utility we do not discover which alternative is *really* our duty, but rather which duty it would be better to perform in the case in question." Sumner takes Mill to be assuming that "in such cases each of the items in conflict is a genuine obligation or duty."[19] This suggests that Mill accepts some form of RT, since it entails that for Mill an agent may violate a genuine obligation no matter what. But both Mill's analysis of the nature of moral obligation and his discussions of specific examples of conflicting obligations suggest that he did not accept RT.[20]

With respect to the former, Mill says that if a person has a moral obligation to do some kind of action X, then the person can rightfully be compelled to do X and can rightfully be blamed and punished for not doing X.[21] The punishment may involve the law, the opinions of others, or the reproach of the person's conscience.[22] Though Mill seems to regard it as a conceptual point, independent of utilitarianism, that a moral obligation has this implication, he thinks the determination of which kinds of actions meet this condition must be based on utilitarian considerations. In order to establish whether a class of actions should be morally obligatory, we must compare (1) the utility of people's performing the actions who otherwise would not perform them, with (2) the disutility of compelling performance and of blaming and punishing nonperformance. Only if (1) outweighs (2) would there be justification for making the kind of action morally obligatory. It is this complex utilitarian calculation that warrants the moral rules stating our obligations.

It follows from this account that, if an overridden obligation remains an obligation, then a person with conflicting obligations may rightfully be compelled to do what cannot be done (that is, to do one thing and to do another, when both cannot be done) and may rightfully be blamed and punished no matter what is done. Mill makes it clear that there is no sense of wrongdoing that does not involve liability to punishment: "we do not call anything wrong unless we mean to imply that a person ought to be punished in some way or other for doing it."[23] Hence, if there were circumstances in which wrongdoing of any kind were inescapable for a person, then the person ought to be punished no matter what.

Mill does not directly address these consequences of his position with regard to the possibility of a conflict of genuine obligations. He does not say that when obligations conflict, the person ought to be compelled to fulfill both obligations and ought to blamed and punished for neglecting either. Since he frequently discusses conflicting obligations, this omission suggests that he does not think moral wrongdoing may be inescapable. On the other hand, since the determination of when it is appropriate to compel, blame, and punish persons is to be made on utilitarian grounds, it would seem that it is not open to Mill to reject out of hand the idea of compelling persons to do what they cannot do, or of blaming or punishing persons no matter what they do. We would need to carry out a utilitarian comparison similar to that used to establish the obligations in the first place.

Because a person cannot be compelled to do what cannot be done, it is not clear that there would be any point to considering the utility of compulsion. But it is possible to blame or punish a person no matter what, so we could consider whether there would be a utilitarian justification for doing this when obligations conflict. Nonetheless, it is prima facie unlikely that Mill believes this would have a utilitarian justification; for if we blame and punish the person no matter what, then we do so even when he or she fulfills the obligation that brings about the greatest happiness in the situation. But the purpose of blame and punishment on a utilitarian account is to encourage persons to do what they ought to do, either to follow the rules of obligation or, when they conflict, to follow the rule with the best consequences in that case. If the person is doing what ought to be done, then it is difficult to see how this end would be promoted by punishing the person.[24] Therefore, it seems doubtful that Mill supposes there are reasons to punish people with conflicting moral obligations no matter what they do.[25]

Mill also states that "a person is only responsible for what he has done voluntarily, or could voluntarily have avoided." The aim of this and other maxims of justice, he says, is "to prevent the just principle of evil for evil from being perverted to the infliction of evil without that justification."[26] But if a person would violate a genuine obligation no matter what, then the person could not voluntarily avoid violating some obligation and hence, on this view, could not be responsible or punished for failing to do so.[27] This suggests again that Mill does not think an overridden obligation remains in force or that wrongdoing of any kind could be inescapable.

This interpretation is confirmed by Mill's discussion of examples of moral conflicts. In the case referred to earlier, Mill says that the obligation not to lie "admits of possible exceptions," as when lying is the only way to fulfill the obligation to prevent undeserved evil. The central concern in both obligations and their exceptions is the promotion of utility. The justification of obligations requires that following them ordinarily promotes utility. But in the simple form in which we are educated to adhere to these obligations, they may sometimes conflict. When they do, we are to follow the obligation that on that occasion has greater utility—in this case, preventing an undeserved evil. Since on a utilitarian analysis violating the rule not to lie is not wrong in itself and since following this rule does not promote utility in this situation, there is nothing wrong with momentarily setting it aside. This is the force of saying it admits of an exception.[28] In this circumstance, there is no genuine obligation not to lie.

That Mill understands the resolution of moral conflicts in this way is explicit in his account of a conflict of obligations concerning justice. An obligation of justice, he says, is a moral obligation in which some person has a corresponding moral right, meaning that the person has a justified claim on society to enforce the obligation. When an obligation of justice is violated, there is not only a wrong action, there is a definite person who has been wronged or harmed by the action and who may rightfully demand protection from this action by society. The basis for determining which kinds of actions are obligations of justice is utilitarian: Only that which is most essential for human happiness, in particular our security, is of sufficiently great utility to warrant the disutility of giving individuals a legitimate claim on society to enforce the obligation.[29]

Since obligations of justice concern such important matters, they generally override other moral obligations with which they may conflict. They are "of more absolute obligation" than other obligations.[30] But a rule of justice does not always override other rules: "particular cases may occur in which some other social duty is so important as to overrule any one of the general maxims of justice."[31] For example, Mill says (anticipating the plight of Craig), the moral obligation to save a life may overrule the obligation of justice not to steal or kidnap. In such cases, he claims, "as we do not call anything justice which is not a virtue, we usually say, not that justice must give way to some other moral principle, but that what is just in ordinary cases is, by reason of that other principle, *not just in the particular case*." Through this "accommodation of language," Mill says, we can maintain the "indefeasibility attributed to justice," and we are "saved from the necessity of maintaining that there can be laudable injustice."[32]

His point is clearly that, in a moral conflict where a life can be saved only by stealing or kidnapping, there is no obligation of justice not to steal or kidnap: In this circumstance the overridden obligation is not an obligation at all. Hence, there is nothing wrong with stealing or kidnapping in this case, and so wrongdoing may be entirely avoided by saving the life.

There is no question, then, but that Mill is committed to the rejection of RT.[33] He acknowledges that there are conflicts of obligations in the sense of conflicts between the moral rules that, for utilitarian reasons, persons are educated to follow. But he states that these conflicts may be resolved by utilitarian considerations, and he makes it clear that the overridden obligations would not in those circumstances be genuine obligations. In these moral conflicts, the agent would avoid all wrongdoing by acting so as to maximize utility.

When combined with his account of internal sanctions, Mill's rejection of RT suggests a critique of the phenomenological argument. Mill supposes that persons ought to be, and generally are, educated to associate internal sanctions with their moral obligations. An internal sanction of duty is "a feeling in our own mind; a pain, more or less intense, attendant on violation of duty."[34] The "binding force" of this sanction, Mill says, "consists in the existence of a mass of feeling which must be broken through in order to do what violates our standard of right, and which, if we do nevertheless violate that standard, will probably have to be encountered afterwards in the form of remorse."[35] This feeling is a form of punishment, and its only justification is utilitarian. Since remorse is painful, persons raised to feel remorse upon violating their obligations are less likely to violate them. So long as the pain of remorse is outweighed by the good brought about by increased compliance, the internal sanction is justified. When a morally well-educated person violates a moral obligation, then, this person will experience a painful feeling such as remorse. Moreover, when these obligations conflict, this person is likely to feel distress no matter what he or she does. For an obligation of the simple kind we are educated to obey will be violated no matter what. Hence, Mill's account implies an explanation of why people sometimes find moral distress inescapable. But since for Mill there is always a course of action available that is entirely free of wrongdoing, this explanation is compatible with the rejection of RT. It shows why, though we sometimes naturally feel moral distress no matter what, it is not the case that we sometimes do something morally wrong no matter what.

The key to this explanation is Mill's claim that, although there is a sense in which moral obligations conflict, nonetheless moral wrongdoing can always be avoided. Mill assumes that the obligations we are educated to follow in daily life have the form of simple rules such as that we ought to tell the truth and ought not to steal. His examples of rules of obligation are always simple, and he believes there are practical reasons why they could not be made complex enough to eliminate all possibility of conflict. But it is to obligations of this simple form that the internal sanctions attach. For example, with respect to the obligation not to lie, Mill says, "the cultivation in ourselves of a sensitive feeling on the subject of veracity is one of the most useful, and the enfeeblement of that feeling one of the most hurtful, things to which our conduct can be instrumental."[36] In general, there are good utilitarian reasons why people ought to feel aversion to lying and to feel remorse when they do lie.

In the absence of conflict, both moral distress and wrongdoing are avoided by following this and other rules. But when the rules do conflict, moral distress is difficult to avoid, since some rule must be broken and since, given our education, there is a tight psychological connection between breaking the rule and moral distress. Still, a conflict of rules does not mean moral wrongdoing cannot be avoided, because a utilitarian analysis is guaranteed to yield an available action which is free of wrongdoing. In this case, the overridden obligation is not a genuine obligation. There is thus no justification for feeling remorse upon violating this obligation. It is not wrong to violate it. But because of our habitual aversion to lying, which exists for good utilitarian reasons, such feeling, though mistaken, is likely to seem natural and appropriate to us.[37]

IV. Hare's Critique of the Phenomenological Argument

Mill's critique of the phenomenological argument is only implied by remarks aimed primarily at the nineteenth-century intuitionists. A similar critique by Hare is explicitly addressed to contemporary defenders of the phenomenological argument. Hare's critique is thus both more precise and more detailed with respect to issues concerning inescapable moral wrongdoing and moral distress. There are also important differences between Mill and Hare. Mill's rejection of inescapable moral wrongdoing depends upon both his utilitarianism and his claim that wrongdoing implies the appropriateness of punishment. These are not Hare's reasons for thinking wrongdoing can always be avoided. There may also be differences in their understanding of the role of rules in moral deliberation. But for my purposes these differences are less important than the similarities in their critiques, and it is on the latter that I will mainly focus attention.

Hare's linguistic analysis of moral judgments implies a denial of inescapable moral wrongdoing, for the logical properties of these judgments revealed by this analysis—universalizability, prescriptivity, and overridingness—preclude the possibility of conflict.[38] Moreover, Hare's emphatic rejection of any appeal to moral intuitions implies a rejection of the phenomenological argument, since this argument makes explicit appeal to moral intuitions embodied in our emotional responses. In view of this, it might be supposed that Hare would have nothing further to say about these issues. Yet by offering an explanation of these responses via his two-level version of utilitarianism, Hare develops a critique of the phenomenological argument on its own terms.[39] That he does so is an indication of the importance our feelings of inescapable moral distress have for us.

At the more fundamental or what Hare calls the "critical" level, "there is a requirement that we resolve the conflict" that may appear between moral duties in everyday deliberation.[40] For the logical properties of moral judgments preclude conflict. Hare takes these same properties to entail act-utilitarianism. Hence, at the critical level, whether a particular action ought to be done is determined on the basis of the goodness of its consequences in comparison with those of available alternative actions. It is assumed that such an analysis will always result in a conflict-free conclusion.

Like Mill, Hare does not believe persons engaged in ordinary moral deliberation should directly apply the act-utilitarian calculus. In most cases, they should simply follow a set of moral rules. Thus, from the act-utilitarian standpoint of the critical level, it is necessary to formulate a set of prima facie principles for use at the everyday, or what Hare calls, the "intuitive" level of moral thinking. These principles are required because it is not possible to engage in an adequate act-utilitarian analysis on each and every occasion, and because we suffer from a tendency to "cook" the results of such an analysis in our own favor. The justification of these prima facie principles is determined by two criteria. On the one hand, they should be simple and general (that is, unspecific) enough that they can be both learned and then applied in everyday situations. On the other hand, they should be principles that, if followed, would result in actions that would closely approximate what would be required by an act-utilitarian analysis at the critical level (they should have "acceptance-utility"). There is a tension between these criteria. Greater coincidence with the results of act-utilitarianism could be achieved by more complicated and specific principles, but these principles would be less easy to learn and apply. Hence, the principles that are justified by the joint application of these criteria will involve a compromise between them. Though their application will generally coincide with what would be justified by an act-utilitarian analysis, this will not always be the case. Still, for Hare, everyday moral thinking should typically be a matter of applying these prima facie principles to concrete situations with no thought of an act-utilitarian evaluation. By proceeding in this way, Hare thinks we are most likely to do what is right in the long run.

Hare's application of this two-level utilitarianism to the phenomenological argument is as follows (parallels with Mill should be evident): Since the prima facie principles employed at the intuitive level must be relatively simple and general, they will occasionally conflict with one another.[41] When this happens, Hare says, we are forced to return to the critical level, where the conflict must and can be resolved via an act-utilitarian analysis.[42] Whatever the outcome of this resolution, we will be required to violate one of the conflicting prima facie principles. For example, an act-utilitarian analysis might require in a particular case that an agent go against the prima facie principle to tell the truth. According to Hare, part of being educated to adhere to such prima facie principles involves acquiring a disposition to feel dislike upon violating them. "*Having* the principles," he says, "is having the disposition to experience the feelings."[43] As for Mill, there is a sound utilitarian reason for this: Persons who feel an aversion to lying will tend to lie less, and on the whole this will be a good thing. Hence, a properly educated person will feel a form of moral distress when telling a lie, and this will be so even when, in a conflict situation, the person correctly believes on the basis of an act-utilitarian analysis that he or she morally ought to tell the lie.

Hare illustrates this argument with the following example.[44] When visiting Prague to speak with some philosophers (during the Communist regime), he believed he would have been justified in lying if asked by officials at the border about the purpose of the visit.[45] Nonetheless, he says, had he done so, he would certainly have had "a feeling of guilt at telling the lie." But if he felt guilty, he says, "it looks as if there is a sense of 'thinking that I ought' in which I could have been correctly described as 'thinking that I ought not to be telling the lie'." For to feel guilt is "inseparable from" the thought that one ought not. "Yet in another sense," he says, "I should certainly have been thinking that I ought to tell the lie."

I take Hare's point to be this. On account of his moral education, for which there is a sound utilitarian justification, he would always feel guilty when violating the rule requiring veracity. Yet in this particular circumstance, for sound utilitarian reasons, he correctly believes he ought to tell a lie, and on the basis of this belief, he would feel guilty if he told the truth. Feeling guilty would thus be unavoidable: He would feel it whether he told the truth or told a lie. But it does not follow from this that there is any sense in which moral wrongdoing is unavoidable. Though the thought or feeling of wrongdoing is unavoidable, wrongdoing itself can be avoided by telling a lie (as an act-utilitarian analysis would show). Hence, there is a convincing explanation of unavoidable feelings of moral distress that does not require the claim that moral wrongdoing is unavoidable.

V. The Utilitarian Account of Moral Rules

The critique of the phenomenological argument suggested by Mill and that explicitly advocated by Hare have enough similarities that they may be evaluated together. I begin with two preliminary points. First, for their critique to succeed it must be the case that their account of moral education and its rationale be operative in the world of persons referred to in the phenomenological argument. If it is not, it cannot be an explanation of why *those* persons would unavoidably have feelings of moral distress in the wake of certain moral conflicts. And it might well be doubted whether anything close to the utilitarian account of morality and moral education is in place in the world today. Utilitarianism, after all, remains controversial, and not only among philosophers.[46]

In one respect, this criticism is less serious than it seems since it is possible to distinguish the general strategy of a two-level response to the phenomenological argument, on the one hand, and its specific utilitarian formulation, on the other.[47] For example, from the perspective of a complex deontological theory, it might be thought that direct application of the theory in everyday moral reasoning would be difficult and that it would be desirable to develop a set of prima facie principles that are simple and general enough to learn and apply, and that would, if followed, lead to approximately the same actions as would a direct application of the theory itself. It might be supposed that these principles would occasionally conflict and that when they did, the conflict would be resolved by a direct application of the theory. Since following this resolution would mean violating one of the prima facie principles, and since sound moral education would instill the disposition to feel guilt whenever violating a prima facie principle, a person who justifiably violates a prima facie principle would feel guilty about doing so—even though the action was in no way wrong. On this basis, a response to the phenomenological argument similar to that of Mill and Hare might be constructed.[48]

The utilitarian critique may thus be seen as an instance of a general approach that might also be employed by nonutilitarian theories. Still, there are two reasons why this approach is especially suited to utilitarianism. First, act-utilitarianism requires, on each occasion of moral choice, an estimation of all the consequences for all persons of all alternative actions and a determination of their overall comparative values. It is thus a particularly difficult theory to employ, and it may be that it is more susceptible, as Hare puts it, to those inclined to "cook" the results in their favor. Second, the idea that persons should be taught to feel moral distress upon violating prima facie moral principles, in order to increase compliance with these principles, is itself a utilitarian idea. It assumes that the inculcation of these feelings may be justified by their overall beneficial effects, even if this occasionally results in situations in which the feelings would be unwarranted. This is an argument that a deontologist might well resist on the ground that no policy can be justified that, when functioning properly, can be expected to cause innocent persons to sometimes feel guilty.

In any case, my concern here is with the utilitarian version of the two-level critique. This version requires that the utilitarian program of moral education be efficacious in the world, something that is at least doubtful. The second preliminary point is that this critique requires that something approximating the plurality of rules of commonsense moral understanding can be justified on the basis of utilitarianism along the lines envisioned by Mill and Hare. There is no doubt that they endorse this understanding, and they obviously think it can be justified on utilitarian grounds. The question is whether it really can.

Commonsense moral understanding does suppose that, in ordinary deliberation, consideration ought to be given to a plurality of relatively simple moral rules, and that often the correct conclusion of deliberation will be that one ought to act in accordance with these rules. It is another matter, however, to show that these rules are the rules that would be justified by the two-level utilitarian strategy. It is necessary to say "would be" because no utilitarian has attempted to show that the commonsense rules are justified by utilitarian considerations. For the most part, utilitarians have simply asserted that this is the case. There is thus a large lacuna in the utilitarian critique, and it is far from obvious that it can be filled. Serious questions have been raised by critics of utilitarianism, early and late, about whether, for example, it would justify rules that are far more demanding than the rules of commonsense morality, or rules that would substantially preclude the very partial behavior towards family, friends and compatriots that is countenanced by commonsense moral understanding.

Much of the appeal of utilitarianism derives from its aspiration to make moral thinking substantially an empirical (or even quasi-scientific) affair. For the two-level approach, everyday moral rules are to be justified by showing that a world in which people were educated to follow these rules would be a world in which people's actions would, as Hare puts it, "do as much good, and as little harm, as possible."[49] Since it is an empirical question exactly which rules these would turn out to be, it might be expected that the claim that these rules are by and large those of commonsense morality would be accompanied by a body of empirical evidence. In fact, no such evidence has been forthcoming.[50] In the absence of this, the empirical pretensions of utilitarianism are an unfulfilled promissory note.

These difficulties are not, however, the principal issues I wish to pursue with respect to the utilitarian critique of the phenomenological argument. There are more fundamental problems to be considered. Let us assume, then, for the sake of argument, that the rules that would be justified by two-level utilitarianism are for the most part the rules recognized by commonsense moral understanding. My argument is that, even on this hypothesis, the utilitarian critique does not account for commonsense moral understanding and is in any case an inadequate account of morality—and this for reasons which have some independence from questions pertaining to inescapable moral wrongdoing. In addition, I maintain in the next section that the utilitarian critique does not explain our feelings of moral distress in the wake of moral conflicts.

Focus first on situations in which the rules do *not* conflict. Two-level utilitarianism assumes that this will almost always be the case. For example, Hare says that when his prima facie principles are selected properly, "conflicts will arise only in exceptional situations."[51] In the absence of conflict, two-level utilitarianism supposes that the moral agent should simply follow the relatively simple and general rules selected by critical thinking, and indeed, as Hare emphasizes, should do so unreflectively on the basis of "very firm and deep dispositions and feelings" acquired by sound upbringing.[52]

It is perhaps true that rather young children should be instructed to proceed in this way, but it is certainly not true that adults should be educated to think that moral deliberation ordinarily consists of nothing more than selecting the applicable rule and acting in accordance with it (the only exception being the unusual conflict cases). Nor is it the case that commonsense moral understanding supposes this. What is lacking in the two-level utilitarian picture, and what is correctly recognized by commonsense understanding, is the idea that moral deliberation often requires an acute sensitivity to the quite particular needs, feelings, relationships, circumstances, backgrounds, and the like of the persons with whom the moral agent is currently engaged, and further that on the basis of this sensitivity, deliberation requires ascertaining those moral responsibilities to these persons that are relevant to the specific situation at hand. On this understanding, rules play a part in deliberation, but their role is to draw our attention to the sorts of things to which we ought to be sensitive and to the kinds of responsibilities that may be pertinent. We are not merely to follow these rules unreflectively, being on the alert only for possible conflicts. For example, in speaking to someone with some ability but lacking assurance it might be appropriate to say confidently, "I really think you can do it if you work at it," even though this overstates the confidence actually felt. The rule to tell the truth is here violated, but only sensitivity to the psychology of the person, the person's ability, the importance of the task at hand, and the like can determine when this is appropriate. With the same person in another circumstance, or another person in the same circumstance, brute honesty might be what is required. By prescribing for ordinary deliberation a mechanical following of the rules, two-level utilitarianism thus advances a morality appropriate at best for children, but not for mature moral agents.

There are two lines of response that a two-level utilitarian might make to this objection: The first is to claim that it can account for this understanding of deliberation; the second is to admit that it cannot, but to make a virtue of this. I consider these in turn.

It may be said that this analysis presents the two-level account in its worst possible light and that in fact this account would insist on an application of the rules that is sensitive to the particularities of the persons and circumstances involved, and hence is not merely a mechanical or unreflective process. There are places where both Mill and Hare seem to suggest this.[53] But it would be self-defeating for the two-level utilitarian to take this position. On this view, the alternative to regarding ordinary deliberation as an unreflective application of rules is, presumably, to regard it as a process in which rules are applied with an eye to whether they are achieving their end. Since for the utilitarian the end is the maximization of the good of the whole, this would mean considering in each case whether following the rule would have the best overall consequences. Yet the point of the two-level theory is to explain why, in ordinary deliberation, we should not think like act-utilitarians. Hence, the two-level view cannot understand a reflective application of the rules in this way.

It might be supposed that there is a third alternative: a way of reflectively applying the rules that does not involve thinking like an act-utilitarian and yet achieves the end of act-utilitarianism. For example, it may be said that in dealing with her child, a mother ought neither to mechanically apply the moral rules nor to apply them in light of the goal of maximizing the good of all human beings. Rather, she ought to apply them with a view to fulfilling the special needs of her child. By thinking in this partial and hence nonutilitarian way, the mother will best achieve the end of utilitarianism.[54] On this view, moral rules are to be applied from the perspective of a set of sensibilities, nonutilitarian in their conscious outlook, and yet utilitarian in their overall results and underlying justification.

Though this may be the position that Mill and Hare intend, it is incompatible with the two-level utilitarian account of conflicts of moral rules. This account supposes that, when rules conflict, the moral agent is to resolve the conflict by engaging in explicit act-utilitarian thinking. It is hard to see why, if nonconflicting rules are to be applied from the perspective of nonutilitarian sensibilities, the resolution of conflicting rules requires the replacement of those sensibilities with a conscious utilitarian outlook. Whatever disadvantages speak against explicit utilitarian thought in ordinary deliberation will also be present when rules conflict. It might be said that only conscious utilitarian thought can properly resolve the conflict. But there is no more reason to think this than there is to think that explicit utilitarian thought is needed to properly apply nonconflicting rules. If nonutilitarian sensibilities can achieve the end of utilitarianism in the latter case, there is no reason to suppose these sensibilities cannot produce the end of utilitarianism in the former case as well. Moreover, this account requires that agents ordinarily maintain nonutilitarian sensibilities while acknowledging the ultimate truth of utilitarianism—and it may be doubted whether this is possible.[55]

A two-level theorist might conceivably acknowledge that the end of utilitarianism is best served if we never think in conscious utilitarian terms. Yet, with or without this claim, there remains a further difficulty with this version of the two-level account. It is central to this account that we are to be educated so that we feel moral distress *whenever* we violate moral rules, even when we regard ourselves as justified in doing so. That we have these feelings is essential to the two-level critique of the phenomenological argument. But we are not likely to regard every violation of these rules as cause for moral distress to the extent that we have been educated to think, not only that moral rules will occasionally conflict, but that in ordinary conflict-free deliberation we are not to mechanically follow the rules but to determine when to follow them from the perspective of a set of nonutilitarian sensibilities. For we will then recognize that in every case successful deliberation need not require conforming to the rules. In short, we will recognize that these rules are important but fallible guidelines to achieving the aims of morality, whether these be understood in terms of nonutilitarian sensibilities or the end of utilitarianism itself.[56] Hence, this formulation of the two-level account cannot be used in a critique of the phenomenological argument.

It is thus not surprising that Hare, at any rate, often insists that in ordinary deliberation we are to unreflectively apply the rules. He emphasizes that we are not to regard his prima facie principles as mere rules of thumb. Rather, we are to have deep dispositions to follow these principles, and this means that in the absence of conflict we are to follow them unreflectively.[57] Moreover, we need these dispositions to achieve the purposes Hare advances for having the rules: to avoid the difficulties of an act-utilitarian analysis, and to prevent cooking the results in our favor. To the extent that it is required that there be sensitivity to the persons and circumstances involved in the application of the rules, these purposes will tend to be defeated (because deliberation will be more difficult and bias more probable). Further, without these dispositions, we are not likely to feel moral distress upon every violation of the rules, as required by the critique of the phenomenological argument.

As applied to the phenomenological argument, the two-level utilitarian critique is thus committed to the view that, in ordinary moral deliberation, we are to mechanically follow a set of relatively general and simple moral rules. But it is a mistake to suppose that mature moral agents should deliberate in this way. Sound deliberation requires that moral rules be applied in a manner that is sensitive to the special features of the persons, relationships, circumstances, histories, and the like involved in a given situation.[58] By rejecting this, the two-level utilitarian view regards moral agents engaged in ordinary deliberation as, in effect, moral bureaucrats. They are pledged to the end of morality—the maximization of the good of the whole—and they have been trained to bring about this end by automatically acting in accordance with a set of rules (except in occasional conflict situations). In applying these rules, they are not to consider the particularities of the persons with whom they are dealing. Rather, they are to apply the rules impersonally, without regard for personal considerations. The relation of the moral agent to other persons is, in a familiar sense, bureaucratic.[59]

Another way of seeing this is to consider the conception of moral responsibility that emerges from the two-level account. The ultimate responsibility of the moral agent, on this view, is to maximize the good of the whole. From this, secondary responsibilities to follow the rules are derived. In a given case, the moral agent has a responsibility to follow a specific rule, and typically another person will benefit from this action. But it cannot be said that in this situation the agent has a responsibility *to* this particular person per se. Rather, the agent has a responsibility *with respect to* this person, namely, to act in accordance with a rule that now requires certain behavior affecting the person. Once again, the moral relation of the agent to other persons is rendered bureaucratic. Not only is the agent to act in accordance with a set of rules impersonally applied, the agent is to regard him- or herself as being ultimately responsible, not to any particular person as such, but to the goal of maximizing the good of human beings taken in the aggregate.[60] In this way, two-level utilitarianism displaces persons as direct objects of moral concern.

For these reasons, the two-level utilitarian theory needed for the critique of the phenomenological argument does not account for ordinary moral consciousness. It is not a feature of this consciousness that in moral deliberation we should typically preclude consideration of the special characteristics of the persons and situations with which we are dealing, and it is a feature of it that we believe ourselves to have moral responsibilities to—and not merely with respect to—specific persons. We do not regard our moral relations with other persons as bureaucratic in these senses.

It may be objected that the two-level account does not require moral agents to consciously think in terms of following a set of rules in order to maximize the good of the whole, it only requires agents to act in a manner which is consistent with these rules. Since it is possible to do this, and at the same time to show concern for the particularities of specific persons and to regard oneself as having responsibilities to these persons, there is nothing in the two-level account that precludes these aspects of our moral relations with others.

Acting in accordance with the rules is often compatible with, for example, showing concern for a particular person as such. Still, this is not sufficient to rescue the two-level account from the aforementioned difficulties. This account requires the moral agent to have enough awareness of what he or she is doing to recognize when the rules conflict and to have enough knowledge of the purpose of these rules to resort to explicit act-utilitarian thinking to resolve the conflict. Hence, the agent must believe that, as a moral agent, he or she is following the rules in order to maximize the good of human beings taken in the aggregate. Of course, as Mill emphasizes,[61] the agent may have other reasons for following the rules, but these reasons are not moral reasons. Understanding of the purpose of the rules need not always be consciously on display, but it can never be far from sight. Otherwise, the agent will fail to properly resolve conflicts. Deception about the purpose of the rules is ruled out on this version of the two-level account.

Moreover, whatever the agent does that is consistent with but not required by these rules cannot be regarded on the two-level account as being of moral significance. On this account, in ordinary circumstances morality requires that we follow the rules. It does not require anything else. An agent who follows the rules and then, off-hours morally speaking, shows sensitivity to the particularities of a specific person, will be no better morally on the two-level account. Once again, ordinary moral consciousness eludes its grasp.

There is a very different response to these issues that may be forthcoming from some proponents of the two-level utilitarian account. It may be said that the moral rules should be applied impersonally, without regard to special features of the persons involved, because morality is fundamentally impersonal. A central thesis of utilitarianism, after all, is that expressed in Bentham's famous slogan, quoted with approval by both Mill and Hare, "everybody to count for one, nobody for more than one."[62] Since the aim of the rules is to maximize the well-being of everyone, where each person counts equally, the rules must be applied without consideration of the particularities of persons. To deny this would be to allow an unwarranted form of partiality or prejudice to enter into moral considerations. Hence, to the extent that the understanding of rules in ordinary moral consciousness involves a rejection of the moral equality of persons, it is defective and should be corrected by utilitarianism.[63]

The point of this response is to suggest that two-level utilitarianism both explains ordinary moral understanding, through its account of the substance of moral rules, and criticizes that understanding, through its insistence on the importance of an impartial application of those rules. Hence, it repudiates rather than accounts for at least some of the aspects of ordinary moral consciousness to which I have been drawing attention. Moreover, the idea of moral equality that underlies its justification of the rules and their impartial application can seem so obviously correct that it is difficult to suppose it could be mistaken. Nonetheless, as understood by utilitarians, it is mistaken. Seeing why helps to illuminate what is amiss in the utilitarian conception of the moral agent as a moral bureaucrat.

It is obvious that there are some contexts, such as relations with the state, where a concept of equality is important. But utilitarianism insists that the idea underlying all morality is a particular conception of equality according to which each person counts equally, meaning that each person is equally entitled to well-being from each person. From this is derived the central claim of utilitarianism, at the fundamental level, that each agent ought to act so as to maximize the goodness of all persons, taking the goodness of each person to be equally important. This is the point of Bentham's slogan, at least as understood by Mill and Hare. If we accept the assumption that, morally speaking, for any two persons, either one counts more than the other, or else they count equally, then it is difficult to find a basis for saying anything except that they count equally. It is because this assumption is made that the utilitarian position seems so hard to resist, however counterintuitive its results turn out to be. What is mistaken in utilitarianism is the assumption itself, that morality ought to assert as its first principle a thesis about whether some human beings are to count more than, less than, or the same amount as others.

The alternative is to reject as morally fundamental the idea of ranking human beings at all and to insist instead that what is essential is the notion that each human being is uniquely, as well as intrinsically, valuable in him- or herself. That we regard each human being in this way is one of the most important features of our understanding of ourselves. It is because of this that we do not regard human beings as fungible creatures such that the loss of one person could be fully made up for by the gain of another.

Utilitarianism either denies or regards as morally irrelevant the unique value of each human being. First, there is the familiar point that at a fundamental level (Hare's critical level) utilitarianism is concerned, not with the well-being of individuals per se, but only with the overall amount of goodness in the world. An individual as such, in virtue of being the particular uniquely valued individual he or she is, has no moral claim to any particular form or amount of well-being. The individual is entitled only to that well-being that results from the maximal amount of well-being in the world as a whole, where in determining this each individual counts for exactly one.[64] This is the source of utilitarianism's well-known difficulties with issues of distributive justice. Second, for the utilitarian, at a basic level each individual is entitled to exactly the same moral consideration. Since human beings are regarded as equally rather than uniquely important, morally speaking, each person should be treated in the same way. It is this feature of utilitarianism that makes it natural, when a plurality of moral rules is introduced, to regard the application of these rules as bureaucratic.

Since we think human beings are uniquely important, we want to respond to each person, not in exactly the same way, but in a way that is appropriate to the unique quality and value of that person. This is why, in applying moral rules, we resist the bureaucratic mentality and strive to be sensitive to the particularities of the persons with whom we are engaged. A two-level utilitarian theory might attempt to accommodate this perspective at the intuitive level, as both Mill and Hare sometimes aim to do, but it is a perspective that in a deep way is at odds with the fundamental commitments of utilitarianism. The difference between the critical and the intuitive level so interpreted cannot be understood merely as the difference between the single rule of act-utilitarianism and the plural rules of commonsense morality. The two levels involve essentially different ways of valuing human beings. For the act-utilitarian, persons are as raindrops in the sea of humanity. Once submerged, they are not easily recovered. This is why it is difficult to suppose that both the critical and intuitive level could reside simultaneously in the conscious awareness of the enlightened moral agent.[65]

VI. The Utilitarian Account of Inescapable Moral Distress

There is a more direct reason why the two-level utilitarian critique of the phenomenological argument fails. The critique purports to explain inescapable feelings of moral distress in the wake of moral conflict. But in fact it does not explain these feelings. In a discussion of an earlier statement of Hare's position, Walzer says, with regard to persons who feel guilty even though they believe they are justified in violating a moral rule, that "the more fully they accept the utilitarian account, the less likely they are to feel that (useful) feeling."[66] His point is that persons will tend to stop feeling guilty once they realize that they are not in fact doing anything wrong and that the only reason they are inclined to feel guilty is because of their moral education, the justification of which is that good effects will generally result if persons are raised to feel guilty when violating a moral rule. "The feeling whose usefulness is being explained," he says, "is most unlikely to be felt by someone who is convinced only of its usefulness."[67] If Walzer is right, then it is not the case that where moral rules conflict feelings of guilt are inescapable (since guilt will tend to disappear as long as one does what is thought to be justified), and so the two-level account does not explain the phenomenon of inescapable moral distress.

Hare's implicit response to this objection is not that moral agents ought to be deceived about the justification of their moral feelings. We are to be aware of the utilitarian justification of our beliefs and feelings. Indeed, we need to be if we are to know how to resolve conflicts. Rather, Hare argues that a properly educated person will not be able to stop feeling guilty in these circumstances, even with this knowledge. For the point of moral education is to instill a deep disposition to feel guilty whenever violating prima facie principles. The justified thought that one is not in fact doing anything wrong on the occasion of a particular violation, and that one feels guilty only on account of this education, will be relatively powerless to affect any such well-placed disposition.

This is not an implausible response. We are often unable to alter our feelings when we know they are unwarranted. Yet it is this very feature of Hare's position that creates difficulties for his challenge to the phenomenological argument. On Hare's account, the agent who feels guilty when justifiably breaking a moral rule knows that the guilt is unwarranted. Despite the feeling, the person knows that he or she is not really doing anything wrong. The agent is thus in a position analogous to the person, in an example of Rawls,[68] who was brought up to accept religious beliefs according to which attending the theater is wrong, and who in later life continues to feel guilty while attending the theater in spite of having rejected those religious beliefs. In both cases, the person cannot help feeling guilty even with the belief that this feeling is unwarranted.

On Hare's account, a form of moral discomfort such as guilt is inescapable when prima facie principles conflict, but the quality of this guilt differs significantly depending on what we do. If we fail to do what we believe, by an act-utilitarian analysis, we really ought to do, then we will both feel guilty and think we are doing something wrong. On the other hand, if we do what we believe we really ought to do, then we will feel guilty but realize that we are not in fact doing anything wrong. In both cases we will find the feeling inescapable, but we will regard it as appropriate only in the first case. However, this is not an adequate description of our inescapable feelings of moral distress in the wake of moral conflicts.

Consider the plight of Craig. Suppose he believes that, all things considered, he ought to grab the girl, wrench the keys from her hand, and steal her car. Upon doing this he feels moral distress. Does he also believe he has done nothing wrong? Insofar as 'wrong' means failing to do what, all things considered, he ought to do, he does believe he has done nothing wrong. But Craig may be expected to believe that, though he has acted for the best, there is nonetheless a sense in which he has done something wrong. In particular, he has wronged the girl, who cannot be said to deserve to be treated in such a fashion. In thinking this, we may suppose, Craig does not believe it is usually wrong to treat a person in this way but perfectly all right in this case. Rather, he believes it is wrong in this case, even though it is morally for the best. He regards his feeling as an entirely appropriate response to the way in which he treated the girl.

On the two-level utilitarian account, Craig's beliefs and feelings are mistaken. Assuming that his action is justified by an act-utilitarian analysis, there is no sense in which he can be said to do anything wrong. Though he will naturally feel guilty, if he has been brought up well, he will also believe, if he is knowledgeable and rational, that this feeling is quite inappropriate in this case. Hence, the two-level utilitarian account fails to explain Craig's feelings of inescapable moral distress.[69] By contrast, the responsibilities to persons account does explain why these feelings can be an appropriate response to the situation.

There is another respect in which the utilitarian critique is inadequate with respect to at least some cases appealed to in the phenomenological argument. To see this, consider an example mentioned earlier. Suppose a woman has just married and then finds out that her widowed mother has suddenly and unexpectedly become disabled. The woman takes herself to have responsibilities to both her husband and her mother, and she believes that no matter how she handles the situation, she would feel, and would find it natural and appropriate to feel, moral distress about failing to fully live up to these responsibilities.

On the responsibilities to persons account, this woman's feelings are a reasonable response to this situation. Whatever she does, she will fail to fulfill her responsibility to each person in a way that is appropriate to the value of that person and the nature of their relationship. Even if she acts for the best, the woman has reason to feel morally pained by the fact that she has neglected or damaged the well-being of at least one of these persons to whom she feels responsible. The source of her distress is not, as the two-level utilitarian critique supposes, that she will violate some rather simple and general moral rule no matter what. No such rule, or conjunction of rules, comes close to capturing her understanding of her various responsibilities to her husband and mother. Moreover, the focus of the distress is not on the violation of a rule, even if complex, but on her failure to respond adequately to these two persons. The origin of the distress is the concrete reality of the unfulfilled needs of these two persons for whom she feels responsible. It is not the violation of a general rule of conduct she has been educated to follow in order to maximize the well-being of all human beings. Hence, by focusing on the rules of commonsense morality, the two-level critique misconstrues the kinds of moral conflicts that are often relevant to the phenomenological argument.[70] It is not always conflicts of simple, general moral rules that make moral distress inescapable. Rather, it is conflicts of specific, concrete, complex, and often multifaceted responsibilities to particular persons. Far from being simple, these responsibilities are frequently difficult to articulate at all. But they are no less real and important for that.

Notes

1. There are other sources of opposition. For example, Santurri argues that Christian moral philosophies, specifically Thomistic natural law theory and the divine command theory, are incompatible with inescapable moral wrongdoing (though he does not clearly distinguish this from the question of irresolvable moral conflicts; see Gowans 1992). However, there are disagreements about "moral dilemmas" within the Christian tradition. Some side with Santurri (see Geach 1969, p. 128); others do not (see Niebuhr 1935 and Quinn 1989).

2. In some respects, the issues I raise here pick up on themes with a long history in the criticism of utilitarian and Kantian theories, going back respectively to early intuitionist and Hegelian objections (in recent years, these themes have received renewed attention, for example in Blum 1980; Stocker 1976; and Williams 1981a; for some representative responses, see Baron 1984 and Railton 1984). But my interest is specifically in the relationship between moral conflict and the tendency to displace persons as direct objects of moral concern, something that has not been given much discussion. Also, my claim is not that something nonmoral in our lives, such as our basic "projects," puts limits on what morality can demand of us. Rather, it is that what is central to morality on this account, namely responsibilities to persons, gives us reason to reject the constraints these moral theories impose on our responsibilities.

3. Slote suggests that it is logically possible, though quite implausible, for there to be a situation in which whatever we do, there is always something with better consequences we could have done (1985, p. 168 note 5).

4. For discussion of some difficulties with this kind of position, see McConnell 1981a. Railton suggests that a utilitarian might regard this situation as a moral dilemma, understood as a conflict in which each side has the same weight (1992, pp. 729–30). But it is hard to see why an act-utilitarian would regard an action as wrong when there was no alternative with better consequences. If I can achieve checkmate by taking your knight or your rook, I make the right move no matter which I chose. That this seems a poor analogy for moral conflict is indicative of the inadequacy of act-utilitarianism.

5. There is one qualification to this. Even with the reference to the aggregate of persons, a form of utilitarianism could allow for inescapable moral wrongdoing if the goods to be maximized were of discrete, inconvertible types. On this view, it might be said that it is morally wrong not to maximize the type-1 good of persons as a whole, morally wrong not to maximize the type-2 good of persons as a whole, and so on. There might then be a moral conflict in which if I do A I maximize the type-1 good but not the type-2 good, and if I do B I maximize the type-2 good but not the type-1 good. These types of goods might still be comparable, so that there is a basis for saying which action overall is morally best. Nonetheless, whatever I do I will fail to maximize some good and hence will do something morally wrong. In effect, this is a form of moral pluralism, and it does support a doctrine of inescapable moral wrongdoing (though it is quite different from the responsibilities to persons account). However, though some utilitarians have not been averse to speaking of types of goods, they have not generally supposed that it would be wrong not to maximize each of these types. In this connection, cf. Railton 1992, pp. 735–37 and Sen 1980–81.

6. Slote tries to show that a form of act-utilitarianism can allow for inescapable moral wrongdoing. On this view, an action is morally right if and only if it produces consequences that (1) are no less good than those of any alternative action, and (2) are better than the way the situation was before the action. Since there may be circumstances in which, whatever a person does, the situation will get worse, it follows from (2) that a person may inescapably do something wrong. There are two difficulties with this analysis. First, (1) expresses the idea of act-utilitarianism as ordinarily conceived, but it is (2) which establishes this conclusion, and (2) is independent of (1). Though Slote claims to find support for the inclusion of (2) in both Bentham and the concept of benevolence, it appears that he has defined a more complex position, which includes act-utilitarianism and which, for a different reason, allows for inescapable wrongdoing. Second, it is implausible to think that situations in which, whatever the person does, things will get worse are necessarily situations in which moral wrongdoing is inescapable. Suppose lives are being lost in a burning building in which, whatever is done, the fire cannot be put out and the lives cannot be saved. Whatever a chance passerby does, the situation will get worse. It is not clear why we should suppose that, for this reason, the person will do something morally wrong no matter what (or that the person will unavoidably fail to be benevolent).

7. For the classic essay, see Urmson 1953. A good summary of this debate is found in Berger 1984, ch. 3, esp. pp. 101–20.

8. On this issue, I am mostly in agreement with the interpretation of Mill developed by Lyons (1976, 1977, and 1978). For critical discussion of Lyons's views, see Berger 1984, pp. 105–20; Brown 1982; Copp 1979; Gaus 1980; and Sumner 1979.

9. It may be that it is not possible to understand everything Mill said as expressions of a coherent moral theory (see Ryan 1990, p. xix; and Sumner 1979, pp. 110–11).

10. Mill 1957, ch. 2 par. 25 .

11. For example, see ch. 2 pars. 19 and 23, and ch. 5 pars. 8 and 37.

12. Mill 1957, ch. 2 par. 25 .

13. *Ibid.*, ch. 2 par. 2. Though there has been much discussion about the correct understanding of the principle of utility in Mill, there is no question that he regards some principle of utility as the foundation of morality. One difficulty is how to reconcile this statement of the principle with the claim, considered later, that wrongness implies liability to punishment.

14. *Ibid.*, ch. 2 par. 10. Though it is clear that the happiness of each human being counts equally (see ch. 2 par. 18 and ch. 5 par. 36), it is not clear whether the happiness of nonhuman sentient creatures counts equally with that of human beings.

15. Mill 1957, ch. 2 par. 25.

16. *Ibid.*, ch. 2 par. 23.

17. Mill does not say here that there is an obligation to protect persons from undeserved harm, though he seems to believe there is such an obligation (see ch. 5 par. 7). If his point were that we ought to violate the rule not to lie whenever doing so would have better consequences than following the rule, it would seem that he is committed to act-utilitarianism (which is difficult to reconcile with his account of obligations and rights). Hence, I take Mill to be implying that there is a conflict of rules here (cf. the passage from Mill cited in Berger 1984, p. 104).

18. Lyons holds that conflicts are not to be resolved "in act utilitarian terms," but "by some more complex utilitarian calculation" (1978, p. 10). It is not clear what this calculation is supposed to be. Mill does not think that the fact that following one rule generally has greater utility than following another rule means we should always follow the first rule when they conflict. We are to look at the consequences of following each rule in

that case. This suggests that conflicting obligations are resolved by an act-utilitarian analysis. I assume that when obligations conflict, we are to perform that action which has the best consequences, among the actions warranted by those obligations, not among all possible actions in that situation (see Hoag 1983).

19. Sumner 1979, p. 108.

20. Sumner's interpretation is criticized by Berger (1984, p. 115).

21. See ch. 5 par. 14. Following Lyons, I give this passage a rule-utilitarian reading (1976, pp. 105–109). For critiques of this interpretation, see Brown 1982, p. 33; and Gaus 1980, pp. 268–70.

22. Lyons takes the internal sanction of guilt to be fundamental (1976, p. 106); by contrast, Brown takes it to be a "rhetorical flourish" (1982, p. 36). I see no reason to doubt that Mill intended internal sanctions such as guilt to be forms of punishment.

23. Mill 1957, ch. 5 par. 14. In ch. 2 Mill says that actions are "wrong as they tend to produce the reverse of happiness" (par. 2). Since an agent could be in a situation in which, whatever was done, unhappiness would be produced, this might be taken to imply that wrongdoing could be inescapable for Mill (cf. Slote's proposal in note 6). But I think we should read this passage as a preliminary expression of Mill's position, to be understood in light of the detailed account of obligation which comes later (and not vice versa).

24. Conflict cases differ from situations in which only one rule applies, but the best consequences are achieved by violating it. Here punishment for violation of the rule might be justified on the ground that it encourages general adherence to the rules, which will lead to the best outcome overall (cf. Sartorius 1975, p. 62). But when rules conflict, punishment no matter what cannot be said to have this effect; indeed it might be undermined by making punishment seem arbitrary.

25. Sumner (1979, p. 106) cites a passage that might be taken to suggest a way around this conclusion. Mill declares that "duty is a thing which may be *exacted* from a person, as one exacts a debt," and he adds that "reasons of prudence, or the interest of other people, may militate against actually exacting it, but the person himself, it is clearly understood, would not be entitled to complain" (1957, ch. 5 par. 14). It might be supposed that Mill could claim that when duties conflict, wrongdoing is inescapable, but that "for reasons of prudence" a person with conflicting duties would not be compelled to perform the overridden duty and would not be punished for not performing it. Yet on this view, the person still "would not be entitled to complain" if he or she were punished no matter what. But if the person has acted for the best, then there would be reason to complain for being punished, because the punishment would serve no good purpose. Moreover, it is not "for reasons of prudence" that a person would not be compelled to perform the overridden duty, but because the person cannot be compelled to perform both conflicting duties.

26. Mill 1957, ch. 5 par. 35.

27. It might be said that a strict application of this principle would not have this result. For, whichever obligation the person violated, the person could have voluntarily avoided violating that obligation (by violating the other one). But it is doubtful that Mill intends the principle to be understood in this way. It goes against the spirit of the principle, and it is unlikely that he supposes there is a utilitarian justification for the principle so understood.

28. This argument might suggest that we should be prepared to set aside an obligation whenever doing so would have better consequences. But Mill does not view obligations in this way. He supposes that better results overall will be achieved if people ordinarily follow their obligations without consideration of consequences. The direct

appeal to act-utilitarian considerations is intended to be an exceptional procedure, activated by conflict of rules.

29. Mill 1957, ch. 5 pars. 15 and 23—25.

30. *Ibid.*, ch. 5 par. 32.

31. *Ibid.*, ch. 5 par. 37.

32. *Ibid.* (Emphasis added.)

33. Similar conclusions are reached by Lyons (1978, p. 6) and Gaus (1980, pp. 277–78).

34. Mill 1957, ch. 3 par. 4.

35. *Ibid.*

36. *Ibid.*, ch. 2 par. 23.

37. It might be said that this argument shows that, for Mill, when obligations conflict wrongdoing *is* inescapable, since there is an overall utilitarian justification for punishment in the form of remorse for violation of each conflicting obligation (even though in the particular case there is no utilitarian justification when the person does what is best). Though this is a possible position (cf. Railton 1992, pp. 740–41), it is not a plausible interpretation of Mill in view of the whole of his comments on moral conflicts. For Mill, moral conflicts are frequent enough that the best overall outcome is achieved by regarding an overridden obligation as not genuine, and hence as not worthy of punishment. External sanctions are relatively easy to withhold in these cases. But internal sanctions are not. Thus remorse may be unavoidable, though it is not justified.

38. Hare is not altogether explicit about this. But it seems clear, for example, that there cannot be conflicts between overriding judgments (see Sinnott-Armstrong 1988, pp. 17–18), and I argued in chapter 4, sec. I that judgments that are prescriptive in Hare's sense cannot conflict. Hare does acknowledge that it is "logical intuitions" having to do with the Kantian principle and the agglomeration principle that create problems for moral conflicts (1981, p. 28). Hence, it is conceptual considerations from the most fundamental level of moral thinking, the metaethical level, that impose the requirement at the critical level that moral judgments cannot conflict. These arguments have no parallel in Mill. For a critique of Hare's rejection of dilemmas, see Dahl 1987, pp. 413–16.

39. See 1981, pp. 25–52, esp. pp. 28–31. It appears that Hare developed the two-level approach at least in part in order to achieve this purpose.

40. 1981, p. 26.

41. To allow for this, Hare qualifies his account of the logical properties of moral principles. See 1981, p. 60.

42. Hare suggests that in some simple cases we may resolve the conflict "intuitively," but he makes it clear that this would be a pragmatic substitute for a proper analysis, which can only be provided by an act-utilitarian evaluation (see 1981, pp. 50–51).

43. Hare 1981, p. 39.

44. *Ibid.*, p. 31.

45. Hare says the justification of lying is that "if they had known they would most probably have expelled me" (1981, p. 31). It is not clear what prima facie principle is thought to be relevant here.

46. More recently, Hare says only that "many people already do think in the way I am trying to clarify" (1988, p. 291).

47. This possibility is implicitly acknowledged by both Mill (1957, ch. 2 par. 24) and Hare (1981, p. 50).

48. Cf. Conee 1982, p. 94 and Santurri 1987, p. 103.

49. 1981, p. 62.

50. The most plausible attempt to justify these rules was made by Sidgwick (1981, bk. IV ch. III). But much of his account consists of pointing out that the rules of commonsense morality typically have some good results. This unsurprising observation is not sufficient. It must be shown that, to a large extent, these rules are more likely to maximize the good of human beings taken as a whole than other rules that might be accepted. Hare has virtually nothing concrete to say on this subject. Mill, on the other hand, suggests that for "the whole past duration of the human species . . . mankind have been learning by experience the tendencies of actions." He adds that "mankind must by this time have acquired positive beliefs as to the effects of some actions on human happiness; and the beliefs which have thus come down are the rules of morality for the multitude" (1957, ch. 2 par. 24). There is, however, a great difference between knowledge of "the effects of some actions on human happiness" and knowledge of the rules that will maximize the happiness of all human beings, much less "the whole sentient creation," taken in the aggregate. It would require an extraordinarily naive view of human history to regard the development of moral beliefs as a trial and error process of discovering such rules.

51. 1981, p. 50.

52. *Ibid.*, p. 38.

53. See Mill, ch. 2 par. 25; and Hare 1981, pp. 39 and 173.

54. In this connection, see Mill 1957, ch. 2 par. 19; and Hare 1981, pp. 136–37 and 202.

55. Cf. Williams 1988, pp. 189–90.

56. So far as this point goes, an agent might be able to rely on nonutilitarian sensibilities in determining what following a rule requires. My argument here concerns determining when to follow a rule.

57. See 1981, pp. 38–39. Cf. 1988 p. 275. On the whole, it is reasonable to interpret Mill's account of rules in this way as well, though this is controversial (for one difficulty, see 1957, ch. 2 par. 24). Yet if Mill's rules are mere rules of thumb, it is harder to discern a critique of the phenomenological argument in his position.

58. It may be said that such sensitivity would put the applicability of a rule in question only when another rule appears to conflict with it, and hence that the situations I am referring to are simply those in which rules conflict. But this is unlikely, at least in the absence of a very large number of rules. Moreover, to the extent to which this is true, it will turn out that a conflict of rules is much more common than the two-level account acknowledges.

59. In saying this, I mean to invoke some but not all features of Weber's classic analysis of bureaucracy, in particular, that the ends of a bureaucratic organization are best achieved when its officials follow, in a "spirit of formalistic impersonality," the rules designed to achieve these ends (see Weber 1946, pp. 196–244).

60. It might be said that Mill and Hare do not intend agents at the intuitive level to regard human beings in this way. Though this may be true, the account of moral rules required by the critique of the phenomenological argument fosters this attitude.

61. 1957, ch. 2 par. 19.

62. See Hare 1981, p. 4; and Mill 1957, ch. 5 par. 36 (cf. ch. 2 par. 18).

63. I do not mean to suggest that Mill or Hare would give this response. But consideration of it can reveal the commitments and resources of a two-level utilitarian approach.

64. It might be said that, by taking into account the preferences of each individual, Hare's theory does accommodate whatever may be unique about persons. But this is not to the point. To aim to maximize the sum of all preferences of all persons counted

equally is precisely not to acknowledge the separate, intrinsic, and unique value of each person: It is to make the value of each person a function of the overall value of the whole. A revealing indication of this is Hare's insistence that while thinking morally "in theory it is not necessary . . . to mention individuals" (1981, p. 42).

65. It is thus not surprising that some two-level theorists have been tempted by the unpromising idea that agents should somehow adopt, for act-utilitarian reasons, moral dispositions that consciously reject the perspective of act-utilitarianism. In this connection, see Railton 1984.

66. Walzer 1973, p. 172.

67. *Ibid.*, p. 171.

68. Rawls 1971, p. 482.

69. Cf. Dahl 1987, p. 423 note 41.

70. Since Mill did not put forward his position as a critique of the phenomenological argument, he cannot be faulted for this. For both Mill and Hare, however, many of the difficulties with the two-level utilitarian account of moral rules can be traced to the fact this account was developed in response to objections raised by traditional intuitionists. Utilitarians have tended to suppose that the intuitionist understanding of ordinary moral consciousness is correct, and they have tried to show that utilitarianism can account for this understanding. But for reasons I have given here, the intuitionist understanding of the role of moral rules may itself be questioned.

8

Kantian Critiques of
the Phenomenological Argument

Besides utilitarianism, the normative standpoint that has been the main source of opposition to the idea of inescapable moral wrongdoing has been that of Kant and positions inspired by Kant. In this chapter I consider Kantian arguments against RT and in particular Kantian critiques of the phenomenological argument for RT. The chapter has two main parts. In the first three sections I focus on Kant himself. It is clear that Kant rejects any form of genuine moral conflict and hence that he rejects inescapable moral wrongdoing. Yet there is a central idea in Kant, that of respect for persons as ends in themselves, that has some similarity to the responsibilities to persons account and that might be thought to allow for the possibility of inescapable moral wrongdoing. I argue that Kant does not allow for this because he interprets respect for persons as ends in light of his conception of moral law as modeled on physical law. In addition, I maintain that Kant's position is ultimately inadequate because, despite the concept of respect for persons as ends, Kant's understanding of the moral law has the effect of significantly displacing persons as direct objects of moral concern.

In the remainder of the chapter, I consider three recent attempts to give Kantian responses to the phenomenological argument. Two of these, those of Donagan and Barbara Herman, take as their starting point Kant's claim that, though there cannot be conflicting obligations, there can be conflicting grounds of obligation. The last, that of Christine Korsgaard, focuses on the specific issue of permissible ways of resisting evil from a Kantian standpoint. As it turns out, some features of these discussions are close to my own position, and in these respects I welcome these allies. But insofar as these authors reject RT and the phenomenological argument for RT, I argue that they are inadequate. On the whole, a Kantian approach offers little prospect of adequately explaining intuitions concerning inescapable moral distress.

I. Respect for Persons as Ends in Themselves

Kant maintains that his moral philosophy is an elucidation of ordinary moral belief. Writing about the "universal law" formula of the categorical imperative, he declares that "the common reason of mankind in its practical judgments is in perfect agreement with this and has this principle constantly in view."[1] Whatever might be thought of this claim, there is no question that there are passages in Kant that have tremendous intuitive appeal and that account for much of the influence of Kant's moral philosophy as a whole. Yet these passages occur mainly in connection with the "end in itself" and "realm of ends" formulas of the categorical imperative. Though Kant thinks the "universal law" formula is the best guide to "moral evaluation," he believes it worthwhile to introduce these latter two formulas "if one wishes to gain a hearing for the moral law." For, he says, compared to the "universal law" formula, they are "closer to intuition" and "nearer to feeling."[2] And indeed they are.

It is important to begin with these passages. Aside from demonstrating the intuitive attraction of Kant's thought, they show immediately that Kant differs sharply from all forms of utilitarianism.[3] At the same time, they indicate that in a significant respect Kant's view is closer to the responsibilities to persons account than is utilitarianism.

In the *Foundations of the Metaphysics of Morals* Kant declares that each human person has "absolute worth," and "exists as an end in itself." For this reason, a person is not to be "used merely as a means," but is to be treated as an "object of respect."[4] These claims are put forward in defense of the "end in itself" formula, which says "act so that you treat humanity, whether in your own person or in that of another, always as an end and never as a means only."[5] Later, Kant draws a distinction between price and dignity. "Whatever has price," he says, "can be replaced by something else or its equivalent." But "whatever is above all price, and therefore admits no equivalent, has a dignity." Again, that which has "relative worth" has a price, while that which has "intrinsic worth" has dignity.[6] Kant then declares that human persons have dignity and not mere price. Hence their value is intrinsic and irreplaceable, and for this reason persons deserve respect. These remarks occur in Kant's argument for the "realm of ends" formula. Our dignity is said to be rooted in our "autonomy," our capacity to legislate for ourselves. According to the "realm of ends" formula, "all maxims which stem from autonomous legislation ought to harmonize with a possible realm of ends as with a realm of nature."[7]

These words are echoed in *The Metaphysic of Morals*. In one respect, a man may be said to have "an *extrinsic* value in terms of his usefulness (*pretium usus*)," and so to have "his *price*." But "man regarded as a *person*," Kant says, "is exalted above any price." As a person, "he is not to be valued as a mere means to the ends of others . . . but as an end in himself." For he possesses "a *dignity* (an absolute inner worth) by which he exacts *respect*."[8] Later Kant says that respect is "the recognition of a *dignity* (*dignitas*) in other men, *i.e.* of a worth that has no price or no equivalent for which the object of esteem (*aestimii*) could be exchanged."[9] Hence, everyone owes respect to others and is owed it in return. This means, again, that a "man cannot be used merely as a means by any man . . . but must always be treated at the same time as an end."[10] The respect that is owed to a person is in an important sense unconditional. It is based on personhood and not on what the person does. Hence, "I cannot deny all respect to even the immoral man as a man; I cannot withdraw at least the respect that belongs to him in his quality as a man, even though by his deed he makes himself unworthy of his humanity." For this reason, though punishment may be justified, "there can be disgraceful punishments which dishonour humanity itself."[11]

These passages exhibit a fundamental and compelling dimension of Kant's moral thought. With these eloquent words, Kant evokes an essential feature of our moral sensibility: that each individual person has an intrinsic worth or dignity, and that on account of this each person deserves to be treated with a respect that is commensurate with this value.[12] It is clear that this idea is incompatible with the utilitarian principle that we are to maximize the well-being of persons taken in the aggregate. This is implied by the statement that we are always to treat a person not merely as a "means" but as an "end in himself," as well as by the categorical rejection of the language of "price" and "exchange" in moral deliberation. For Kant, respect for a person means that some ways of treating a person are absolutely required, or absolutely forbidden, irrespective of the consequences. For example, to make a deceitful promise to someone is "to use another man merely as a means."[13] Hence, it is always wrong to make a deceitful promise, even if in a given case doing so would maximize the well-being of the aggregate of persons. No person can be used as a means to maximizing the well-being of the whole if this violates the person's dignity. Hence, the "end in itself" formula is "the supreme limiting condition on freedom of the actions of each man."[14]

At the same time, these passages show that in an important respect Kant's position is similar to the responsibilities to persons account. A key feature of that account is that persons are to be regarded as intrinsically valuable, as valuable in and of themselves. It is partly because of this that we come to have moral responsibilities to persons. In saying that persons have a worth that has "no equivalent," it might seem that Kant also believes that persons are uniquely valuable. But it is hard to find an affirmation of this in Kant's moral philosophy since what gives a person worth is the fact that he or she is a rational and autonomous being, a feature common to every person.[15] There are also other important differences between Kant and the responsibilities to persons account. Still, the similarity with respect to the idea of persons as ends in themselves is significant.

If we focus on this idea, taken by itself, it would seem that there may be situations in which it is not possible to respect each person as an end. For example, it might reasonably be thought that protecting an innocent child from undeserved harm is required by respecting persons as ends. Since the child is an end in itself, is a being with intrinsic worth and dignity, and since it is quite defenseless, surely our respect for it requires us to provide it with protection. But suppose that another person with evil intentions will harm, or even kill, this child unless I divert this person by making a deceitful promise. If respecting the child as an end requires such protection, then whatever I do I will fail to respect someone and hence will do something wrong. It seems possible that the concept of respecting persons as ends could result in inescapable moral wrongdoing. Thus Nussbaum can write with some plausibility that "we can claim to be following a part of the deep motivation behind Kant's own view of duty when we insist that duty does not go away because of the world's contingent interventions."[16] On this view, the duty to respect each person remains even when contingent circumstances prevent fulfilling both duties.

In fact, of course, this is not Kant's view. He interprets the concept of respect for persons as ends in themselves in such a way that it is always possible to respect each and every person. This interpretation is necessary because, for Kant, there cannot be a conflict of duties. This has already been suggested in the aforementioned "realm of ends" formula of the categorical imperative. To be moral, Kant says, our maxims "ought to harmonize with a possible realm of ends as with a realm of nature." The requirement that there be harmony among our duties introduces another dimension of Kant's thought. Hence, in order to understand his full position, it is important to see both why he thinks duties cannot conflict and how this affects his understanding of the concept of respecting persons as ends in themselves.

II. The Impossibility of Conflicting Obligations

Kant declares explicitly that moral obligations or duties cannot conflict. In a well-known passage in *The Metaphysic of Morals* he writes:

> A *conflict of duties* (*collisio officiorum s. obligationum*) would be a relation of duties in which one of them would annul the other (wholly or in part).—But a *conflict of duties* and obligations is inconceivable (*obligationes non colliduntur*). For the concepts of duty and obligation as such express the objective practical *necessity* of certain actions, and two conflicting rules cannot both be necessary at the same time: if it is our duty to act according to one of these rules, then to act according to the opposite one is not our duty and is even contrary to duty.[17]

Though widely quoted, this passage is rarely elucidated. It has not attracted much attention from Kant's commentators.[18] Yet it is not an isolated thought in Kant: His writings on moral philosophy are replete with admonitions about conflict within the moral sphere. For example, in the *Foundations* he declares that an absolutely good will "is a will whose maxim, when made a universal law, can never conflict with itself."[19]

In the passage from *The Metaphysic of Morals* Kant purports to give an argument for the claim that there cannot be conflicting duties. Perhaps Kant's sympathetic readers have regarded this argument as obvious and thus as not requiring explanation. Indeed, I will suggest that it is based on the most fundamental features of Kant's moral philosophy. Nonetheless, it is not evident on its face exactly how the argument is to be understood. Its two premises are, first, that duty or obligation expresses "the objective practical *necessity* of certain actions," and second that "two conflicting rules cannot both be necessary at the same time." Hence, it is a concept of practical necessity that is meant to be instrumental in the argument.

It might be supposed that Kant is tacitly relying on an idea that has been made explicit in some traditional deontic logics, namely that there is an analogy between moral obligation and logical necessity (and their related concepts).[20] This analogy has led to the thought that many theorems in alethic modal logic have parallels in deontic logic, parallels that imply that there cannot be conflicting obligations. Thus, in modal logic, if P is logically necessary and Q is logically necessary, then the conjunction of P and Q is logically possible. Likewise, it might be supposed, in the deontic case, if there is an obligation to do A and an obligation to do B, then the conjunction of A and B can always be done. Hence, a conflict of obligations is impossible.

There is, however, an obvious disanalogy between the concepts of necessity and obligation, which makes this and related arguments unconvincing. It is fundamental to modal logic that necessity implies actuality and that actuality implies possibility. But in deontic logic, we cannot infer actuality from obligation: Obligations often go unfulfilled, something Kant clearly did not deny. This difference surely casts doubt on the aforementioned argument. In modal logic, if P is necessary and Q is necessary, then the conjunction of P and Q is necessary. From this it immediately follows that the conjunction of P and Q is actual and hence that it is possible. In the deontic case, on the other hand, even if we assume that if there is an obligation to do A and an obligation to do B, then there is an obligation to do the conjunction of A and B, it does not follow that the conjunction of A and B is done. Hence, it does not follow in turn that it can be done. The route from obligation to possibility via actuality is blocked in the deontic argument.

Kant thinks obligation involves a notion of necessity, namely "practical necessity," and as will be seen he thinks this relates to another notion of necessity. But we are not likely to understand his argument merely by assimilating it to the analogy with logical necessity exploited in some deontic logics. A more fruitful approach is suggested by Donagan.[21] After quoting Kant's argument with approval, he goes on to defend its conclusion on the basis of the familiar argument from the agglomeration principle and the Kantian principle that 'ought' implies 'can'. Though he does not present this directly as an interpretation of Kant's argument, he offers no other interpretation of what Kant intends, and he implies that Kant is committed to this argument.

Donagan formulates the argument in terms of conflicting 'ought' statements. To review: According to the agglomeration principle, if X ought to be done and Y ought to be done, then both X and Y ought to be done, and according to the Kantian principle, if X ought to be done, then X can be done. Now, if A ought to be done and B ought to be done, then by agglomeration both A and B ought to be done, and by the Kantian principle it follows that A and B can both be done. But this is inconsistent with the claim that A and B cannot both be done. Therefore, it is not possible that A ought to be done and B ought to be done even though A and B cannot both be done.

Kant does not explicitly state this argument. But there is some reason to think he does accept it, or at least is committed to it. The Kantian principle is so-called because Kant frequently and famously endorses it. For example, in the *The Metaphysic of Morals* he says that an agent "must judge that he *can* do what the law commands unconditionally that he *ought* to do."[22] Again, in the *Critique of Practical Reason* he declares that "it is always in everyone's power to satisfy the commands of the categorical command of morality."[23] Matters are less clear with respect to the agglomeration principle. I know of no place where Kant directly endorses this principle, but many find it obvious and perhaps Kant does as well.[24] In addition, Kant sometimes formulates the Kantian principle with respect to the *actions* required by morality (rather than *an action*), and this might be read as implicit acceptance of the notion of agglomeration. Thus in the *Critique of Pure Reason* he says with respect to morally required actions, "since reason commands that such actions should take place, it must be possible for them to take place."[25] If this is interpreted as stating that it is possible for all morally required actions, taken together, to take place, then it would seem that Kant is endorsing both the agglomeration principle and the argument itself.[26]

On the other hand, there is no direct indication in the argument from the *Metaphysic of Morals* that Kant has this specific argument in mind. In any case, assuming that Kant does accept this argument, it remains to be shown why he supposes that obligations, taken collectively, can always be fulfilled. My suggestion is that the underlying explanation of why Kant believes moral obligations cannot conflict is rooted in the most fundamental idea of his moral philosophy: that morality is determined by the "moral law," variously referred to as the "categorical imperative" or the "law of freedom." In a passage just prior to the *Metaphysic of Morals* argument, he states that "*obligation* is the necessity of a free action under a categorical imperative."[27] Kant's understanding of the moral law, and of the relationship of moral obligations to it, explains why he believes these obligations cannot conflict.

Kant supposes that the moral law must be known on the basis of reason and not experience. It is an a priori principle and hence is characterized by necessity and universality. In addition, he emphasizes that we can know the moral law only on the basis of its "form." In the second *Critique* he says that a practical rule of pure reason "implies necessity with reference to the occurrence of an action," and he adds that this rule is "a law of freedom by which the will is determinable independently of everything empirical and merely through the conception of a law in general and its form."[28] But in order to know the form of law in general, Kant says, we can rely on the form of the law of nature (that is, of the physical world) provided by the understanding: "this natural law can, for the purpose of judgment, be used only in its formal aspect, and it may, therefore, be called the *type* of the moral law."[29] Thus the law of nature provides us with "a type for the estimation of maxims according to moral principles."[30] In particular, if a "maxim of action" cannot "stand the test of being made the form of a natural law in general," then it is morally prohibited.[31]

It is a central theme of Kant's philosophy that reason is unified but has two applications, resulting in two forms of knowledge: theoretical and practical. "Theoretical knowledge," he says in the first *Critique*, "may be defined as knowledge of what *is*, practical knowledge as the representation of what *ought to be*."[32] In each domain there is an a priori law: The law of nature determines what is, and the law of freedom determines what ought to be. But these two laws must have the same form, the form of any law. This is what makes it possible to use the form of the law of nature as a "type" for the law of freedom.

The common form is universality. But it also involves necessity, though this is understood differently in the two cases. The law of nature states what necessarily and universally happens in the realm of nature. The law of freedom declares what necessarily and universally ought to be done in the domain of autonomous beings. In nature, "necessity" means everything is causally determined by universal rules of reason and so cannot be otherwise. But autonomous beings, as noumena, are not causally determined: They are free from the necessity imposed by the law of nature. However, there is another sense in which they are under a rule of necessity, for the law of freedom requires that every autonomous being act in accordance with universal rules of reason. Since autonomous beings are free to choose whether or not to act in accordance with these rules, it is given as a categorical imperative. "It is," Kant says in the second *Critique*, "a rule characterized by an 'ought', which expresses the objective necessitation of the act." He adds that this means that, "if reason completely determined the will, the action would without exception take place according to the rule."[33] Moral necessity is a requirement of rules of reason imposed on every autonomous being. An autonomous being may choose not to act in accordance with these rules. But insofar as this being acts rationally, he or she does act in accordance with them.[34]

It is in light of this account of the relationship between the law of nature and the law of freedom that the "universal law" formula in the *Foundations* should be understood. In his clearest formulation of this connection, Kant writes:

> Because the validity of the will, as a universal law for possible actions, has an analogy with the universal connection of the existence of things under universal laws, which is the formal element of nature in general, the categorical imperative can also be expressed as follows: Act according to maxims which can at the same time have themselves as universal laws of nature as their object.[35]

The moral law requires us to act in accordance with rules of reason. The form of these rules is universality, and the "type" of this form—our model for understanding it—is found in the laws of nature. Hence, we are to act as if our maxims were universal laws of nature, that is, as if everyone did in fact act according to these maxims (even though they often do not). There is considerable controversy about the precise meaning of this formula of the categorical imperative.[36] But for the purpose of this discussion, it is sufficient to emphasize that Kant understands the form of moral obligations as modeled on the form of physical laws and that he regards both of these as rules of reason imposing, in different ways, necessary requirements upon their respective domains.

In view of this, it is not difficult to understand why Kant thinks there cannot be conflicting obligations. There are several ways to bring out this point. Intuitively, it is inconceivable that there could be physical laws that determine that something is (at the same time and in the same respect) both moving and not moving, or both liquid and solid, or both large and small. As a requirement of reason, the law of nature could not have such a result. Likewise, since the law of nature and the law of freedom are formally the same, it is inconceivable that there could be moral obligations or duties that determine that an action (at the same time and in the same respect) is both commanded and forbidden, or both right and wrong, or both good and evil. Since the law of freedom is also a requirement of reason, it could not have such an outcome either.

For Kant, it is impossible that a law, whether of nature or of freedom, could require an inconsistent state of affairs, since a law is a requirement of reason. It expresses universal and necessary rules. The sense of "necessity" differs in the two cases, but in both the concept of law connotes a requirement of reason. The law of nature states that physical objects are causally determined to conform to its rules of reason. The law of freedom states, not that autonomous beings will in fact conform to its rules of reason (which would be incompatible with freedom), but that *insofar as they are acting rationally* they will so conform.[37] Hence, if there were conflicting obligations, then it would sometimes be the case that agents acting rationally would both do and not do something. Since this is not possible, conflicting obligations would mean that it is not possible to act rationally.[38] Put differently, it would mean that reason would require us to act irrationally. Nothing could be more incomprehensible for Kant.

Another way to bring this out is to focus on the "universal law" formula of the categorical imperative. We are to act as if our maxims were universal laws of nature. In particular (in one manner of application), we are to consider whether a world in which every agent acts according to our maxims is a logically possible world. If it is not, then our maxims are not in conformity with the moral law. But it would violate this requirement if a set of maxims were such that, sometimes, following one maxim required doing A and following another required doing B, when A and B could not both be done. A world in which every agent acts in accordance with these maxims is not a possible world, for in such a world agents would sometimes do both A and B even though A and B cannot both be done. Thus the requirement to act as if our maxims were universal laws of nature preclude conflicting moral obligations.

This account of Kant's understanding of the moral law explains in what sense he thinks obligations "express the objective practical *necessity* of certain actions," and why he thinks these obligations cannot conflict. It also suggests that the analogy proposed by some deontic logicians between moral obligation and logical necessity does have a counterpart in Kant. For Kant, there is an analogy between the law of freedom and the law of nature: Both are universal and necessary requirements of reason. Moreover, the disanalogy between obligation and necessity—that the latter but not the former entails actuality—is, in a sense, addressed by Kant. It is true that, whereas physical laws entail actuality (conformity of nature to their requirements), moral obligations do not entail actuality (conformity of autonomous beings to their requirements). But there is another sense in which obligations do entail actuality since the law of freedom entails that autonomous agents conform to moral obligations insofar as these agents act rationally. Since for Kant it must be possible to act rationally, he would say both that physical objects must be able to conform to the law of nature and that autonomous agents must be able to conform to the law of morality.

This makes it clear why Kant accepts the Kantian principle. In addition, this account suggests that Kant is committed to what might be considered the functional equivalent of the agglomeration principle. That is, he assumes that moral obligations are to be regarded as applying collectively. This is implied by the analogy with physical laws, which are clearly understood to apply collectively, as well as by the fact that Kant repeatedly speaks in terms of moral obligations as constituting a system. Thus, we are to "make possible a system of freedom comparable to a system of nature."[39] Moreover, Kant often expresses the "universal law" formula in the plural: We are to act in accordance with maxims that could be universal laws of nature.[40] This suggests that we are not to universalize maxims individually but collectively: It must be possible for maxims, taken together, to be universal laws.[41] There is thus considerable reason to suppose that Kant does accept, at least implicitly, a version of the argument against conflicting obligations based on the Kantian principle and the agglomeration principle.

III. The Displacement of Persons

Insofar as Kant is claiming that there cannot be conflicting conclusions of moral deliberation I have no disagreement with him. It is clear, however, that there is no place in Kant for any form of genuine moral conflict that would make wrongdoing inescapable. It is true, as will be seen, that Kant does allow for what he calls conflicting "grounds of obligation." But this is not intended to be an admission of inescapable moral wrongdoing.[42] The entire conception of moral obligations as grounded in a moral law with the same formal structure as physical law makes it evident that Kant's theory precludes genuine moral conflict of any kind. Conflict may appear in the derivation of conclusions of moral deliberation from the categorical imperative, but such conflict is merely appearance. There is no substructure beneath sound deliberative conclusions in which actual conflicts giving rise to inescapable moral wrongdoing may persist. Kant manifestly rejects RT as well as DT.

Kant's rejection of inescapable moral wrongdoing is based on his understanding of the moral law as at once the source of moral obligations and the product of pure practical reason. A direct argument against Kant would need to show that the foundation of morality cannot be deduced solely on the basis of pure practical reason. Though I am skeptical about Kant's claim, I will not undertake a refutation of it here. Rather, I will present an indirect argument against Kant by showing that his position is inadequate because his understanding of the moral law has the effect of displacing concrete persons as immediate objects of moral concern. Thus I will pursue a theme related to my critique of utilitarianism. There is, however, an important difference between the two critiques. Whereas the responsibilities to persons account is flatly incompatible with utilitarianism, it has some affinity with Kant. This is due to Kant's concept of respect for persons as ends in themselves. There is a sense in which this concept is fundamental for Kant. Yet his understanding of morality as grounded in an a priori moral law leads him to interpret respect for persons in such a way that persons tend to be displaced as direct objects of moral concern. This displacement is closely connected to Kant's rejection of conflicting moral duties: Paradoxically, it is because persons are displaced that it is always possible to respect each and every person. From Kant's point of view, the concept of the moral law and the idea of respect for persons as ends are but two descriptions of the same reality.[43] From my perspective, there is an inherent tension between them.

The idea that moral duties are grounded in the law of reason might be seen as placing Kant in the natural law tradition that goes back to the Stoics.[44] But it is more significant to interpret Kant as a figure with the modern concern of reconciling morality (and also religion) with modern science, in particular with the physics of Newton. There are two related aspects to this project, both relevant to the rejection of moral conflicts and the displacement of persons. The first is methodological: to show that one and the same reason has two employments, a theoretical use and a practical use.[45] This results in the thesis that a common form of law is involved in both. The other concern is substantive: to establish that "the doctrine of morality and the doctrine of nature may each . . . make good its position."[46] The doctrine of morality entails freedom; the doctrine of nature entails causal determination. What allows each to "make good its position" is the division of objects into noumena and phenomena. The person as phenomenon is causally determined by the law of nature. But the person as noumenon is free from such determination and is subject only to the moral law. There is a tacit assumption in many recent discussions of Kantian moral philosophy to the effect that the categorical imperative may be accepted without commitment to the noumenal-phenomenal distinction. But to thus sever the two is not merely an amputation, as if the former could live perfectly well without the latter, it is a decapitation of Kant's moral theory. His understanding of the categorical imperative is unintelligible without the noumenal-phenomenal distinction. An analysis of the meaning of respect for persons as ends reveals this.

The person which is to be respected as an end in itself is given various descriptions by Kant. For example, the person is said to have "the power to set an end," or "the capacity of giving universal laws."[47] What underlies these different statements are the coordinate concepts of freedom and rationality. It is "the will of a rational being as such" that we are to respect.[48] This is important as much for what it excludes as for what it includes since it amounts to saying that we are to respect persons as noumenal entities but not as phenomenal entities. "It is only as intelligence," that is, as noumenon, that man "is his proper self."[49] On the other hand, "man in the system of nature," that is, as phenomenon, "is a being of slight importance," a being with the same value as animals.[50] As phenomenon man is a creature of inclinations, and inclinations "are so lacking in absolute worth that the universal wish of every rational being must be indeed to free himself completely from them."[51] Inclinations are not really attributes of man's "proper self" at all.

For Kant, then, the concrete person of ordinary experience is sharply divided into the noumenal and phenomenal, and only the former deserves respect.[52] This has several important consequences. First, since feelings and desires fall on the phenomenal side of this division as "inclinations," it is not persons with whom we are emotionally engaged who are as such deserving of our respect. Second, since each person is equally deserving of respect as a free and rational being, there is no respect for the person as a unique individual. What is respected about each person is always the same thing. Those features of persons that distinguish them from one another, that lead us to think of persons as uniquely valuable, are irrelevant to respect. Frequently these features are associated with the phenomenal person and hence are irrelevant for that reason. But even when they might be associated with the noumenal person, as when persons exhibit different styles of *esprit*, they are not relevant to respect.[53] More generally, any characteristic of a person that depends on the fact that the person is a spatial-temporal physical entity is irrelevant to respect since everything in the spatial-temporal framework of the physical world is phenomenal and hence not deserving of respect. Hence, it would seem that someone's physical comportment in the world, or someone's growth as a person, can have no bearing on respect.

In comparison with the understanding of persons in ordinary experience, the "persons" owed respect for Kant are severely truncated. The persons whom we encounter in everyday life are displaced by noumenal selves.[54] In fact, it is problematic to what extent even noumenal selves deserve respect for Kant. He declares that "the only object of respect is the law," and he adds, "all respect for a person is only respect for the law (of righteousness, etc.) of which the person provides an example."[55] This suggests that the primary object of our respect is not persons in any sense, but the moral law. Respect for (noumenal) persons is in some way secondary to respect for the law. It might be said that for Kant in respecting the law we thereby respect persons.

It is clear in any case that it is respect for the moral law that is of fundamental importance for Kant. In the *Foundations* he says that actions have moral worth only if they are done from duty, and duty is defined as "the necessity of an action executed from respect for law."[56] What gives actions moral worth is that they are done out of respect for the moral law. It is not an attitude to particular persons as such that generates moral worth, but an attitude to the law.

Kant explains the notion of respect for the law at length in the second *Critique*. Whereas all other feelings are inclinations associated with the phenomenal self, "respect for the moral law . . . is a feeling produced by an intellectual cause, and this feeling is the only one which we can know completely a priori."[57] It is reason itself, in the form of the moral law, that causes the feeling of respect for this law. Moreover, this feeling is concerned only "with the idea of a law simply as to its form."[58] The primary feeling of moral respect for Kant is neither caused by nor directed to particular persons as such. It is reason that is both cause and object of moral respect. On the other hand, though in this sense purely intellectual, the feeling of moral respect has tremendous emotive import for Kant.

Indeed, he frequently speaks of this respect in language ordinarily reserved for religious worship, for example, "Duty! Thou sublime and mighty name that dost embrace nothing charming or insinuating but requirest submission . . . only holdest forth a law which of itself finds entrance into the mind and yet gains reluctant reverence (though not always obedience)."[59] The emotive quality of the language of respect for the moral law is rarely that associated with love and concern for particular persons. Rather, it is that used to express humility and submission before God.

Respect for persons, then, turns out to mean respect for the law of reason. "We stand under a *discipline* of reason," Kant writes, "and in all our maxims we must not forget our subjection to it."[60] This is why he is committed to interpreting respect for persons in such a way that it is always possible to respect each and every person. Since respect for persons means respect for the law and since the law cannot generate conflict, respect for persons cannot generate conflict either. But conflict is avoided by displacing persons, whether phenomenal or noumenal, as immediate objects of moral concern. This is not to say that persons are eliminated altogether. For Kant, in respecting the law we do respect persons as noumenal beings. Nonetheless, there is a clear primacy of respect for the law over respect for persons in Kant. The orientation of Kant's moral agent is, so to speak, always upwards towards the moral law rather than outwards towards those particular persons in his or her immediate environment. This attitude manifests itself in a variety of ways in Kant. Here are some examples.

First, though he regards the three formulas as objectively equivalent, Kant maintains that "it is better in moral evaluation to follow the rigorous method and to make the universal formula of the categorical imperative the basis."[61] Kant apparently thinks we are more likely to understand our obligations by considering whether our maxims can be universal laws than by thinking about persons as ends in themselves. Second, he repeatedly makes remarks such as the following: "I should seek to further the happiness of others, not as though its realization was any concern of mine . . . I should do so merely because the maxim which excludes it from my duty cannot be comprehended as a universal law."[62] Kant is deeply skeptical about the value of direct concern for persons. Only concern for persons produced by a prior respect for universal law can have moral value.

Finally, there is Kant's famous essay in which he rejects Constant's claim that we are justified in lying in order to prevent the murder of a friend. Though Kant's position here is confirmed by his discussion of lying in *The Metaphysic of Morals*,[63] his friendly interpreters commonly argue that for one reason or another Kant's theory does not compel him to reach this conclusion.[64] Whether or not this is so, Kant does think it would be wrong to lie even to prevent a murder, and his articulation of this view betrays in stark fashion an attitude that in more subtle form pervades all his writings on ethics. In discussing this issue, the focus of Kant's attention is simply on whether or not the maxim to lie could be a universal law of reason. His conclusion is that honesty is "a sacred and absolutely commanding decree of reason, limited by no expediency."[65] To limit this command by expediency—here, in order to prevent the murder of your friend—is unjustified because to do so would be to admit an exception to the rule, and to add such exceptions to moral rules "would nullify their universality."⁶⁶ In making this argument, Kant does not suggest that the moral agent should show the least concern or responsibility for the friend who is about to be murdered. After all, he says, "it was only an accident (*casus*) that the truth of the statement harmed" the friend.⁶⁷ There is no better testimony to the tendency of Kantian ethics to displace persons by focusing on the concept of moral law. Even if the conclusion is in fact unwarranted on Kantian grounds, his discussion reveals the overwhelming importance Kant attaches to acting out of respect for the moral law irrespective of the implications of doing so for particular persons. He is prepared to say that nothing, even the preventable murder of a friend, can count against acting on a maxim that can have the form of law.

IV. Donagan on Conflicting Grounds of Obligation

Though Kant rejects the idea of inescapable moral wrongdoing, he does not offer anything that can be construed as a direct response to the phenomenological argument. Since he sometimes describes moral philosophy as an elucidation of the moral beliefs of ordinary persons, it might be supposed that he would be open to the possibility of this argument. But any such supposition is quickly undermined by Kant's categorical repudiation of the idea that we might learn something from our moral intuitions or feelings.⁶⁸ Kant would have flatly rejected the methodology of the phenomenological argument. Nonetheless, some contemporary philosophers have given Kantian responses to this argument. That they have done so suggests once again the importance that intuitions concerning inescapable moral distress have for us. I devote the remainder of this chapter to discussion of these responses, beginning with that of Donagan.⁶⁹ His expressed aim is to argue against the thesis that there may be conflicting moral obligations. But it is evident that he intends to reject both DT and RT, as well as to criticize the phenomenological argument.

There are two oddities in Donagan's account. The first is that he regards the rationalist moral theory upon which he bases his argument as being common to Kant and Aquinas. There are some affinities between Kantian and Thomistic moral thought. But there are also substantial differences, especially with respect to classical metaphysics and Aristotle. Second, Donagan's rejection of conflicting moral obligations has an important qualification: He claims that an agent who has violated no obligation cannot be confronted with conflicting obligations, but an agent who has violated an obligation may thereby create a conflict of obligations (what he calls a "perplexity *secundum quid*"). Though he thinks the former conflict involves an inconsistency, he regards the latter as unproblematic. These two oddities are connected by a third: Donagan purports to find the account of perplexity *secundum quid* in Aquinas, but it is not to be found there. In any case, though I briefly consider Donagan's discussion of perplexity *secundum quid*, I otherwise read him as presenting a Kantian theory and have nothing further to say about Aquinas.

Donagan's rationalist moral theory largely conforms to the covering law model. There is an abstract, universal first moral principle, best expressed by the "end in itself" formula of the categorical imperative. This principle is not self-evident, Donagan says, but it is justifiable by rational reflection. It also requires articulation on the basis of additional premises specifying what counts as respecting rational nature, premises that are established by "unformalized analytical" or "dialectical" reasoning.[70] On the basis of the first principle and these additional premises, it is a matter of deduction to establish various moral precepts. From these precepts and the facts of particular cases, specific deliberative conclusions may be deduced. When moral theory is properly understood, Donagan thinks, at whatever level we consider—first principle, moral precepts, or particular deliberative conclusions—there can be no moral conflicts (leaving aside the question of perplexity *secundum quid*). But he thinks there are several reasons why it might mistakenly appear that there are moral conflicts. His analyses of these purported mistakes suggest responses to the phenomenological argument.

Donagan begins with a passage from *The Metaphysic of Morals* that immediately follows the argument that a conflict of obligations is impossible. According to Kant:

> It may, however, happen that two grounds of obligation, one or the other of which is inadequate to bind as a duty (*rationes obligandi non obligantes*), are conjoined in a subject and in the rule that he prescribes to himself, and then one of the grounds is not a duty. When two such grounds are in conflict, practical philosophy does not say that the stronger obligation holds the upper hand (*fortior obligatio vincit*), but that the stronger ground binding to a duty holds the field (*fortior obligandi ratio vincit*).[71]

There are two claims here. This first is that there cannot be conflicting obligations but there can be conflicting grounds of obligations. The second is that when grounds conflict, we are not to say that there are two obligations the stronger of which "holds the upper hand" (which would deny the first claim), rather we are to say that there are two grounds of obligation the stronger of which "holds the field." The first claim is perplexing in that Kant here explains neither how conflicting grounds of obligation are generated nor how these conflicts are resolved so that no conflict of obligations results. But there is no perplexity about the meaning of the second claim: The relation of ground of obligation to obligation is that of appearance to reality. Donagan points out the significance of Kant's metaphors. "Kant avoided the metaphor for victorious struggle, namely, 'holding the upper hand', which he employed in depicting what a putative conflict of obligations would be." Rather, Donagan says, Kant "represented it as a conflict in which one ground 'holds the field', while the other, a mere *ratio obligandi non obligans*, simply vacates it, as being inadequate to bind as a duty."[72] Herman makes a similar point.[73] When grounds of obligation conflict, proper understanding reveals that at most one ground remains on the field as an actual obligation, while the other leaves the field altogether.[74]

The distinction between grounds and obligations suggests a possible response to the phenomenological argument, for it may be that inescapable moral distress can be explained by reference to conflicting grounds of obligation. On this account, only violation of an obligation would warrant moral distress, but by mistakenly taking conflicting grounds to be conflicting obligations persons sometimes incorrectly think moral distress is inescapable. In this way, inescapable distress is explained without supposing that obligations conflict.

The difficulty with this response is suggested by the metaphor of holding and leaving the field. This is indeed an apt metaphor for describing the elimination view. The discovery of conflicting grounds is like walking onto a tennis court for a singles match and finding two opponents on the other side of the net. This appears to create a problem. But when the situation is understood correctly, it is determined that one of these opponents has to leave the court altogether. So far as the game is concerned, you need pay attention only to the opponent on the court and can ignore the person now on the sideline. Likewise, in the case of conflicting moral grounds, once understood properly, you need concern yourself only with fulfilling the obligation established by one of them, and so far as morality is concerned, you can ignore the other.

On some occasions this may be an accurate description of the resolution of a moral conflict. For example, if I think I have conflicting lunch engagements this afternoon and then discover that one is actually for next week, then so far as today's obligations are concerned, I can focus on the one engagement and forget the other (it has left today's moral field). But the moral conflicts relevant to the phenomenological argument are not like this. In deciding whether or not to steal the car in order to help his hiking companion, Craig is not trying to figure out which moral responsibility—to help his friend and not to steal the girl's car—is allowed on the moral field. They are both plainly on the field: The question is what is the best thing to do under the circumstances. In deciding this, Craig does not suppose that if only he had understood morality properly in the first place he would have realized that one of these alleged responsibilities should never have been allowed on the field at all. From the perspective of this critique, of course, Craig is mistaken in thinking this. He should be attempting to determine which "responsibility" should leave the field and, morally speaking, no longer be his concern. But this just goes to show how removed this critique is from our moral experience. It repudiates rather than explains that experience.

Donagan says that Kant should be understood as claiming that conflicting grounds of obligation must involve an imperfect duty.[75] As an example, he considers a fireman who can save some but not all persons in a burning building. The need of each person is a ground of an imperfect duty to help. If there were only one person who could be saved, then the ground "would hold the field as a ground binding to a duty." But since there are several persons who cannot all be helped and since each ground has equal force, "none of them holds the field as a ground binding to a duty."[76] In this situation, Donagan says, the fireman has a duty only to act on as many of these grounds as possible.

The metaphor of grounds vacating the field does not comport well with this analysis, for if all the grounds leave the field, then it is unclear why there should be a duty to act on as many of them as possible.[77] In any case, this analysis maintains that when grounds conflict, each ground is such that in some circumstance it would "bind as a duty," even though in this circumstance at least one of these grounds does not so bind. This might again suggest a critique of the phenomenological argument. Since a ground is something that sometimes holds the field and binds as a duty and sometimes does not, in a particular situation it is easy to confuse grounds of duties with duties themselves. When grounds conflict, the confusion of grounds and duties may make it seem that duties conflict and hence that moral distress is inescapable.

This critique requires an account of why specific grounds bind in some circumstances and do not bind in others. For Donagan, since duties cannot conflict, when grounds conflict at least one ground does not bind as a duty. But this is not sufficient to show *why* it does not bind. If it binds in other situations, then why not here as well? In particular, if respecting a person as an end requires this action in some circumstances, then why does it not require it in this circumstance? There must be something specific to this situation, in contrast with those others, that shows that the ground does not bind here. The reason cannot simply be the presence of conflict. Conflict by itself does not establish which ground binds as a duty and which does not. Donagan himself acknowledges that the explanation cannot be *ad hoc*, but must be supported by "dialectical reasoning."[78]

Whatever the explanation, a consequence of this view is that what respecting a person as an end requires depends upon the particular circumstances of each situation. From one perspective, this analysis is unexceptionable. Deliberative conclusions necessarily depend upon the specific features of each situation. In deciding what is morally best here and now, all the circumstances of here and now must be considered. If conflicting grounds are really equally significant, then the correct conclusion of moral deliberation is to do one action or the other. But suppose, to modify the example, a father acts on this conclusion by saving one of his children rather than another, and yet feels moral distress nonetheless. For Donagan this can only result from a mistake, a confusion of duty and nonbinding ground. Since the father has done what the moral law requires in this case, there is no justification for any form of moral distress. Though the analysis is different, the conclusion of this argument is substantially the same as that of the two-level utilitarian critique: that an agent who does what is morally best and yet feels, and finds it appropriate to feel, moral distress is making some kind of mistake.

In the absence of an alternative to Kantian and utilitarian theories, the attribution of a mistake in these feelings may appear plausible. But the responsibilities to persons account shows that these feelings need not be seen as involving a mistake. Though the correct deliberative conclusion is to save one or the other child, there may still be a moral responsibility to save each. Our responsibilities have contextual determinants, yet they are not defined by what is possible in every situation. Because they are based primarily on our responses to the intrinsic and unique value of particular persons with whom we are connected, it is possible for these responsibilities to conflict. When they do, justified moral distress is inescapable. Moral distress at not being able to save the life of a person for whom one is responsible need not involve a misunderstanding. With respect to moral feelings we consider natural and appropriate, an account that regards them as reasonable responses to a situation is superior, *ceteris paribus*, to an account that is forced to regard them as involving a mistake.

Donagan uses the fireman example to make a more general point. The conclusion that the only obligation is to save one or the other victim obviously leaves a deliberative question about exactly which to save. For Donagan, this is a special case of a common phenomenon: Though moral deliberation typically constrains what we may do, it often leaves unanswered the question specifically what to do. "In most cases," he says, "moral considerations do not suffice to answer the question, What shall I do?."[79] When this happens, only practical but nonmoral reasons can answer this question. Since there is an irreducible plurality of these reasons and they may conflict, genuine practical conflicts are possible. But a practical conflict is not a moral conflict, Though it may be "readily mistaken" for it.[80] On this view, inescapable moral distress may be said to arise from confusing practical conflicts with moral conflicts. Practical conflict may occasion its own form of inescapable distress, but this is not moral distress. Mistaking practical conflict for moral conflict may make moral distress seem inescapable even though in fact there are no moral conflicts and moral distress can always be avoided.

The claim that many deliberative questions are not moral questions is characteristic of Kantian morality. On Kant's view, it would seem that much of life falls under the category of the morally permissible. Since what is morally permissible is neither commanded nor forbidden by the moral law, conflicts that arise within this domain are by definition not moral conflicts.[81] But even assuming that many deliberative questions are not moral, it is implausible to suppose that the conflicts appealed to in the phenomenological argument are not moral conflicts: The conflicts of Vere, Craig, Jennifer, and the like clearly involve conflicting moral considerations. It may be said that this only appears to be so, that any such conflict involves a conflict of considerations that are sometimes moral considerations but that, on account of conflict, are not both genuine moral considerations in this case. Once it is determined what the moral law requires or permits in each of these cases, any further practical conflict is nonmoral. This response is what is to be expected from the Kantian standpoint. What it shows, however, is how Kantian morality displaces persons as direct objects of moral concern. As long as an agent acts out of respect for the moral law, he or she has met the requirement to respect persons as ends. Further issues about how to relate to persons are not moral questions. They are matters of inclination and have no moral significance.

The remainder of Donagan's critique concerns obligations arising in connection with promises. It is surprising to discover that here Donagan allows for inescapable moral wrongdoing, in one case intentionally and in another case, it seems, unwittingly. He correctly observes that the duty to keep promises has loomed large in the "moral dilemmas" literature, in the form of either conflicts between promises or conflicts between promises and other duties. Donagan sets out to show that these situations are often misunderstood because they suppose that there is a duty to keep any and all promises. On his view, promises are made conditionally: "most promises are made and accepted on the twofold condition that the promiser has acceptable reason to believe that he can and may do what he promises, and that if nevertheless it turns out that he either cannot or may not, the promisee will not be entitled to performance."[82] Donagan adds that the two parties "can often be confident, whether from a shared culture or from personal intimacy, that they would agree about the acceptability or unacceptability of any reason that might be put to them for believing that a particular promise could be kept."[83] Thus, if a person makes a promise in the belief that it will be morally permissible to keep it and it later turns out unexpectedly on account of a conflicting duty that keeping it is not permissible, then there is no obligation to keep it. In this way, apparent moral conflicts involving promises are shown not to be conflicts at all. Conflict is precluded by a condition tacitly attached to the promise itself.

It may be doubted whether promises are always made with the understanding of this condition, and also whether there will always be agreement about which circumstances are relevant to the condition. Nonetheless, this does suggest a plausible strategy for resolving conflicts involving promises. Even if this strategy were accepted, however, it would not follow that moral wrongdoing can always be avoided in these cases. The condition may establish only what ought to be done all things considered. It need not state that in following this deliberative conclusion there is no wrongdoing. Indeed, Donagan himself seems to sense this. When a promise cannot or may not be kept, he says, we promisees "would not be entitled to demand that it be kept, although, depending on circumstances, we might be entitled to amends for the breach."[84] Again, this time from the perspective of the promiser, Donagan says that in a case of this kind, "I am not bound to do what I promised her, although I may have amends to make for not doing it."[85] The language of "amends for the breach" surely implies a compensatory response to some form of wrongdoing. Donagan seems to commit himself here to a doctrine of inescapable moral wrongdoing, though he neither acknowledges this nor offers an account of it in terms of his Kantian framework.

This is a welcome concession. Yet it is important to understand why wrongdoing may be inescapable in promising cases. On the responsibilities to persons account, it is rare that promises are merely isolated, contractual acts between consenting adults, as Donagan's account suggests. Very often promises are made in the context of ongoing relationships between persons in which the promise is a way of carrying out, making explicit, qualifying, extending, or specifying already existing responsibilities that are constitutive of the relationship. For example, a promise to have lunch with a friend may part of a more inclusive effort to maintain, enlarge, revitalize, enhance, or redirect the friendship. When the promise is broken, albeit justifiably, it remains the case that this effort has been damaged or at least derailed. Depending on the circumstances, this may have greater or lesser significance, but sometimes it may have sufficient import to call for a compensatory response—an apology, a special effort to meet again soon, an offer to do a favor, and so on. It is constitutive of flourishing human relationships that we sometimes respond to broken promises, whether justified or not, in these restorative ways. Such responses are ways of affirming the value of persons, our relationships with them, and our responsibilities to them. To regard the unfulfilled promise as of no import because after all we acted for the best is to deny that there has been a disruption in our standing with the promisee. It is to act as if the person has no independent importance to us, but is of value only as a function of some larger set of concerns. Both Kantian and utilitarian theories encourage precisely this attitude, and for this reason they are poorly equipped to explain why amends for a justifiably broken promise may be called for.[86]

There is one situation where Donagan explicitly accepts inescapable wrongdoing. If a person promises to do something wrong, then whatever the person does will be wrong in some respect. Though it is wrong to make such a promise, once it is made either it is kept (and wrong because the action promised is wrong) or it is broken (and wrong because it is wrong to break the promise). Hence, a person making a "wrongful promise" would make wrongdoing inescapable.[87] This is Donagan's example of "perplexity *secundum quid.*"

Donagan seems to think that philosophers may have endorsed inescapable moral wrongdoing in general at least partly because they have failed to distinguish this special case in which wrongdoing makes further wrongdoing unavoidable from all other cases in which wrongdoing can always be avoided. There are, however, several respects in which it is puzzling that Donagan endorses this view. First, he claims to have discovered this position in Aquinas although Aquinas does not accept it.[88] In the passages to which Donagan refers, Aquinas maintains that a person in a sinful state such as voluntary false conscience may do something wrong no matter what. But the person can at any time forgo that state and thereby make it possible to avoid wrongdoing. For Aquinas there is never a time, as on Donagan's view, at which wrongdoing is inescapable. Second, as Alasdair MacIntyre points out, Aquinas elsewhere suggests what from Donagan's own perspective is surely the more plausible analysis of this case: namely, that a wrongful promise is not binding, and so no wrong is committed by breaking it.[89] It is hard to believe that, if I promise to murder your business competitor, I thereby acquire a moral obligation to do so.

Finally, as several critics have pointed out, on Donagan's view conflicting obligations are inconsistent and it would seem that an inconsistency is unacceptable with or without prior wrongdoing.[90] On this last point there may be a response, for the inconsistency arises only in conjunction with the agglomeration principle and the Kantian principle. Perhaps Donagan would say that one or both of these principles does not apply in this case. His thought seems to be that the moral law by itself could not generate conflicting obligations, but that conjoined with a wrongful promise it could.[91] He may regard these principles as constraining what the moral law itself, as a law of reason, could require, but not as constraining what could be required as a result of the moral law in conjunction with an act by an agent that is wrongful and hence contrary to reason. By analogy, were an event to violate a physical law this might make other violations of the law inevitable. Yet Donagan elsewhere seems to block this rejoinder. In response to the claim that morality is an ideal which cannot always be applied in an evil world, he declares that the moral law is intended to constrain actions in "the actual world—in Cicero's cesspool of Romulus" and not merely in Plato's ideal republic.[92] Since wrongful promises are part of our less than ideal world, one might think that for Donagan the moral law would entail nonconflicting obligations for agents confronting any morally imperfect action, whether by others or themselves.

In any case, there is no basis for thinking that the phenomenological argument gains unwarranted plausibility from failing to distinguish the special case of wrongful promises from other moral conflicts. Though the examples appealed to in the phenomenological argument have sometimes involved promises, they have not featured wrongful promises. On the responsibilities to persons account, since inescapable moral wrongdoing is possible, there is no reason to deny that it may arise from previous wrongdoing. But neither is there reason to think it only arises from it.

V. Herman on Conflicting Grounds of Obligation

Herman gives a more direct Kantian response to the phenomenological argument.[93] She acknowledges that "the phenomenon of moral conflict is an ordinary part of moral experience," or at least that "agents may be faced with situations . . . that leave them with no choice that does not also involve apparent wrongdoing."[94] Yet she agrees with Kant that there can be no actual conflict of obligations. Herman regards his reference to the possibility of conflicting grounds of obligation as the key to saving the facts of moral experience that seem to suggest inescapable wrongdoing: "the shift from conflict of obligations (or duties) to conflicting *grounds* of obligation 'saves the phenomena' directly."[95] In particular, she says, "moral conflict is experienced by an agent in circumstances where she is responsive to more than one [conflicting] ground of obligation."[96] Thus she argues that a Kantian account can reject inescapable moral wrongdoing and yet not have to "explain away the phenomena of conflict in moral experience."[97] It "saves both phenomenon and theory."[98]

Herman admits that for Kant, when grounds conflict, "the weaker ground of obligation cannot gain the field at all—it has no effective weight in these circumstances."[99] I have suggested that this implies that our experience of moral conflict involves a mistake. But Herman thinks there is more to be said on behalf of the Kantian account. She maintains that grounds of obligation are "that which constrains what can be willed a universal law," and this means they are "*facts* of a certain sort." For example, the ground of the obligation of mutual aid is "the fact that we are dependent beings."[100] Because facts cannot conflict, it is not grounds per se that conflict. Rather, moral conflict occurs in an agent's maxim of action: If she acknowledges more than one relevant ground, "she *may* adopt a maxim of action that brings them into conflict."[101] An agent with a friend in need and a promise to keep may set out to do both only to discover that this is impossible. She then has a conflict in her maxim of action. When this happens only one ground is sufficient to establish an obligation, and deliberation is needed to determine which. In deliberation, the presumption is that a ground generates an obligation, but this presumption can be rebutted by other grounds. Obligation is "the *result* of deliberation."[102]

Herman contrasts this account with what she calls "the performance model," according to which "duties (or obligations) are conceived of as *performance* requirements, that is, as obligations to *do* certain actions (or kinds of action)."[103] By comparison, according to her Kantian model, "what it is to be obliged is to be under the practical necessity of acting as moral deliberation directs." Hence, "obligation is not a matter of required performances but of commitment to a way of determining how one is to act."[104] This is not to say that obligation has no implications for action. But on the Kantian model there is only one obligation: to act as deliberation directs. Since sound deliberation cannot give conflicting directions, there cannot be conflicting obligations. By contrast, on the performance model, there are multiple duties and "conflicts of duty are unavoidable."[105]

Herman thinks philosophers have endorsed inescapable wrongdoing because they have accepted the performance model. She anticipates the objection that Kant himself accepts this model, at least insofar as he regularly appears to speak of a plurality of obligations to perform kinds of actions. Through an analysis of two purported "Buridan cases" of inescapable wrongdoing, she tries to show that Kant's model is in fact the Kantian model.

Suppose an agent can save the life of only one of two twins, but there is no basis for choosing which. For Herman, what the duty of mutual aid requires is not the action of saving one or the other twin. That is the view of the performance model. Rather, "one is obliged to acknowledge claims of need and to be prepared to help as and if one can." Though only one twin can be saved, she says, "this obligation can be met for *both* twins." Hence, if one saves A rather than B, "one has *not* left one's obligation to B unfulfilled." For, she says, "one had no obligation to save B (or A)."[106]

In the second case, an agent can keep only one of two promises and there is no basis for choosing which. What the duty of promise-keeping requires for Herman is not, as on the performance model, that the actions promised be performed. Rather, "the content of the promising obligation" is a "constraint on deliberation." This constraint creates a presumption that one must choose to keep the promise, but this presumption can be rebutted if there is sufficient moral reason. In the case at hand, only one promised action can be performed. In performing this action, she says, "it does *not* follow that I have not done what I ought to have done *with regard to the promise I have not kept*." In fact, she claims, "I can have satisfied the obligation (in the sense of deliberative constraint) imposed by both promises."[107]

Questions may be raised about this account as an interpretation of Kant. Herman's explanation of deliberation does not explain the metaphor that one conflicting ground "holds the field" while the other leaves it. To say that the presumption to keep a promise may by rebutted by a sufficient moral reason does not show why when so rebutted the ground of obligation has "no effective weight." In addition, though Kant does think our obligation is to act as deliberation directs, it is not clear why this should be regarded as an alternative to the performance model, the idea that obligations are "obligations to do certain actions (or kinds of action)." Kant certainly speaks as if there are performance obligations, for example, to be honest. It need not be assumed that performance obligations must conflict. They may be specified in such a way that conflicts are precluded.

Kant's reference to conflicting grounds might be interpreted as a stage in the process of specification. Suppose analysis in terms of universalizability has shown there is an obligation to do actions of kind X and kind Y. The fact that an action is X is thus a ground for the obligation to do the action, and likewise for Y. We then encounter a situation in which action A is X and action B is Y, but it is not possible to do both A and B. There are conflicting grounds of obligation. This occasions deliberation, but what deliberation achieves is a new analysis in terms of universalizability such that there is, say, an obligation to do actions of kind Y* rather than Y (where Y* is a modification of Y), and B is not Y*. This analysis shows that one ground holds the field—there remains a ground for the obligation to do A—while the other leaves it—there is no longer a ground for the obligation to do B (since the fact that B is Y is no longer a ground for the obligation to do B). On this account, deliberation establishes an obligation to do actions of kind X and hence the particular action A.

Whatever Kant in himself may think, Herman argues that Kant as she understands him—that is, as accepting the Kantian model and repudiating the performance model—is able to explain the experience of moral conflict even though he denies that obligations conflict. The basic idea is that an agent may adopt a maxim that brings grounds into conflict. With a friend in need of help and a promise to be kept, an agent may set out to do both, and discover that these actions are incompatible. Thus it may appear to the agent that wrongdoing is inescapable. This appearance, however, merely sets the stage for deliberation that, when correctly performed, will result in conflict-free direction. But Herman acknowledges that proponents of the phenomenological argument have appealed to features of moral experience that go beyond the thought that there are conflicting grounds of obligation as she understands them. In particular, she correctly recognizes two aspects of moral experience that have been emphasized in this argument.

First, there are moral conflicts in which, no matter what was done, agents would feel, and find it appropriate to feel, some form of moral distress such as guilt or remorse. Second, whatever was done, agents would also feel, and find it appropriate to feel, the need to make up for the action they did not perform, by an apology or some more concrete form of restitution. The phenomenological argument claims that these feelings are often best explained by supposing that these agents would do something wrong in some sense no matter which action they performed. These are the sorts of phenomena that must be accommodated by theory.[108]

Herman grants that these phenomena "in their customary presentation do not fit in the Kantian account."[109] Nonetheless they can be explained. With respect to inescapable feelings of moral distress, Herman first insists that remorse or guilt are justified only if there has been wrongdoing. Since wrongdoing is never inescapable on the Kantian model, agents in conflicts who would feel remorse or guilt no matter what are making a mistake. Some course of action is always available for which it would be unwarranted to feel these things. Though Herman does not deny that people may feel guilt when doing as they ought, she expresses skepticism about the epistemic value of these feelings. "I do not think we are clear enough about guilt," she says, ". . . to have much confidence in our guilt responses as foundations for theoretical claims."[110] On the other hand, she allows that other feelings, such as compunction, repugnance, and regret, may be justified in the absence of wrongdoing. To the extent that we think it a good thing that agents feel some distress about, say, breaking a promise, even when it is obligatory to do so, she says these feelings are sufficient but give no rationale for thinking wrongdoing inescapable.

This is a common critique: Distressful moral feelings are divided into those that do and do not imply the thought of wrongdoing, and it is claimed that the former cannot be inescapable without error, although the latter can. With respect to inescapable feelings of guilt and remorse, there is no explanation of these feelings here except to say that they involve a mistake, perhaps a confusion of grounds of obligations with actual obligations. This too is a common claim. But it is not a claim that saves the phenomenon. In Herman's terms, it explains it away. Indeed, her skeptical remark about guilt suggests that for her there is no point in trying to save this particular aspect of moral experience.

The explanation of inescapable feelings of moral distress rests on the claim that other feelings such as regret, repugnance, and compunction may be justifiable when acting as deliberation directs. Thus, it may be inescapable that a person will justifiably either feel these things (when so acting) or else feel guilt or remorse (when not). Regret and the like do not imply the thought of wrongdoing. What makes them appropriate is the fact that some kinds of actions "should be hard to do." These actions are those that are "normally forbidden." When justifiably breaking a promise, it is appropriate to feel regret and so on because normally it is forbidden to break a promise. These feelings are warranted because they do "the required instrumental work" of preventing us from becoming too comfortable about doing what ordinarily is wrong. They are "appropriate constraints for imperfectly rational beings."[111]

It is not clear what contribution the Kantian model is making to the justification of this account. Feelings such as regret are supposed to be appropriate for persons with the thought, "I am doing nothing wrong, although usually actions of this kind are wrong." As is the case with Hare's not dissimilar analysis of guilt, it is hard to see why a person with this thought should feel any form of moral distress (though it might be an understandable mistake). The knowledge that such distress would have instrumental value is not sufficient to make it appear appropriate. Perhaps the idea is that persons with sound moral education would nonetheless find it appropriate, but Herman is clearly unsympathetic with any program that would instill these feelings via deception.[112] If our only obligation is to act as deliberation directs, then the most straightforward approach would be to educate people to feel moral distress if and only if they do not so act.

In addition, the feelings Herman sanctions do not fully capture the thought of persons in examples referred to in the phenomenological argument. If Jennifer decides to turn her son into the authorities because she believes this is morally for the best, she may well regret it. But she may also think she is doing something in some sense wrong. Herman's account cannot make sense of this. It supposes that 'wrong' can only mean failing to do what deliberation directs. Jennifer's feeling must then be confused or mistaken. But we need not interpret her feeling in this way. On the responsibilities to persons account, it is possible to believe one is acting as deliberation directs (and so in one sense doing nothing wrong) and at the same time think one is failing to fulfill a responsibility to someone (and thus doing something wrong in that sense).

Herman's response to the restitution argument is rather different. With respect to conflicting promises, when one promise is kept and the other is not, she says there arises a new situation, which includes the unkept promise and which may call for further deliberation. The broken promise is not an unfulfilled obligation: It was not wrong to break it. Still, she says, the broken promise may have future "deliberative significance."[113] If breaking the promise causes some harm, the agent may have some responsibility for relieving this harm. Acknowledging this responsibility is part of the deliberative constraint that arises from making the promise in the first place.

Herman does not say much about when and in what ways a broken promise that was not wrongly broken may result in further responsibilities. But it is clear that her account does partially capture an important aspect of moral experience: the feeling that, because the promise was broken, something ought to be done that need not have been done had the promise been kept. Yet it also clearly excludes a key aspect of this experience. This is most evident with respect to apologizing. An agent who breaks one promise in order to keep another is likely to feel that she ought to apologize to the first promisee, especially if great harm, inconvenience, or disappointment has been caused. On Herman's account it would not make sense to apologize: In the absence of wrongdoing there is nothing to apologize for. Sometimes all one can do is apologize. In these cases, Herman's agent can do nothing at all, except perhaps give notification of the circumstances and express concern. In general, no future responsibility could be understood on her analysis as being a response to prior wrongdoing. But this is often how such actions are understood. A mother who on account of an overriding professional responsibility is unable to attend her child's recital, as promised, naturally feels a sense of moral shortcoming. Further action with respect to her child is called for, and this cannot be understood except in terms of a kind of reparation or restoration of the relationship with her child.

The responsibilities to persons account can make sense of this. Though the mother acted as deliberation required, she failed to fulfill an important responsibility to her child. In this sense she acted wrongly, and she correctly feels the need to apologize and make up for it. Herman criticizes accounts of this kind for employing "economic metaphors." When an obligation is not met, "there is a balance due, a debt that is owed," and a responsible agent must discharge the debt in order "to clear her balance."[114] Herman also maintains that the performance model, which she believes gives rise to these accounts, regards morality as an unwelcome interruption into ordinary life, as something imposed from without. On this view, she says, "obligations are burdens to be discharged, interfering with the real business of our lives."[115] The "hero" of this view, she claims, is "the individual of liberal theory: triumphant in the face of obstacles (including morality) in the pursuit of private goals."[116] By contrast, she argues that the Kantian model is "able to integrate morality more intimately into an agent's life."[117]

These are perplexing remarks. There is no reason to think the restorative activity involved here must be understood on the model of economic transactions. This model implies that there is some unit of moral value such that a broken promise costs so many units and thus requires repayment with an equivalent number of units. It also implies that we would just as soon not repay if we could. But it is implausible to suppose that the mother who seeks to make up for missing her child's recital is thinking in these terms. It is hard to understand why Herman assumes that those who speak of inescapable moral wrongdoing are committed to understanding human relationships in this economic way. On the responsibility to persons account, moral responsibilities, far from being an external intrusion into life, are intrinsic to what makes life worthwhile. For they are constitutive of those relationships which give significance to our life. They are not something we generally wish to avoid. In confronting conflicting responsibilities, we are not thinking in terms of balancing our moral account. We are trying to be properly responsive to each of the persons with whom we are connected.

It is also surprising that Herman should offer this critique on behalf of Kant, for whom the relationship between morality and ordinary personal concerns is frequently described in the language of antagonism and hostility. Kant regularly portrays human life as a battle between the higher noumenal self and the lower phenomenal self, between reason and inclination, between the uncompromising demands of the moral law and the unruly and rebellious disruptions of our desires and emotions. To say that, by comparison, those who defend inescapable moral wrongdoing are committed to an understanding of human life into which morality is less integrated is doubtful. And it is simply false of the responsibilities to persons account.

VI. Korsgaard on Resisting Evil

Unlike Donagan and Herman, Korsgaard is not primarily concerned with the "moral dilemmas" literature. But in a discussion of the problem of resisting evil in Kantian ethics, she develops a response to the phenomenological argument, one that in some ways is more accommodating than others from the Kantian tradition.[118] She does not present her position as a straightforward interpretation of Kant, but as a modification of his views with which he might have some sympathy. Regardless, she offers an interesting strategy for understanding at least some purported cases of inescapable moral wrongdoing.

Korsgaard begins with Kant's claim that it would be wrong to lie to someone in order to prevent a murder. She argues that the "universal law" formula of the categorical imperative does not have this result, that in this case it would be permissible though not obligatory to lie. Yet she thinks the "end in itself" formula makes it wrong to lie in every case, including this one.[119] According to this formula, "coercion and deception are the most fundamental forms of wrongdoing to others—the roots of all evil."[120] On this analysis, then, these two formulas are not equivalent, but they are related. The "end in itself" formula is stricter than the "universal law" formula, although both make our rational nature the source of moral justification.

Korsgaard suggests that the "end in itself" formula is an attractive doctrine for free and rational beings. It specifies "a determinate *ideal* of conduct to live up to rather than setting a *goal* of action to strive for." Its advantage is its doctrine of limited responsibility: "your share of the responsibility for the way the world is is well-defined and limited, and if you act as you ought, bad outcomes are not your responsibility."[121] On this account, we can attempt to reason with others, but beyond that we have no responsibility for what they do. We are not permitted to coerce or deceive them in order to achieve our ends, even when good. But Korsgaard adds, "the trouble is that in cases such as that of the murderer at the door it seems grotesque simply to say that I have done my part by telling the truth and the bad results are not my responsibility."[122] More generally, she says, the "end in itself" formula "gives implausible answers when we are dealing with the misconduct of others and the recalcitrance of nature."[123]

Her response to this problem is a "double-level theory" based on the two formulas of the categorical imperative. The "end in itself" formula is the ideal for everyday life. But when dealing with "evil circumstances," whether moral or natural, we may set this ideal aside. In these cases, the "end in itself" formula "is inapplicable because it is not designed for use when dealing with evil."[124] This opens the way for the duty of mutual aid and the duty of self-respect (not to be used as a tool of evil) to justify or make obligatory the prevention of evil. In confronting evil, though we may violate the "end in itself" formula, we must never violate the less restrictive "universal law" formula: "this provides the point at which morality becomes uncompromising."[125] Moreover, even in these cases, the "end in itself" formula "defines the goal towards which we are working" and may guide us in formulating priority rules specifying the least objectionable means.[126]

In sum, according to Korsgaard's double-level theory, the less demanding "universal law" formula is an ideal standard that must be met in all circumstances. However, the more demanding "end in itself" formula functions differently in different circumstances. In daily life, it too is an ideal standard that must always be met. But when confronting evil, it is only a goal to be achieved, providing guidance as to means. Thus, although it is always wrong to lie in daily life, it may be permissible or obligatory to lie to evildoers such as the murderer at the door.

Korsgaard says one of the advantages of her theory is that it addresses the phenomenological argument. For it provides an explanation of Williams's claim that there can be regret for doing the morally correct action. She writes:

A double-level theory offers an account of at least some of the occasions for this kind of regret. We will regret having to depart from the ideal standard of conduct, for we identify with this standard and think of our autonomy in terms of it. Regret for an action we would not do under ideal circumstances seems appropriate even if we have done what is clearly the right thing.[127]

Korsgaard notes that there are two kinds of exceptions. Some exceptions are built into the moral practices of daily life. Thus there are exceptions, which provide conditions under which promises are canceled. When breaking a promise for this kind of exception, she says, "regret would be inappropriate and obsessive." She distinguishes this from "the kind of exception one makes when dealing with evil."[128]

Korsgaard clearly means to restrict her remark about the appropriateness of regret to a special class of cases: those circumstances in which we confront significant evil as contrasted with the ordinary circumstances of everyday life. Hence, this is not a response to all cases that have been put forward in defenses of the phenomenological argument. Yet it may be questioned how useful this distinction among circumstances is. In a world in which large numbers of men regard it as normal to abuse women, in which racial and religious prejudice structures the activities of a great deal of ordinary life, and in which political and economic institutions often promote or perpetuate oppression, it is hardly a typical person whose daily routine does not involve confrontation with some measure of evil. Though there are important differences among forms and degrees of evil in the world, it is doubtful whether Korsgaard can avoid dealing with what she regards as the danger of the slippery slope of saying simply that we may violate the "end in itself" formula when consequences are very bad.

With respect to obvious encounters with great evil such as the murderer at the door, it is hard to know exactly how to interpret Korsgaard's position. If deception is one of "the most fundamental forms of wrongdoing" (as the "end in itself" formula says), and yet in this case "not to tell the lie is morally bad," then it would seem that she is endorsing a doctrine of inescapable wrongdoing.[129] But she says that when confronting evil the "end in itself" formula is "inapplicable."[130] This may be taken in different ways. It might mean the formula has no relevance in these circumstances, in which case it would seem that lying to the murderer is not wrong in any sense. On this interpretation, she is offering an alternative to inescapable wrongdoing. The lie is not at all wrong: It is "clearly the right thing." Yet there is "regret for an action we would not do under ideal circumstances." However, it is not clear why, if the formula says that lying is wrong there but not here, we should have any regret for lying here.

Korsgaard seems to want to say something stronger. 'Inapplicable' may mean that, although the formula shows this lying action to be wrong in some significant sense, the correct conclusion of deliberation is that this action is permissible or obligatory. On this view, the "end in itself" formula states that every lie is "wrong." Nonetheless we are sometimes morally justified in not following this formula. In these cases we regret this departure because "we identify with this standard and think of our autonomy in terms of it." This interpretation is perhaps implied by Korsgaard's remark that it may be that "suicide is wrong from an ideal point of view, though justifiable in circumstances of very great natural or moral evil."[131] Here she looks to be embracing a form of inescapable wrongdoing: An action that is wrong according to a standard "we identify with" is nonetheless morally justified.

The main difficulty with Korsgaard's position on either interpretation is that it is unclear what the warrant for it is from a Kantian standpoint. Her intuitions are obviously sound: It is morally disturbing both to lie and to allow a murder, and the latter is considerably more disturbing than the former. On her reading of Kant, however, the "end in itself" formula entails that lying is always wrong, and she rightly admits that Kant believes the formula must always be obeyed.[132] The problem, she says, is that doing so is sometimes "grotesque," "implausible," or "not feasible."[133] But this does not show why, from Kant's perspective, we should put aside the "end in itself" formula in these cases. Kant himself is quite prepared, in this and other circumstances, to accept terrible consequences that might ensue from obeying the moral law as he understands it.[134]

Kant does give us a reason for preventing a murder: the duty of helping one another. But he says this duty cannot be fulfilled by means that are impermissible, and on Korsgaard's interpretation of the "end in itself" formula lying is always impermissible. More needs to be said to show why in special cases of confronting evil Kant would have reason to modify this view. By themselves, intuitions about what is grotesque or implausible have no weight for Kant. The problem is not simply that Kant believes the various formulas of the categorical imperative are equivalent and so is not in a position to consider a double-level theory presupposing that they are not. The difficulty is to explain why, assuming they are not equivalent, there is justification within the resources of Kant's outlook for sometimes setting aside the stricter standard.[135]

Earlier I suggested that the concept of respect for persons, understood intuitively, could give rise to inescapable moral wrongdoing. This might offer an avenue for developing Korsgaard's position. The problem is that, as Kant interprets this concept, all forms of genuine moral conflict are ruled out. I argued that this interpretation is a result of Kant's understanding of morality as respect for the moral law as the law of reason. To be genuinely Kantian, a double-level theory must be shown to be the product, not of intuitions about what is morally feasible, but of pure practical reason.

Notes

1. Kant 1959, p. 18 (402). In referring to Kant's ethical works, the page reference of the edition cited is followed by the standard *Preussische Akademie* page reference (specific volumes are listed in the Bibliography); references to the first *Critique* are to the Smith translation followed by the conventional A and B references to the first and second editions. Kant distinguishes three basic statements of the categorical imperative; see 1959, pp. 54–55 (436). Though each of these is itself given various formulations, I follow Kant in this threefold division and refer to these respectively as the "universal law" formula, the "end in itself" formula, and the "realm of ends" formula.

2. Kant 1959, pp. 54–55 (436–37).

3. It is significant that Hare's attempt to bring the categorical imperative in support of utilitarianism relies on the "universal law" formula of it (1981, pp. 4–5). However plausible this might be, such an argument could not even begin to look feasible with respect to the other two formulas.

4. Kant 1959, p. 46 (428).

5. *Ibid.*, p. 47 (429).

6. *Ibid.*, p. 53 (434–35).

7. *Ibid.*, p. 55 (436).

8. Kant 1971, p. 99 (434–5).

9. *Ibid.*, p. 132 (462).

10. *Ibid.*

11. *Ibid.*, p. 133 (463).

12. Kant nonetheless refers to the person as a "man," a designation that cannot be interpreted as an innocuous reference to persons of both sexes. For critical discussion of Kant's views concerning women, see Tuana 1992, pp. 61–70.

13. Kant 1959, p. 48 (429).

14. *Ibid.*, p. 49 (430–31).

15. The terms "price" and "equivalence" are employed to elucidate the idea that persons are valuable as ends and not merely as means. "That which constitutes the condition under which alone something can be an end in itself," Kant writes, "does not have mere relative worth, i.e., a price, but an intrinsic worth, i.e., *dignity*" [1959 p. 53 (435)]. Since a thing may be used merely as means, it can be replaced by some other thing that is an equally effective means. In this sense, things have equivalents. By contrast, because a person is an end in itself, he or she cannot be used merely as a means and so in this respect cannot simply be replaced by another person the way a thing can. In this sense, the worth of persons has no equivalent. But since what makes persons ends is autonomy and rationality, a property common to all persons, persons are equally ends, and in this respect they have equivalents. As ends, Kant does not deny that one person is equivalent in value to another. Though I have argued that we need uniqueness of value to fully explain the fact that we regard persons as in some respects irreplaceable, there is nothing in Kant which suggests such an argument. In this connection, see Blustein 1991, ch. 18; and Hill 1980, p. 88; and 1992, pp. 755–57.

16. Nussbaum 1986, p. 49. Cf. Hill 1992, pp. 756–57. Both recognize that Kant does not think respecting persons as ends could warrant "moral dilemmas."

17. Kant 1971, p. 23 (224).

18. There is a brief explication in Herman 1990, p. 317. The sentences that immediately follow this passage, where Kant says that there can be conflicting "*grounds* of obligation," have received more consideration. I discuss this claim later.

19. Kant 1959, p. 55 (437). See also 1956, p. 118 (114).

20. I discuss this analogy in connection with the "moral dilemmas" literature in my Introduction to Gowans 1987, pp. 23–24. I was more impressed with the analogy then than I am now. In this connection, see also McConnell 1978, p. 274.

21. Donagan 1984.

22. Kant 1971, p. 37 (380).

23. Kant 1956, p. 38 (36). Herman interprets this principle as stating only that in general we can do the *kinds* of actions morality requires (see 1990, pp. 315–16). So understood, it would not support this argument.

24. Donagan declares that the rejection of the agglomeration principle is incompatible with a rationalist moral system such as he attributes to Kant, but he does not provide

specific textual evidence to show that Kant accepted it (1984, pp. 299–300). As far as I know, no one disputed the principle until Williams in 1973a, p. 182.

25. Kant 1929, p. 637 (A807/B835).

26. The passage does not decisively support this reading. For the plural 'actions' could refer to all actions taken collectively or to each action taken individually. Consider "All the players in the tournament can win." This is ordinarily taken to mean that any one player can win, not that it might turn out that they all win.

27. Kant 1971, p. 20 (222).

28. Kant 1956, p. 70 (67–68). Cf. p. 26 (26–27).

29. *Ibid.*, p. 72 (69). Of course, for Kant, 'natural law' has a special meaning, since the laws of nature have their origin in the understanding, where 'nature' refers to objects given in experience. I take this analysis as assumed throughout my account. For discussion of Kant's use of the analogy between natural law and moral law, see Paton 1963, pp. 157–64.

30. Kant 1956, p. 72 (69).

31. *Ibid.*, p. 72 (69–70).

32. Kant 1929, p. 526 (A633/B661). Cf. pp. 633–34 (A802/B830) and 658–59 (A840/B868-A842/B870).

33. Kant 1956, p. 18 (20).

34. For presentations of this account, see 1971, pp. 11–15 (215–18); 1956, pp. 15–19 (15–21); and 1959, pp. 3–4 (387–88) and 64–65 (446).

35. Kant 1959, pp. 55–56 (437). For other statements of this idea, see pp. 39 (421) and 57 (438).

36. Kant himself immediately notes that it is applied in two different ways depending on the case [1959, pp. 41–42 (424)].

37. See the quotation from the second *Critique* three paragraphs back, p. 190.

38. It would also mean than an absolutely good or holy will is impossible, since such a will always acts in accordance with the moral law; see 1959, pp. 30–31 (413–41) and 58 (439); and 1956, p. 32 (32). But it is an essential tenet of Kant's critical philosophy that a holy will is possible.

39. Kant 1971, p. 15 (218). See also 1959, p. 57 (438); and 1956 p. 45 (44).

40. For example, see Kant 1959, pp. 55–58 (437–39).

41. As before, this interpretation is not decisive (see note 26). But in view of Kant's overall position, it is reasonable to read him in this way.

42. I discuss this claim in the next two sections.

43. Though often disputed by commentators, Kant insists that the various formulas of the categorical imperative "are fundamentally only so many formulas of the very same law" [1959, p. 54 (436)]. Thus the idea that moral obligations have the form of universal laws of nature and the idea that we are to respect persons as ends are said to be "objectively" equivalent, though they appear "subjectively" different.

44. This reading of Kant is emphasized in Donagan 1977, esp. pp. 1–9.

45. See 1959, p. 8 (391). Kant was much influenced by the Enlightenment idea that the method of the sciences could in some way serve as a model for our thinking in morality. See, for example, his suggestion at the end of the second *Critique* that we ought to use an analytical "process similar to that of chemistry" in understanding ordinary moral judgments [1956, p. 167 (163)].

46. Kant 1929, p. 29 (Bxxix).

47. Kant 1971, p. 51 (392) and 1959, pp. 58–59 (440). For a good discussion of the idea of persons as ends in themselves, see Hill 1980.

48. Kant 1959, p. 44 (426).

49. *Ibid.*, p. 77 (457).

50. Kant 1971, p. 99 (433).

51. Kant 1959, p. 46 (428). Though the passage is hardly atypical, Kant does sometimes speak more favorably of the inclinations.

52. It may be said that for Kant the noumenal and the phenomenal are but two aspects of the same thing, and hence that in respecting the person as noumenon we are also respecting the person as phenomenon. But this dual aspect conception of the person puts considerable pressure on the intelligibility of Kant's already troublesome attempt to reconcile freedom and determinism. In any case, as the passages just cited indicate, Kant did not believe that persons as phenomena are deserving of respect.

53. There is one possible exception to this. Kant sometimes speaks as if some persons deserve more respect than others in proportion to their moral merits [for example, see 1971, p. 133 (463)]. But no other differences among persons regarding reason or will are relevant to respect or are a basis for differential respect. Moreover, this is not a basis for respecting persons as unique individuals, but for adjusting respect on a scale of moral worth.

54. The way in which persons, as objects of moral concern, are displaced is quite different in Kant than in utilitarianism. For the latter, persons are displaced by being aggregated with other persons: The person becomes a drop in the sea of humanity. For Kant, persons are displaced by being stripped of their ordinary attributes: The person becomes the core of the onion, or nearly so. But in both cases, direct concern for the person of concrete experience is significantly diminished.

55. Kant 1959, p. 18 (401) note 2. See also 1959, p. 57 (439); and 1956, p. 81 (78).

56. Kant 1959, p. 16 (400).

57. Kant 1956, p. 76 (73).

58. *Ibid.*, p. 83 (80).

59. *Ibid.*, p. 89 (86). See also 1971, pp. 100–101 (435–36).

60. Kant 1956, p. 85 (82).

61. Kant 1959, p. 55 (436).

62. *Ibid.*, p. 60 (441).

63. Kant 1971, pp. 92–96 (429–31).

64. See, for example, Hill 1983; Korsgaard 1986; Paton 1953–54; and Sullivan 1989, pp. 173–77. I discuss Korsgaard's essay in Sec. VI.

65. Kant 1949, p. 348 (427).

66. *Ibid.*, p. 350 (429).

67. *Ibid.*, p. 349 (428).

68. For example, see 1959, pp. 22–29 (406–12).

69. See Donagan 1984. There are related discussions in 1977, esp. pp. 143–89.

70. See 1977, p. 72; and 1984, p. 293.

71. The translation is from Donagan 1984, p. 294. For a different translation, see Kant, 1971 p. 23 (224).

72. Donagan 1984, p. 295.

73. See Herman 1990, p. 318. Cf. Hill 1992, pp. 754–57.

74. There has been some temptation to interpret grounds of obligation as Rossian prima facie duties (see Nell 1975, p. 133; and Aune 1979, pp. 196–97). Ross clearly rejects DT, but depending on how "prima facie duties" are understood, his claim that these duties can conflict may or may not be taken as endorsing some form of RT. He says that when violating an overridden prima facie duty, we feel "not indeed shame or repentance, but certainly compunction, for behaving as we do" (p. 28). For criticism of a Ross-

ian reading of Kant, see Donagan 1984, pp. 291–95 and Herman 1990, pp. 317–18. Kant's acknowledgment of conflicting grounds of obligation clearly cannot be interpreted as implying RT much less DT. This is consonant with standard interpretations (for example, see Sullivan 1989, pp. 72–75), though there has been some speculation, in deference to presentations of moral experience, that there must be a more substantial doctrine of moral conflict to be found in Kant [see Aune 1979, pp. 192–93; and Louden 1992, p. 110, both of whom rely on one of Kant's unanswered casuistical questions in 1971, p. 89 (426)]. The passage under discussion here together with the considerations adduced in Sec. II undermine any such reading. Whether a revision of Kant could allow for some conception of "moral dilemmas" is a further question, one raised by some issues in the remainder of this chapter (see also Railton 1992, pp. 731–34).

75. Donagan 1984, p. 295. It is not clear what textual basis there is for this restriction; Herman does not accept it.

76. *Ibid.*, p. 307.

77. Indeed, apparently setting the metaphor aside, Donagan says that though none of the "grounds binds as a duty, they remain grounds and they are in conflict" (1984, p. 308).

78. Donagan 1984, p. 293. Even sympathetic readers of Kant have noted his lack of guidance on this issue (for example, see Aune 1979, pp. 192–97; Nell 1975, pp. 132–37; and Sullivan 1989, pp. 72–75).

79. Donagan 1984, p. 308.

80. *Ibid.*

81. See Kant 1971, pp. 21–22 (223).

82. Donagan 1984, p. 303. The original is italicized.

83. *Ibid.*, p. 304.

84. *Ibid.*, p. 303.

85. *Ibid.*, p. 304.

86. An act-utilitarian might say that amends are required when this would have the best overall results. This is a curious position. We are to apologize, not because we have something to apologize for but because doing so will have the best results. This verges on incoherence. If the promisee realizes that this is a *faux* apology, then it will no longer have its anticipated good results. Only a two-level theory with deception at the everyday level could circumvent this outcome.

87. See Donagan 1984, pp. 305–306; and 1977, pp. 144–45. Cf. McConnell 1978, pp. 276–77; and Zimmerman 1989.

88. Donagan's reading of Aquinas is criticized by Santurri 1987, pp. 91–94; and MacIntyre 1990, pp. 379–81. MacIntyre previously endorsed Donagan's interpretation (see 1981 p. 167).

89. MacIntyre 1990, p. 380. In the text cited by MacIntyre, Aquinas considers the argument that if a person swears to do something wrong such as murder, then whether he murders or not "he sins either way." Against this, Aquinas declares that "he who takes an oath to do what is wrong commits perjury through lack of justice, but not if he fails to keep his oath, since what he swore to do is not fit matter for an oath" (1964–75, IIa—IIae 98, 2, 1).

90. See Conee 1989, pp. 135–36; Feldman 1986, p. 205; and MacIntyre 1990, pp. 379–80.

91. There appears to be a widespread intuition that inescapable wrongdoing caused by one's previous wrongdoing is less troubling than inescapable wrongdoing not so caused. For example, in addition to the references in note 87, see Foot 1983, p. 388; Nagel 1979a, p. 74; and Raz 1986, p. 362. I discuss this intuition in chapter 9, sec. I.

92. Donagan 1984, p. 301.

93. Herman 1990. Some features of her argument are anticipated in 1985, esp. pp. 420–22.

94. Herman 1990, p. 314.

95. *Ibid.*, p. 317.

96. *Ibid.*, p. 324.

97. *Ibid.*, p. 311.

98. *Ibid.*, p. 316.

99. *Ibid.*, p. 318. Later she allows that some moral considerations "can occupy a higher ground in the deliberative field" than others (p. 331).

100. *Ibid.*, p. 318.

101. *Ibid.*, p. 319.

102. *Ibid.*, p. 320.

103. *Ibid.*

104. *Ibid.*, p. 329.

105. *Ibid.*, p. 320.

106. *Ibid.*, p. 321.

107. *Ibid.*, p. 323.

108. Herman also identifies a third feature, which she calls "remainders." But I take the idea of remainders not to be a feature of experience in addition to the first two, but an account of what must be the case to explain the first two (as she seems to acknowledge on p. 325).

109. Herman 1990, p. 324.

110. *Ibid.*, p. 325.

111. *Ibid.*, p. 326 (for all phrases quoted in this paragraph).

112. It might seem that a two-level theory is in the offing, where persons are educated to feel regret, compunction, repugnance, and so on whenever doing certain kinds of actions which are usually but not always wrong. But Herman rejects "indirection" arguments (see 1990, pp. 313–14).

113. Herman 1990, p. 329.

114. *Ibid.*, p. 327.

115. *Ibid.*

116. *Ibid.*, p. 332.

117. *Ibid.*, p. 329.

118. See Korsgaard 1986, esp. pp. 341–49.

119. The same is true of the "realm of ends" formula, which Korsgaard regards as a corollary of the "end in itself" formula.

120. Korsgaard 1986, p. 333.

121. *Ibid.*, p. 345. See also p. 337.

122. *Ibid.*

123. *Ibid.*, p. 346.

124. *Ibid.*

125. *Ibid.*, p. 349.

126. *Ibid.*, p. 347.

127. *Ibid.*, p. 346. Korsgaard refers to Williams's argument in 1973a. Cf. Hill 1983, pp. 228–29.

128. Korsgaard 1986, p. 346 note 21.

129. *Ibid.*, pp. 333 and 340, respectively.

130. *Ibid.*, p. 346.

131. *Ibid.*, p. 347.

132. *Ibid.*, p. 344. Cf. Donagan 1984, pp. 301–302; and Hill 1983, p. 219.

133. Korsgaard 1986, pp. 345, 346, and 349.

134. For example, Kant claims that there can "be no legitimate resistance of the people to the legislative chief of the state," that "it is the people's duty to endure even the most intolerable abuse of supreme authority" [1985, p. 86 (320)]. It should be noted that Kant nonetheless expresses enthusiasm for the French Revolution (whether these attitudes can be reconciled is a vexed interpretive question).

135. Korsgaard suggests that Kant's views about just war might provide an opening for such a justification, but she does not develop this point (1986, p. 349). As she notes, it is Kant's religious beliefs that provide his solution to these intuitive concerns. This raises the further issue to what extent "Kantian" moral philosophers who reject these beliefs can remain true to Kant's outlook.

9

Innocence Lost

My argument in the last three chapters has been that the responsibilities to persons account provides a better explanation of inescapable moral distress than accounts rooted in either the utilitarian or the Kantian traditions. On the basis of this, along with considerations developed in Chapter 5, it is reasonable to accept the conclusion of the phenomenological argument that there is a sense in which moral wrongdoing is sometimes inescapable. The differences between my account and the theories of these influential traditions turn centrally on contrasting conceptions of valuing and relating to particular persons and associations of persons in our lives. Nothing could be more fundamental to the understanding of morality than these issues. For this reason, the full ramifications of the responsibilities to persons account, and the whole range of its differences with utilitarianism and Kantianism, go well beyond the questions pertaining to moral conflicts I have considered here. The holism of the method of reflective intuitionism pushes us towards an overall assessment of contrasting approaches apropos our moral intuitions, and hence urges evaluation of these further topics. But this evaluation is beyond the scope of my present concerns.

I conclude with some brief and somewhat more speculative comments on three topics, each related to the remainders view, but only loosely related to one another. The last, the problem of dirty hands, has already received a good deal of attention. Since the literature on dirty hands is closely connected to the themes of this book, it is worthwhile to evaluate this literature from the perspective of the position I have defended. On the other hand, the first two topics, the ideal of moral innocence and the nature of moral tragedy, have been very much in the background of the "moral dilemmas" debate. My remarks are intended to suggest that they deserve more explicit consideration.

I. The Ideal of Moral Innocence

I have maintained that beneath the myriad of arguments for and against the idea that moral wrongdoing is sometimes inescapable lie deeper dispositions of thought, reflecting fundamental differences in the understanding of morality and moral philosophy. With respect to methodology, those who believe that moral wrongdoing cannot be inescapable often incline to defend this view on the basis of rather abstract and a priori concerns—hence the prominence of inconsistency arguments in their objections, with their reliance on conceptual principles drawn from the domain of deontic logic. By contrast, those who maintain that wrongdoing is sometimes inescapable tend to base their arguments on relatively more concrete and experiential considerations—hence the widespread acceptance of various forms of the phenomenological argument, with its appeal to our moral feelings, and more generally the frequent reference to particular examples of moral conflicts. Again, this time with respect to substantive normative outlooks, opponents of the idea of inescapable moral wrongdoing often accept forms of the covering law model with its ideal of deliberation as deductive inference from abstract first principle, while proponents of this idea usually favor more pluralistic accounts of moral value, accounts that resist systematic or algorithmic models of moral deliberation.

These are only tendencies of thought, not strict conceptual connections, and they can be obscured by countervailing commitments as well as the necessity of each side in the debate to engage the arguments of the other. But as common differences in philosophical disposition they are real and revealing. In my own defense of the remainders view, I have tried to be responsive to all the concerns expressed in the "moral dilemmas" literature. But I have also made manifest my belief in the importance of the more experiential and pluralistic approach of proponents of the possibility of inescapable moral wrongdoing.

I now suggest that there is a third underlying difference here, one that is perhaps at once more fundamental and less obvious. This difference is not a matter of method, nor indeed of specific normative perspective per se. Rather, it concerns visions of what is morally possible in human life. In brief, those who reject the idea of inescapable moral wrongdoing suppose that moral innocence is possible, while those who accept this idea think that moral tragedy is possible. I begin by discussing what may be called the ideal of moral innocence. In the next section I turn to the nature of moral tragedy.

Assuming we have come to the point of understanding our lives in moral terms, it is obvious that it is better to be more rather than less responsive to moral concerns. The ideal of moral innocence goes beyond this: It puts forward a standard of perfection that, though difficult to attain, is nonetheless thought to be within the reach of each of us. The standard is moral innocence, or moral purity, the ideal of living one's life in such a way as to fully, comprehensively, and harmoniously understand and respond to the requirements of morality, and thereby to entirely exclude all forms of wrongdoing.[1]

It is hard not to feel the appeal of the ideal of innocence. In one respect at least, it expresses a deeply hopeful and optimistic outlook on human life. There are a variety of perspectives from which this ideal might be thought compelling. What unifies them, or at any rate stands out as prominent among them, is the following line of thought: There is much that happens to us in our lives which is bad: disappointment, betrayal, the loss of love, injury, disease, and ultimately death. We can strive to forestall these events, with occasional or temporary success, but in the end they are largely or entirely beyond our control. Human life is irreparably subject to the vicissitudes of an existence plagued by variety of psychological and physical ills whose origin is external to us. However, in contrast to what happens to us, there is who we are and what we do, and this is a matter which is not due to factors beyond our control. Here, at least, goodness must be possible. It has to be acknowledged, of course, that there are obstacles to goodness: our selfishness, our negligence, our lack of courage and temperance, and perhaps our propensity for evil as well. But these impurities of the will—or self, or soul, however it may be described—are all internal. In the end, they are not things which happen to us, but things which we are, and more importantly, things which through sheer effort of will we may overcome. Though moral innocence is perhaps never actually achieved, and is certainly not typically achieved, it is nonetheless crucially important that it remain as an ideal to which we can aspire. At some deep level it must be possible for us to attain it. For we believe, and perhaps need to believe, that the obstacles to innocence are all internal and hence surmountable by effort. We find it intolerable to suppose that the obstacles might also be external and hence beyond our control. It is bad enough that we are subject to the multiplicity of arbitrary ills which assault us from the outside. If there were no preserve of goodness which even our best efforts could achieve, the moral universe would be fundamentally unfair if not absurd. For with respect to every aspect of value in our lives, we would be subject to the contingencies of the world.[2]

This argument is one of the principal reasons for acceptance of the ideal of moral innocence. The belief that, though much harm may befall us, we can remain pure of heart in confronting it, if only we choose, is a powerful and widespread human sentiment. It is a recurrent theme in the Western philosophical tradition. Often it finds expression in religious faith and is there frequently coupled with additional beliefs, or hopes, such as that our moral goodness will be rewarded in the end, or that the bad things that happen to us are ultimately unimportant, merely apparent, or of hidden design.[3] Yet the ideal that through effort of will alone moral innocence may be achieved need not take religious form to have a forceful hold upon us. For most contemporary moral philosophers it does not appear in this form, at least not in any explicit or recognizable way. Indeed, it hardly appears at all as a consciously maintained or articulated belief. Still, the ideal of moral innocence may well be operative as a central albeit unspoken motivation among many philosophers opposing the idea of inescapable moral wrongdoing.

If the responsibilities to persons account were correct, then moral innocence would be virtually impossible to attain, regardless of how pure of heart we may be. For on this account, we will sometimes violate a moral responsibility to a person no matter what and hence will do something morally wrong no matter what. To admit this is tantamount to abandoning the ideal of moral innocence. Of course, we can aspire to act as deliberation directs, and when this means violating a moral responsibility to someone, to be as attentive as possible to the consequent harm to, or neglect of, that person. Here the obstacles might all be internal. But this is not really moral purity. It is making the best of impurity.[4] The aspiration to be fully responsive to the entire range of our moral responsibilities is destined for frustration. Hence, if we are committed to the ideal of innocence, we are likely to regard the possibility of inescapable moral wrongdoing as a deeply offensive idea. In fact, to accept this idea might be thought to succumb to an intolerable cynicism: In an already troubled and morally vexatious world, it is to abandon our only hope for goodness, that through power of individual will alone we may attain moral innocence.

It might be supposed that this ideal could be maintained in the face of inescapable moral wrongdoing by sharply distinguishing what we do from what we are, our acts from the quality of our will. Thus it may be said that though the world may compel me to act wrongly, my will can remain morally innocent throughout. Montaigne, for whom politics could be a vicious business, declared that "I have been able to take part in public office without departing one nail's breadth from myself." "The mayor and Montaigne have always been two," he said, "with a very clear separation."[5] Among other difficulties, this attenuated conception of moral identity makes it unclear why I should be distressed by acting wrongly, if my real self continues to be pure of heart. Indeed, on this account it is unclear to what extent, morally speaking, these wrongful acts can be said to be my acts at all. But on any understanding of moral identity in which what one is, is inseparable from what one does, inescapable moral wrongdoing will appear problematic from the standpoint of the ideal of moral innocence.

In the recent "moral dilemmas" literature, objections to inescapable moral wrongdoing are virtually never put in this form. Yet there is an important indication that the ideal of innocence is an underlying concern in these objections. As seen in the last chapter, Donagan distinguishes between inescapable wrongdoing caused by the agent's prior, avoidable wrongdoing (perplexity *secundum quid*) and inescapable wrongdoing not so caused (perplexity *simpliciter*).[6] He finds the latter deeply problematic. But he thinks the former is quite possible, despite the fact that the problem of consistency he raises would seem to apply to both. Though Donagan's specific position is not commonly accepted, the sentiment does appear widespread, on both sides of the "moral dilemmas" debate, that perplexity *secundum quid* would not be nearly as objectionable as perplexity *simpliciter*. For example, Nagel writes that a situation in which "there is no course one can take which is not wrong" is "perfectly intelligible" if one brings it upon oneself, for example, by making incompatible promises. "It is possible to get into such a situation by one's own fault, and people do it all the time." Such cases, Nagel says, are "not morally disturbing" since "we feel that the situation was not unavoidable." But, he says, "our intuitions rebel" at the thought that "the world itself . . . could face a previously innocent person with a choice between morally abominable courses of action."[7]

The ideal of moral innocence explains the thought that there is an important difference between the two situations. Cases of perplexity *secundum quid* are brought about by oneself, they are not imposed by the world. When I cannot escape wrongdoing on account of previous wrongdoing I have only myself to blame. I could have acted in such a way that wrongdoing would not now be inescapable. Innocence, a life free from all wrongdoing, was a possibility for me. But I chose another path. All this seems quite compatible with the ideal of innocence, and so from this standpoint is unproblematic. On the other hand, cases of perplexity *simpliciter* are imposed by the world. Here wrongdoing is unavoidable, not because I have already done something wrong, but because of what happens to me. Hence, I could not have chosen a life of moral purity. This runs directly against the ideal of innocence. If we are committed to this ideal, "our intuitions rebel" at the idea of perplexity *simpliciter* in a way that they do not rebel at the idea of perplexity *secundum quid*.

The common perception of the importance of the difference between these two cases suggests that the ideal of moral innocence is one significant source of the opposition to the notion of inescapable moral wrongdoing brought on by the world. If we accept this ideal, we are compelled to find an account of morality that precludes externally imposed conflict among moral values it is wrong to transgress and that also explains the appearance of such conflict in ordinary experience as mistaken. There are a variety of ways in which this goal might be achieved. In religious doctrines, for example, it might be declared that our only moral obligation is to do what God requires and that God's requirements do not conflict. Apparent conflicts among responsibilities to persons are interpreted as misunderstandings of God's commands. Nussbaum suggests that a different strategy is a theme of Sophocles's *Antigone*.[8] Faced with a family obligation to bury a relative and an incompatible civic obligation to not bury a traitor (the relative and traitor both being Polyneices), Creon declares that there is no conflict because our only real obligations are civic obligations. Likewise, faced with similar demands of family and state, Antigone declares that her only genuine obligation is a family obligation. In both cases, the conflict of values they might be expected to have experienced is eliminated by a strategy of simplification: The apparent multiplicity of potentially conflicting values to family and state is reduced to a single, presumably nonconflicting source of obligation.

Both of these strategies for maintaining the ideal of moral innocence are important, historically as well as in the everyday moral beliefs of many persons today. Yet neither strategy has been prominent in the critiques of inescapable wrongdoing by moral philosophers. The approach of these philosophers is almost always secular, so a religious account is ruled out. Moreover, the commitment to conceptions of equality or impartiality, which is commonly taken for granted, precludes any approach that would appeal to something such as the family or the state as the ultimate source of moral value. The vehicle for promulgating the ideal of innocence for these philosophers is typically the covering law model, usually as articulated by versions of utilitarianism or Kantianism. On these views, moral innocence is not a matter of obeying God's commands, but of occupying God's standpoint—or at any rate the place left vacant by God in the secular world. Sidgwick's idea that morality requires us to act from "the point of view . . . of the Universe" continues to be influential.[9] Thus Rawls says that "purity of heart . . . would be to see clearly and to act with grace and self-command" from "the perspective of eternity."[10] For many contemporary moral philosophers it is supposed that, by approaching our lives from this standpoint, a standpoint that allows justification of the first moral principle, our experience of moral conflict can be shown to be an illusion resulting from the limited perspective of our particular relationships and commitments.

If in pursuit of the ideal of moral innocence it is regarded as a sine qua non of moral value that there be no genuine conflict, then there are any number of accounts of moral value available that meet this requirement. There is no difficulty describing such a position. The question is whether we should accept this requirement in the first place. The ideal of innocence is based on a consideration of morality from the point of view of the agent: It owes its appeal to a concern for the quality of one's life as a moral agent, to the desire that one be morally pure. By itself, this is obviously an important concern and need not be seen as moral self-centeredness. On the other hand, it can be so interpreted if it is given such importance that it distorts one's understanding of moral value, of what in one's life requires moral response. In my view, as construed by the ideal of moral innocence, the concern for one's own goodness does precisely this. It precludes recognition of the plurality of potentially conflicting moral responsibilities that ordinarily constitutes a person's life.

On the responsibilities to persons account, the importance of one's own moral purity is obviously not rejected. But it is complemented by another concern, which is not directed to the quality of one's life as a moral agent but to those agents other than oneself and those social entities to which one is responsible. From this second perspective, the focus of attention is not so much on the question "How can *I* be morally pure?" as it is on the question "How can I properly respond to *each* of these persons and institutions to which I am responsible?" There is an important difference in emphasis here. Exclusive attention to the first question can prompt a strategy of value-elimination. The apparent conflicts of ordinary experience cannot be genuine conflicts. Otherwise, moral innocence would be impossible. By contrast, consideration of the second question suggests a different outlook. Conflicts among our responsibilities may well be real. What needs to be determined is not which may be eliminated, but how best to respond to these conflicting requirements.

The responsibilities to persons account regards as fundamental the diverse and potentially conflicting responsibilities to persons that naturally and appropriately develop in our lives. It takes seriously the importance of fulfilling each of these responsibilities. To this extent, it may be said to be concerned with moral innocence. But it rejects the ideal of moral innocence, understood as entailing a guarantee that there can be no genuine moral conflicts.

Proponents of this ideal might object that fairness requires that moral innocence be fully available to each person, on the ground that it would be unfair if our goodness depended on factors outside the will.[11] Yet there is much about morality in our lives that might be regarded as similarly unfair. The demands of morality are unequally distributed, and they are certainly not distributed in accordance with the moral quality of the will. The temptations of immorality are much greater for persons in some circumstances than for those in others. The opportunities for moral heroism are sporadically given. In each case, these differences occur through no fault of our own. As a result, persons with the

same underlying moral quality of will but situated in substantially different circumstances may live lives that differ radically in moral goodness. We may think
this is unfair, even as we think it unfair that some suffer much more than others.
But this does not make it unreal. That inescapable moral wrongdoing may likewise be unfair is no basis for denying its reality.

II. The Nature of Moral Tragedy

Wrongdoing that is *not* inescapable, that can be avoided, may involve a variety
of moral configurations. It may be a matter of trivial import, of substantial but
short-term concern, or of deadly seriousness. It may result in virtually no harm,
in a real but limited harm, or in a harm of catastrophic proportion. It may be the
product of the best of intentions, of the most malicious of them, or merely of
negligence. It may reflect diverse moral characters—the good, the bad, or the
indifferent. From the standpoint of others, it may be ground for severe repri-
mand, for understanding with the hope of better behavior in the future, or for
little if any critical response. For the agent performing the action, it may occasion various emotional responses, from severe moral distress to mild disquiet to
at most passing concern.

In general, the same diversity of configurations may accompany wrongdoing
that is inescapable. It too may be a matter of greater or lesser import. It too may
result in harms ranging from the negligible to the disastrous. It too may be the
product of various motives and characters. And as I have already argued, it too
may warrant a variety of responses regarding responsibility and blame on the
part of others as well as the agent. In defenses of inescapable moral wrongdoing,
there has been a tendency to dwell on examples of grave and dramatic significance, such as those involving the moral conflicts in *Agamemnon*, *Sophie's Choice*,
or in my own case *Billy Budd*. In one way, this has been unfortunate. These
moral conflicts are no more representative of the varieties of inescapable wrongdoing than Iago's plot against Othello is representative of the varieties of
escapable wrongdoing. There is no reason to deny that inescapable wrongdoing
may involve matters of little or modest significance.

Nevertheless, there are instances of inescapable moral wrongdoing that take
on tragic dimensions, which are what I call "moral tragedies." In saying this, I
do not mean to imply that human life in general is deeply and irrevocably tragic
in this sense, that moral tragedy is part and parcel of every person's life. This is
certainly not true. Still, inescapable moral wrongdoing of some form may well
be involved in every human life, and that form which is morally tragic is a *possibility* for each of us. Recognition that moral tragedy is possible in one's life, even
if it never occurs, brings an outlook on life that is quite different than if this possibility is denied. For the ideal of moral innocence, it may be said that our most
important possibility is absolute moral purity: Regarding this as possible can
shape one's entire moral perspective. By contrast, to regarding moral tragedy as
possible lends a very different, and far less sanguine, complexion to one's life.

Philosophical discussions of tragedy have generally been concerned with tragedy as a genre of dramatic or literary works of art. On this subject, there appear to be nearly as many theories of tragedy as there are proponents of such theories. My interest here is not with tragedy in this sense; I do not propose to take issue with the themes of Aristotle's *Poetics*. Rather, I am concerned with tragedy, in particular moral tragedy, as a feature of human life. Though the two cannot be neatly separated—tragic works of art presumably aim to express something real in our lives—discussion of tragedy as a characteristic of human existence, which need not be defined by reference to an artistic genre, is a relatively recent phenomenon, beginning as near as I can tell in the nineteenth century and reaching its culmination with the existentialists. In the contemporary literature about "moral dilemmas," allusions to tragedy have not been uncommon. Thus Williams speaks of "drastic cases of tragic choice, where one might say that whatever the agent did was wrong."[12] Such remarks have sometimes been received with scorn. There are, Hare says, "some people who like there to be what they call 'tragic situations'; the world would be less enjoyable without them."[13] In any case, the nature of tragedy has been for the most part at the periphery of the "moral dilemmas" debate.[14]

What I have to say regarding tragedy does not have much to do with most of the concerns of the existentialists. For example, Nietzsche famously supposed tragedy to be a product of the synergy of Apollinian and Dionysian forces, while Unamuno connected "the tragic sense of life" to the desire for immortality. On the other hand, Sartre did speak of returning to "the concept of tragedy as the Greeks saw it," a concept according to which "right may conflict with right."[15] The most important historical antecedent for a philosophical account of tragedy as involving moral conflict is found in Hegel. Writing about Greek tragedy, but also about tragedy as a feature of human life, he maintained that tragedy involves a conflict between "ethical powers." "The original essence of tragedy," he wrote, consists "in the fact that within such a conflict each of the opposed sides, if taken by itself, has *justification*." He added that "the consequence is that in its moral life, and because of it, each is nevertheless involved in *guilt*."[16] Having made this brief acknowledgment, I will not attempt to further relate my discussion of tragedy to other accounts.

When we speak of tragedy, we often have in mind the terrible things that can happen to people, especially when they are particularly undeserved. Events such as children being swept away in a flood or the assassination of Martin Luther King are commonly referred to as tragedies. In this sense, tragedy is an extreme form of the phenomenon acknowledged in the argument for the ideal of innocence: It concerns *what happens to us*. There is no reference to the agency of the person who suffers the tragedy. The tragedy comes entirely from without.[17] But we sometimes speak of tragedy as something that does involve a person's agency, as when we say that someone is faced with a tragic choice. Tragedy in this sense brings us closer to moral tragedy, but a tragic choice need not involve moral conflict. It may simply be a case in which whatever one chooses there will or may be serious losses, as when one must decide whether to have one's leg amputated or risk death. This would be a tragic choice, but it need not involve a conflict of moral responsibilities. Tragic choices concern *what we do* as much as what happens to us. They present us with a painful decision about what to do, but that a person confronts a tragic choice may well be a matter of happenstance.

Moral tragedy is a special case of tragic choice, one that necessarily involves conflicting moral responsibilities. The ideal of moral innocence acknowledges tragic events that happen to us and perhaps also nonmoral tragic choices. But it rejects tragic choices that involve genuine moral conflicts. It supposes that there is a realm of life that is immune to the tragic. This is the source of the hope and optimism which this ideal inspires. No matter how bad things might be, there is one thing—who I am and what I do morally—that cannot be tarnished by outside events. By contrast, on the view I am putting forward, there is no sphere of life that guarantees a safe haven from tragedy: Not only may we suffer tragic events, we may be compelled to make tragic choices, some of which are inescapably and seriously flawed moral choices.

A necessary condition for moral tragedy is inescapable moral wrongdoing. Moral tragedy concerns certain extreme cases where whatever the agent does, he or she will do something wrong in the sense of violating some moral responsibility. But there is no reason to suppose that a precise specification of these cases is possible. We often speak of actions as being more and less tragic; this suggests that the difference between the tragic and the nontragic is not always sharp. Moreover, there are a variety of factors relevant to the presence of tragedy. It would be a mistake to seek an exact set of necessary and sufficient conditions for the existence of moral tragedy. Rather, we should try to identify those factors that contribute to making a case of inescapable moral wrongdoing tragic. I call these "tragic-making characteristics." Whether a given moral conflict is tragic depends on whether there are more rather than fewer of these characteristics and on whether they are present to a greater rather than a lesser degree. Some cases are clearly tragic, while others are clearly not. But there may be moral conflicts about which it would be pointless to insist on a definitive answer to the question whether or not they are really tragic. In addition, among those cases that are tragic, different configurations of tragedy may be expected, depending on the combination and degree of tragic-making characteristics present.

In sum, a moral tragedy is a moral conflict in which moral wrongdoing in the sense of violating a moral responsibility is inescapable, and the action that all things considered morally ought to be done, or may be done, nonetheless has one or more tragic-making characteristics. There are numerous kinds of tragedy-making characteristics that, though not unrelated to one another, are worth separately identifying. Some of these may generally be more important than others, but I make no attempt to arrange them in a hierarchy. In accordance with the preceding definition, they are described by reference to the action that all things considered morally ought to be or may be done. For shorthand, I refer to this as "the morally best action."[18] Here, then, are some prominent tragic-making characteristics.

The morally best action seriously harms or allows to be harmed a person or social entity to whom the agent is morally responsible. The more serious the harm, the greater the tragedy. Death is among the most serious harms that can strike a person. For this reason, we naturally think of tragedy in all its senses as commonly involving death or its imminent likelihood. But there are other serious harms besides death, and it may be that there are more serious harms than death. Torture and human degradation, as well as such things as the destruction of a community, may be worse than death.

The morally best action results in a harm that is either irreversible or extremely difficult to repair. Harms that are easily remedied are generally not tragic, and harms that are more difficult to rectify are more tragic than those that are less so. Since death is utterly irreversible, it is especially tragic in this regard. But death is not the only harm meeting this criterion. There are many harms— physical, psychological, and social—that are irreversible even though life goes on.

The morally best action results in a harm that is far-reaching in its consequences. Harms that affect many people, or an entire society, are more tragic than those that affect one or a few persons.

The morally best action not only fails to fulfill a moral responsibility but actively works against that responsibility. If someone has a responsibility to provide for the welfare of a person, it is bad enough not to do so. But it is worse to interfere with that person's welfare. An action that undoes that which a responsibility requires to be done is more tragic than an action that merely does nothing regarding the responsibility.

The morally best action harms or neglects a person whom the agent especially values, or with whom the agent has an intimate relation. The meaning of our lives is in large measure constituted by personal relationships that are both close and partial. To act in such a way as to damage these relationships, or to harm the persons with whom we are so related, can be among the most tragic of occurrences.

The morally best action harms or neglects a person who is especially undeserving of this harm or neglect. For this reason, an action is more tragic than otherwise if the person affected is a child or is particularly virtuous.

The morally best action renders the agent a tool in the evil projects of others. When we act for the best, and yet in doing so nonetheless help promote the sinister aims of others—for example, by making a political concession to a despotic government in order to obtain freedom for a hostage—we feel tarnished by the fact that we have been used to implement these aims.

More generally, the morally best action involves doing something that is degrading to the agent. There are actions that on rare occasions may be morally justified all things considered and yet degrade us. Such things as treachery, intimidation, and humiliation may sometimes be what is morally for the best. Yet they involve treating persons in ways that we believe human beings should not be treated, and we find it morally repugnant to relate to persons in this way.

Finally, the moral conflict is one in which the moral reasons for two conflicting actions do not override each other, and yet each overrides the reasons for all other alternative actions. Much has been made of moral conflicts of this kind in the "moral dilemmas" literature. I have argued that there may be such conflicts, since conflicting moral reasons may be equally strong, and that in such cases the correct conclusion of moral deliberation is that one action or the other ought to be done. A troublesome feature of these cases, however, is that an agent who performs one of the actions cannot say, "I had no moral choice but to do this," even if the action results in harm to someone. The agent did have a moral choice. With equal moral justification, he or she could have performed the other action, an action that may have resulted in harm to someone else. The agent can give no conclusive moral reason to the person harmed why that action rather than the other was taken, and it is disturbing to act under this condition. Situations of this kind are quite rare. But they are not impossible, and when they occur the inability to perform an action that is the one and only action required by deliberation can contribute to the tragedy of the conflict.

These are the kinds of factors that can render a conflict in which moral wrongdoing is inescapable into a morally tragic conflict. Are there any moral tragedies so understood? It is difficult to imagine moral conflicts in which wrongdoing is inescapable and *all* these factors are present. But I am not suggesting that these tragic-making characteristics are necessary conditions for moral tragedy. Rather, these are characteristics that, in various combinations, make for tragedy. Once it is acknowledged that there are conflicts in which moral wrongdoing is inescapable, it is hard to see a reason for denying that moral tragedy so understood may occur; for it is easy to envision circumstances in which wrongdoing cannot be avoided and several of these factors are present. The conflict of Captain Vere in *Billy Budd* is plausibly regarded as a moral tragedy and so too, perhaps, is that of Sophie in *Sophie's Choice*. Other examples are not hard to come by. On the other hand, there is less reason to consider the plights of Craig and Jennifer as tragic. Moral tragedy is not an occurrence in most people's personal lives. But it is a possible occurrence, and it is an extreme form of something that is, if not common, at least not uncommon in our lives— namely, the more ordinary cases of inescapable moral wrongdoing. This is why we are engaged by moral tragedy as represented in the arts. In heightened form, these works portray something that is real for us, something that we recognize as among the range of moral possibilities for human lives. A moral theory that cannot account for this is missing something of fundamental importance.

III. The Problem of Dirty Hands

Inescapable moral wrongdoing is often thought to occur in one area of life above all others. The area is politics. That this is so is typically referred to as "the problem of dirty hands," or sometimes as "Machiavelli's problem." The latter designation is due to the fact that Machiavelli is believed to have been the first to publicly advocate "immorality" in politics. "It is necessary," he declared, "for a prince . . . to learn how not to be good."[19] In fact, the issue has a more ancient lineage than Machiavelli. Plato argued that the rulers of his ideal society sometimes ought to lie, although no one else should.[20] Perhaps Plato did not suppose, as it seems Machiavelli did, that such lying by rulers, though necessary, would still be wrong. Still, Plato did suggest that the moral situation of political leaders is strikingly different than that of others, that what is at least ordinarily wrong is sometimes morally required of them. It is this thought that animates recent discussions of dirty hands, and it is this thought that, in connection with the remainders view, I wish to examine here.

The term "dirty hands" appears to have its origin in the title of a play by Sartre, though in fact *Les Mains sales* is rather more concerned with *mauvaise foi* and the possibility of creating significance for our actions than it is with dirty hands per se.[21] The term was made popular by Walzer's classic essay, which continues to be the starting point for most discussions of the issue.[22] Walzer proposes two examples of dirty hands. In the first, a moral politician can win an important election only by making a corrupt deal. In the second, the bombing of innocents can be prevented only by torturing a captured terrorist with likely knowledge of the location of the bombs. Walzer maintains that in both cases moral wrongdoing may be inescapable, though making the deal and torturing the prisoner may be morally for the best. No one denies the possibility of situations of this sort, though it is possible to exaggerate their frequency. Those who reject the idea of inescapable wrongdoing altogether are faced with the twofold challenge of showing which action is morally best in these circumstances and explaining why that action is in no way wrong. Utilitarians have not had much to say about Walzer's claims but may be presumed to allow that his deliberative conclusions could well be correct. Kantians and other nonutilitarians appear to have been rather more vexed by the issue, but have also, perhaps surprisingly, sometimes been prepared to accept these conclusions as well.[23]

Since I have argued that inescapable moral wrongdoing is possible, I see no reason to deny that it is possible in politics. Nonetheless, there is reason to consider two theses on this topic, both suggested by Walzer and others, as well as by the way in which dirty hands is often singled out for special consideration. According to the first:

> *The Dirty Hands Thesis* Inescapable moral wrongdoing is a common or pervasive feature of political life, but is either nonexistent or of negligible importance in the rest of life.

The second may be thought of as a corollary of the first:

> *The Moral Sacrifice Thesis* Politicians are required to make moral sacrifices that other persons at least typically need not make.

Walzer does not deny that inescapable wrongdoing is possible in "private life," but he thinks politics is where it is most likely to occur. "It is easy," he says, "to get one's hands dirty in politics."[24] On account of this, Walzer is troubled by the moral sacrifice that politicians must make, and he is concerned with how they, as well as the rest of us, should deal with it. Though he is critical of Weber's striking claim that "he who seeks the salvation of the soul . . . should not seek it along the avenue of politics,"[25] he nevertheless thinks, with many others, that there is a special problem about the moral character of politicians, a problem not generally shared by others.

In my view, the first thesis requires significant modification and the second should be accepted only in light of this. We should be wary of the suggestion conveyed by much of the dirty hands literature that politics and politicians generally require differential treatment apropos inescapable moral wrongdoing. It will help to begin with two preliminary observations. First, while inescapable wrongdoing may arise in various aspects of political life, the most poignant cases—and those most supportive of these two theses—occur in connection with the executive branch of a legitimate government in confronting threats to the safety and security of the community, whether these threats be of domestic or of foreign origin. I confine my attention to these. Second, there is no reason to doubt the claim that there are moral questions that are distinctive of politics and political actors. There are many moral issues that cannot be coherently described except by reference to the fact that the agents in question occupy particular social roles. In this respect, politics is one among many arenas of life that give rise to special moral problems. But to acknowledge this is not to suggest that we need a special morality to deal with these problems. We need only to bring ordinary moral considerations to bear on the special circumstances created by the complex social and institutional arrangements of our world.

My argument concerning the Dirty Hands Thesis and the Moral Sacrifice Thesis is based in part on a claim that has been implicit throughout my defense of the remainders view: that inescapable moral wrongdoing may occur in any area of life. If this is so, then the assertion that outside politics inescapable wrongdoing is nonexistent or of negligible importance is false and so too is the suggestion that moral sacrifices occur mainly within politics. Here I will focus attention on the comparative claim suggested by these two theses: that inescapable wrongdoing is significantly more common within political life than elsewhere. A number of arguments have been advanced to show why this is so.

First, in politics it is necessary to deal with immoral, and sometimes evil, persons and institutions. Confronting the threats posed by these increases the likelihood of inescapable moral wrongdoing. Second, the state may use violence systematically and sometimes massively to achieve certain of its objectives. This too increases opportunities for inescapable wrongdoing. Third, in politics the stakes are so high that situations are not uncommon in which the deontological constraints operative in ordinary life must yield to overwhelming consequentialist considerations. This is the one area in which consequences are likely to be significant enough to justify the conclusion that the morally best act is one that violates a deontological requirement.[26] All three arguments may be illustrated by Walzer's second example. Thus it may be said that though it is wrong to torture a person, it would be morally best to torture a terrorist in order to prevent the death of thousands of innocent people. A situation of this sort is hardly likely to come up in ordinary life, but it could arise for a government official.

These arguments do not establish that there is a categorical difference between political and nonpolitical life. Outside of politics, it is certainly possible to encounter evil persons and institutions, and (assuming it is possible at all) it is also possible to be justified in using violence and in violating deontological constraints for consequentialist reasons. Nonetheless, these arguments do show that certain kinds of inescapable wrongdoing are far more likely in politics than elsewhere. Yet there are other kinds of inescapable wrongdoing that are far more likely outside of political life than within it—for example, those of family life and intimate friendship. To identify a class of cases as more or less distinctive of political life is not sufficient to establish the Dirty Hands Thesis.

It may be objected that cases of inescapable moral wrongdoing in politics are significantly worse, by involving goods and harms of greater magnitude, than other cases. For example, they often concern situations in which the morally best action involves killing or seriously injuring people, even large numbers of people, something that cannot be said about most personal lives. This is clearly true. Indeed, it is indicative of a truth which may be properly substituted for the Dirty Hands Thesis: that moral tragedy is more likely to occur in politics than elsewhere. This is not to say that moral tragedy does not take place in private lives or in other professions. But on account of the use of violence, the encounter with evil forces, and the great consequences that may be at stake for the community as a whole, inescapable wrongdoing with several of those tragic-making characteristics earlier identified is more prevalent in political life than the rest of life. It is the probability of moral tragedy, and not of inescapable moral wrongdoing per se, that has given birth to the thought that politics is the special province of dirty hands.

There is a further difficulty with the Dirty Hands Thesis, one that has been acknowledged but not sufficiently appreciated in the dirty hands literature.[27] The thesis rests on a distinction between "political life" and "the rest of life." But modern Western countries such as the United States are, albeit imperfectly, democracies. In principle, government officials act with our consent, and they act on our behalf. If they are involved in moral tragedy, then so are the rest of us. Perhaps not *all* the rest of us. Those who actively oppose the government may have some claim for denying any such involvement. But it can hardly be the case, in democratic regimes, that all of us, or even most of us, can make such a claim. Democracy renders "the rest of life" inclusive of "political life." Politics is not, as it was for Machiavelli, a special concern of the few. For this reason, the differential suggested by the Dirty Hands Thesis is misleading. Though moral tragedy is more likely in politics than elsewhere, citizens of a democratic society cannot generally seek moral refuge in a life free from political responsibility.

It must be admitted, however, that putting matters this way is too simple, given the complexities of modern democratic rule. In general, it is problematic to determine to what extent we can be said to consent to the actions of our political leaders, even if we are not actively opposed to their policies. In some situations where wrongdoing is inescapable, we may not know of their actions, and sometimes we cannot know of them if they are to succeed. For example, if what makes an action wrong is that it is intended to deceive another country, this cannot very well be made public. Though government secrecy is all too frequently used to shield ineptitude and corruption, it would be naive to suppose that every government action should be made public as or before it is undertaken. This is especially true in those circumstances where inescapable wrong-doing is most likely to arise.

But without knowledge, how can we be said to consent? Locke suggested that the people grant to the executive a power of prerogative to act for the public good in extraordinary circumstances even if this means going beyond or against what is required by law.[28] Something of this sort may be supposed to be operative for those situations that genuinely require secrecy or immediate, unannounced action, including those where wrongdoing may be inescapable. We grant a power of prerogative to the executive to do what is morally best, and in this way we consent to those actions properly taken under this authority. Or we may assign to our legislators the responsibility to oversee these actions on our behalf. Eventually such actions ought to be made public, at least in most cases, even though this may occur well after the fact. These disclosures may give us reason to express our retrospective disapproval and may lead us to remove those in charge or to modify our understanding of the prerogative. This is not unrealistic. The problem of dirty hands is typically discussed by persons outside government who nonetheless have a fair idea of what goes on within it. In this way, a real albeit approximate measure of consent may be achieved, even though it is not specific and direct consent to each and every action. Under these circumstances, citizens of democratic regimes participate in the morally tragic actions of their leaders. In a real sense, these actions are their actions. It is offensive to the concept of civic responsibility that comes with self-government to deny this.[29]

Thus far I have argued that what is more likely in politics is not inescapable moral wrongdoing itself, but moral tragedy, and that in democratic systems these morally tragic actions are to some extent the actions of all or most of us, and are not simply the actions of our political leaders. The Dirty Hands Thesis is mistaken insofar as it does not recognize these complexities. But what of the Moral Sacrifice Thesis? Discussions of dirty hands often suggest that there is a special problem about the moral character of political leaders. Is this not in fact the case?

One discreditable way of affirming this thesis is suggested by the passage from Weber quoted earlier. On this view, we the electorate are concerned with our own moral purity, with the salvation of our souls. But we recognize that, the world being what it is, politics is a necessary albeit morally questionable business. Since it is questionable, we ourselves should stay clear of politics, concerned as we are with our own moral innocence. But since it is necessary, it is fortunate that there are those who do not have this concern. They are not worried about the salvation of their souls, and hence they are the ones who should go into politics. By this convenient division of moral labor, the essential work of politics will get done while we keep our own souls morally pure. Of course—and this is why there is a special problem about the character of politicians—we are naturally uneasy about putting political power into the hands of those who have eschewed the ideal of moral innocence.

I have already suggested why this is an untenable position, both in its supposition that moral purity is possible independent of political life and in its assumption that in democratic society it is possible to disassociate ourselves from the actions of our political leaders. Still, there does remain a special problem about the moral character of politicians with great power and responsibility. More so than others, these political leaders may have to decide to command the morally tragic action, and to make this decision is to occupy a distinct moral position. The position is not that of carrying out the command. This is typically the work of operatives who are closer to the action in one way but are more remote from it in another: They are merely carrying out the decision of their superiors.[30] On the other hand, those of us who have elected these leaders and granted them the power of prerogative to do such things, nonetheless do not make the specific decision to so act. Though as consenting citizens we cannot deny all responsibility, our responsibility is nonetheless refracted, both because there are many of us who have expressed consent, and because we are not the ones to exercise the prerogative and decide that this particular morally tragic action is in fact for the best. The action is not uniquely the action of the political leader, but he or she stands in a special authorial relation to it.

This makes a moral difference. In comparison with others, the political leader who makes morally tragic decisions is in a position of greater culpability. These actions are a direct expression of the particular deliberation and choice of the leader, and they are a prominent feature of the leader's moral identity. By contrast, for consenting citizens, the responsibility is indirect, broadly distributed, and only one among many in life. Likewise, for operatives, the responsibility is constrained by obligations of their roles and limited access to the overall deliberative framework. Though others share in responsibility, the political leader necessarily bears a greater proportion of responsibility for the tragic dimensions of the choice, as well as for its beneficial objectives. In this respect, the Moral Sacrifice Thesis is correct.

Direct and regular involvement in morally tragic decisions raises questions about the moral character of political leaders. We wonder what kind of person could make such decisions, and whether a person of this kind should make other important decisions affecting our lives. The sheer magnitude of these decisions—the enormous import of the wrong done, the harm averted, the good achieved—can overwhelm an otherwise virtuous moral disposition. On account of this, some politicians may face moral dangers that the rest of us do not typically face. Political leaders may become morally disoriented, losing the ability to determine what is morally best, and perhaps simply acquiescing to the course of events. They may become morally corrupt, no longer concerned with what is morally best but only with advancing their own careers or private interests. They may become morally callous, in one sense doing what is morally best and yet failing to appreciate the significance of the wrongs that are involved in these actions. These are the dangers that come with great power and responsibility. In confronting these dangers, political leaders take unusual moral risks. They put their character to the test in circumstances not routinely encountered.[31] At the same time, if they survive the test, they may achieve heroism beyond the reach of ordinary lives. They may be pivotal in preventing the destruction of a community or in raising it to new levels of collective achievement.

We want political leaders who can make morally tragic decisions and yet avoid these dangers. When wrongdoing is inescapable, we hope they will act for the best while remaining conscious of the wrong involved. Writing about dirty hands, Williams correctly suggests that our politicians should be "reluctant or disinclined to do the morally disagreeable when it is really necessary." This is both because only such politicians "have much chance of not doing it when it is not necessary" and because this is "a correct reaction *to that case*, because that case does involve a genuine moral cost."[32] Walzer, however, goes further. Of the politician with dirty hands, he says, "we want a record of his anguish."[33] We want politicians who "acknowledge their responsibility for the violation by accepting punishment or doing penance."[34] This is surely overdrawn. What we want are politicians who understand and appropriately respond to the realities of a morally complex world. As anguish sometimes is the appropriate response, we want not so much a record of anguish (indeed the perilous circumstances may call instead for a display of fortitude) as evidence of a moral character that we know would feel anguish when appropriate. As for punishment, it would be extraordinary for us to undertake to punish leaders who, acting with our consent and on our behalf, have done what is morally best when wrongdoing is inescapable. Rather than looking to punish, we should be vigilant in demanding of them what we should demand of ourselves: continued moral sensitivity, balance, and courage while engaging a world of distressing and occasionally tragic moral conflicts.

Notes

1. Cf. Hill 1983.
2. These considerations suggest a connection between inescapable moral wrongdoing and what has been called "moral luck." Though this connection is a theme in Nussbaum 1986, it has not otherwise received much attention. It deserves more. On moral luck, see Walker 1991.
3. It may also be denied in religious faith, as on some understandings of original sin and grace (for example, see the reading of Augustine in Gilson 1960, pp. 148–57).
4. To say that moral purity is possible in the sense of being able to do what moral deliberation requires is by itself a hollow claim since a constraint on successful deliberation is that we can do what all things considered we ought to do. This claim can be given substance only in terms of an account of moral value that makes it possible for us always to be fully responsive to the exigencies of morality.
5. Montaigne 1965, pp. 770 and 774. Montaigne was mayor of Bordeaux for four years during a period of considerable strife on account of the religious wars.
6. See Donagan 1977, pp. 144–45, and 1984, pp. 305–306.
7. Nagel, 1979a, p. 74. Unlike Donagan, Nagel is nonetheless prepared to accept perplexity *simpliciter*. In this connection, see also Foot 1983, p. 388; McConnell 1978, pp. 276–77; Raz 1986, p. 362; and Zimmerman 1989.
8. See Nussbaum 1986, ch. 3.
9. Sidgwick 1981, p. 382.

10. Rawls 1971, p. 587.

11. This objection is analogous to the concern that it would be unfair if our capacity for goodness depended on the gratuitous grace of God (see note 3).

12. Williams 1981b, p. 60. See also 1981c, p. 74.

13. Hare 1981, pp. 31–32. Hare later implies that he himself finds a part of the world "enjoyable" in this sense. In defense of the view that there are situations where "there may be no completely just solution," he says by way of example that, "there is probably no solution to the Palestinian problem which will be just to both the Israelis and the displaced Arabs" (pp. 158–59). He adds that "those who like to agonize" about such situations "may well be right."

14. Nussbaum relates her account of the Greek tragedians to the "moral dilemmas" literature (see 1986).

15. Cited in Bradby 1971, p. 265. See also p. 281.

16. Hegel 1975, vol. 2 p. 1196. Hegel also says that in these conflicts there is a "tragic resolution" by means of "eternal justice" (p. 1197). This looks to make his position rather different than mine. For a helpful discussion of interpretations of Hegel's theory of tragedy, see Donougho 1989. Also in this connection, see Scheler 1963.

17. Insofar as we emphasize the point that the harm suffered is undeserved, there is reference, by way of background condition, to the person's agency (except in the case of young children who are regarded as undeserving, not because of what they have done, but because of their station in life). It may be that in the most extreme cases of tragedy we always suppose there is some combination of moral goodness and harm suffered. For example, when an especially vile person suffers a great harm—say, when a child rapist is murdered by another prisoner—we are inclined to say, "There is no tragedy in that."

18. In cases in which, all things considered, two actions are morally better than any alternative actions but neither of the two is better than the other, this expression is somewhat misleading; for there is no single action which is *the* morally best one. Nonetheless, for the sake of simplicity, I will say that an agent who does one of these two actions is doing the morally best action. The final tragic-making characteristic concerns cases of this sort.

19. Machiavelli 1952, p. 84.

20. See Plato 1974, 382c-d and 389b-d.

21. See Sartre 1955. For a philosophical consideration of dirty hands from the same milieu—leftist intellectuals in postwar France—see Merleau-Ponty 1969.

22. In addition to Walzer and the works cited in the next note, I have benefited from the following: Benn 1983; Hampshire 1983a and 1989, ch. 5; Hollis 1982; Nagel 1979a and 1979b; Stocker 1990, chs. 1 and 3; Thompson 1987, ch. 1; and Williams 1981b.

23. At any rate, see Donagan 1977, pp. 180–89; and Goldman 1980, pp. 62–76. For criticism of the former, see McConnell 1981b. Also relevant in this regard is Korsgaard 1986.

24. Walzer 1973, p. 174.

25. Weber 1946, p. 126.

26. The violation of ordinary deontological constraints for consequentialist reasons is virtually the paradigmatic description of dirty hands cases. Though not entirely wrong, this description can be misleading. Politicians do not typically think in utilitarian terms. Their consequentialist reasons aim to promote at most the interests of their constituencies; they are not trying to maximize the well-being of all human beings. Moreover, these consequentialist considerations are often the result of responsibilities that do not, as ordinarily understood, have a consequentialist justification. The politician has an obligation to promote certain interests because he or she has pledged to do so.

27. An exception is Thompson 1987, ch. 1. I have found his discussion especially helpful.

28. See Locke 1980, ch. 14.

29. To the extent that politicians act without our consent, even under the authority of prerogative, their actions lack the sanction of democratic principles. Ordinarily this would be sufficient to render them morally unjustified all things considered. But Thompson argues that such actions might sometimes be morally for the best: "we may simply have to accept, indefinitely, that officials will dirty their hands without democratic legitimacy" (p. 33). In these cases, he says, there are "doubly dirty hands." For, "the decision itself incorporates a wrong, and the making of the decision without democratic legitimacy represents a further wrong" (p. 32). It may be that such cases are possible, though I believe they would be quite rare.

30. Other moral issues arise for these operatives, since they cannot deny all moral responsibility for their actions, even if they are "only following orders." The problem of dirty hands is generally considered to concern political leaders who are at or near the top of the political hierarchy and hence are the ones who give the orders. This is the problem I am concerned with here.

31. We should not lose sight of the fact that there are other professions such as medicine, law, and the military that also involve great responsibilities and in which analogous problems of moral character may arise.

32. Williams 1981b, pp. 62–63.

33. Walzer 1973, p. 176.

34. *Ibid.*, p. 178.

Bibliography

Adler, Joyce Sparer. 1976. "*Billy Budd* and Melville's Philosophy of War." *PMLA* 91: 266–78.

Aquinas, St. Thomas. 1964–75. *Summa Theologiae.* translated by Thomas Gilby, O. P., *et al.* 60 vols. New York: McGraw-Hill.

Arendt, Hannah. 1963. *On Revolution.* New York: Viking Press.

Aune, Bruce. 1979. *Kant's Theory of Morals.* Princeton, N.J.: Princeton University Press.

Badhwar, Neera Kapur. 1987. "Friends as Ends in Themselves." *Philosophy and Phenomenological Research* 48: 1–23.

Baier, Annette C. 1970. "Act and Intent." *The Journal of Philosophy* 67: 648–58.

Baron, Marcia. 1984. "The Alleged Moral Repugnance of Acting from Duty." *The Journal of Philosophy* 81: 197–220.

Barry, Brian. 1984. "Tragic Choices." *Ethics* 94: 303–18.

Benhabib, Seyla. 1987. "The Generalized and the Concrete Other: The Kohlberg-Gilligan Controversy and Moral Theory." *Women and Moral Theory*, edited by Eva Feder Kittay and Diana T. Meyers. Totowa, N.J.: Rowman and Littlefield.

Benn, Stanley I. 1983. "Private and Public Morality: Clean Living and Dirty Hands." In *Public and Private in Social Life*, edited by S. I. Benn and G. F. Gaus. New York: St. Martin's Press.

Berger, Fred R. 1984. *Happiness, Justice, and Freedom: The Moral and Political Philosophy of John Stuart Mill.* Berkeley: University of California Press.

Bishop, Sharon. 1987. "Connections and Guilt." *Hypatia* 2: 7–23.

Blum, Lawrence A. 1980. *Friendship, Altruism, and Morality.* London: Routledge & Kegan Paul.

Blustein, Jeffrey. 1991. *Care and Commitment: Taking the Personal Point of View.* New York: Oxford University Press.

Bolt, Robert. 1962. *A Man for All Seasons.* New York: Vintage Books.

Bonjour, Laurence. 1985. *The Structure of Empirical Knowledge.* Cambridge, Mass.: Harvard University Press.

Bradby, David. 1971. "Sartre as Dramatist." In *Sartre: A Collection of Critical Essays*, edited by Mary Warnock. Garden City, N.Y.: Anchor Books.

Bradley, F. H. 1927. *Ethical Studies*, 2nd ed. Oxford: Oxford University Press.

Brandt, Richard B. 1958. "Blameworthiness and Obligation." In *Essays in Moral Philosophy* edited by A. I. Melden. Seattle: University of Washington Press.

———.1979. *A Theory of the Right and the Good.* Oxford: Clarendon Press.

———.1990. "The Science of Man and Wide Reflective Equilibrium." *Ethics* 100: 259–78.

Bratman, Michael E. 1987. *Intention, Plans, and Practical Reason.* Cambridge, Mass.: Harvard University Press.

Brink, David O. 1989. *Moral Realism and the Foundations of Ethics*. Cambridge, U.K.:
    Cambridge University Press.
Brodtkorb, Paul, Jr. 1967. "The Definitive *Billy Budd:* 'But Aren't It All Sham?'" *PMLA*
    82: 602–12.
Brown, D. G. 1982. "Mill's Criterion of Wrong Conduct." *Dialogue* 21: 27–44.
Brown, James. 1977. "Moral Theory and the Ought-Can Principle." *Mind* 86: 206–33.
Castañeda, Hector-Neri. 1966. "Imperatives, Oughts, and Moral Oughts." *The Aus-
    tralasian Journal of Philosophy* 44: 275–300.
———.1982. *Thinking and Doing: The Philosophical Foundations of Institutions*. Dordrecht,
    Holland: D. Reidel Publishing Co.
Clarke, Stanley G. 1987. "Anti-Theory in Ethics." *American Philosophical Quarterly* 24:
    237–44.
Clarke, Stanley G., and Evan Simpson. Eds. 1989. *Anti-Theory in Ethics and Moral Conser-
    vatism*. Albany: State University of New York Press.
Conee, Earl. 1982. "Against Moral Dilemmas." *Philosophical Review* 91: 87–97.
———.1989. "Why Moral Dilemmas Are Impossible." *American Philosophical Quarterly*
    26: 133–41.
Copp, David. 1979. "The Iterated-Utilitarianism of J. S. Mill." In *New Essays on John Stu-
    art Mill and Utilitarianism. Canadian Journal of Philosophy* supp. vol. 5: 75–98.
Dahl, Norman O. 1974. "'Ought' Implies 'Can'" and Deontic Logic." *Philosophia* 4:
    485–511.
———.1987. "A Prognosis for Universal Prescriptivism." *Philosophical Studies* 51:
    383–424.
Dancy, Jonathan. 1986. "Two Conceptions of Moral Realism." *Proceedings of the Aris-
    totelian Society* supp. vol. 60: 167–87.
Daniels, Norman. 1979. "Wide Reflective Equilibrium and Theory Acceptance in
    Ethics." *The Journal of Philosophy* 76: 256–82.
———.1980. "Reflective Equilibrium and Archimedean Points." *Canadian Journal of Phi-
    losophy* 10: 83–103.
DeCew, Judith Wagner. 1990. "Moral Conflicts and Ethical Relativism." *Ethics* 101:
    27–41.
DePaul, Michael R. 1988. "Argument and Perception: The Role of Literature in Moral
    Inquiry." *The Journal of Philosophy* 85: 552–65.
De Sousa, Ronald B. 1974. "The Good and the True." *Mind* 83: 534–51.
Donagan, Alan. 1977. *The Theory of Morality*. Chicago: University of Chicago Press.
———.1984. "Consistency in Rationalist Moral Systems." *The Journal of Philosophy* 81:
    291–309.
———.1987. *Choice: The Essential Element in Human Action*. London: Routledge & Kegan
    Paul.
Donougho, Martin. 1989. "The Woman in White: On the Reception of Hegel's *Antigone*."
    The Owl of Minerva 21: 65–89.
Dworkin, Ronald. 1975. "The Original Position." In *Reading Rawls: Critical Studies on
    Rawls' "A Theory of Justice,"* edited by Norman Daniels. New York: Basic Books.
Feldman, Fred. 1986. *Doing the Best We Can: An Essay in Informal Deontic Logic*. Dor-
    drecht, Holland: D. Reidel Publishing Co.
Finnis, John. 1980. *Natural Law and Natural Rights*. Oxford: Clarendon Press.
———.1983. *Fundamentals of Ethics*. Washington D.C.: Georgetown University Press.
Foot, Philippa. 1983. "Moral Realism and Moral Dilemma." *The Journal of Philosophy* 80:
    379–98.

Frankena, William K. 1950. "Obligation and Ability." In *Philosophical Analysis: A Collection of Essays*, edited by Max Black. Ithaca, N.Y.: Cornell University Press.

Friedman, Marilyn. 1991. "The Social Self and the Partiality Debates." In *Feminist Ethics*, edited by Claudia Card. Lawrence: University Press of Kansas.

Gaus, Gerald F. 1980. "Mill's Theory of Moral Rules." *Australasian Journal of Philosophy* 58: 265–79.

Geach, Peter. 1969. *God and the Soul.* London: Routledge & Kegan Paul.

Gewirth, Alan. 1978. *Reason and Morality.* Chicago: University of Chicago Press.

Gilson, Etienne. 1960. *The Christian Philosophy of Saint Augustine* translated by L. E. M. Lynch. New York: Random House.

Goldman, Alan H. 1980. *The Moral Foundations of Professional Ethics.* Totowa, N.J.: Rowman and Littlefield.

———.1988. *Moral Knowledge.* London: Routledge and Kegan Paul.

Goldman, Alvin I. 1970. *A Theory of Human Action.* Englewood Cliffs, N.J.: Prentice-Hall.

Gowans, Christopher W. Ed. 1987. *Moral Dilemmas.* New York: Oxford University Press.

———.1992. "Review of Edmund N. Santurri, *Perplexity in the Moral Life: Philosophical and Theological Considerations* and Walter Sinnott-Armstrong, *Moral Dilemmas.*" *Noûs* 26: 252–61.

Greenspan, Patricia S. 1983. "Moral Dilemmas and Guilt." *Philosophical Studies* 43: 117–25.

Griffin, James. 1977. "Are There Incommensurable Values?" *Philosophy & Public Affairs* 7: 39–59.

———.1986. *Well-Being: Its Meaning, Measurement, and Moral Importance.* Oxford: Clarendon Press.

Guttenplan, Samuel. 1979–80. "Moral Realism and Moral Dilemmas." *Proceedings of the Aristotelian Society* 80: 61–80.

Halfon, Mark S. 1989. *Integrity: A Philosophical Inquiry.* Philadelphia: Temple University Press.

Hampshire, Stuart. 1983a. "Public and Private Morality." *Morality and Conflict.* Cambridge, Mass.: Harvard University Press. 101–25.

———.1983b. "Morality and Conflict." *Morality and Conflict.* Cambridge, Mass.: Harvard University Press. 140–69.

———.1989. *Innocence and Experience.* Cambridge, Mass.: Harvard University Press.

Hare, R. M. 1952. *The Language of Morals.* Oxford: Clarendon Press.

———. 1963. *Freedom and Reason.* Oxford: Clarendon Press.

———. 1971. "The Argument from Received Opinion." *Essays on Philosophical Method.* London: Macmillan. 117–135.

———. 1975. "Rawls' Theory of Justice." In *Reading Rawls: Critical Studies on Rawls' "A Theory of Justice,"* edited by Norman Daniels. New York: Basic Books.

———. 1981. *Moral Thinking: Its Levels, Method and Point.* Oxford: Clarendon Press.

———. 1985. "Ontology in Ethics." In *Morality and Objectivity: A Tribute to J. L. Mackie,* edited by Ted Honderich. London: Routledge & Kegan Paul.

———. 1988. "Comments." *In Hare and Critics: Essays on Moral Thinking,* edited by Douglas Seanor and N. Fotion. Oxford: Clarendon Press.

Harman, Gilbert. 1986. *Change in View: Principles of Reasoning.* Cambridge, Mass.: MIT Press.

Harrison, Ross. 1979. "Ethical Consistency." In *Rational Action: Studies in Philosophy and*

Social Science, edited by Ross Harrison. Cambridge, U.K.: Cambridge University Press.

Hegel, G.W.F. 1975. *Aesthetics: Lectures on Fine Art*, translated by T. M. Knox. 2 vols. Oxford: Clarendon Press.

Henderson, G. P. 1966. ""Ought" Implies "Can"'." *Philosophy* 41: 101–12.

Herman, Barbara. 1985. "The Practice of Moral Judgment." *The Journal of Philosophy* 82: 414–36.

———. 1990. "Obligation and Performance: A Kantian Account of Moral Conflict." In *Identity, Character, and Morality: Essays in Moral Psychology*, edited by Owen Flanagan and Amélie Oksenberg Rorty. Cambridge, Mass.: MIT Press.

Hill, Thomas E., Jr. 1980. "Humanity as an End in Itself." *Ethics* 91: 84–99.

———. 1983. "Moral Purity and the Lesser Evil." *Monist* 66: 213–32.

———. 1992. "Kantian Pluralism." *Ethics* 102: 743–62.

Hoag, Robert W. 1983. "Mill on Conflicting Moral Obligations." *Analysis* 43: 49–54.

Hollis, Martin. 1982. "Dirty Hands." *British Journal of Political Science* 12: 385–98.

Hook, Sidney. 1974. "Pragmatism and the Tragic Sense of Life." In *Pragmatism and the Tragic Sense of Life*. New York: Basic Books.

Hurley, S. L. 1985–86. "Conflict, *Akrasia* and Cognitivism." *Proceedings of the Aristotelian Society* 86: 23–49.

Ives, C. B. 1962. "*Billy Budd* and the Articles of War." *American Literature* 34: 31–39.

Jonsen, Albert R., and Stephen Toulmin. 1988. *The Abuse of Casuistry: A History of Moral Reasoning*. Berkeley: University of California Press.

Kagan, Shelly. 1989. *The Limits of Morality*. Oxford: Clarendon Press.

Kalin, Jesse. 1992. "Knowing Novels: Nussbaum on Fiction and Moral Theory." *Ethics* 103: 135–51.

Kant, Immanuel. 1929. *Critique of Pure Reason*, translated by Norman Kemp Smith. New York: St. Martin's Press.

———. 1949. "On a Supposed Right to Lie from Altruistic Motives" (*Preussische Akademie* vol. VIII). In *Critique of Practical Reason and Other Writings in Moral Philosophy*, translated and edited by Lewis White Beck. Chicago: University of Chicago Press.

———. 1956. *Critique of Practical Reason* (*Preussische Akademie* vol. V), translated by Lewis White Beck. Indianapolis, Ind.: Bobbs-Merrill.

———. 1959. *Foundations of the Metaphysics of Morals* (*Preussische Akademie* vol. IV.), translated by Lewis White Beck. Indianapolis: Bobbs-Merrill.

———. 1971. *The Doctrine of Virtue: Part II of The Metaphysic of Morals*. (*Preussische Akademie* vol. VI.), translated by Mary J. Gregor. Philadelphia: University of Pennsylvania Press.

———. 1985. *The Metaphysical Elements of Justice: Part I of the Metaphysics of Morals* (*Preussische Akademie* vol. VI), translated by John Ladd. New York: Macmillan Publishing Company.

Korsgaard, Christine M. 1986. "The Right to Lie: Kant on Dealing with Evil." *Philosophy & Public Affairs* 15: 325–49.

Ladd, John. 1958. "Remarks on the Conflict of Obligations." *The Journal of Philosophy* 55: 811–19.

Larmore, Charles E. 1987. *Patterns of Moral Complexity*. Cambridge, U.K.: Cambridge University Press.

Lemmon, E. J. 1962. "Moral Dilemmas." *Philosophical Review* 70: 139–58.

Levi, Isaac. 1986. *Hard Choices: Decision Making under Unresolved Conflict*. Cambridge, U.K.: Cambridge University Press.

————. 1992. "Conflict and Inquiry." *Ethics* 102: 814–34.

Locke, John. 1980. *Second Treatise of Government*, edited by C. B. Macpherson. Indianapolis, Ind.: Hackett Publishing Company.

Louden, Robert B. 1992. *Morality and Moral Theory: A Reappraisal and Reaffirmation*. New York: Oxford University Press.

Lukes, Steven. 1974. "Relativism: Cognitive and Moral." *Proceedings of the Aristotelian Society* supp. vol. 48: 165–89.

Lyons, David. 1975. "Nature and Soundness of the Contract and Coherence Arguments." In *Reading Rawls: Critical Studies on Rawls' "A Theory of Justice*," edited by Norman Daniels. New York: Basic Books.

————. 1976. "Mill's Theory of Morality." *Noûs* 10: 101–120.

————. 1977. "Human Rights and the General Welfare." *Philosophy & Public Affairs* 6: 113–29.

————. 1978. "Mill's Theory of Justice." In *Values and Morals*, edited by A. I. Goldman and J. Kim. Dordrecht, Holland: D. Reidel Publishing Co.

Machiavelli, Niccolo. 1952. *The Prince*, translated by Luigi Ricci, revised by E.R.P. Vincent. New York: The New American Library.

MacIntyre, Alasdair. 1981. *After Virtue*. Notre Dame, Ind.: University of Notre Dame Press.

————. 1988. *Whose Justice? Which Rationality?*. Notre Dame, Ind.: University of Notre Dame Press.

————. 1990. "Moral Dilemmas." *Philosophy and Phenomenological Research* supp. vol. 50: 367–82.

Mallock, David. 1967. "Moral Dilemmas and Moral Failure." *Australasian Journal of Philosophy* 45: 159–78.

Marcus, Ruth Barcan. 1980. "Moral Dilemmas and Consistency." *The Journal of Philosophy* 77: 121–36.

McConnell, Terrance C. 1978. "Moral Dilemmas and Consistency in Ethics." *Canadian Journal of Philosophy* 8: 269–87.

————. 1981a. "Utilitarianism and Conflict Resolution." *Logique et Analysis* 24: 245–57.

————. 1981b. "Moral Absolutism and the Problem of Hard Cases." *Journal of Religious Ethics* 9: 286–97.

Meiland, Jack W. 1970. *The Nature of Intention*. London: Methuen & Co.

Mele, Alfred R. 1987. *Irrationality: An Essay on Akrasia, Self-Deception, and Self-Control*. New York: Oxford University Press.

Melville, Herman. 1956. *The Shorter Novels of Herman Melville*, edited by Raymond Weaver. Greenwich, Conn.: Fawcett Publications.

————. 1962. *Billy Budd, Sailor (An Inside Narrative)*, edited by Harrison Hayford and Merton M. Sealts, Jr. Chicago: University of Chicago Press.

————. 1975. *Billy Budd, Sailor (An Inside Narrative)*, edited by Milton R. Stern. Indianapolis, Ind.: Bobbs-Merrill.

Merleau-Ponty, Maurice. 1969. *Humanism and Terror: An Essay on the Communist Problem*, translated by John O'Neill. Boston: Beacon Press.

Milder, Robert. 1989. "Introduction." In *Critical Essays on Melville's Billy Budd, Sailor*, edited by Robert Milder. Boston: G. K. Hall..

Mill, John Stuart. 1957. *Utilitarianism*. Indianapolis, Ind.: Bobbs-Merrill.

Montaigne, Michel de. 1965. "Of Husbanding Your Will." *The Complete Essays of Montaigne*, translated by Donald M. Frame. Stanford, Calif.: Stanford University Press. 766–84.

Mooney, Edward F. 1986. "Abraham and Dilemma: Kierkegaard's Teleological Suspension Revisited" *International Journal for Philosophy of Religion* 19: 23–41.

Morris, Herbert. 1987. "Nonmoral Guilt." In *Responsibility, Character, and the Emotions: New Essays in Moral Psychology*, edited by Ferdinand Schoeman. Cambridge, U.K.: Cambridge University Press.

Morris, Michael K. 1992. "Moral Conflict and Ordinary Emotional Experience." *The Journal of Value Inquiry* 26: 223–37.

Mumford, Lewis. 1929. *Herman Melville*. New York: Harcourt, Brace & Co.

Nagel, Thomas. 1979a. "War and Massacre." *Mortal Questions*. Cambridge, U.K.: Cambridge University Press. 53–74.

———. 1979b. "Ruthlessness in Public Life." *Mortal Questions*. Cambridge, U.K.: Cambridge University Press. 75–90.

———. 1979c. "The Fragmentation of Value." *Mortal Questions*. Cambridge, U.K.: Cambridge University Press. 128–41.

———. 1986. *The View from Nowhere*. New York: Oxford University Press.

Nell, Onora. (now O'Neill). 1975. *Acting on Principle: An Essay on Kantian Ethics*. New York: Columbia University Press.

Niebuhr, Reinhold. 1935. *An Interpretation of Christian Ethics*. San Francisco: Harper & Row.

Nielsen, Kai. 1977. "Our Considered Judgments." *Ratio* 19: 39–46.

Nozick, Robert. 1981. *Philosophical Explanations*. Cambridge, Mass.: Harvard University Press.

Nussbaum, Martha C. 1986. *The Fragility of Goodness: Luck and Ethics in Greek Tragedy and Philosophy*. Cambridge, U.K.: Cambridge University Press.

———. 1990. *Love's Knowledge: Essays on Philosophy and Literature*. New York: Oxford University Press.

Odegard, Douglas. 1987. "Deep Moral Dilemmas." *Theoria* 53: 73–86.

O'Neill, Onora. 1986. "The Power of Example." *Philosophy* 61: 5–29.

Orwell, George. 1956. "Reflections on Gandhi." *The Orwell Reader*. New York: Harcourt, Brace & Company.

Paske, Gerald H. 1990. "Genuine Moral Dilemmas and the Containment of Incoherence." *The Journal of Value Inquiry* 24: 315–23.

Paton, H. J. 1953–54. "An Alleged Right to Lie: A Problem in Kantian Ethics." *Kant-Studien* 45: 190–203.

———. 1963. *The Categorical Imperative: A Study in Kant's Moral Philosophy*. 4th. ed. London: Hutchinson.

Phillips, D. Z., and H. O. Mounce. 1970. *Moral Practices*. New York: Schocken Books.

Plantinga, Alvin. 1974. *The Nature of Necessity*. Oxford: Clarendon Press.

Plato. 1974. *The Republic*, translated by Desmond Lee. 2nd ed. Harmondsworth, U.K.: Penguin Books.

Platts, Mark de Bretton. 1979. *Ways of Meaning: An Introduction to the Philosophy of Language*. London: Routledge and Kegan Paul.

Posner, Richard A. 1988. *Law and Literature: A Misunderstood Relation*. Cambridge, Mass.: Harvard University Press.

Putnam, Hilary. 1979. "Literature, Science, and Reflection." *Meaning and the Moral Sciences*. Boston: Routledge & Kegan Paul. 83–94.

———. 1981. *Reason, Truth and History*. Cambridge, U.K.: Cambridge University Press.

Quinn, Philip L. 1986. "Moral Obligation, Religious Demand, and Practical Conflict." In *Rationality, Religious Belief, and Moral Commitment*, edited by Robert Audi and William I. Wainwright. Ithaca, N.Y.: Cornell University Press.

———. 1989. "Tragic Dilemmas, Suffering Love, and Christian Life." *Journal of Religious Ethics* 17: 151–83.

Railton, Peter. 1984. "Alienation, Consequentialism, and the Demands of Morality." *Philosophy & Public Affairs* 13: 134–71.

———. 1992. "Pluralism, Determinacy, and Dilemma." *Ethics* 102: 720–42.

Rawls, John. 1971. *A Theory of Justice*. Cambridge, Mass.: Harvard University Press.

———. 1974–75. "The Independence of Moral Theory." *Proceedings and Addresses of the American Philosophical Association* 48: 5–22.

———. 1980. "Kantian Constructivism in Moral Theory." *The Journal of Philosophy* 77: 515–72.

———. 1985. "Justice as Fairness: Political Not Metaphysical." *Philosophy & Public Affairs* 14: 223–51.

———. 1988. "The Priority of Right and Ideas of the Good." *Philosophy & Public Affairs* 17: 251–76.

Raz, Joseph. 1986. *The Morality of Freedom*. Oxford: Clarendon Press.

Rescher, Nicholas. 1987. *Ethical Idealism: An Inquiry into the Nature and Function of Ideals*. Berkeley: University of California Press.

Ross, W. D. 1988. *The Right and the Good*. Indianapolis, Ind.: Hackett Publishing Co.

Ryan, Alan. 1990. *The Philosophy of John Stuart Mill*. 2nd ed. Atlantic Highlands, N.J.: Humanities Press International.

Santurri, Edmund N. 1987. *Perplexity in the Moral Life: Philosophical and Theological Considerations*. Charlottesville: University Press of Virginia.

Sartorius, Rolf E. 1975. *Individual Conduct and Social Norms: A Utilitarian Account of Social Union and the Rule of Law*. Encino, Calif.: Dickenson Publishing Co.

Sartre, Jean-Paul. 1955. *Dirty Hands*, translated by Lionel Abel. In *No Exit and Three Other Plays*. New York: Vintage Books.

———. 1975. "Existentialism Is a Humanism," translated by Philip Mairet. In *Existentialism from Dostoevsky to Sartre*, edited by Walter Kaufmann. Rev. ed. New York: Meridian-New American.

Sayre-McCord, Geoffrey. 1985. "Coherence and Models for Moral Theorizing." *Pacific Philosophical Quarterly* 66: 170–90.

———. 1986. "Deontic Logic and the Priority of Moral Theory." *Noûs* 20: 179–97.

———. 1988. "The Many Moral Realisms." In *Essays on Moral Realism*, edited by Geoffrey Sayre-McCord. Ithaca, N.Y.: Cornell University Press. 1–23.

Scheler, Max. 1963. "On the Tragic," translated by Bernard Stambler. In *Tragedy: Modern Essays in Criticism*, edited by Laurence Michel and Richard B. Sewall. Englewood Cliffs, N.J.: Prentice-Hall.

Sealts, Merton M., Jr. 1986. "Innocence and Infamy: *Billy Budd, Sailor*." In *A Companion to Melville Studies*, edited by John Bryant. New York: Greenwood Press.

Sellars, Wilfrid. 1963. "Imperatives, Intentions, and the Logic of 'Ought'." In *Morality and the Language of Conduct*, edited by Hector-Neri Castañeda and George Nakhnikian. Detroit, Mich.: Wayne State University Press.

———. 1966. "Thought and Action." In *Freedom and Determinism*, edited by Keith Lehrer. New York: Random House.

———. 1968. *Science and Metaphysics: Variations on Kantian Themes*. London: Routledge & Kegan Paul.

Sen, Amartya. 1980–81. "Plural Utility." *Proceedings of the Aristotelian Society* 81: 193–215.

Short, Raymond W. 1946. *Four Great American Novels*. New York: Henry Holt & Co.

Sidgwick, Henry. 1981. *The Methods of Ethics*, 7th ed. Indianapolis, Ind.: Hackett Publishing Company.

Singer, Peter. 1974. "Sidgwick and Reflective Equilibrium." *Monist* 58: 490–517.

Sinnott-Armstrong, Walter. 1988. *Moral Dilemmas.* Oxford: Basil Blackwell.

Slote, Michael. 1985. "Utilitarianism, Moral Dilemmas, and Moral Cost." *American Philosophical Quarterly* 22: 161–68.

Solomon, W. David. 1985. "Moral Realism and Moral Knowledge." *Proceedings of the American Catholic Philosophical Association* 59: 41–57.

Sophocles. 1973. *Antigone,* translated by Elizabeth Wyckoff. In *Sophocles I,* edited by David Grene and Richmond Lattimore. Chicago: University of Chicago Press.

Sorensen, Roy A. 1991. "Moral Dilemmas, Thought Experiments, and Conflict Vagueness." *Philosophical Studies* 63: 291–308.

Steiner, Hillel. 1973. "Moral Conflict and Prescriptivism." *Mind* 82: 586–91.

Stocker, Michael. 1971. "'Ought' and 'Can'." *The Australasian Journal of Philosophy* 49: 303–316.

———. 1976. "The Schizophrenia of Modern Ethical Theories." *The Journal of Philosophy* 73: 453–66.

———. 1990. *Plural and Conflicting Values.* Oxford: Clarendon Press.

Styron, William. 1980. *Sophie's Choice.* New York: Bantam Books.

Sullivan, Roger J. 1989. *Immanuel Kant's Moral Theory.* Cambridge, U.K.: Cambridge University Press.

Sumner, L. W. 1979. "The Good and the Right." In *New Essays on John Stuart Mill and Utilitarianism. Canadian Journal of Philosophy* supp. vol. 5: 99–114.

Tännsjö, Torbjörn. 1985. "Moral Conflict and Moral Realism." *The Journal of Philosophy* 82: 113–17.

Taylor, Charles. 1989. *Sources of the Self: The Making of the Modern Identity.* Cambridge, Mass.: Harvard University Press.

Taylor, Gabriele. 1985. *Pride, Shame, and Guilt: Emotions of Self-Assessment.* Oxford: Clarendon Press.

Thompson, Dennis F. 1987. *Political Ethics and Public Office.* Cambridge, Mass.: Harvard University Press.

Thompson, Lawrance. 1952. *Melville's Quarrel with God.* Princeton, N.J.: Princeton University Press.

Trigg, Roger. 1971. "Moral Conflict." *Mind* 80: 41–55.

Trotsky, Leon. 1973. "Their Morals and Ours." In *Their Morals and Ours: Marxist vs. Liberal Views on Morality.* Leon Trotsky, John Dewey, and George Novack. 5th ed. New York: Pathfinder Press.

Tuana, Nancy. 1992. *Woman and the History of Philosophy.* New York: Paragon House.

Urmson, J. O. 1953. "The Interpretation of the Moral Philosophy of J. S. Mill." *The Philosophical Quarterly* 3: 33–39.

Vallentyne, Peter. 1987. "Prohibition Dilemmas and Deontic Logic." *Logic et Analysis* 30: 113–22.

———. 1989. "Two Types of Moral Dilemmas." *Erkenntnis* 30: 301–318.

van Fraassen, Bas C. 1973. "Values and the Heart's Command." *The Journal of Philosophy* 70: 5–19.

Vlastos, Gregory. 1973. "The Individual as Object of Love in Plato." *Platonic Studies.* Princeton, N.J.: Princeton University Press. 3–34.

Walker, Margaret Urban. 1989. "Moral Understandings: Alternative 'Epistemology' for a Feminist Ethics." *Hypatia* 4: 15–28.

———. 1991. "Moral Luck and the Virtues of Impure Agency." *Metaphilosophy* 22: 14–27.

Walzer, Michael. 1973. "Political Action: The Problem of Dirty Hands." *Philosophy & Public Affairs* 2: 160–80.

Weber, Max. 1946. *From Max Weber: Essays in Sociology*, edited by H. H. Gerth and C. Wright Mills. New York: Oxford University Press.

Weisberg, Richard. 1982. "How Judges Speak: Some Lessons on Adjudication in *Billy Budd, Sailor* with an Application to Justice Rehnquist." *New York University Law Review* 57: 1–69.

White, Alan R. 1975. *Modal Thinking*. Ithaca, N.Y.: Cornell University Press.

Wiggins, David. 1987. "Truth, Invention, and the Meaning of Life." *Needs, Values, Truth: Essays in the Philosophy of Value*. Aristotelian Society Series, vol. 6. Oxford: Basil Blackwell. 87–137.

Williams, Bernard. 1973a. "Ethical Consistency." *Problems of the Self: Philosophical Papers 1956–1972*. Cambridge, U.K.: Cambridge University Press. 166–86.

———. 1973b. "Consistency and Realism." *Problems of the Self: Philosophical Papers 1956–1972*. Cambridge, U.K.: Cambridge University Press. 187–206.

———. 1978. "Introduction." In *Concepts and Categories: Philosophical Essays by Isaiah Berlin*, edited by Henry Hardy. New York: Viking Press.

———. 1981a. "Persons, Character and Morality." *Moral Luck: Philosophical Papers 1973–1980*. Cambridge, U.K.: Cambridge University Press. 1–19.

———. 1981b. "Politics and Moral Character." *Moral Luck: Philosophical Papers 1973–1980*. Cambridge, U.K.: Cambridge University Press. 54–70.

———. 1981c. "Conflicts of Values." *Moral Luck: Philosophical Papers 1973–1980*. Cambridge, U.K.: Cambridge University Press. 71–82.

———. 1988. "The Structure of Hare's Theory." In *Hare and Critics: Essays on Moral Thinking*, edited by Douglas Seanor and N. Fotion. Oxford: Clarendon Press.

Winch, Peter. 1965. "The Universalizability of Moral Judgements." *Monist* 49: 196–214.

Zimmerman, Michael J. 1987. "Remote Obligation." *American Philosophical Quarterly* 24: 199–205.

———. 1989. "Lapses and Dilemmas." *Philosophical Papers* 17: 103–112.

Zink, Karl E. 1952. "Herman Melville and the Forms—Irony and Social Criticism in '*Billy Budd*'." *Accent* 12: 131–39.

Index